NORTH OF THE PLATTE, SOUTH OF THE NIOBRARA: A LITTLE FURTHER INTO THE NEBRASKA SAND HILLS

by

Bryan L. Jones

Forward by Linda M. Hasselstrom

STEPHEN F. AUSTIN STATE UNIVERSITY PRESS

For more information:
Stephen F. Austin State University Press
P.O. Box 13007 SFA Station
Nacogdoches, Texas 75962
sfapress@sfasu.edu
www.sfasu.edu/sfapress

BOOK DESIGN CREDIT

Cover photo: Taken by Chris Amundson, publisher of *Nebraska Life Magazine*, north of Osh-kosh, Nebraska, on an unusually humid late summer day. He was flying his 1948 single-engine Stinson 108-3 tail dragger when the heat and humidity forced him up to 10,000 feet. The striking view of dunes and mist stretching into an infinite horizon forced him to reach for his Mark II Canon with a 300 mm telephoto lens. Cover design by Thomas Sims.

Foreword: By Linda M. Hasselstrom, rancher, poet and author of 17 books, including *Going Over East* and her most recent, *Gathering from the Grassland: A Plains Journal*.

ISBN: 978-1-62288-225-0

www.bryanjoneswriter.com
Facebook - Bryan L. Jones author

for Kathy
who makes all things possible

Foreword

A Writer Follows His Nose

North of the Platte, South of the Niobrara: A Little Further into the Nebraska Sand Hills is unlike any other book I've read. Filled with adventurous writing, sharp scrutiny, meticulous and audacious use of language, it winds around its subjects the way the rivers and creeks of the Great Plains twist around humps of prairie grass, ranches and rock outcroppings.

One minute you are reading about history, like the Kinkaid Act which brought homesteaders to the region. A few pages later, you are immersed in a Mari Sandoz novel. In short order, you are watching the "official castrator" collect calf testicles which will be roasted and eaten. These may sound like different stories, but they are all linked in surprising, sometimes subtle, ways. The book's people and events are woven together like a warm shawl that settles around the reader's shoulders. The supervisor of the rural school teacher is the daughter-in-law of the woman who provided shelter for Celia Sandoz and her pupils in the winter of 1949, as portrayed by Mari Sandoz' book *Winter Thunder*. A teacher of one of the bull rider subjects was a sister to Bryan's Uncle Leo's widow. And, Bryan adds in a note to me, "The Loup Valley Cemetery not only holds C.B. and Ruby McIntosh and most of the Lamb family, but a good percentage of my Tupper relatives."

This book shows the Nebraska Sand Hills as they are known by a man of widespread interests and deep roots in the neighborhood. No one is safe from his eagle-eyed scrutiny and sharp commentary. Besides the unique characters and terrain of the Sand Hills and tracing the ways they are connected, Bryan offers trenchant comments on how to float down a river in a stock tank, blowout penstemon, pesky river otters, Mormon cows, grave dowsing and bull riding. He reflects with almost unbearable poignancy on war and its consequences and with fierce advocacy on two beloved Nebraska poets. He brings humor and occasional cynicism to reflections about "the metaphysical and metaphorical aspects" of the Sand Hills, newcomers, like Ted Turner, the Sandoz family and other long-time residents and a considerable chunk of Western history.

Attending the auction of an historic Sand Hills ranch, he observes the room packed with ranchers in jeans and big hats, and comments:

"Except for a few token pairs of cowboy boots the entire crowd is shod in sneakers, a sure sign, if one were needed, of the fast approaching end of civilization as we know it."

The successful bidder at the auction is Ted Turner's agent and Bryan notes in fairness that the man did not blow out the other bidders by jumping the offer fifty or a hundred bucks at a time. Instead, he upped the price a dollar with each bid, not behavior expected from billionaires. The favorable opinion of the crowd, Bryan reports:

"He may be a billionaire with weird politics, once married to a certified wing nut, but at least he watches his pennies like a normal person."

One of my favorite chapters is "Winter School," describing a visit to a one-room grade school southwest of Valentine, Nebraska, told with the kind of informed remarks about education in general that only a dedicated teacher like Bryan could manage. I attended a small country school, though never one quite this small. I recall and cherish the flexibility and dedication shown by a teacher who taught first, second, third, fourth, and fifth-grade students all in one room. This tiny school has all the modern equipment parents expect these days: a television with VCR/DVD player, laptop computers, desktop PCs. But when "the girl in the yellow dress," who is supposed to be practicing her handwriting, asks a question about golden eagles, Miss Winter behaves just the way my first teacher did. She sends the girl to consult the E volume of the encyclopedia and a book on Nebraska birds. Soon all the students are gathered around their teacher, learning by doing. One source said the wingspan of a golden eagle averages seven feet, so Miss Winter uses a yardstick, a ball of string, and the little girl's outstretched arms, to demonstrate just how long that is. Bryan writes: "I'm pretty certain no one in the room will soon forget the wingspan of a golden eagle."

Bryan traveled 70,000 miles and conducted 370 interviews collecting the diverse material from which he conjured this book. Because my day is often enhanced by my West Highland White Terriers, Cosmo and Toby, I like knowing that on many trips Bryan was accompanied by his Westie, Finlay, an inquisitive and intrepid traveler who sleeps at his feet while he writes. Fortunately, Finlay was smarter than Bryan and refused to join him in the plane which crashed during this research, seriously injuring Bryan and the pilot. If that didn't stop him, I doubt this is his last book. I'm already looking forward to the next one.

Linda M. Hasselstrom

Hermosa, South Dakota

Preface

The Nebraska Sand Hills have a feeling of emptiness and newness belying the thousands of homesteaders who dug wells, built fences, plowed and planted, before most gave up and sold out. The names of a few of those pioneers remain on surviving ranches and in the memories of ranch families, who still refer to the different portions of their holdings by the names of the original homesteaders. The land itself, except for expansive herds of cattle, miles of fences, thousands of creaking windmills and a few widely scattered clusters of ranch buildings, has returned to its natural state, largely unscathed by man's determined efforts at the end of the 19th and beginning of the 20th century to turn 20,000 square miles of grassed sand dunes into a rough approximation of Illinois.

People new to the Sand Hills often struggle to describe how they are affected by them. Many, particularly urban dwellers, express a sense of disquiet occasioned by the undifferentiated landscape, the paucity of signs of human habitation, the shortage of landmarks. And becoming lost in the Sand Hills is ridiculously easy. I've done it hundreds of times.

I don't experience trepidation in the Sand Hills, but more a child-like sense of wonder. Why do the dunes, which are to some degree constantly moving, seem so solid and utterly reliable? Even a faint breeze skitters a few grains of sand among grass roots. The next extended drouthy period, which will likely occur some time in the coming 500,000 years, will kill much of the grass and loosen the sand to reshape entirely new dunes or, more likely, new and interesting additions to old dunes. Nothing solid and reliable in that picture. Yet there exists a strong mysterious presence, almost tactile, which has nothing to do with humans or beef cattle or unpredictable grains of sand, hovering over the undulating dunes to the far circumference of the horizon. And that presence strongly suggests a peaceful permanence, as only a pristine landscape can, and to some, a presence with mysterious healing properties.

Once visitors fully comprehend the distances between ranches and small towns, and realize how geographically isolated Sand Hill ranch families can be, they often declare they could never live in the middle of so much empty and speculate on what sort of person could manage it. Their voices betray a grudging respect tinged with a little bit of fear. What strange species of humans are these anyway?

The lives of Sand Hills residents revolve around the seasonal demands of cattle ranching. And, as with all herders, whether they be living on the Mongolian steppes or the high plateaus of western Kenya, the welfare of the animals has the highest priority. Herding, no matter where it takes place, entails hard physical work, exposure to harsh weather, surrendering control of the family's financial future to the whims of markets, disease and drought. Although every form of human endeavor attracts its share of 14 carat jackasses, the realities of herding tend to weed out the indolent, the narcissistic braggarts and those uncomfortable in their own skins.

I crossed paths with only a handful of 14 carat jackasses during my extended visits to the Nebraska Sand Hills. Some might attribute this happy circumstance to small sample size and extraordinary good fortune, a reasonable supposition. However, occasional trips to other geographies have resulted in more numerous 14 carat jackass sightings leading to the tentative belief the Sand Hills suffer from a relative shortage of 14 carat jackasses.

Sand Hills residents remind me of the older customers on my 1950s era small town paper route, people who as youngsters campaigned for William Jennings Bryan, people who buried young adult children during the 1919 flu epidemic, survivors of the Great Depression and two World Wars. Honesty was a given. Good manners were a given. Quiet personal courage was a given. Veneration for the past provided personal histories rich with tragedy and adversity, but enough examples of modest success to have kept the storytellers from hanging themselves from windmills. These were people who knew where they had been and who they were and, if not completely satisfied with that knowledge, had made their peace with it. Like my paper route customers, Sand Hills residents most definitely know who they are.

Even people who know who they are may not agree on how to spell where they live. Both the Sandhills and Sand Hills spellings have adherents. University of Nebraska geographer/cartographer Charles Barron McIntosh, who knew more about the area than anyone, religiously used Sand Hills, plenty good enough for me.

It would be a fool's errand to attempt to replicate McIntosh's painstaking research. My more modest goal: using personal interviews, Sand Hills explorations and family histories to create fresh understandings of the place, the inhabitants and the scholars who have devoted their professional lives to unlocking its secrets.

Welcome to the Nebraska Sand Hills.

Contents

NORTH OF THE PLATTE, SOUTH OF THE NIOBRARA: A LITTLE FURTHER INTO THE NEBRASKA SAND HILLS

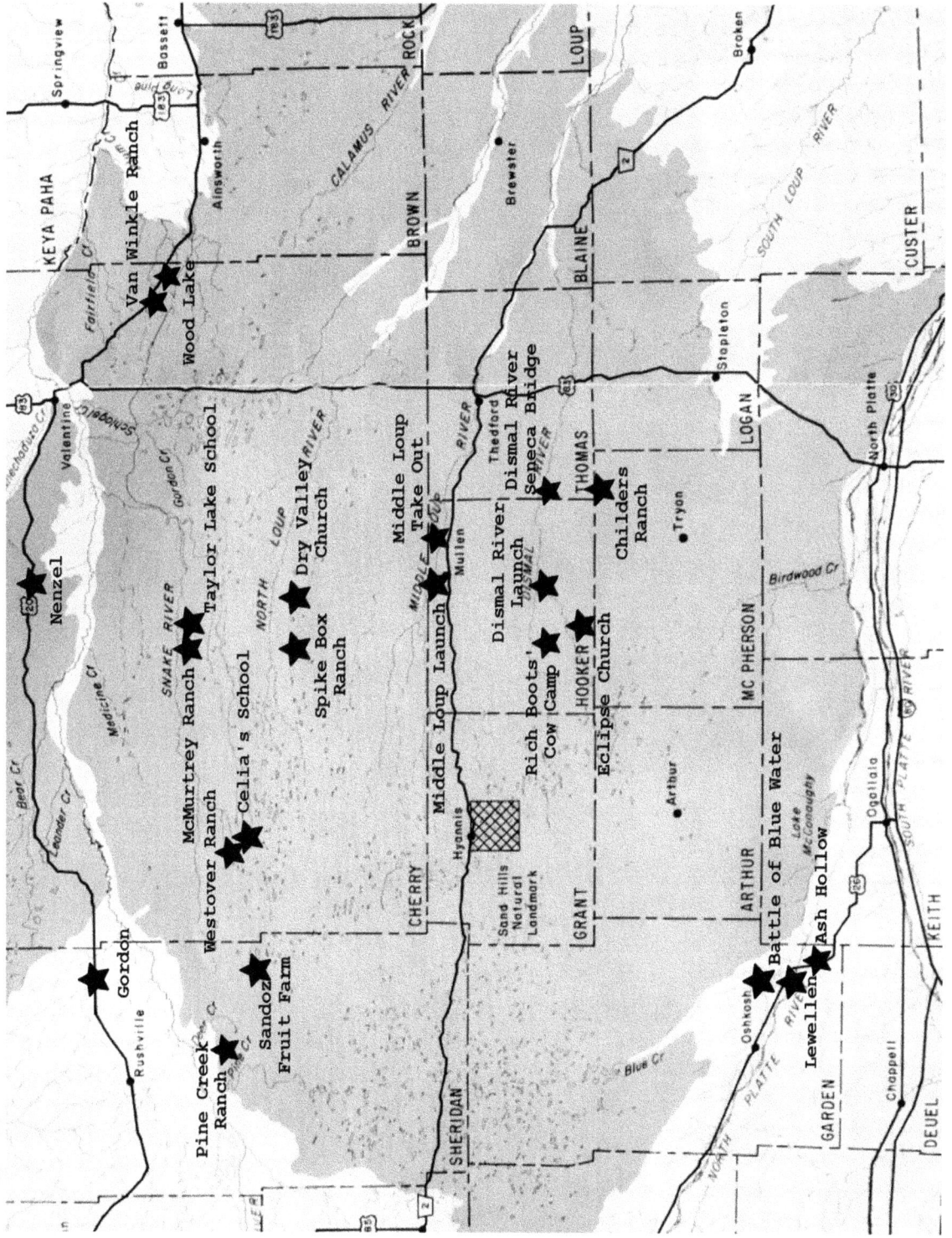

Chapter 1
Dismal River

We call it the Divorce River, because we've known
several couples who split the sheets after one trip.
— Denver kayaker

Do I look like I'm crazy?
— Cousin Julie Pettit,
when asked if she ever
canoed the Dismal River

Mid-afternoon, early May, Red's Cafe, Mullen, Nebraska. A dozen miles north of the Dismal River where Kathy and I launched Mitch Glidden's Dodger blue kayak early this morning. Despite the clattering of hot crockery from Red's overheated kitchen and multiple cups of scalding coffee, Kathy's bones have yet to thaw. She claims she's "fine."

At a nearby table, next to a wall covered with sale bills, three elderly ranch couples take a late lunch. In a much better collective mood than we are, they exchange news briefs, local, state and international, punctuated by easy laughter. One of the men waves a hand in our general direction, describes the day Jane Fonda and Ted Turner sat where we are sitting, declares Ted, then in the process of converting his recently purchased Spike Box Ranch into a bison operation, was an okay guy when you got to know him, but that Jane Fonda, everyone knew right away she thought she was really something.

Easy to picture the always earnest Miss Fonda showing up in Red's Cafe dressed in her best guess of what a Mullen area ranch wife of a certain age might wear. Might have overestimated the amount of jewelry and make up she'd need to fit in. Might have underestimated how accurately the denizens of Red's Cafe would guess the cost of her recent cosmetic implants, tucks and pleats. Chances are she wasn't wearing the type of inexpensive wash and wear casual slacks and blouses outfitting the women sitting by the wall covered with sale bills. Chances are she wasn't wearing Adidas sneakers like they are, nor the sturdy Justin boots favored by their husbands. Billionaire invader Ted Turner, whose ranch acquisition spree in the Nebraska Sand Hills eventually totaled over 500,000 acres, gets a pass as an "okay guy." Miss Fonda, whose father spent his early years in not so far away in Omaha, earns a curled lip. On some level this makes perfect sense.

Perhaps if Ted and Jane had run the Dismal, then trailed up to Red's Cafe, Jane's perfect teeth chattering, hair rudely coifed by river water, clad in sopping wet off the rack clothing, she might, at the very least, have received points for grit. Although memories of a wide-eyed Miss Fonda manning a North Vietnamese anti-aircraft battery won't disappear any time soon, that sorry business might be grudgingly excused as youthful indiscretion. However, no social crime is more serious in a region famous for social democracy than showing up at Red's Cafe in Mullen, Nebraska, "thinking you're really something." We may be sitting in Red's Cafe at the table where Ted Turner and Jane Fonda sat, but we sure as hell don't think we're really something.

From Red's Cafe it's a little over twelve miles south to where the north and south forks of the Dismal join forces, an area rich in Western lore. The north branch meanders west through the magnificent Ben Crenshaw designed Sand Hills Golf Course, ranked by *Golf Magazine* as the best American golf course constructed in the last 50 years. A few miles farther you'll come to University of Nebraska hydrologist Jim Goeke's sacred patch of Sand Hills ground and to yet another signature golf course, the Dismal River Golf Club, offering a Jack Nicklaus course and prime building lots at astonishing prices.

Follow the south branch of the Dismal and you'll pass the pristine Eclipse Church, waiting unlocked through a century of seasons for the occasional wedding or funeral. A few miles farther west you'll come to the site of the short-lived cattle operation established by Buffalo Bill Cody and Pawnee Scouts Frank and Luther North. To the northwest you'll spot the impressive mass of Big Baldy, where the intrepid John Bratt established the first permanent ranch in the interior of the Sand Hills, the bull camp where his men dodged Cheyenne arrows for most of one bitter winter during the storied Cheyenne breakout from Oklahoma.

Most people launch their canoes or kayaks in a pool next to Highway 97 below the forks, where the river is much deeper than upstream. The favored launching area sits below a prominent hill, once favored by migrating Plains Indians as a camp site and lookout, later serving as the designated staging area where the wealthy eastern guests of the Black Ranch were royally entertained on their trips down the Dismal in a massive plate steel Jon boat. The trail from the highway down to the river, eroded nearly to extinction, ends abruptly 50 feet short and 25 feet above the river. A strong companion, like Kathy, who once made a living wrestling 55 gallon chemical drums, comes in handy lowering the kayak down a series of steep drop offs.

Wade your kayak onto the spring fed Dismal, bubbling straight out of the zillion gallon Ogallala aquifer on a cold 40 degree overcast day like today and you'll likely raise a decent crop of goose bumps. Upend your kayak in the middle of a snag, which we managed to do before we'd floated a quarter of a mile, and you'll spend the rest of the day wishing vainly for sunshine and matches in a waterproof container. The Dismal, as deceptive a stream as you'll ever lay eyes on, has a way of subverting the best anti-dump measures.

On the stretch between the forks and the Seneca Bridge the tortuous river runs straight for as long as a hundred yards in only a couple of places. And though stream flows hold as steady as any river in the state, if the river is slightly lower than usual, say in mid-July, the distance between the bank and the numerous snags or "strainers," invariably situated on the outside of every sharp river bend, narrows to a couple of feet. Should the intrepid paddler lose concentration for a fleeting moment, causing a fractional miscalculation negotiating the narrow slot between bank and strainer, the kayak swings broadside to the current and slams against the snag, a thicket of sharp dead limbs scratching and poking. Vain attempts to push off against the current tip the kayak to the upstream side and it promptly fills with water and capsizes in a pool often eight to fifteen feet deep. Coolers float merrily away, cameras sink. The persistent can repeat this action many times during one trip between the forks and the Seneca bridge, where most people call it a day. My brother-in-law Lenny and I, on a considerably warmer day than this one, once flipped 30 times without raising a sweat.

When occasional upstream rains swell the river, the distance between bank and snag increases and becomes more forgiving. However, the swifter current often carries a boat directly into the snag, or worse, behind the snag on the lee side. Once caught between the snag and the lee bank the only way to keep the craft upright is to abandon ship and manhandle the kayak back upstream to regroup.

Mitch Glidden, who supplies most of the rental canoes and kayaks for the Dismal trip, occasionally floats the river with a chain saw, clearing a path through the worst of the new strainers. He checks the barbed wire fences across the river, makes sure the bottom strands are covered with plastic pipe. During the summer season his customers do small repairs on fence crossings as needed, keep him up to date on conditions.

There is little danger the Dismal will ever be completely free of snags. Whenever the local beaver population determines the strainer population to be dangerously low, they fell a few more large trees directly into the river, where they lodge on the outside of bends, slyly waiting for the unwary.

Our inaugural spill, a scant 300 yards below the launch site, like most Dismal River spills, results from a loss of concentration and a tiny error in judgement. Sliding by a strainer we paddle a smidgen too slowly, swing broadside to the current, impaling the kayak in the prickly remains of a huge cedar. Seconds later we are leaning precariously to the upstream side, water pouring into the boat. We sink like a rock, dumping our entire supply of sandwiches. The swift current wedges the upended kayak under the cedar. After muscling the kayak out from under the strainer and swimming it to back to some shallows, we dump out the water and begin shivering in earnest. Concentration considerably sharpened, we do a better job of staying focused and avoid multiple dunking opportunities for the next four or five miles.

Every so often, after a few spills, a half-drowned pilgrim throws in the towel, trudges up though the timber to the steep grassy dunes rimming the Dismal River valley, and lights out for civilization. Mitch Glidden discourages this option, warning his clients of the vast spaces between ranch houses. Chances of marching out of the Dismal Valley and colliding with a set of buildings are remote at best. Any one foolish enough to abandon the river mid-trip can count on a lonely 13 mile hike north up and over the dunes to Highway 2.

One of the things first-timers notice about the Dismal is the absence of trash, indeed any trace of human occupation. No beer cans, no water bottles, no potato chip bags. The more popular Niobrara River to the north regularly hosts 1200 people on a summer day. The Dismal might see 700 daring souls a year. Mitch makes sure his customers know the banks are private land, mostly owned by ranchers with dim views of littering. The few people who bring their own kayaks and canoes every year to run the Dismal, folks usually physically fit and environmentally conscious, seldom leave a footprint. Perhaps the most important reason for the lack of beer cans is the concentration the river demands. Nobody can kick back, relax, set to work on a cold beer and expect to remain dry.

On one relatively straight section we notice several muddy seeps along a line of bluffs close to the south bank. This is the site where a young lad drowned a few years ago. Beaver-felled trees blocked river navigation and funneled the current into a narrow tunnel under the trees. When the boy's family beached their canoes above the blockage and prepared to portage, the current grabbed the little guy and sucked him under the trees, where he lodged so firmly a rescue crew took most of a day recovering the body. Today we encounter no obstructive trees along this stretch. I am relieved we won't have to portage through the mud, and a little awestruck at the power of the steady Dismal, which seldom floods, to wipe a hundred yards of river clear of tons of mud and trees.

A half hour later we pull off on the north bank to explore "the pool," a 150-foot deep cold water spring boiling up out of the Ogallala aquifer, carrying so much sand it suspends anyone who wades in. With sopping clothes, wet hair plastered to our skulls, we decide today is not the ideal time to test the suspension characteristics of a frigid spring. Maybe next trip.

As things turn out, a swim in the pool could hardly have made us colder. We capsize a quarter mile downstream, failing to negotiate a tricky passage between strainers anchored in opposite banks. If Kathy was ever going to throw in the towel and launch a death march up to Highway 2, this would have been the spot. But she was born game, and although tinted blue around the gills, she carries on, claiming through gritted teeth she's "fine."

Forewarned by Mitch and previous experience, we beach well above The Falls, a stretch where the Dismal narrows, tumbling down a narrow rocky chute. We study the falls, decide to try them another time. Mitch says it is theoretically possible to bang down the chute and into the deep pool below without flipping, that it's been done many times. However, he says those who try often lose the bet, and sometimes a good chunk of their possessions. On a warmer day I'd argue for adventure. Today we portage around through the cockleburs, only two and a half hours of river in front of us.

The next section of the Dismal goes much more quickly, river bends less tortuous, strainers and snags less intrusive. We come to an impressive elk proof fence across the river. We pull the kayak up a steep bank and push it through the plywood trap door, climb over the metal stairs to join our kayak on the other side. A half hour later we repeat the process without spotting a single elk. Unlike on previous trips down the river we've seen little wildlife, only a few pairs of nesting mallards, a couple dozen turkey vultures, ominously circling above us on the worst stretches, a lone buck white tail deer running easily up a couloir. Maybe all the smart critters have gone into hibernation mode until this unseasonable cold spell passes.

A nervous blue heron leads us down stream, each landing and takeoff as inelegant as the last. On an extended stretch where high banks border the river we encounter a small horse herd. The brood mares take exception to our blue kayak, snort, kick water, fart in our general direction. I think the heron, which has flown far out of sight down river, has the right idea.

We keep a sharp eye along this section for signs of a crossing, an old trail leading away from the river, the place where in early February, 1916, Anna Hora, an 18-year-old school teacher, died crossing the Dismal on her way to school. Although a large search party found her drowned horse in a patch of quicksand, her calcified body did not appear until two years later. Discovered by an area trapper, the body was found on a sandbar "as though seated in a chair" missing a head and one arm. Relatives identified the corpse by the clothing, which survived in good condition, including the corset strings, which held "despite the ravages of the water."

No signs of an old crossing, although there could be hundreds of ancient sand hills tracks trailing down to the river hidden by trees and sumac. The Dismal Valley is more heavily wooded than it was in 1916. After a century of unusually high rainfall and better control of prairie fires, lush grass now covers the banks and the steeply sloping dunes are dotted with sumac, eastern red cedar, green ash, box elder, burr oak and a smattering of eastern cotton-wood.

We see no signs of calcified, school teacher heads or any other calcified critters spewed out by whimsical quicksand patches. We make good time after we pass through the horses. The river has fewer sharp bends below the falls. Negotiating snags on a straight stretch is child's play compared to weaving through strainers on a sharp bend. We catch an occasional glimpse of a canoe following a hundred yards to our stern. A 30ish couple in brightly colored, new-fangled, moisture-wicking clothing. Now there's the ideal garment for a 40 degree day on the Dismal. They are slow to navigate a snag, lose momentum, swing sideways to the current, the canoe fills with water, disappears from sight. I take no pleasure in their troubles, only a minuscule acknowledgment a young, physically upscale, fashion-conscious couple can make the same mistake a fat old fart dressed in raggedy-assed sweatpants made a couple of hours ago.

We float under the Seneca Bridge, pull the kayak up on the north bank. Since our ride back to Mullen hasn't arrived, we wander the bridge, wishing vainly for sunshine, trying to restore circulation in frozen limbs. We stroll south to inspect the pristine camp ground Mitch leases from the landowner. About 50 intrepid folks a year canoe as far as the campground, spend a night and the next day tackle the 18 mile stretch of the Dismal from the Seneca Bridge to the Highway 83 bridge south of Thedford. Pretty much everyone who has floated both sections considers the lower section to be more challenging. The river, fed by springs all along the way, has more water and fewer bends, but there are more low hanging barbed wire fences, and many more tough strainers to negotiate, some of them near impossible.

The trailing couple finally comes into sight. From our vantage point up on the bridge we spot an inch of Dismal River water in the bottom of their canoe. We ask if they had an enjoyable trip. The trip, they say, was a breeze. Not a single spill. But, of course, they run this river every year so they know what to expect. An extremely fit sales rep from Omaha and his extremely perky dentist wife. He has 100 percent of the answers to any question you haven't asked. No telling how much knowledge we would have acquired had not the lecture been interrupted by the approach of Mitch Glidden's vintage Suburban towing a canoe trailer.

We help Mitch's elderly driver load our Dodger blue kayak and the smartly dressed couple's canoe on the trailer, sit directly behind the driver on the trip back to Mullen so we can visit over the engine noise. We learn something of the surrounding country and the current state of the canoe rental business.

*

The three ranch couples finish their leisurely meal at Red's Cafe, aim a friendly nod in our direction as they trail up to the register to pay their bills, passing close by the very table Ted Turner and Jane Fonda occupied back when they were still blissfully married. Impossible to know what these folks make of the two wet pilgrims in their midst. Maybe we think we're really something. Maybe we'd be okay if they got to know us, even if we're a little bit stupid for spending time on a river only a crazy person would tackle. Talking a mile a minute they head off for parts unknown, perhaps a supply gathering expedition to North Platte or a late season bull sale. They'll spot our 48 County license plate in the parking lot and know we're from Red Willow County, an indicator we may be okay. Not as good a resume as a license plate from Hooker or Thomas or McPherson or any other Sand Hills county, but it sure beats the heck out of a license plate from Omaha or Lincoln or Denver, places where just about everyone thinks they're really something.

An attentive waitress keeps our coffee cups filled. She is enthused about the Sand Hills Golf Club, says the managers and owners are quality people, who treat the hired help like human beings. She sometimes works there on busy summer weekends. We wouldn't believe the tips. Some of those guests think nothing of leaving a 100 dollar bill after a hamburger lunch.

The newer course, the one Jack Nicklaus designed, is a whole different animal. The manager irritated people here in Mullen from the git go. Hired outsiders, who didn't stay long enough to do jack squat. They didn't sell many building lots, which isn't surprising given the crazy prices. Enough to make your eyes bleed. Finally the whole kit 'n caboodle went blewie, the lenders took over, brought in new management, which is trying to get the townspeople back on board. They have a chance of sliding back on the rails, but they've got a long way to go. Nobody from here would take a job at the new course if they had the chance of working for the old one. That's just how it is.

Hot coffee and comfort grub finally work their magic. Kathy is no longer quite as blue around the gills. More importantly, she no longer replies to solicitous inquiries with a tight-lipped "fine." As we reminisce about the lowlights of our river trip she laughs. The twinkle returns to her eyes. Perhaps our marriage will survive the Dismal after all. I wonder if she'd be up for another stab at the Dismal. After all, we have valuable experience. It will surely be much warmer the next time. Our next trip will be as smooth as buttah. We could tackle the next stretch between the Seneca Bridge and Highway 83 south of Thedford. Maybe we'll locate the quicksand crossing that swallowed and spit out Anna Hora. We might even find the cedar posts set in the river marking the river bridge between the house and the barn on the old Black Ranch. Wouldn't that be something? The world outside lightens perceptibly as the sun makes its first appearance of the day. Things are looking up.

The largest sale bill on the wall of Red's Cafe catches my eye. Agri Affiliates of North Platte is offering at public auction, the historic McMurtrey Ranch — 26,332 deeded acres, 28,252 total acres including school leases. Referee's sale, which likely means the heirs, because they don't get along and don't trust each other, had to go to the additional expense of hiring a neutral legal representative to hold the sale, collect payment, disburse legal fees and pay the various heirs from the balance. Twenty-six thousand acres in one compact chunk. I wonder if Ted Turner will bid. If he does, will anyone bid against him?

Might be worth a drive to Valentine to find out.

Chapter 2
The Kinkaid Act

In 1904, Nebraska Republican Congressman Moses P. Kinkaid proposed a bill, later known as the Kinkaid Act, which allowed settlers in 37 counties of western Nebraska, comprising the Sand Hills, to claim up to 640 acres (a full section) rather than the standard 160 provided by the Homestead Act of 1862. Kinkaid argued the additional acreage was necessary to support agriculture in an area of sparse rainfall and nonproductive soils. Congress, in 1909, amended the original Homestead Act to allow homesteaders in other arid regions of the west to claim 320 acres, which in 1914 prompted my maternal grandparents, Bryan and Edith Tupper, to file on 320 acres north of Upton, Wyoming.

Chapter 3
McMurtrey Ranch Auction

I don't want to own every ranch, I just
want to own the ranch next door.

— Ted Turner, quoted in *Fortune Magazine*

I head out in the black predawn, Finlay, our copacetic West Highland White Terrier, sacked out on the passenger seat beside me. Early morning showers have dampened the two-lane highway from McCook to Valentine 200 miles to the north. If we mind our Ps and Qs and the crick don't rise, we might make the trip in three and a half hours. John Childears, head broker for Agri Affilates in North Platte, the real estate firm staging this morning's auction of the McMurtrey ranch, has promised introductions to the current renters and to Bob Childers (no relation), one of his salesmen, a relative of the McMurtrey heirs. By the end of the day perhaps I'll know why the heirs couldn't settle on a mutually agreeable real estate agent and had to hire Eric Scott, County Attorney of Cherry County, to hold a referee's sale.

Highway 83 tracks through a portion of the Lincoln County dune fields south of the Platte River. Though impressive in their own right, these dunes, the easternmost of which are often liberally sprinkled with red cedar, have different origins from the 20,000 square mile expanse of sand dunes north of the Platte. The sand making up the Lincoln County dunes is a mixture of K-feldspar rich sand from the neighboring Yuma Dune fields, originating in the Rocky Mountains near what is now Ft. Collins, Colorado, and sands with high quartz content, also found in the Nebraska Sand Hills, which can be traced back to the mountains west of Laramie, Wyoming.

A stop in North Platte for a coffee refill and to top off my gas tank, something that becomes habitual when heading into the sparsely populated Nebraska Sand Hills. As usual, Finlay wakes up when the car stops moving, retreats into his coma once we're back on the road. Climbing out of the Platte Valley we are soon in large dune country, the pastures short after five years of drought, but greening up nicely under the steady drizzle. Winking lights from low-lying clouds materialize into cell phone towers, mute testimony to the recent intrusion of cell phone service in these parts. It has become increasingly common in the past few years for a contemporary pilgrim crossing the Sand Hills to happen into an area where his cell phone actually works.

Stapleton, surrounded by more hard land farming and pivot irrigation than most towns in the heart of the Sand Hills, is home to the Logan County Fair & Rodeo, scheduled this year for August 24-27, the rodeo where cousin Willis Ruby rode bulls in the 1940s. I make a mental note to mark the calendar. To the west of Stapleton, a few miles up the South Loup, lies the Loup Valley Cemetery, picturesque home to Sand Hills geographer extraordinaire Charles Barron McIntosh, his wife Ruby and several storied relatives on my mother's side of the family tree.

Eight miles north of Stapleton we pass a narrow road leading east to Wild Horse Flat, site of the 200 horse hay operation of the legendary Black Ranch. If I weren't in an all-fired hurry to get to Valentine I'd scout it out, see if any building foundations survive.

A blink of an eyelash to cross the highway bridge over the Dismal. By the time the spring-fed Dismal River flows under Highway 83 south of Thedford it resembles an actual river rather than a narrow twisting creek cunningly designed to bust up marriages.

Highway 83 jogs east then north at Thedford, host of the Thomas County Fair & Rodeo every July. Loaded cattle semis head south through the rain towards feedlot country. SUVs and sedans sporting out-of-state license plates — Colorado, Oregon, Iowa, Minnesota appear and disappear in the mist. Why here? Are half the people in creation floating the Niobrara this summer?

Seven miles north of Thedford we cross into Cherry County, a county larger than the entire state of Connecticut, larger than the states of Rhode Island and Delaware put together, a county containing portions of two national forests, two ginormous national wildlife refuges and over 100 miles of the stunning Niobrara River Valley. A faded sign at the county line announces "God's Cattle Country." Some ranchers west and south of Cherry County, folks who obviously have never met Buzz Kime, regard the cattlemen in Cherry County as a hair too smug, a condition they blame on Cherry County's higher rainfall, higher stocking rates and bigger spreads. In my experience, cattle ranchers are among the least smug human beings on the planet. But I suppose there could be highly calibrated degrees of smug, and in an area deeply imbued with social democracy, anything smacking of smug, the first cousin to "thinking they're really something," would be easy to detect.

About the time we tool into Valentine, a half-hearted sun finally rouses itself and pokes a few holes in the clouds. Valentine, the commercial and medical hub of the north central Sand Hills, serves as base camp for thousands of hunters and Niobrara river floaters every year. Valentine's summer beer sales are always robust.

We pull into the crowded parking lot of the newish Holiday Inn Express. Mostly Cherry County license plates, except for Montana, home to the headquarters of Ted Turner's bison operations, and assorted individual plates from Wisconsin, Missouri, New Mexico, Arizona, Texas and neighboring South Dakota. No luxury cars, although there are a few tricked out six passenger one ton pickup trucks that cost more than a Mercedes Benz automobile.

The lobby swarms with beaming real estate people in matching yellow blazers. I accept a slick four color brochure, complete with a detailed map of the McMurtrey Ranch.

Livestock water on McMurtrey "is provided by Gordon and Betsy Creeks, approximately 62 wells/windmills, 7 good flowing wells (artesian) and 2 of smaller volume." To a person who once owned one balky windmill that ate leathers like lifesavers, 62 windmills is a staggering number. How many days' labor would it take to check the gear oil on all those wells? Replace the leathers once or maybe several times a year?

"Twenty-eight thousand, two hundred fifty-two acres divided into 55 separate pastures." How many miles of fence? Fifty? One hundred? One hundred fifty? How many rolls of barbed wire per year just to keep things spiffy? How many loads of posts? How many pounds of fence staples? And how many days to set the posts, stretch the wire, pound the staples? Any owner operator who purchases the McMurtrey will be buying years of hard labor. If Turner buys it he'll have wood posts and barbed wire fences torn out and replaced with high tensile electric wire, solar powered fence chargers and plastic posts, creating months of hard work for the men and women who work for him.

"Productive capacity 1250-1400 cows plus replacement heifers and breeding bulls." At today's cattle prices a buyer would need several million dollars just to stock the place.

"One thousand seven hundred fifty acres of wet hay meadow produce between 2000 and 2500 tons per year." That translates into 5000 big round hay bales every year and the equipment to cut, rake, bale and move, representing multiples of a hundred thousand dollars. And long hours of hard manual labor. Hours to calve out the cows, hours to work the calves, hours to help all the neighbors who helped you work your calves, long days to fix fence, hours to check windmills, hours to move the cattle between pastures, hours to put up the hay in the summer, feed the hay in the winter and early spring, hours to wean the calves, pregnancy test the cows and replacement heifers, market the calves, yearlings and cull cows. Based on recent prices the McMurtrey will likely bring roughly $10 million at today's auction. Even if I had the 10 million lying around, plus the 3 million it would take in operating money and some chump change to buy hay equipment, even if I had that kind of money, which I don't, the thought of all those hours of hard work shrinks my puny ambition like a spider on a hot stove.

A cheerful Wells Fargo representative points across the lobby to where John Childears chats up a potential buyer. Once he's finished, I remind him of his promise to introduce me to the renters and one or more of the heirs. He hasn't forgotten, but clearly has bigger fish to fry, makes noises about something similar to what we talked about maybe happening after the sale. That will have to do.

I give a pass to the table where bidders sign up for numbers. Obtaining an official bidding number requires too much personal financial information. Because I don't have a number a blazer guy steers me to the back of the room, the part of the room packed with ranchers and rancher wives. Except for a few token pairs of cowboy boots the entire crowd is shod in sneakers, a sure sign, if one were needed, of the fast approaching end of civilization as we know it.

By definition, all of the spectators are millionaires, many of them land poor millionaires to be sure, but millionaires nonetheless. 8,000 acres of Cherry County sand hills grass will, if properly managed, provide a living for one family. Most full time ranch families have larger spreads, but a ranch consisting of 8,000 acres is usually sufficient to free family members from taking second jobs in town. 8,000 acres, depending on the price set at today's auction, would sell for between 2.5 and 3.4 million dollars. Throw in $750,000 in livestock and machinery and without counting savings or brokerage accounts, most full time ranchers in the room own enterprises worth a minimum of 3 to 5 million dollars, with many in charge of larger operations.

None of those seated near me in the peanut gallery have buyer's numbers, even though the price of the McMurtrey is likely to be in reach for most. They might be satisfied with the amount of land and cattle and work and debt they already have. Their base of operations may be so distant from the McMurtrey, 72 miles southwest of the Holiday Inn Express where we're sitting, as to make management problematic and expensive. Some of those seated near me are pulling for the Kime family, the current renters, to outbid Ted Turner and don't wish to run up the price. Nobody hopes for an exorbitant price, which would make their holdings more valuable, but raise their property taxes significantly. For a rancher, property taxes often represent the single largest out of pocket annual expense.

Jim Wright takes an open seat beside me. Long time neighbor to the McMurtreys. Soft spoken. Big fella. One of the few men wearing cowboy hats, he, too, is shod in sneakers. I peek at my own shoes. Right in style.

Jim says Hub McMurtrey was a legend in the neighborhood. "Nobody worked harder than Hub. Nobody worked harder than when they were working for Hub. Hub didn't believe in Daylight Saving Time, never changed his clocks. Out there south of Nenzel everybody was on 'Hub time,' it just made sense."

Jim's father landed in Normandy on D Day and fought all the way to Germany before the war ended. A successful poker player in the army, he sent home enough winnings to purchase his first ranch. When he came home from Europe he quit poker for good, and by virtue of hard work built a sizable ranching operation. Turner purchased Jim's father's ranch three years ago. Jim says his daughters weren't interested in ranching.

Most good weather days Jim flew his daughters in a small plane to the one room Taylor Lake School near the McMurtrey ranch to avoid the two hour round trip by car. Jim says he still flies every chance he gets. Maybe if Jim and I become better acquainted he might take me up in a small plane, fly us over his old ranch, the Spike Box, the McMurtrey, point out the landmarks, tell me who used to own what. Wouldn't that be a kick?

Jim was especially fond of Hub and Muriel McMurtrey, who he says were good neighbors and classy people. Sad to watch the ranch pass out of the McMurtrey family, Jim says the heirs just can't get along.

The first time Turner turned out bison on the Spike Box, just south of Jim's ranch, he woke up the next morning with a couple of hundred bison in his yard after they'd stampeded through five barbed wire fences. Now Turner's fences are comprised of six electric wires with solar chargers every five or six miles. The bison respect the fences, which send out a half inch long spark. When he used to move cows across the Spike Box and had to drive them through a gate in the electric fence the cows hesitated, then scooted through like their butts were on fire. Jim figures they'd been bitten a few times by that arcing solar powered spark.

One of the yellow blazer-wearing guys turns on a wall-sized TV and a PowerPoint presentation flicks by with photos of the McMurtrey ranch and the same information contained in the slick, four-color brochure. Any assemblage of Sand Hills ranchers is usually dominated by people with college educations, many with Master's degrees, who have the ability and the inclination to read a four color real estate brochure, but Agri Affiliates takes no chances. This sale is not only about showcasing a legendary Cherry County ranch to best advantage, but a golden opportunity to market Agri Affiliates' real estate expertise. Unbeknownst to anyone but the feuding heirs and their lawyers, Agri Affiliates has been hired to conduct the sale for a flat $5000 fee plus promotional expenses ($10,000 in advertising, $541 miscellaneous fees, $1000 in title work and $150 to rent the room at the Holiday Inn Express). The big money, an even three-way split of $468,838.17, will eventually be paid out to referee Eric Scott and attorneys Mike Smith and Jeffery Orr, representing the two factions of the McMurtrey clan. None of the blazer guys will get a much of a pay out from today's sale, but future business may increase if potential sellers like what they see.

John Childears opens the festivities by asking people in the peanut gallery, "especially you ladies," to move up to the mostly empty front rows. Nobody moves. He asks all the veterans to stand and be recognized. One of the veterans is wearing a yellow blazer. Childears says Leland Johnson fought his way across the Philippines during W. W. II. I bookmark him for a later conversation. Childears introduces a weazened little guy under a humongous cowboy hat as a Korean War veteran. I bookmark him as well. Childears leads us in the Pledge of Allegiance to "the greatest flag on earth." Childears assures us he starts all his auctions with "The Pledge."

Sitting three rows in front of me in the seats reserved for actual bidders is a multigenerational family group, the men clad in golf shirts and sporting high dollar haircuts. The oldest guy has a bidding number. Jim doesn't know the names, but thinks they may be shirttail relation to the McMurtrey clan. My question circulates in the crowd behind us. Two minutes later the name Eric Rapp surfaces, along with the information his grandmother was a McMurtrey, who homesteaded near Hub McMurtrey and his brother Alf before selling out and returning home to Missouri. Someone else says Rapp made some real money "in the glass business back east." The Rapps visit with Bob Childers, a tall, good-natured guy in a blazer, assigned to give their bids his personal attention. I learn Bob's mother was related to Hub and Alf McMurtrey and he spent his childhood on the ranch where his dad worked for wages. On the other end of the row sits a line of ranchers and their wives and a broad-shouldered guy built like a steer wrestler. Jim says the ranchers are the Kime family, the renters, and the Ravenscrofts, their close neighbors. The steer wrestler-looking guy is Russ Miller, general manager of Turner's North American bison operations.

Childears runs through the nuts and bolts of the auction process. 15 percent of the purchase price due today, closing in 10 days, $71,065 in real estate taxes prorated between buyer and seller, fences owned by the ranch on leased school land included in the purchase price, all oil, gas and mineral rights going to the buyer. Childears says the McMurtrey will handle 1250 cow/calf pairs. Jim thinks 1250 pairs would be a stretch. Eric Scott, Cherry County attorney and dapper estate referee, rises to acknowledge his introduction.

A younger auctioneer takes over, starts his chant at $290 per acre, taking bids in $5 increments until the process stalls at $340. Childears calls a five minute recess. Bob Childers jokes with Eric Rapp. I can't tell if Rapp has been a participant in the bidding, but on closer inspection he strikes me as a self-assured, savvy person who will not bid above his self-imposed limit, even if he has the means to go higher. The Kimes and Ravenscrofts huddle. The auction resumes. Everyone in the peanut gallery strains to see who's bidding what. Another recess at $350 an acre. During most land auctions this is when the auctioneer wheels out the "speech," a long-winded sermon boiling down to "nobody can know for certain what a piece of land is worth, but what we do know for certain is the good Lord isn't making any more land, especially prime land like this, blah, blah, blah." But not today, perhaps a reflection of the relative sophistication of the bidders, bidders well-known to Childears and the auctioneer. Bob Childers works his side of the room. An anonymous buyer from California bids by phone. The bidding resumes in $1 increments until it reaches $364 an acre, a total of $9,584,848. After a brief consultation with referee Scott to make sure the auction lasted the legally required one hour, Childears pronounces the ranch sold. Someone behind me announces Turner won the bid. Jim confirms. Many in the room might have wished for a different outcome, but nobody is much surprised, and there is a palpable sense of relief the price wasn't as high as two recent area sales of $407 and $425 an acre. Taxes is taxes.

Adding the McMurtrey Ranch's 26,332 deeded acres to what he already owns in Cherry County brings Turner's holdings to 225,342 acres, a significant percentage of the 2 million acres he owns in Nebraska, South Dakota, Kansas, Oklahoma, New Mexico and Montana. No doubt some folks begrudge him his purchase. But he made this one at public auction, not in a sly, secretive transaction. Anyone in the room with the dough-re-me could have joined the fray. The last few minutes of the auction, when the bid increased one dollar at a time, made an impression. Clearly Turner's bidder was trying to buy the ranch as cheaply as possible. Had he chosen he could have blown out the other bidders by jumping the bid by $50 or a $100 an acre. We expect that sort of behavior from billionaires. That Turner's man didn't jump the bid in an ostentatious manner earns Turner some grudging respect. He may be a billionaire with weird politics, once married to a certified wing nut, but at least he watches his pennies like any normal person.

The room clears rapidly. John Childears, referee Scott and Turner's representative Miller disappear into side room to deal with the paperwork. Kimes and their neighbors engage in deep conversation. The weazened Korean War vet and his impressive hat have vanished. The World War II vet, the one wearing a blazer who fought his way across the Philippines, strolls up the aisle. I ask Leland Johnston if he were a draftee in World War II. Johnston was working as a ranch hand when the draft notice came. He and several Cherry County boys rode an ancient Northwestern Railroad coach into Lincoln for their induction physicals. He remembers the old style carbide lights, how they smoked and stung his eyes. He saw MacArthur riding in a jeep a few times in the Philippines. The malaria he contracted in the Pacific acted up recently after he had a stent put in his heart. Didn't make him that sick, just weak. He figures he trucked pretty much every artillery shell used against the Japanese in the Philippines, who by the way made a huge mess of Manila. The Japanese didn't give up easily. You usually had to kill them to get them to quit.

Johnson doesn't think the price the McMurtrey ranch brought today is any big shucks, says ranch land has never been profitable, even when it only cost a dollar an acre and a family could live on cream and egg money. He agrees to visit at a later date about his experiences in the Pacific.

I catch up with Bob Childers and his wife Susan as they're headed out the door. They live three miles south of the Seneca Bridge over the Dismal River. Bob and his wife admit to floating the Dismal at least once, but don't say if it was an enjoyable experience. They are still married, if that means anything. Come on up, we'll talk about the McMurtrey Ranch.

Losing bidder Duane Kime, who, along with his cousin, Shane and uncle, Kenneth "Buzz" Kime leases the McMurtrey from the McMurtrey estate, says he will be happy to visit, but wants first to finalize his leasing arrangements with John Hansen, Turner's ranch manager. During the year or two it will take for the Spike Box crew to convert the McMurtrey to handle bison Kimes are hoping to extend their lease. The McMurtrey comprises half the Kime's grazing capacity and a good chunk of their wet hay meadow. The eventual loss, unless replaced by other rental or purchased capacity, may mean some members of the Kime family will have to leave the operation. The Kime family faces the frustrating kind of decisions with no pain-free options.

Duane Kime said he and his uncle approached the auction with an agreement with John Ravenscroft, their neighbor to the east, (operator of the old Three Bar, formerly owned by the Brandies merchant family from Omaha) to buy the McMurtrey and split it. They had a price of $325 an acre in mind, but bid $360 after the final recess. "There are people who don't know the place or the ground who thought it sold cheap. The price of fuel this far out is a factor, whether it's hauling cattle in or out or hauling in hay or feed. It just costs us more."

We both know there is no more certain path to financial ruin than paying too much for land, borrowing too much of the purchase price, over leveraging the land you already own, leaving you only one killer blizzard or one stretch of low cattle prices from bankruptcy. But he seems not so much relieved he didn't pay too much than worried about the future of the Kime Ranch without access to the McMurtrey.

As usual, Finlay is happy to see me. Dogs are dependable that way. He's also happy in the knowledge we'll be going for a walk soon. We hike the hills above Minnechaduza Creek where it runs through the city park on the north edge of Valentine. The trail is mostly mud — part sand, part slippery clay. Finlay turns from brilliant white to gooey gray in a matter of minutes. Muddy Westies are the reason God invented protective tarps for car seats. Slogging through a steady drizzle makes the memory of the hard drought years recede a bit, although I am constantly reminded as we pass through charred stumps marking the path of the Valentine forest fire in July of 2006, which burned 3,100 acres and destroyed 10 homes. Big fire. Forty-seven volunteer fire departments helped out, along with three air tankers and a couple of helicopters. Plenty of trees and grape vines and underbrush still to burn, but not today. Way too wet.

Finlay, his legs stretched, a virgin territory well-marked, his coat a mess of muddy dingle-berries, clambers into the car and nestles down on the tarped front seat.

The four color real estate brochure contains a map of the McMurtrey and driving directions. Might as well check it out. Finlay loses consciousness as soon as we hit Highway 20 headed west out of Valentine. Twelve miles to Crookston, 11 miles to Kilgore, 8 miles to Nenzel, where we turn south for the last 42 miles, crossing the narrow upper Niobrara and passing through the Samuel R. McKelvie National Forest, which is long on grass, mighty short on trees. The road jogs west, then south, then west. We pass a well-maintained one-room school, empty of teachers or students until fall. Recently retired from 27 years in the classroom, I'm intrigued by the idea of visiting a modern one-room school when classes resume in the fall, observing how a single teacher handles multiple grades in one classroom. Another bookmark.

Finlay growls at a small horse herd. For some reason horses always make him suspicious. I snap photos of the horses against the backdrop of the sprawling headquarters of the McMurtrey Ranch, a small village of scattered barns and houses backlit by the dying sun. How much of what Hub and Muriel and brother Alf built and inhabited all those years will Turner leave standing? What will become of Hub's Kinkaider shack, the one he moved from his original homestead and was fond of showing visitors?

I pull into the driveway for a closer photo. A fading hand painted red and white wooden sign announcing "The McMurtrey Ranch" lies beside the road where it has fallen in tall grass

Chapter 4
A KINKAIDER COMES AND STAYS

Forty miles to water, thirty miles to wood, twenty
miles to hell, and I've gone there for good.

— Inscription left behind by a disgruntled homesteader, quoted
by Mari Sandoz in *Great American Desert*

Alf never intended to be that big, just wanted
to own all the land that joined him.

— Erba "Hub" McMurtrey

I never wanted my kids to work as hard as I did.

— Muriel McMurtrey

In tracing the history of the McMurtrey Ranch, I understood I'd be sifting through conflicting accounts. People who knew the McMurtreys said the family "just doesn't get along." And it soon became apparent some of the heirs flat didn't like each other. Even the handful who could tolerate being in the same room had honest differences over the future of the ranch. With a few exceptions, no interview with a member of the immediate family was complete without a jab at someone on the other side. The old nostrum that time heals all wounds is one of my personal favorites, but when it comes to the McMurtrey heirs it might be bullshit.

Every community has mean-spirited gossips who enjoy rolling around in the misfortunes of others. The neighborhood south of Nenzel in Cherry County is probably no exception. I just didn't happen to run into any mean-spirited gossips. The people who shared their stories universally regarded the disintegration of the McMurtrey family as a Greek tragedy, the roots of the implosion plain to see long before it happened. For them, the inevitability in no way made the situation any less regrettable.

I found the heirs to be in general agreement about only three things: their genuine love and admiration for Hub and Muriel McMurtrey, their abiding respect for Alf McMurtrey's keen business sense and their sorrow the McMurtrey Ranch was no more because of those lazy, greedy relatives on the other side of the family divide they'd been telling me about.

Talking to the principals, starting with Hub and Muriel's eldest son Dr. George Boone McMurtrey, was the easy part. Sorting through wildly different versions of family history was a whole nother level of difficulty.

Dr. George Boone McMurtrey

Everyone who knew George describes him as brilliant — brilliant mind, brilliant surgeon. I bumped into friends and relatives who'd made special arrangements to have their surgeries done by George in Omaha or Valentine. And on the phone George sounded smart. Smart in a stentorian kind of way. He managed to tell me twice he'd "proudly" served his Wyoming district in the state legislature for 10 years. "Come on up," he bellowed, "I'll meet you in town."

The next day after lunch, Kathy and I are on now familiar Highway 26 following the Oregon Trail up the North Platte Valley from Ogallala past Lake McConaughy, Ash Hollow, over Blue Water Creek, past Lisco, Broadwater and Bridgeport. We're well into January and by six p.m. it's plumb dark. The floodlit spire of Chimney Rock, 300 feet above the valley floor, emerges from the gloom. Oregon Trail emigrants could see Chimney Rock for two days before they arrived. Despite erosion and lightning strikes, and apocryphal artillery assault, Chimney Rock remains a distinctive landmark.

Priceline, as you probably know, can be a wonderful thing. Kathy found a motel on the outskirts of Gering, Nebraska, for a pittance. The two friendly women at the check-in desk, wearing fishnet stockings and otherwise abbreviated costumes, show an interest in pursuing a closer acquaintance. Assaulted by the aroma of rotting marijuana and sinus-clearing perfume, I back out of the office and mobile to our room — which turns out to be not for the squeamish. Crusted carpet, dingy towels. inoperative heat. And a random .38 caliber bullet casing lying smack in the middle of the crusty floor. Kathy gingerly pulls back the covers to examine the sheets, grayish with artistic sprinklings of short, dark, curly hairs. Naturally, she has to make a big deal out of it, ignoring my attempts at levity. "Do you think those sheets have always been gray or do you think someone dyed them?" She huffs around, donning her winter parka, two pairs of heavy socks and ski gloves and spends a sleepless night, rigid as any Egyptian mummy, atop the DNA stained bedspread. I, on the other hand, jump between the sheets and sleep the sleep of the innocent.

Let's just say we were not completely blindsided a few months later when a sheriff's deputy serving a warrant at the motel and the criminal in question engaged in a bloody shootout.

Except for an unsuccessful half hour search for a breakfast cafe in Torrington, we make good time on the trip to Gillette. So good we have a few extra minutes for a quick tour of Upton, Wyoming, near where my maternal grandparents homesteaded just prior to World War I and where my mother was born. You might not consider Upton a large place (pop. 876), but I would estimate Upton and surrounding Weston County must employ approximately five law enforcement officers for every each and every citizen. The massive police presence was no doubt an anticipation of civil insurrection, which would have been danged interesting to watch, but after l meekly accepted the speeding ticket for being a crummy five miles over the limit we had no time to spare before rushing off to meet George in Gillette.

For our interview site George chose a large hotel on the east side of Gillette with a spacious seating area and an imposing gas fireplace. Cozy. He marches in wearing a luxurious cashmere overcoat and erect military bearing from his years in the service. With a hearty, booming voice George greets everyone in sight, desk clerks, hotel maids, guests coming and going. Easy to see why he spent 10 years in the Wyoming legislature. First rule of politics: never leave a potential voter unacknowledged. After delivering a good dose of impeccable old school manners and polished meet and greet all around, George settles into the soft leather sofa across from us and gets down to the business at hand: his childhood and the sale of the McMurtrey. And boy, can George McMurtrey enunciate once he gets on a roll. I'm half deaf and don't miss a syllable, neither does the tape recorder.

George has nothing but fond memories of an idyllic childhood, says he was born on April 2, 1920. "You can probably do the arithmetic," which I take to mean his mother's pregnancy lasted less than nine months after the wedding (actually four and a half months). While George was growing up on a Kinkaid claim on Boardman Creek in western Cherry County, his father Erba (Hub) and uncle Alfred (Alf) continually added to the holdings of the Bar Lazy 8, usually by purchasing the proved up claims of neighboring Kinkaiders, sometimes for fifty cents an acre, sometimes for as much as a dollar and a half. Several of these purchases, especially those bordering the expanding McMurtrey spread, were from Missouri relatives, including sister Luvecia McMurtrey Babcock, grandmother of Eric Rapp, bidder at the McMurtrey Ranch auction a few months ago.

In a country where hard work was unremarkable, both Muriel and Hub were considered to be extraordinary, working from "can't see to can't see," only leaving the ranch for town when supplies ran low. "I can still see my father, always impatient, trotting from house to barn to hayfield." During haying season Muriel took responsibility for the milking, laundry, meals and lunches for twenty men, sometimes with the help of a hired girl, sometimes with only daughter Mary Alice's assistance. The wash house, where Hub and Alf shaved every morning with cold well water, had a wringer washer and three tubs. "In later years my mother said the automatic washing machine was the single most important invention during her lifetime." Muriel gradually built a reputation as a cook, famous for her baked goods. "I can remember walking home from our little country school. If it was baking day I could smell the cinnamon rolls and ran the last 100 yards." Hub and Muriel kept the operation humming during the times when Alf absented himself.

"Now Alf, he was a little different from my father. He had more of a business head. My father concentrated on overseeing the hired help and the livestock." Alf, in keeping with his solitary nature, roamed when he could, always packing cash or a checkbook in case he encountered a bargain on livestock, supplies or land. Alf returned from an early expedition to Grand Island with a set of broken down thoroughbred mares, which Hub successfully bred to Morgan and Steel Dust (Quarter Horse) studs. Alf wasn't opposed to hitchhiking or traveling on foot. Much more aggressive than Hub when it came to land purchases, Alf was fond of buying a new piece of land, walking in the front door and telling Hub and Muriel "time to tighten our belts again."

An elderly man wearing cowboy boots and a stark white cowboy hat enters the hotel lobby, pardons his interruption, shakes George's hand, thanks him for his service in the legislature. George promises to keep up the fight. "We'll stop those crooked Democrats, do whatever it takes. Either you're an honest politician or you're a Democrat and you lie about everything." The man chuckles, tugs his hat brim in Kathy's general direction, strolls out of the hotel.

"Alf lived with us. Sometimes my mother grumbled because he was never too clean." On his long distance rambles Alf adopted a hobo appearance, unshaven, dressed in dirty, ragged overalls. And although he typically carried large amounts of cash, he was never robbed. Alf returned to Missouri on several occasions to succor relatives going through hard times.

He took older sister Cora and her tubercular daughter to Arizona in a doomed search for a cure, helped his mother on the family farm for several months after his father died. During the Depression he often returned from Missouri with hungry, destitute relatives, who worked on the ranch for little more than board and room. Any down on their luck nephew, niece or third cousin once removed could count on a job and a place at Muriel's table. And a diet heavy on peanut butter. "Mother bought peanut butter in gallon cans and she bought a lot of cans."

"Alf's the one who tracked down the horse thieves." This was back in the 1930s after the McMurtreys built a sizable horse herd. "We always had 15-20 saddle mares and raised Belgian colts every year." Led by "Rat" Peters, a handful of pool hall trash ran off fifty head of McMurtrey mares and colts and set off cross country for the railroad livestock pens at Wood Lake. "Alf tracked them until he figured out where they were going, hoofed it back to the ranch, drove to Wood Lake, where he spotted some of our horses. Sheriff Otho Kime and Deputy Allen Ward, my son-in-law Charlie Ward's father, made the arrests."

Alf died unexpectedly. During haying season in the summer of 1949 when Alf was 63 he spent an entire day in the shop welding on a galvanized air tank trying to close a leak. Late that night, his lungs affected by the fumes, Alf died of a heart attack, his longtime dream of purchasing 640 acres of his great-great grandfather Joseph's original Spanish land grant in Missouri and restoring it to the family unrealized. The family took him back to his beloved Missouri Ozarks to the cemetery where his parents were buried.

Alf died without a will. Neighbors said Alf saw no need to formalize his estate because he assumed he would outlive his younger brother Hub, who Alf thought would kill himself by working too hard. Alf likely considered his share of the ranch as the common property of all of his brothers and sisters. With some difficulty Hub was able to satisfy the obligations of his intestate brother by selling off 3000 acres of range and a set of replacement heifers and distributing the money to Alf's siblings. Although Hub added back a few acres to the Bar Lazy 8 in the succeeding years, the expansionary era of the McMurtrey ranch effectively ended with Alf's death. The experience, according to George, made Hub particularly mindful of the difficulties one heir might encounter purchasing the interests of the multiple heirs of a large ranch.

Hub and Muriel might have been obsessive worker bees, but as Muriel said on more than one occasion, "I never wanted you kids to work as hard as we did." George and his younger sister Mary Alice performed the normal chores of children of the era. Mary Alice helped her mother cook for large crews of hired men, gathered eggs, scavenged corn cobs for the cook stove, scalded the cream separator. George, in the dark pre-dawn, rounded up the 140 head work horse herd for harnessing. As he grew older George not only rounded up horses, but spent long days mowing the vast McMurtrey hay meadows and dug hundreds of post holes. Post hole digging was not, we can tell, his most favorite thing to do.

The McMurtreys doted on their children, showering them with books and clothing ordered from catalogs. "We wanted for nothing," George said. Always precocious, George read everything, including his father's Lincoln Star newspaper. His intelligence and photographic memory soon caught the attention of his teachers, one of whom encouraged him to take up science. When George told Muriel he was considering a career in medicine she adopted his ambition as her own.

After high school graduation, George enrolled in the University of Nebraska. "I was in all kinds of campus organizations, made many friends, joined the Corn Cobs, ever hear of it? We were the student pep squad. I'll never forget the trip to the 1941 Rose Bowl. That's back when Nebraska had a good football team." Medical school led to a tour of duty as a battle surgeon with the 82nd Airborne Division towards the end of World War II. He spent his early surgical career in Omaha, then Texas, then Valentine, divorced and remarried before a brief stint with the Indian Health Service in South Dakota and his move to Gillette in 1978.

What did Hub want to see happen to the ranch after he died?

"He would have liked to see the ranch stay in the family, but his lawyers talked him into putting it in a trust. My sister's (Mary Alice's) family, they're the ones who forced the sale. They went to court and got it done. Some of her kids were overcome by a surplus of greed and I don't like them very well. They sold my old home out from under me. My sister shares their sentiments. I don't dislike her, but I don't spend any time with her."

I am thinking George is gilding the lily a little bit. Nobody sold the ranch out from under him, because he had given up his interest in the ranch years before in exchange for Hub bailing him out of a bad financial bind. It's all right there in the Cherry County courthouse. But it's George's story to tell any way he wants.

"My sister is a widow who lives in Valentine. She lived in Denver a long time before her husband died or maybe they got divorced. Herb was in real estate, one of those guys who had a champagne appetite and beer pocketbook." Ouch.

George does not approve of Ted Turner buying the ranch. "Ted Turner is a thug. I don't like that guy. Turner will be dead one of these days and then what's he going to do with all that? Of course, Jane Fonda dumped him. I don't know where she is now, still insulting Vietnam veterans probably." Probably.

Mary Alice McMurtrey Williams

Mary Alice may be an octogenarian, but you'd never know it. She enjoys a full social calendar and doesn't regret the move back to Valentine to be close to her mother Muriel during her last years. "I still have friends from high school living here." Some of Mary Alice's chums accompany her to daily exercise class.

Mary Alice's spacious ranch style house just north of Valentine's downtown, while more than adequate for her needs, is not in any way ostentatious or speaks of newly minted millionaire status. She asks Kathy about our three-hour drive this morning, wonders if spring in McCook is as far advanced as Valentine's. Kathy assures her the tulips blooming along the sidewalk would challenge anything we have at home. She clearly dotes on the weepy-eyed white toy poodle presently barking at Finlay, who is wagging his tail in the front seat of the car. We let him out to become better acquainted, but once Mary Alice discovers he is an intact male (always has been, always will be) it's back in the slammer for Finlay.

Like her brother George, Mary Alice is not pleased about Turner buying the ranch. "We knew he was going to buy it. He'd asked about it for two years. My daughter Dianne went out and talked to his people in Montana.

"I have a cousin from Wisconsin, Eric Rapp, who made his money in the glass business.

He wanted to buy it and we would have loved to sell it to him at private treaty, which would have kept it in the family. You get people like my brother George's second set of kids, they were younger, had no sentimental ties to the ranch, no feeling about anything except just being obnoxious.

"In order to buy it Eric would have needed my brother's second set of children to agree. My brother wasn't in the trust because when he divorced his first wife she was entitled to alimony and he got stubborn and wouldn't pay it. After her lawyer slapped a lien on the trust, my father paid her off and took George out of the trust. His second set of children weren't specifically mentioned in the trust because they were born later. But in order to have a private sale they needed to sign off and at least one of them, a boy, even refused to talk to Eric. I hear he's a grown man living in George's basement. I don't think my brother even tried to convince them. I wouldn't know them if they walked down the street. They didn't gain a dollar by doing that. The only thing they did was make enemies. So what was the point? To be obnoxious." Ouch.

Like her brother George, Mary Alice grew up wanting for nothing. "I never felt poor, because we always had plenty to eat and warm clothes. Mom only had one dress most of the time we were growing up. At home she mostly wore striped overalls. But she bought me new dresses from the catalogue whenever she thought I needed one.

"It was about a mile and a half to school. If it were really bad weather my brother rode a horse and I rode up behind my dad. I remember walking back from school some days and smelling my mother's cinnamon rolls. That's when we started running."

Mary Alice never wanted to stay on the ranch after high school, had no interest in boys from the neighborhood. "My mother and father never put any pressure on my brother or me to stay." She attended Colorado Woman's College in Denver with a high school classmate Ruby Gale her freshman year, then switched to the University of Nebraska. "I think my mother and Mrs. Gale got together and decided to send us to a women's college. The next year I made up my mind to go to Lincoln where my brother was. I intended to be a teacher. I got my degree in elementary education but I never did teach. I was what you would call a flub up."

Following Muriel's death, lease payments from the ranch provided Mary Alice with a decent income after taxes and expenses. However, the grandchildren split the balance into much smaller shares, representing a fraction of the ranch's worth. "There were several who wanted to sell — myself and my three children and my brother's two surviving children from his first marriage. The grandchildren were getting less than two percent a year on the investment. You could get that in a CD."

Did any of her children express an interest in running the ranch?

"Oh yes, but we have a dysfunctional family. Nobody could have run that ranch because a few of them would have had their noses in there from daylight to dark. My daughter (Dianne Yarbrough) and her husband would have run it. Charlie Ward, do you know him? No? That's good. He was married to George's daughter. She died of cancer."

Charlie Ward couldn't have run the ranch?

Mary Alice laughs, "Take my word for it, there probably wouldn't be anything left by now."

We take our leave on Mary Alice's manicured front lawn. A gracious hostess, as she's been all afternoon, she says to call anytime if we have more questions. "I don't know much, but I'll do my best." She bows her head for a moment, when she looks up she is smiling. "My father was a very generous, kind, lovable man, who never said no to me for anything."

Charlie Ward

Charlie Ward lives on an immaculately groomed acreage on the northeast edge of Valentine along meandering Minnechaduza Creek. Minnechaduza Creek, you may remember, is Finlay's all-time favorite place for collecting wet, greasy clay balls on his undercarriage.

Charlie's daily schedule would put a much younger person to shame. Connecting with him hasn't been easy. His lock shop services clients within a 100 mile radius. If you're a co-op manager who's forgotten the combination to the safe Charlie Ward's your guy. If some mope high school kid used a borrowed key to break into your school last night and trashed the computer lab, Charlie Ward will have all your locks changed out in record time. Then there's the ready-mix concrete plant he recently launched and the human transport business, which has him shuttling prisoners and suicidal folks back and forth from jails to penitentiaries to psych facilities to courts across the state. He also serves on the Nebraska Board of Educational Land and Funds, which administers 1.3 million acres of state-owned land, making decisions on leasing for agricultural use and for mineral, oil and gas development. The board, not so well known in more densely populated areas of the state, is a big deal in ranch country, where state-owned "school sections" make up a percentage of most large land holdings, Ted Turner's Spike Box being no exception.

Charlie's wife Phyllis says he's out in the corral messing with a horse. She hopes tonight will be the exception, but she expects him to be late for every meal. By the time Charlie finishes with the horse and we enter the kitchen it's obvious dinner has been ready and waiting for a good long time.

The first thing you notice about Charlie is he has so much energy he practically vibrates. The second thing you notice is Charlie does not mince words.

"Gimme, gimme, gimme. You gave him fifty cents more than you gave me. Gimme. That's what it was. Greed. Mary Alice was so jealous it's unbelievable. George, he's the same way, although he probably won't admit it. Like when Granny (Muriel) built Mary Alice her house in Valentine. She had to give George the equivalent amount of money in cash."

Charlie Ward's first marriage to George's daughter Mary Margaret gave him a ringside seat to the dysfunctional McMurtrey family. After Hub's fatal heart attack and before Mary Margaret's death from cancer, Charlie took a zealous role in guarding Muriel's interests, keeping an eye on ranch buildings, repairing windmills, working with renters, all the while viewing the rest of the family as lazy, greedy parasites. Despite his best advice, the always generous Muriel continued to fund grandchildren's educations, buy family members automobiles and bail descendants out of unwise financial choices. After Muriel died, management of the ranch reverted to two family trustees, Mary Alice's daughter Dianne Yarbrough and Rella Hallman, George's daughter and Mary Margaret's twin sister. As part of the trust agreement an employee of the Bank of the West served as the third trustee. Charlie signed over his share of the ranch to the boys. "I didn't think the ranch was mine. I went to the rest of 'em, told this is the time to give it to your kids. They said 'We can spend that money.'"

"Once Dianne got in there she kept trying to sell it. The boys and I prevented her from doing that on more than one occasion. She kept at it. We'd have meetings at the bank and we'd say no and the bank stuck with us."

Charlie served in the military, graduated from Chadron State College, met and married Mary Margaret McMurtrey, who graduated from SMU in computer science. Charlie taught industrial arts at Niobrara and Sidney, Nebraska, before returning to Valentine to take over his father's plumbing business. "Dad bought this acreage in 1956. I was a plumber for 30 years before a horse tried to kill me. I've got two rods and four great big screws in my back holding it together." The injury prompted Charlie's exit from the plumbing business. His entrance into the locksmith, prisoner transportation and the concrete businesses followed soon after.

Charlie takes the first of several phone calls, moves outside for privacy.

Phyllis, who clearly dotes on her husband, says I have to understand Charlie is very energetic. "He has a brilliant mind like a lot of the family members. He challenged himself to teach school, went to the service, obtained another degree in refrigeration and electrical work, got a well driller's license, then learned how to fly a plane. He's always challenging himself with something else. I was the latest challenge. Charlie's political. I'm political too."

Charlie, returning to the kitchen, overhears. "Oh, God, she's a Democrat. I'm a Republican naturally. She went down to the courthouse to register. The next time I'm in the courthouse people kept popping out of doorways asking me if I knew she was a registered Democrat. When I got down to the sheriff's office he said we've got another Democrat in the county."

Phyllis grins, "We have some good discussions."

"When I was helping Granny run things I was out at the ranch a lot. I took money from the rent, plowed it back in the ranch. I didn't think the heirs deserved any of it. That twisted some tails, especially Dianne's. If my wife Mary had lived she would have had her sister Rella's position as trustee and she would have stood up to Dianne and would have prevented the ranch from being sold. Once Granny died Mary Alice gave her trustee position to Dianne and I had nothing to do with running the ranch. If I had been a position to manage things Ted Turner's holdings would never have reached the border of the ranch because all the neighbor ground that came up for sale would have been added to the McMurtrey. Jim Wright's was probably ten or twelve thousand acres, Younkin's was probably six or seven thousand. Ranch income could have made payments on both properties, which lay between the Spike Box and the McMurtrey."

There was a section of the will instructing the trustees to give added consideration to any heir who wanted to operate the ranch. Did any heir ask to lease it?

"Nobody had the backing or the capital to lease and stock something of that size. It was just too big. I regret it (the sale) ever happened. If I could redo anything that's one thing I would undo. Desperate people do desperate things. I don't know how badly they needed the money. Maybe I was fortunate not to need the money, didn't want the money."

Phyllis offers me a dish of butter pecan ice cream covered in fresh strawberries, an unusual combination, but I accept. The strawberries and ice cream are delicious. Meanwhile, Charlie's cell phone is ringing off the hook. Clearly I am keeping him from conducting important business. Three hours from home and plumb dark, it's past time to ease on down the road.

"Granny was my in-law grandmother. I don't think I ever loved a grandmother the way I loved her. She was a great, great lady. If anyone has a place in heaven she should have the throne. In fact, I could goddamn near cry at her loss and I'm an old man. She was never better than anybody, would never ask anyone to do something she wouldn't do herself. One time I was upset with some family stuff that was going on and telling Granny about it. She said, 'Charlie, don't expect so much from people and you won't be so disappointed.'"

Dianne Yarbrough

I catch up with Dianne Yarbrough by phone at her home in New Mexico. She is talking about her childhood on the McMurtrey. "From the time we were 10 years old us kids spent our summers there. I don't think my grandparents trusted my parents or my cousins' parents to raise children properly. When we were with Grandma we cleaned house and carried lunches to the men in the hay fields. When we went with Grandpa to check windmills and cattle we opened gates and helped put out salt.

"I learned to ride a horse almost before I could walk. My first horse was named Paint and had been my mother's horse. The grandkids were roping and branding by the time they were 7 or 8 years old. By the time we got to be 11 or 12, we were in the hay meadows taking turns on a side delivery rake.

"Grandma made the work fun and there was always a reward. She took us to town, took us to the movies at the drive in, took us to country dances. George and my mother brought current wives and husbands and all the cousins every Christmas. There'd be dances and skating and card parties. Before Grandpa and Grandma built the new house all the family stayed at their old house. There were only three bedrooms so the kids all slept wherever. We had so much fun getting ready for dances, using flashlights in the hallway to put on our makeup.

"After Hub died, my uncle George, my grandmother and Bill Quigley, the attorney from Valentine, were the trustees and it was a mess. Uncle George and grandmother left everything up to Quigley and he didn't know shit from applesauce. Judge Moursund leased the ranch for 17 years and he ran the place into the ground. He didn't make repairs, overgrazed, did not take care of the meadows or the fences. Moursund had the option of matching anyone else's offer to lease the place. The Kime's made an offer right after Grandma died and he didn't match it. In 1994 Moursund was stealing it for maybe $5.75 an acre. With the Kimes it went straight to $8 an acre. Mother and George were totally dependent on the ranch income in their later years.

"Rella and I became trustees and were able to make the repairs and still pay the heirs more than they'd ever been paid. The Kimes also were better stewards of the land. We worked with Jim Van Winkle and the Sand Hills Task Force on some riparian reclamation projects and restored the overgrazed pastures by adding fences and windmills. Back when Alf and my grandfather were getting started they dredged the meadows to gain more hay land, which dropped the water table. We restored some of the old meadows, created bends in the creeks that had been straightened. Although the Kimes were doing some of this on their own land, they didn't like the fact I was putting so much water back in the meadows, which made the haying season shorter.

"When I was a young woman and was seriously dating someone in the area I asked my grandfather if I could be on the ranch and be a part of it and he said he wouldn't allow it. He never gave a reason. Later, when I was working so hard managing the ranch I thought about leasing it, running it myself. I hired a consulting firm to figure out what it would take to stock it with cattle, get all the machinery. It was prohibitive. Too much capital. And we had in-laws that just couldn't be gotten along with. The only reason we finally sold it, and I'm sure this is a decision most families make in this instance, Rella and I were getting to the age when it was a hardship to spend four to six weeks up there managing the ranch. The next generation didn't know anything about the ranch, had no interest in the ranch and ownership would have become more fractured and more diluted.

"It was downright impossible to convince the others. Rella and my mother were okay with selling. Rella's sister Alice was okay with it. Only one of Uncle George's second family was okay with it. We finally got them to see the light by bribing them with a larger share. The people who got a huge pay day were the lawyers, Jeff Orr, Eric Scott and Mike Smith. Mike Smith was the lawyer for the Ward boys. He got a huge chunk because without him we could never have got the Ward boys to sign off on the dissolution of the trust and the sale. Gary Peterson, Rella's attorney son-in-law got a piece for going up to Gillette and persuading Uncle George's second family. I think the lawyers divided up about a half million dollars.

"Hub was a wonderful man. He loved us children. I'll always remember in the evening when he sat on the porch peeling apples for us and tell stories about when he first came into the country and his growing up years in Missouri."

Eric Rapp

Eric Rapp, retired glass industry executive from Wisconsin, learned from his mother, Hub and Alf's niece, the heirs were leaning towards selling the McMurtrey, part of which was homesteaded by his grandmother Luvecia.

He had conversations with Dianne, but soon ran up against the family's inability to agree on much of anything. The breaking of Hub's trust meant the ranch would have to be sold at public auction, ending his chance at a private treaty sale. "The family probably could have gotten more money (from me) rather than paying all the fees."

Leading up to the auction, he visited the ranch for the first time since he was a boy, when he'd ridden a horse, done "the kind of cowboy things kids do." Rapp met with the Kimes, gauging their interest in leasing the ranch. He liked them, decided they were the kind of people he could trust over the long term. "I liked Buzz, he was rock solid.

"A couple of years after the sale — it is what it is and we're moving on. If Ted Turner ever wanted to sell I'd think about buying it, but I don't think Ted's going to do that."

Rella McMurtrey Hallman

Rella Hallman: "The only reason it got sold was because the attorney in Valentine worded one of the trusts wrong so it got broke. Not by me! Because I was perfectly happy with things the way they were."

James Boone Ward

James Ward, son of Charlie and Mary Ward, is a practicing attorney. He and his family opposed the sale of the McMurtrey for as long as was practical. "The whole process drug out three or four years, starting with the entire rest of the family suing my family to break up the trust and sell the ranch. We engaged Mike Smith, personal friend and a well-respected attorney out here, to represent our interests. I was a little too emotionally attached to make rational choices on what needed to be done.

"The other side engaged Mr. Orr and both sides agreed on Eric Scott as the referee. It basically came down to nobody trusted anybody. The lawsuit was filed the instant Nebraska law changed. The law changed on January 1st and on January 10th we were sued, no warning given, even from my Aunt Rella. The revised law allowed a trust to be broken without unanimous consent. We could have chewed up the entire assets of the ranch in litigation and everyone would have walked away with nothing. With the change in Nebraska law we'd have only been postponing the inevitable.

"The attorneys agreed to be compensated by a percentage of the sale split between them. I believe that proposal came from Mr. Orr and it's not an unusual way of doing things.

"The ranch could still be in existence, a usable place for the family to visit. Nobody would have gotten rich from it, but it could have been a family heirloom in perpetuity. There were pieces of the ranch, and this is what pisses me off the most, that were the original homestead, signed over and deeded to Hub McMurtrey. Just about all the land could be traced back to individual homesteads of family of Granny or Hub's.

"This deal split us off from the rest of the family. The last time I talked to any of them was at the auction. Nothing will ever put that ranch back together. It will never happen in my lifetime or my kids' lifetime or my grandkids' lifetime, not in one contiguous piece like that. I think Ted Turner would have paid whatever it took to get it bought. He'd have gone five or six hundred an acre if someone would have been there to push him. It fit right in. There's probably 70 miles of fence between the McMurtrey and the Spike Box. It might have been different if someone would have talked to us. We expected it from Dianne, just because of her personality and the way she'd behaved in the past, we didn't expect it from my mom's sister or my grandfather. But it's neither here nor there now."

Bob Childers

Any old excuse will do when it comes to visiting Bob and Susan Childers, as warm and genuine a couple as walk the earth. Sometimes, like on this sunny March morning, when the dissolution of the McMurtrey family weighs heavily, another hour or two with Bob and Susan can be just the stout medicine the doctor ordered.

We first drive to Mullen for lunch at Red's Cafe. Unlike almost every other television set in America, Red's television is not broadcasting college basketball. Instead, the classic western *Monte Walsh*, starring the inimitable Lee Marvin and the lovely Jeanne Moreau, occupies the big screen. As we munch on our burgers Monte Walsh's disappearing world of itinerant cowboys minding someone else's cattle and their friendships with aging town prostitutes with hearts of gold fades to sepia.

The Mullen cemetery houses the grave of Suell Babcock, Alf McMurtrey's Missouri contact when he came west. The marker lists Suell and Suell's wife, but no death date for the wife. She was fifteen years younger. Could be she remarried and blew town. The grave of Thomas A. Boots, son of famous Nebraska bull rider Rich Boots, lies a stone's throw from Suell's, marked by stone engraved with his name and the inscription "A Top Hand" — a large cross fashioned from welded horseshoes on one side, a coiled lariat mounted on a wrought iron stand on the other side.

In the cemetery's southwest corner an honor guard of six Air Force guys in full dress uniforms huddle under a blue undertaker's tent against the brisk March breeze waiting for the internment crowd to arrive from the funeral dinner at the bowling alley.

Another cemetery, a few miles to the east, on a hill overlooking the village of Seneca and the docile Middle Fork of the Loup River. Kathy has never visited the grave of teenager Fredrick David McMurtry (no relation to the Cherry County McMurtreys), September 9, 1894 - March 30, 1908, who died eating Loup River Valley sand after a cave he and his mates were digging in the side of a blowout collapsed. He is buried next to Frederick, a 3-year-old brother and a sister and brother who died in infancy. The Seneca McMurtrys, it would seem, had no luck at all.

You may remember Bob Childers from the McMurtrey ranch auction as the tall, good-natured guy in an Agri Affiliates blazer whose main job was to hold Eric Rapp's hand and answer questions. Bob's mother is a niece of Hub and Alf's and Bob spent a good share of his life living and working on the McMurtrey. One of the few family members to be held in esteem by rest of the McMurtreys, Bob's unique position does not prevent him from being forthright. When I assured him I would be careful with what he told me so as not to cause hard feelings with other family members he said "I don't give a good goddamn whether you quote me or not. I'm long past caring what those people think of me."

The recent drought-busting heavy snows have receded, leaving the hills tinged with the faint green of new grass pushing up through the old. The smells of warming soil and live animals come through the open car windows. Spring is almost here.

The Childers ranch lies just south of the Seneca bridge over the Dismal River, where most people, if they haven't previously drowned underneath an infamous Dismal River strainer, take out their canoes and kayaks and wait for outfitter Mitch Glidden to ferry their thoroughly drenched asses back to Mullen. Susan Childers, during a recent phone conversation, spoke kindly of the Dismal. "I had a good time on the river. But if you go on down the stretch from the Seneca bridge to the Thedford bridge you want to take a fiberglass canoe. They don't tip as easy."

As we follow the twisting driveway to the Childers' modest bungalow I keep a sharp watch for Bob's three border collies, especially the one who, for no discernible reason other than perhaps the smell of Finlay on my clothing, has taken a strong dislike to me. On previous visits Bob locked the dog on the back porch to keep me out of harm's way. I have never seen the dog work cattle, but Bob says it's something special. Since he purchased the dog from one of my shirt tail relatives let me just say it's probably one helluva working dog.

No dog in sight, no Bob either. Susan says he's checking cows, now entering the tail end of calving season. In the sheltered field south of the house about 30 contented cows and nursing calves enjoy the sunshine. Bob shows up five minutes later in a recently minted Chevrolet Suburban trailed by three border collies. He immediately hustles the dog which doesn't like me onto the back porch. I am relieved and grateful.

As the first order of business we visit his horse corrals west of the house. Bob has two horses anyone would be proud to own — if they were only for sale. Both are quarter horse-thoroughbred crosses, giving them adequate muscle for roping duty and enough leg and stamina to cover plenty of ground. His favorite of the two is also part-Morgan. The other day he used the part-Morgan mare to drive an outlaw bull away from a set of heifers. The bull crowded the horse. She bit a hunk out of his ass and he went away. I am jealous, having always wanted to own a horse that would do that.

Bob snaps a halter rope on his prize possession, a handsome, 1200-pound mule, a mule who towers over me, a mule exuding preternatural intelligence and the faint exotic aroma of what might be Africa. I've never been to Africa, but if I went I'd expect it to smell like this mule. I am wishing my grandfather Bryan Tupper could see this magnificent animal. He was an admirer of big mules, bred them, broke them to the harness, thought they were smarter and way tougher than horses. He always said, "If a mule won't look at you, Bryan Lee, he will never recognize your authority." One early morning on the Thompson Creek farm north of Riverton my grandfather found a dimwitted hired man out in the barn beating a young mule over the head with a bridle. Bryan Jay Tupper, he of the legendary volcanic temper, was not into fisticuffs, but he knocked the ignoramus to the ground with one mighty blow and kicked him a hundred yards downhill to the road, went back to the house for the man's kit and threw it on top of the mostly unconscious former hired man. B. J. Tupper was just about the best man-kicker Franklin County, Nebraska, ever produced.

The mule is staring intently at Bob. Bob asks him to walk a narrow plank, stand with all four feet on a tiny platform, back into the traces of a small cart. Whatever Bob asks the mule to do, he does. You can tell this is only because Bob is the one doing the asking. The mule ignores me when I stand beside him, but you can almost see the wheels turning in his enormous head. He will never welcome my company or affection and knows everything he needs to know about me — I am not Bob Childers, the only human being in his world who matters.

"He hates dogs. If any of our dogs went into a pasture with him they'd get killed." One particularly risk-happy Border Collie sneaks up behind me in the corral. The mule, aware of everything going on in the entire known universe, whirls, and had I not skipped this fat carcass out of the way, would have run me over trying to get at the dog, last seen hightailing it under the corral fence and on up towards the house. Bob laughs. "He really hates dogs."

Bob shows us a small pen next to the barn enclosed by a six-foot high set of panels. The mule continually jumped out of this pen from a flat-footed stance before Bob gave up and let him run with the horses. "He's just too goddamned smart." I agree. This is by far the most intelligent non-human animal I have ever been around. There's way more going on inside the mule's head than inside the collective brains of 500 of our nation's most prominent educrats. Which, when I think about it, is underestimating the mule's IQ by a country mile.

Horses and mules fully admired, we troop in the house for coffee, keeping a wary eye out for that mean-assed Border Collie in case it gets loose from the back porch. While Susan rounds up some coffee cups and gets the coffee pot in gear Bob talks about his grandfather Jody, who homesteaded with his brothers Hub and Alf. "He was born with a withered arm, so he couldn't fix fence. But he sure as hell could break a horse and fix windmills. Both Hub and Granddad lied about their age when they filed for a homestead.

"Granddad's homestead touched Hub's on the south end, one corner where the house sat was on the wet hay meadow. The rest extended up north into the steepest goddamned dry hills you ever set eyes on. I suppose all the better ground had already been claimed. He sold out to Hub and Alf and returned to Missouri. He came back, went to work for his brothers until he died.

"My grandmother slaved her whole life, big garden, lots of chickens, milked cows. Never had a pot to piss in or hardly a window to throw it out of. She was awful religious. She told me when I was little it would be easier for a camel to pass through the eye of a needle than for a rich man to get into heaven. She made goddamned sure she didn't have any money when she died.

"My mom Maribeth and her brother Johnny McMurtrey grew up on that old homestead. Johnny never left the ranch. One time after eighth grade Aunt Muriel loaded him up and took him to Valentine to high school. I don't think he ever unpacked his suitcase. He rode home with her a couple of days later and never went back. He took over as the ranch trail boss, often trailing cattle with neighbor Edson Gale* on drives to the Cody rail yards twice a year. It took a day and half with cattle and a full day coming back with the horses and chuck wagon. Johnny was the best goddamned hand with horses I've ever seen. Best goddamned hand anybody's ever seen. I learned a lot from him.

"After Dad and Mom got married Dad served as Hub's ramrod. Dad was a hard driver, worse than Hub. If he'd stuck around the ranch I wouldn't have. Not long after Alf died Dad made a deal with Hub to run the place on shares. That worked for a few months, but when Hub couldn't stand not being the boss any longer they had a falling out. Things didn't heal for a long time, even though Hub gave Mom a milk cow as a no-hard-feelings present when they left.

"I finished high school at Ansley in 1955 when I was 16, graduated on May 10, went to work for Hub on May 12, worked for him until I was 27. Later on Hub and I had a share deal worked out so I could run his cattle and some of my own, use his machinery. Then he came back and said Muriel wouldn't go for it. She wanted the ranch to stay intact for the kids.

"That's when Dan McMurtrey, Mom's younger brother, and I went down on the Spike Box. Charlie Kramer owned the Spike Box and wanted a share deal. For the first three years we ran cattle on all 26,000 acres. Charlie had the land, the cattle and the machinery. He sold us half the cattle and we split the calf check right down the middle. Made a helluva good way for me to get started.

"The bulls had been allowed to run with the cows year round. We had calves dropping in the middle of the worst goddamned winter we'd seen since 1948-49. Snow up to here and cold down to there. I bet I sewed up 40 goddamned prolapsed cows the first winter. We had calves all over our trailer house tryin' to keep 'em alive.

"Dan left after the third year. He was a helluva mechanic, but his lungs were shot and we were working awful damned hard. He'd spent nine months on Eniwetok in the early 1950s, witnessed four nuclear bomb tests, got exposed to ionizing radiation. It eventually ruined his health. He was sent home from the service without explanation. Never even had a goddamned mustering out physical. Since then he's made a lot of trips to the Vets' hospital. They've taken tumors off his brain.

---

* Edson Gale Jr. was inducted into the Nebraska Sandhills Cowboy Hall of Fame in 2008, primarily for his sterling character and skills at breaking horses and open pasture roping. Gale was married to Barbara, Buzz Kime's sister.

"Susan and I stuck it out on the Spike Box for six more years, built up our herd, then bought this place, just as land and cattle prices were peaking. We paid too damned much for it. The year we brought 375 cows down to this place calves were selling for seventy-five cents a pound. The next year you couldn't get thirty cents a pound. It was nip and tuck until we went into the hog business. The hogs saved us."

Susan doesn't think her generation or the younger generation of ranchers measures up to the ranchers who came before. "Of all the people who got started from scratch the same time we did we're the only ones left. The only family of the next generation in this neighborhood to start their own operation came from Colorado where they had a dairy. They only left Colorado because they found a dead body in their manure pile. Many long-time ranch families are selling out because their kids aren't interested. Basically the parents forgot to teach their children how to work."

Bob says most Sand Hills ranchers still help at neighborhood brandings. "Although this neighborhood is a little peculiar. Most of them are related and they fight like cats and dogs. We're outsiders and get along with everyone. Don't know, don't care about the politics. We have close neighbors who always brand on the same goddamned day."

Susan: "It splits up the help and all the neighbors have to decide which sister they're going to irritate. It's so weird. They're sisters who don't speak to each other. You show up at a doin's and you sit next to one the other one's nose will be all out of joint. It's ridiculous."

Hmmmm. I just might have shirt tail relation living very near here. I sure hope Bob and Susan are talking about someone else's family. It would be a little awkward to spend all this time and effort looking into the dysfunctional McMurtrey family when...

"Hub was a helluva horseman. He was riding horses until the day he had that big boomin' heart attack trottin' from the house to the barn. They hauled him up to Dr. George in Martin, South Dakota, then flew him to Rapid City, but he was too far gone. Back when he came into the country he broke horses for Al Prey for several years. He knew horses. And he loved to swap. Any horse trader in the country knew Hub liked the action. Sometimes he got the short end, but not often. Hub's word was gold on a land deal or a $50,000 cattle deal, but with horse trades it was different. He'd skin you if he could, even on a $25 horse.

"When Hub died Muriel was overwhelmed. To operate she needed large amounts of capital, which scared her. She'd never made major business decisions. That was Hub's responsibility. Dan and I were already gone. We had taken care of a lot of stuff, windmill repair, wells and mechanical work. Muriel then had the added expense of hiring outsiders to do what we'd done for ranch wages. Johnny McMurtrey and Jerry Shelbourne were still on the ranch, and they were terrific workers, but there was just way too much work for two people. But I think it was worrying over finances that made her decide to sell the cattle and rent the place to Judge Moursund.

"Charlie Ward is a good business man and a helluva mechanic. I don't know if he could have learned the cattle part, but he's a smart man. I think it would have taken more capital to operate than he could manage.

"You know Kimes tried to buy the north part of the Spike Box, the old Roseberry place, about 5400 acres that bordered them on the south. This was before Paul Engler sold the whole shootin' match to Turner. Leonard (brother to Buzz Kime) even gave the realtor an earnest money check. The realtor came back a few days later, returned the check. I wasn't there, but I understand Leonard followed him until he left the county, wanted to make sure he was gone and wouldn't come back. If Kimes had bought the Roseberry they would have blocked Turner and maybe he wouldn't have considered buying the McMurtrey."

Bob and Susan walk us out to the car. Even though it's not yet 5 o'clock the sun has about given up poking through the late forming clouds to the west. Past time for the Childers to take the Suburban on another round of cow checking. Bob says to call anytime if I have more McMurtrey questions.

"Hub told me before he died the kids weren't supposed to sell the place for at least 99 years. He was afraid they'd sell the ranch and blow the money. I don't know how they broke the trust. I know Dianne wanted her money. She was the oldest granddaughter.

"Aunt Muriel always said she didn't want her kids to work as hard as she did and she worked awful goddamned hard. Of course, there's worse things than having to work. But I blame it all onto Hub. He never did a goddamned thing to keep those kids on the ranch."

Chapter 5
Judge Moursund

They'll forgive you for anything except being weak.
— A. W. Moursund advising LBJ to escalate
the war in Vietnam

Bill Quigley, Muriel's attorney and Democrat Party stalwart, scouted ranch leases for Judge A. W. Moursund (Albert Waddel Moursund, III), a larger than life Texas wheeler-dealer and close confident of President Lyndon Baines Johnson. Quigley brokered a deal for Judge Moursund to rent the McMurtrey. Moursund had the requisite deep pockets and was already leasing ranch land west of the McMurtrey.

According to Judge Moursund's son Will, the Moursunds initially brought cattle into the Sand Hills to graze on cornstalks. "We had 380 toothless old cows with big calves and not much to feed them. A trucker we'd used said he knew just the place. We rented corn stalks near Thedford. Not only did the calves gain 200 pounds over the winter, but the cows also gained 200 pounds. That's when we started leasing Sand Hills ranches."

The high interest rate environment of the late 1970s and 1980s depressed land prices and stressed any ranch operation reliant on bank credit. Investors with adequate funding saw an opportunity to pick up prime Sand Hills land at bargain prices. Moursund was not the only well-heeled Texan moving into the Sand Hills in the 1980s. Paul Engler, owner of one of the largest cattle feeding operation in the world, Cactus Feeders, purchased the Spike Box, just south of the McMurtrey. Other Texans, some acquainted with either Engler or Moursund, made smaller investments, not always for the long haul.

Moursund helped Johnson put the LBJ ranch together, served as LBJ's tax preparer, investment counselor, ranch advisor and partnered with him on several business deals. When Johnson went to Washington he gave Judge Moursund irrevocable power of attorney over all his business interests and investments and had a direct phone line to the White House installed in Moursund's home. The direct line had two benefits: Johnson could reach Moursund during the odd hours when LBJ's hyperactive brain did most of its creative thinking and the direct line bypassed the White House switchboard, which meant there would be no official record of the calls. Sometimes Johnson phoned Moursund in the wee hours to give instructions on business matters. The next morning, Moursund delivered those instructions to Clark, Thomas & Winters, Lyndon Johnson's favorite Austin law firm.*

When LBJ visited Texas, Moursund's companionship was a constant. If they weren't playing dominoes or discussing purebred bulls, they talked about affairs of state. Moursund advised Johnson not to withdraw from Vietnam.

---

* Partner Ed Clark, another Texas power broker and close friend of Johnson's, served Texas Secretary of State and was appointed ambassador to Australia by Johnson. During the infamous "Landslide Lyndon" 1948 Senate campaign, featuring widespread corruption and ballot stuffing, which Johnson won by 87 votes, Ed Clark provided invaluable service as Johnson's chief legal counsel.

"Goddamn, there's not anything that'll destroy you as quick as pulling up stakes and running." On one occasion, Moursund, sitting in the den at the LBJ ranch, overheard Johnson on the phone arm-twist a reluctant Sen. Richard Russell into serving on the Warren Commission. Johnson told Russell, who was balking at being appointed to the same commission as the hated Earl Warren, "I don't give a damn if you have to serve with a Republican, if you have to serve with a communist, if you have to serve with a Negro or if you have to serve with a thug or if you have to serve with A. W. Moursund." Russell eventually caved.

The year before Johnson died Moursund and Johnson had a falling out over a prospective joint bank purchase. The two men never reconciled, although Lady Bird and the Moursund family remained close. In the mid-1980s Muriel McMurtrey was flattered, and not a little surprised, to receive an invitation from Lady Bird Johnson to a social function at the LBJ Ranch. She was tempted, but thought it too far to drive.

Moursund's association with Lyndon Johnson and Gov. John Connally, Texas power brokers instrumental in creating the Pedernales Electric Cooperative (PEC), the largest electric co-op in the nation, led to Moursund's long-term position as general counsel and de facto head decision maker at PEC. Moursund parlayed his position into lucrative business for his banks, law firm, insurance agency, title and abstract companies.

During an effort in the early 1980s by PEC and Bluebonnet Electric Cooperative to build a lignite fueled power plant they created Texland, a brand new jointly owned utility. When the project died due to opposition from the politically powerful Lower Colorado River Authority, PEC, Bluebonnet and Texland sued and received a settlement of $18,000,000, from which Moursund extracted $150,000.

Between 1980 and 1987 Moursund and his associated businesses earned $1,409,787 from Texland alone, in addition to the substantial fees earned from PEC. Between 1988 and 2002, the year Moursund died, his banks and related businesses took in an additional $3,093,148 from PEC.

Perhaps because of his aversion to the limelight, Moursund, unlike Ted Turner, preferred acquiring property in smaller parcels rather than buying larger trophy spreads. He often chose to make acquisitions far from the prying eyes of his Texas hill country neighbors. After leasing the McMurtrey in 1978, Moursund quietly purchased 56,000 acres in Cherry and neighboring Sheridan Counties in Nebraska. During the same time frame, Elman Fuchs, Moursund's brother-in-law, purchased 30 connected parcels totaling over 6500 acres in western Cherry County.

Moursund's attorney son Will served as chief bird dog, scouting potential acquisitions and negotiating sale terms. This burst of Sand Hills ranch buying occurred at a time when Judge Moursund was mining outsized fees from Texland and PEC.

Several years after Moursund died, PEC auditors uncovered a sizable mystery non-interest bearing PEC bank account in Moursund's bank and began investigating the complicated history of hidden payments to Moursund, PEC officials and to the Austin law firm of Clark, Thomas & Winters. Two current PEC officers were eventually indicted and sentenced to prison, but the bitter struggle between the board and the customer shareholders for control of PEC persists.

Despite the scandal and investigations, the family fortune Judge Moursund assembled remains largely intact. In 2009, after selling 35,000 acres of South Dakota grass land, the

Moursund family still owned 115,000 acres on the High Plains, good for 78th place on *Fortune Magazine's* list of American landowners.

When he initially leased the McMurtrey, Judge Moursund paid Muriel market rental rates and always treated her with great kindness. Meanwhile, Moursund over stocked the ranch, which had been primarily a purebred Hereford operation, with a colorful assortment of extravagantly branded Tex-Mex cattle, not one resembling another. Moursund's cattle used the ranch hard, fences and windmills received minimal attention. Some buildings at headquarters and at the Russell place disappeared, either burned or torn down.

Charlie Ward, Dr. George's energetic son-in-law, took responsibility for tasks Moursund's men weren't performing. Charlie numbered the 61 windmills, kept servicing records on each, often doing the service and repairs himself. He provided Moursund's men with plenty of replacement fence posts, whether they used them or not. He and his sons fixed fence, dug thistles, crawled windmills, used a back hoe to dig out the auto gates. Charlie checked the ranch furnaces every fall, made sure they had new filters and were working properly. For his troubles, Charlie excited suspicions of overcharging the ranch and having undue influence over Muriel. Once his wife Mary Margaret died in 1992 and his sister-in-law Rella and her cousin Dianne Yarbrough took control, he detached himself from the operation.

Moursund's 17-year lease of the McMurtrey provided Muriel with regular income, enough to pay for property insurance, real estate taxes and finance sporadic generosity to children and grandchildren. The Moursund period also effectively postponed the contentious family decision on the eventual fate of the Bar Lazy 8, a postponement which only added to the accumulation of resentment and hard feelings.

Chapter 6
WINTER SCHOOL

I have come to believe that a great teacher is a great artist and that there are as few as there are any other great artists. Teaching might even be the greatest of the arts since the medium is the human mind and spirit.

— John Steinbeck

The greatest sign of success for a teacher... is to be able to say, "The children are now working as if I did not exist."

— Maria Montessori

I am an hour late, headed west on the narrow blacktop traversing the largely treeless Samuel R. McKelvie National Forest southwest of Valentine. Finlay, who can be counted on to sleep through anything short nuclear war, stands alert on the seat beside me, paying wary attention to the chunks of snow flying up over the hood as we bust two foot high drifts. Long milky snow patches dotting the surrounding dunes are reminders of the three-day blizzard, which roared in with impressive violence last Thursday morning. Alongside the unfenced road, month-old red and white Gelbvieh-cross calves, none the worse for wear, gamboling in the bright sun, stop to stare curiously at the passing vehicle. I wonder if the Kimes have finished sorting their mismatched cows and calves. I wonder if the Ostrander family herds out in Sheridan County fared any better in the same storm.

The unflappable Deborah Winter welcomes me to the Taylor Lake School, waves off my apologies, says most outsiders underestimate driving time in the Sand Hills. I take possession of a short chair at a short table, conduct a reconnaissance of the room over the tops of my fat knees. Cheryl Ravenscroft is a long-time neighbor of the McMurtreys and a retired teacher. She volunteers as a teacher's aide once or twice a week, waves at me from the corner, where she's tutoring a reluctant first-grader on his reading vocabulary. Five other students scattered around the one-room school work diligently on their own business.

The first-grader, more interested in alien presences than in strange new words, fidgets, plays with his mechanical pencil, sneaks glances in my direction. Mrs. Ravenscroft coaxes him back on task. As a guy who spent nearly 30 years in the classroom I've always admired patience in school teachers, a virtue I consider vastly underrated and almost impossible to emulate. Miss Winter, who also shows remarkable patience, particularly for a rookie school teacher, helps two fifth-graders engage an interactive computer blog over a shared reading book. I noted the roof mounted satellite dishes as I drove up. The Taylor Lake School is wired for internet and educational television.

In one corner behind the teacher's desk sit a photocopy machine, a television with VCR/DVD player and a book shelf with four lap top computers. The bloggers behind me are using newish desktop PCs. Screens refresh instantly, indicating plenty of horsepower.

Posted on the west wall are Miss Winter's SCHOOL RULES:

LISTEN

BE KIND TO OTHERS

BE CAREFUL OF ANIMALS

STAY TOGETHER

FOLLOW DIRECTIONS

Hard to argue with any of these, although it's unclear if the animals in question pose a threat to the children or if the livestock-savvy children, most of them handy with a rope and experienced in castration and branding, might endanger the animals.

A fourth-grade boy checks the large clock on the wall, stuffs his backpack with homework, announces he's accompanying his family to Hastings to visit relatives and won't be back for two days. He says he has all his assignments and textbooks. Miss Winter and Mrs. Ravenscroft wish him a good trip as he heads outside to a waiting pickup.

Miss Winter rescues Mrs. Ravenscroft from the first-grader, sets him to work on his handwriting, while Mrs. Ravenscroft helps a sixth-grader with mixed number fractions. Miss Winter then checks the kindergartner's completed vocabulary work. Obviously bright and interested in everything going on around him, he pulls out a book and turns to page 37. Miss Winter asks him to look at the pictures and guess what they might predict about what happens in the story.

A wispy third-grade girl in a highway yellow dress practices her handwriting on a large marker board. Miss Winter notes the words slant upwards to the right. The girl fetches a ruler, rewrites the words, which still climb to the right, but not as much.

The first-grader, finished with his handwriting exercise, reads uncertainly to Miss Winter. He stops periodically to fool with his mechanical pencil. Miss Winter explains a Venn diagram, asks the little guy to compare two characters by making two circles on a piece of paper. He balks, but she waits him out and he eventually retrieves a piece of paper from his desk. His pencil quickly regains his full attention. Miss Winter gently suggests he may want to bring different pencils to school, the wooden kind with erasers. She offers him one of these newfangled wooden pencils, which he ignores. I am tempted to offer Miss Winter the loan of a stout pair of pliers with which she might tug on a prominent first-grade ear or perhaps obtain a firm grip on a disinterested first-grade nose, but she is clearly driving this buggy and I'm betting she will eventually get the desired results in her own patient way.

The girl at the board asks Miss Winter if her handwriting has improved. I wish my handwriting were half as good. Miss Winter praises her, makes suggestions on a couple of letters. Mrs. Ravenscroft echoes the praise, asks Miss Winter which student might need her help next before stopping by my table for a brief visit. From my position very close to the floor, I give her the short version of why I'm sitting in the Taylor Lake School on a fine April afternoon. She says the Ravenscrofts have been in the community since 1959 when they purchased the ranch from the Brandies family, the Omaha department store magnates. Cheryl taught before and after she was married, including a stint in the Valentine School while her own children attended high school and she and her kids stayed in town during the week. She enjoys volunteering whenever she's needed, says she's always liked teaching. I've seen her in action and believe her.

The first-grader finally has his pencil up and running. Tongue clamped to one side, he makes two elaborate circles. Miss Winter asks him to look at his pattern. Inspired by what he sees, he goes to work in earnest, finishes the diagram and hands it in. She reminds him it belongs in his textbook, reminds him to put his spelling words in his backpack so he can work on them at home.

The girl in the yellow dress, who practiced her handwriting so diligently on the marker board, asks a completely random question about golden eagles. Miss Winter sends her to the library, which occupies the east end of the room, for the E-volume of the encyclopedia and a book on Nebraska birds. Soon the students not working on literature blogs have abandoned their assigned tasks, are gathered around Miss Winter, knee deep in the whys and wherefores of golden eagles, which we learn, if we didn't already know, are not uncommon in the neighborhood, often choosing lone cottonwood trees for their nests. The class and I discover the wing span of a golden eagle averages seven feet. Miss Winter sends a boy for a yardstick and a ball of string from her desk, suggests he measure out seven feet of string. Miss Winter has the girl in the yellow dress extend her arms, puts one end of the string in the right hand, pulls it across the girl's chest to show how many feet it stretches beyond her left hand. I'm pretty certain no one in the room will soon forget the wingspan of a golden eagle.

I've always thought classroom awareness separates truly gifted teachers from the merely adequate. An exceptional few know what is unfolding in every corner of the classroom, sense when a student is struggling, understand when he needs help or should be left to figure it out on his own, know when a student's attention has wandered away from an assigned task, like a Venn diagram, and how to bring it back with a minimum of fuss. Like the knack for singing on pitch, classroom awareness cannot be taught. You either have it or you don't. There is no hope for improvement among the blissfully unaware droners, who dominate too many classrooms. These teachers typically make liberal use of the fatuous rhetorical question, inevitably forcing students to think dangerously homicidal thoughts and causing the mathematically inclined to keep a running tally of how many times they hear "okay, now" or "you people." These dreary well-meaning functionaries have no earthly clue what their students are thinking. In contrast, the aware teacher, much like the conductor of an orchestra, maintains a harmonious, purposeful classroom by knowing when and how to elicit the best performance from each student.

This afternoon in the Taylor Lake School watching two exceptional teachers, both whip-smart, self-assured, completely focused on helping children learn, both fully aware of what's going on with every student, I'm reminded of the talented women who found their way into the teaching profession prior to the 1970s. It's impossible to define a similar golden age for male teachers. Since the days of Ichabod Crane, with a relative handful of notable exceptions, the kindest thing you could say about the average male who tried his hand at teaching — "He probably wasn't the sharpest kid in his graduating class."

Until the invention of the pill and a general weakening of the barriers excluding women from a wide range of professions, many formidable women, often among the top students in their classes, gravitated into teaching, where they could earn a modest, but dependable living. The undervalued impact of the intelligent women who became teachers by default has grown noticeable by its absence, as they were replaced by succeeding waves of increasingly less gifted (i.e., doltish, unimaginative, unaware) teachers, with concurrent deterioration in student performance.

I'm sitting on a short chair in the Taylor Lake School on a sunny April afternoon, peering over fat knees at an unfolding minor miracle of extraordinary competence in a contemporary classroom, wondering how a government educrat, assuming he or she might ever stumble into this remote classroom, would interpret what I'm seeing, how many study commissions and faculty sub-committees would, in response, eventually promulgate which brand of numb-skulled nationalized pedagogy, complete with mandatory jargon-riddled mission statements, guaranteed to cost billions, employ thousands of low IQ educrats to dictate and verify, in order to make absolutely goddamned certain the phenomenon I'm witnessing would never be replicated.

P. E. Period — Mrs. Ravenscroft volunteers to watch the students while I visit with Miss Winter. I suggest we observe a few minutes of the P. E. period before we dig into the interview. Children file out to the hall, where they don winter coats against a chilly south wind. No afternoon basketball today with the court still covered with snow drifts. Finlay quietly watches unobserved from his perch on the top of the car's back seat as children run hither and thither. Eventually someone remembers to fetch a Frisbee from the school. The first grader-immediately sails it over a barbed wire fence. The kindergartner retrieves the Frisbee, is temporarily stumped on how to recross the fence, but quickly figures it out before help can reach him.

Miss Winter and I retreat to the short table inside the school. Born and raised in northeast Kansas, Miss Winter attended college and practice taught in Minneapolis, a fur piece in every respect from Cherry County, Nebraska. Her maternal grandparents live near Taylor, on the southeastern edge of the Sand Hills, where she enjoyed childhood visits, attended brandings, took a liking to her grandparents' neighbors.

"I just loved the land. The Sand Hills are where my family came from. My great-grandpa settled in the Sand Hills. The few times I drove down from Minneapolis to visit my grandparents it felt like coming home. There's just something about the Sand Hills; the land and the people that live here, the culture that I love."

Not too surprising after graduation, when she launched her search for employment, a rural school in the Nebraska Sand Hills was at the top of her want list.

Miss Winter talks about her job interview with Jolyne Westover, principal of Cherry County's rural schools. After the initial interview in Valentine, Mrs. Westover drove her 70 miles to inspect the Taylor Lake School and the teacher's residence on the Ravenscroft ranch just down the road. "I remember thinking 'are we ever going to get there?' It seemed like we were driving for hours, although it isn't that far."

I'm curious what she thinks, after nearly a year's experience, of teaching in a multi-grade one-room school.

"My older students can help the younger ones, read directions, answer questions. Daniel, my kindergartner, when I'm teaching the fifth-graders a science concept, he'll be listening and go home and tell his mother, 'Guess what I learned today?'

Every night after school Miss Winter composes individual lesson plans for each student and the next day checks off each task as they finish. Any unfinished work goes home to be completed overnight, strong incentive to complete the work in school.

"With this many grades it's hard to get everything accomplished. You just have to be flexible. I post the basic learning plan where all students can check it. If I'm busy they can see they should be working on handwriting or spelling or if they have a project. The older kids know what they're supposed to accomplish, what their homework will be if they don't get done. It allows them to work while they're waiting for me to finish with the younger students."

I wonder how many 20-something fresh college graduates could survive living 70 miles from small rural town, 130 miles from the nearest Walmart. For Miss Winter, making sure she has full tank of gas is a top priority.

"I try not to go to town every weekend, so I plan groceries to last at least two weeks, longer in winter. During college there was a Walmart or a Target right there. Sometimes we'd go twice a week. Since I came here I took up quilting, but teaching has been pretty much my life. I get home, eat supper, finish grading papers, go to bed. Last week with the blizzard it got a little long. We let out school Thursday morning and it was still blowing on Saturday. I'd run out of work to do long before that."

Although her supervisor, Mrs. Westover, is only a phone call or an e-mail away, she might drop by Taylor Lake once or twice a month in making her regular rounds of rural schools. She also makes special visits, like when she accompanied the fine arts representatives from the University of Nebraska on their rounds of Cherry County's rural schools as they conducted storytelling workshops. If Miss Winter needs a particular piece of equipment or a book she can e-mail a request to the other rural schools. Mrs. Westover usually grants requisitions if she has room in the budget. Except for a shortage of middle school science equipment Miss Winter feels the Taylor Lake school is as well-equipped as the suburban Minneapolis school where she practice taught.

She doesn't know how long Taylor Lake will remain open. For the time being there are enough pupils, but that could change once the McMurtrey ranch is taken over by Ted Turner's operation. The parents of two current students work for the Kimes. Turner might not hire workers with school-age children.

No matter what the future holds for the Taylor Lake School Miss Winter plans to stay in the Sand Hills. She will begin working on her Master's degree in the near future, and continue looking for "an opportunity to become involved with a ranch. I do like being outside working."

Mrs. Ravenscroft sticks her head in the door, wondering if she needs to keep the children outside for a while longer. We're wrapping things up, mindful of the approaching dismissal hour. Breathless, rosy-cheeked children traipse into the room. All of them immediately volunteer to lower the American flag outside.

Miss Winter chooses two who haven't had a recent turn, everyone else goes outside to watch. A few moments later, the flag folded and secured in the hall closet for tomorrow morning's flag-raising ceremony, the students get back to work. The girl in the yellow dress finds a reading book, brings it to Miss Winter for approval. The first-grader discovers a forgotten reading book in his desk, joins the girl on the comfortable bean bag chairs in the library. Wonder of wonders, he soon becomes immersed in his book. The last student on the computer, a studious sixth-grade lad, explains his history project to me as he puts the finishing touches on a paper about the Oregon Trail. He says history is his favorite subject.

When the little hand and the big hand on the wall clock arrive at the magic number, the room begins to stir. Students empty desks of homework and reading books, stuff their backpacks for the long drives to their home ranches. With perfect timing 4-wheel drive pickup trucks appear outside, white exhaust plumes whisked away by the stiff wind across the narrow, winding blacktop where Jim Wright used to land his airplane, ferrying his daughters back and forth to school.

I tell my gracious hostesses I'm off to interview Buzz Kime, offer inadequate thanks for an interesting afternoon. They tell me I'm going to enjoy talking with Buzz, invite me to come back any time. From my own experience, I know hosting strangers in a classroom is seldom an unmixed blessing. Students, like my new favorite first-grader, can be stimulated by a visitor's presence into atypical behaviors, may fail to complete work, may sometimes cause a teacher to expend finite disciplinary resources. I'm confident I've been at least a minor inconvenience, but neither Deborah Winter nor Cheryl Ravenscroft show a particle of annoyance.

WESTERN CHERRY COUNTY
JANUARY 2, 1949

To My Niece, Celia,
daughter of Young Jules, who, with her pupils,
was lost and found in the blizzard of 1949.

— Mari Sandoz, Dedication to *Winter Thunder*

Winter Thunder was supposed to be my story.
The magazines from back east wanted me to write it.
Dad said, 'Leave it alone, that's Marie's.' She had an imagination.
She could make things up and make stories. She had truth in it here and there.
But we didn't get caught out in any blizzard. Nobody was in danger.

— Celia Sandoz Ostrander Barth

Sunday morning, scattered downy flakes falling out of a sunny sky, an ominous blue gray mass building above the northwest horizon. The few ranchers in the neighborhood with battery radios hear the KOA Denver announcer predict another unseasonably warm day for the morrow. The evil-looking clouds and large snowflakes suggest otherwise. Ernest Sandoz, driving his father Young Jules Sandoz's Jeep, brings his older sister Celia eight miles cross country on Sand Hills trails to Cal and Irene Westover's place in western Cherry County, where she boards during the school year. Come Monday morning, Celia, favorite niece of author Mari Sandoz, will be available to teach her eight students, no matter what the weather. Cal Westover hurries to feed his cattle and load his hay cart for the next morning. He's able to spend most of the afternoon relaxing in the ranch house.

Cal Westover's 16-year-old nephew Alton, who makes his home with the Westovers and their three children, has yet to return from a holiday visit to his mother in Gordon. Alton is a hard worker, who would much rather help his uncle than attend the rural school a mile and a half south of the ranch. If he weren't so infatuated with his new teacher, he might quit school altogether.

By daylight the next morning all roads have drifted shut and snow is piled half way up the sides of the chicken house. The Westovers will have to manage without Alton for a couple of weeks. Cal, 10-year-old son Joe and wife Irene battle gale force winds, blocked gates and five foot drifts to keep their cattle fed and watered. The Westovers always raise surplus hay, but they can only reach a few stacks where the wind has blown the ground clear of snow. Cal cables the stacks on a two-wheeled sled and drives his four-horse team on a round about route through the few gates not blocked by drifts. By midmorning Cal's face bleeds freely from the ice caked on his nose and cheeks. Weeks later his face remains too sore to shave. It takes him until 11 a.m. to finish feeding the cattle near the house, another three hours to milk and water the milk cows and feed a herd of spring calves, a few cows and late calves huddled under a big hill on the north side of Gordon Creek valley. The last minute decision to haul feed up the valley probably saves his spring calves from drifting with the wind to flounder and die in the lakes to the south.

At nightfall the exhausted family roll up their mattresses, haul them from the cold bedrooms to the kitchen nearer the wood stove and oil heater to bed down on the floor. Irene remembers "we were fairly warm, but the snow was blowing in around our new weather stripped windows and... it sounded as though that wind would just lift the roof from over our heads."

The next day the blizzard roared unabated. The well froze up, leaving the flowing spring 100 yards north of the house as the only source of water for man and beast, every drop carried in buckets through deep drifts and blinding snow.

Even after it quit snowing on the 5th of January temperatures stayed far below zero and the 50 mile an hour winds created fierce ground blizzards, turning the world into a white wall of flying powder, deadly conditions for any man or critter who ventured out in the maelstrom.

Thirty-five miles east down the Gordon Creek valley, young Dan McMurtrey searched the much larger McMurtrey Ranch for his uncle Alf and Hub's missing 30 heifers, riding the ridges, hoping for an occasional glimpse of the valleys through frozen eyelids. "I finally spotted some steam coming from a valley. Those heifers were completely buried under the snow. I got Hub and we dug them out, drove 'em home and fed and watered 'em. They lived, but for a couple of years afterwards they weren't quite right. Their coats were bad and they didn't do as good."

Vicious ground blizzards and extreme cold for the next few days made it impossible for most of Celia's students to attend school, although she walked to school several days with the Westover children in tow. When weather permitted Celia walked to neighbors' houses to trade supplies and gather news. She was especially eager to learn how her parents were faring. "When I found out I'd be teaching country school I bought a warm ski suit. I could walk to school and walk to the neighbors no matter how cold it got."

Snow storms on January 10th and 17th piled snow and misery on ranchers and their livestock, and frustrated efforts to travel to town for supplies. Ranchers sometimes scooped drifts for a full day without getting more than three miles from home.

Two weeks after the big blizzard nephew Alton Westover, still marooned in Gordon with his mother, grew impatient to get back to help his uncle with cattle chores and to see his favorite teacher. He managed to catch a ride with Boris Kickens, in town for supplies, as far as the Jules Sandoz fruit farm:

"Boris was married to Flora (sister to Mari Sandoz) and he had a tiny old Army jeep. He followed the maintainer from his place into Gordon. The road blew shut right away and he had to stay in town overnight. The next day I rode with him and we followed the maintainer as far as the turn-off to his place. Boris was always good to me. He played for dances with Celia and taught me how to play the guitar. I stayed with Boris and Flora until the next day, when it quit snowing and the wind went down a little. He loaned me this big old long-legged horse and a saddle. It was 12 miles east of Flora's place to Uncle Cal's. When I left the wind was blowing about 40 miles an hour. Ground blizzards. Cold. It must have been 15 or 20 below. I had to stay on the hills and pick my way around the snow banks. Sometimes I'd run into six or eight foot snow banks, have to back out and find another way around."

By 1 o'clock in the afternoon Alton and his horse were desperately cold. He rode down into a hay meadow and found a hay stack on a small rise, where the vicious wind had blown the snow clear.

"There was just room between the stack and a five foot snow bank to get my horse between the bank and the stack. I dug a hole in the stack, crawled in there, left enough opening for me to see the horse and hold on to the reins. I ate the sandwiches Flora gave me and warmed up some. I figured I had four more miles to Cal's, so I headed out again. Got to Cal's about dark, just getting to where you couldn't see nothing. When I got to the west end of the (Gordon Creek) valley I spotted a light in the ranch house. I don't know how I ever got home. There were cattle freezing standing up."

On January 19, Celia and the Westovers decided to hold school in the Westover ranch house. Celia, Joe and Alton walked to the school house where they filled a washtub with school books, loaded it on Alton's toboggan and dragged it back to Westovers. For the next month Celia taught eight pupils in the Westover living room: Alton, when he wasn't helping Cal with cattle chores, Irene's three children, her sister Norma Merrill's three children, and Robena Freeman, Irene's niece. Students learned their lessons during the day and most slept on mattresses on the floor near the wood stove at night. Norma's children walked back and forth from home when weather permitted.

Although effectively isolated from the outside world, the Westover household kept fully occupied, making full use of the Westover's piano and accordion, school book collections of the school and the Westovers, and Irene's stockpile of materials for fancy work. Cal, who worked outside every waking moment, lost 10 pounds from an already spare frame.

Irene says providing food for all the extra mouths wasn't a problem.

"I always canned a lot of wild fruit, plums, currants and chokecherries, garden stuff, beef. We always canned our beef and we usually bought ten or fifteen 50 lb. sacks of flour in the fall. I baked lots of bread, something I always did anyway. Even in normal times we didn't go to town but once a month. It was harder once I ran out of yeast and had to go to starter bread. It wasn't too good, but people ate it anyway. We ran out of coffee, but we only drank coffee in the mornings, so didn't miss it that much".

Westovers traded flour to their neighbors for lard and other staples. Generous neighbors sent Cal cartons of cigarettes.

The McMurtrey Ranch ran out of peanut butter. When young David Childers, Hub's great-nephew, heard about airplanes (flying boxcars) dropping supplies to isolated ranches, he began the laborious process of stamping out over-sized letters for peanut butter in the snow.

David's older brother Bob remembers when the Fifth Army showed up a few days later with three 6 X 6 trucks and a couple of bulldozers.

"They plowed their way in and had to plow their way out. Ground blizzards closed up the roads almost as fast as they cleared them. One 6 X 6 had a snow plow on the front. The other two had steel plates welded front and back. If the snow plow got stuck the two 6 X 6s behind would ram the snow plow and drive it on through the drifts"

It would not be until March 23rd when Alf drove his 4 X 6 weapons carrier into Valentine with Hub, Bob and Bob's dad along to scoop if they ran into trouble. They made it safely into town and purchased an impressive pile of provisions, including several gallons of peanut butter, but the roads had blown shut by the time they returned and they were soon stuck fast. It took a neighbor's tractor to free them and send them the last few miles home.

On February 9th, the Fifth Army showed up at Westover's with two bulldozers and two maintainers. Irene remembers Celia dismissing school for the day, "there was no use trying to study with something as interesting as bulldozers outside."

The school children who had not been lost had been found.

Members of the Fifth Army, once they returned to Omaha, told a wild tale of Celia and her school children marooned in a drafty line shack for 23 days after their school bus upset. The soldiers couldn't imagine schools without school buses. Omaha newspapers published the story, without checking with the principals, admittedly a difficult task at a time when few ranchers in western Cherry County had telephones and with Sand Hills trails still frequently blocked by ground blizzards. Mari, then living in New York, read the story in eastern newspapers. Nearly out of money during a drawn out search for a publisher for *Cheyenne Autumn*, Mari spent several months writing *The Lost School Bus*, a novella loosely based on the newspaper accounts, and sold it to the *Saturday Evening Post* for $3000.

In Mari's telling, the story became allegorical, with the children representing conflicting social classes and family backgrounds. A daughter of a ne'er-do-well drunkard suffers from gangrene after her cheap overshoes fail to keep her feet from freezing. The smug child of a wealthier family steals milk from the communal larder. Celia's actual students were not only a homogenous bunch, but made up entirely of brothers and sisters and cousins. It's possible Mari modeled her characters on students she taught in rural schools before she moved to the east coast. Nor had Mari forgotten the painful incidents from her years as a rural school student. As the eldest child of Old Jules Sandoz, a man who frequently set neighborhood tongues wagging with his multiple wives, frequent feuds and unpaid bills, she had plenty of experience with the cruelties school children visit on those they view as their social inferiors.

Mari, as usual, included plenty of drama in her version. Once the bus tips over and the students escape just before it explodes, Mari's intrepid young schoolmarm Lecia (anagram of Celia) and her students construct a rough shelter of blankets, willow branches and packed snow, where they huddle for the next eight days. At least once a day the teacher sends Chuck, the rebellious teen-aged student, out to seek food or firewood, never certain if he will come back to the group or strike out on his own. Creating the romantic tension between teacher and the teenaged boy would not have been a reach for any writer familiar with Alton's feelings toward Celia. However, Celia says she and Mari never once discussed the blizzard of '49, before or after she wrote about it, nor did Mari make any inquiries or have any knowledge of Celia's students or their families. She was, after all, writing a work of fiction based primarily on her own experiences as a child of the Nebraska Sand Hills.

In Mari's story, the marooned students expect to be rescued by Lecia's wheeler-dealer fiancé, who is so rich he owns an airplane. And he eventually appears as part of the massive rescue team including a doctor, several airplanes and even an improbable helicopter. Mari, when she taught in rural schools, always had an abundance of beaus, some of them well-heeled. In contrast, Celia, a couple of years after the blizzard, married Orville Ostrander, a hard-working local rancher/hay contractor, a young man blessed with much more energy and ambition than money.

Celia's path to becoming a teacher had a few more twists than Miss Winter's. After high school in Hiawatha, Kansas, Deborah graduated from college in four years and began her teaching career. Celia needed the intervention of her Aunt Flora to even attend high school.

Celia's father, Young Jules, although a voracious reader and a self-educated expert in geology and well-versed in many other subjects, was not in favor of Celia attending high school in town. "He said, 'Women don't need to go to high school. You won't learn nothing up there.' He went to the school and talked to the teachers. He said they couldn't even answer his questions."

"My Aunt Flora had better sense." Flora Sandoz, with her sister Mari's assistance, graduated from the University of Minnesota with a degree in horticulture and returned to revitalize the fruit farm her father Old Jules Sandoz established. She found a place in town for Celia, paid the $25 a month for board and room and gave Celia $5 a month for spending money. "At the end of every month I still had the $5."

Like many high school graduates at the time, Celia, after passing the teacher's exam, began teaching in rural schools without any formal teacher training. After teaching for a couple of years she took courses at Chadron State College and renewed her certificate. She taught for six years at four different schools, returning home to help her mother in the summer. She followed the curriculum given her by the Cherry County school superintendent, and like Deborah Winter, planned individual lessons at night. "I often sat up until midnight. You had to plan for the whole month ahead, scheduling what you were going to teach, how you were going to teach it, and then you had to find the books to go with it."

Celia, like all good teachers, has a simple philosophy, refreshingly free of edujargon: "The most important thing to teach grade school kids is how to study, much more important than the subjects you teach. They'll learn if they know how to study."

Celia, like Deborah Winter, rarely saw her superintendent. "The only way she could come to my school was to fly out in an airplane." Even from long distance the superintendent helped with books and supplies. And minimal advice. "I liked her."

In a neat bit of symmetry, during the 1949 blizzard Celia taught her pupils in the ranch house where her future husband was born and raised. Jolyne Westover, principal of rural schools in Cherry County and Deborah Winter's immediate supervisor, is married to Irene's youngest son Roy. They live on the ranch a hundred feet north of Irene's house.

Celia shrugs off any suggestion that what she and her pupils went through during the Blizzard of '49 was anything special.

"I was no different than any other teacher in the hills. I grew up in the hills. It was just a normal thing to me, just another storm. Most of the children felt the same way. It was no big thing. The ranchers had to worry about feeding their cattle. We didn't want to miss too many days so we didn't have to go to school all summer.

Chapter 7
Kenneth "Buzz" Kime

Lord, who shall abide in thy tabernacle?
Who shall dwell in thy holy hill?
He that backbiteth not with his tongue, nor doeth evil to his
neighbour, nor taketh up a reproach against his neighbour.

— Psalm 15, 1 & 3

McMurtrey ranch headquarters, 10 months after Ted Turner bought the place and leased it to Buzz and Duane Kime for two more years. After hearing "If you're going to write about the McMurtreys, you really need to talk to Buzz Kime" for the past several months I've finally landed an appointment. Fortunately, I was able to schedule a visit to the neighborhood rural school for earlier in the day where classes have just concluded. Unfortunately, Buzz has spent the past few days on horseback pairing up cows and calves separated during the freakish spring blizzard. The last thing he'll be wanting to do when he gets back to his house is an interview.

I park in front of the sturdy brick ranch-style house, the 'new' house Hub and Muriel built in 1957. I approach the house, gawking around, walk squarely into a sizable cactus guarding Buzz's front stoop. I pluck out a few annoying spines while banging on Buzz's door. I'm not having any luck with either chore when a callow hired man stops by. He radios Buzz, who tells him he will be home at the time he told me last night.

I ask the hired man how far it is to Edson and Barbara Gale's ranch, the next interview on the list. The hired man suggests I call before I drive that far, says cell phones don't work in these parts, offers me the use of his phone, located in Hub and Muriel's original house 50 yards to the west. No one answers the phone at Gale's. I have an hour and a half until Buzz is due, probably not enough time to drive to the Gale Ranch and back, much less do much of an interview.

We stop beside the hired man's pickup, beached for the past five months with a balky transmission. He says before his pickup broke down the price of gas was chewing his salary pretty good. A hundred dollars to fill his tank for a trip to town and back. He likes to go to town several times a week to hang out with his friends.

"You just can't trust anybody these days." His previous vehicle, a thrifty Ford Escort, ran out of gas on the way to town and he left it overnight on the side of the highway. When he returned someone had bashed out all the windows and taken parts from the car. He has a $2200 estimate in hand from a guy he trusts for a rebuilt transmission for the pickup. It's only a matter of time before he pulls the trigger and gets his wheels back, although he might trade for something with better mileage. I'm thinking the pickup sitting without a transmission in front of his house is getting fantastic mileage.

He waves at a guy driving past with a sick calf in the back of his pickup, one of the casualties of the recent violent snow storm. He makes no move to help with the calf. Another calf arrives in a different pickup. The hired man waves again. "We've lost six already and keep finding more sick ones." I become nervous, thinking I am detaining him from his job. He, on the other hand, seems happy to visit about gas prices and vehicle options.

He likes the looks of my little SUV, the very vehicle he's keen on purchasing. He asks, not about the purchase price, but about mileage. Twenty-six miles to the gallon on the highway is not what he was hoping to hear. I suggest driving at less than top speed can improve mileage substantially, but he takes no comfort. Perhaps he's a man who gets where he's going as rapidly as possible. Time, they always say, is money, and he lives 70 miles from Valentine.

We could have whiled away the rest of the day and probably most of the evening talking cars and transmissions and gas mileage, but I worry a highly irritated boss will show up and assume I am keeping the hired help from earning his wages. Buzz Kime sounded crusty on the phone last night, even more so on the radio a few minutes ago, probably not a man especially tolerant of dawdling workers.

After excusing myself to drive over to Edson Gale's ranch, I pass by the rural school house where I spent the afternoon observing. The schoolmarm's car parked outside, two hours after school dismissal, serves as mute testimony to her dedication. I hole up a few miles north on the road to the Gale Ranch, let Finlay stretch his legs, review my files, make some notes, check the tape recorder batteries. The sun drops behind the placid waters of School-house Lake and the dry dunes to the west, flooding the snow drifted valley with muted reds and oranges.

Buzz time.

Buzz Kime would qualify as semi-famous, since he's appeared in at least two Sand Hills coffee table books, both times in the act of lighting a cigarette with a smokin' hot branding iron. Shaggy brows. Stern visage. On the phone a few days earlier the guy who posed for two semi-famous photographs wasn't all that interested in being interviewed. He made it clear from the git go he was not going to tell tales on the McMurtreys. They're neighbors. They're friends. The Kimes and the McMurtreys go back for years. If it's dirt I've come for I might as well drive right on by. I'm not particularly interested in dirt, but it's hard to talk about the McMurtreys at any length without something popping up that might be vaguely embarrassing to someone. I do not expect my interview with Buzz to start smoothly. It doesn't.

Buzz greets me from the mud room west of the kitchen. Fierce-looking doesn't quite cover it. Buzz's face is a perfect ruin of wild eyebrows and eroded crevices. He coughs hollowly, walks the concave walk of a life-time horseman with chronic back trouble. It appears these days Buzz is doing his smoking outside the interior of his house in the mud room. Perhaps this isolation is his idea, perhaps the inspiration belongs to his wife. I'm thinking Buzz might feel more relaxed if he were smoking multiple cigarettes during the interview. Instead, we sit in a smoke free zone at the kitchen table. Buzz, between suspicious looks at the tape recorder, occasionally aims a longing glance toward the mud room.

I ask a general question. He asks me to shut off the tape recorder, states emphatically he will not say anything against the McMurtreys. I assure him I'm not interested in gossip, only in his memories of when Alf and Hub were running the ranch. He repeats the message. I repeat my assurances. If I could only scribble notes someone could read I'd throw the tape recorder in the crick. Make things much simpler. By now I have decided if on the off chance Buzz says something that violates his code of ethics, I will not only never repeat it, but will burn the tapes in a fiery furnace and smash my typing fingers to smithereens with a sledge hammer. I pose another general question and snap on the recorder, holding my breath. He says he will not tell tales on the McMurtreys. The recorder runs and he begins to answer, but painfully slow. At times he stops talking entirely while he sorts through what he's about to say, censoring anything remotely scandalous. The McMurtreys being the McMurtreys, the formidable task of delivering scandal free information frequently dries up Buzz entirely. Of course, he's 73 years old and exhausted from being in the saddle for most of a three day blizzard. I'm humbled, after what he's been through, that he's submitting to an interview he clearly has no interest in doing. Earlier in the week he agreed to an interview and Buzz's word is gold. I also suspect he's too naturally considerate to send me on the four-hour drive home with nothing but empty audio tape.

"I am going to be a little careful what I say because we moved up here and became neighbors in 1943 when I was 8 years old. I've known Hub ever since then. I think I was a freshman in high school when Alf died. "Because of family relationships of many years I'm not going to tell you anything that would degrade the family. We leased this place from the family for 11 years and, of course, they sold it to Turner.

"I have no idea what Turner will do with this building site. If I were them I'd dig a hole and put most of the buildings in it. That's what they've done most places. I haven't gotten to shake hands with Mr. Turner. I know John Hansen, a nice man, but I think he knows who he works for. But it's that kind of operation. You'd better know who you work for.

"We've been in a wreck the last three days with this storm. Had a bunch of pairs that drifted and got mismated. We thought they were in a good place, but they busted a fence down and went out on the meadow. We're goddamn lucky they didn't go in the crick. We found two under a snow drift where they'd been tromped. Thawed one out. Dallas (hired man) said the one they doctored yesterday died. That's the third victim. Shane (Buzz's son) found one had been mismated since the storm started. You don't know which pasture they come from. Two hundred from this pasture, 100 from the other, all drifted together. I thought there'd be 100 dead calves floating down the crick. The wind was blowing terrible. We couldn't move 'em so we just fed 'em.

"Bunch of goddamn heifers. When the storm hit they just went nuts. We've had worse spring storms that'd kill a lot of cattle, but they'd only last 24 hours. One time there was a snow drift so big it covered this house and went clear out in the driveway. Hub couldn't even get out of the house. He said it was the goddamndest thing he'd ever seen. Couldn't get a door open on this house. Must have been about 1975."

We discuss my afternoon visit to the school a few miles down the road. Buzz tells about his father Jake Kime, lawyer Quigley and neighbor Willis Ravenscroft hatching a plan to pay for a much needed new school building from their own pockets and being reimbursed later out of tax revenues. Ravenscroft approached Hub, the only other tax payer in the school district. Hub said, "Sure, just let me know how much you need."

"Up until we moved here Hub and Alf did all their own work. They were progressive and their neighbors weren't, so they didn't get along so well. When my dad bought that place over there the fence was all down. It had been quite a few years since it had been looked after and it was in terrible shape. Dad sent the hired man and my brother early in the spring, told them to stand the fence up, not try to fix it, but make it turn cattle. They did that. McMurtreys didn't come around much or speak much. The next year, earlier in the spring than this, Alf came riding in on horseback. He visited a little bit, told my dad, 'You're the first people to fix fence on that place in thirty years. Don't even look at it this year, by God, we're going to fix it,' and they did. That's when we got to be neighbors. From then on we traded work. They helped us wean and brand and then they got to branching out and eventually helped other neighbors. But they hadn't gotten along real well before, because they could be progressive and putting this place together and the neighbors were kind of a clan and were jealous. Dad traded work with them one time and we've been neighbors ever since. Dad was a real progressive man and had a helluva personality, just moved in and started ranching, went around and shook hands with the neighbors and said I'm here to stay and I'd like to get along. We got along with everybody.

"Hub and Alf done everything together and put everything together, but Alf was the businessman. He did the business, went to town, got supplies. Hub never went to town. But Hub managed the work. Hub went out every morning, told the crew what to do. Alf was there most of the time, but he got things fixed up in the shop. He wasn't lazy, but he didn't really go out with them and work when I knew him. When Alf died Hub hadn't kept up on business. I guess he thought Alf would go on forever. Alf would go clear to Missouri and buy bulls, haul in hardwood in his old pickup, bring Missourians in here to work. Hub never looked up. He probably didn't go to town more than once a year. He always got car sick and if he went to town he had to ride in the back of a pickup.

"Merle (Muriel) didn't go to town much either. They done the work. Alf went to town and hauled all the groceries. Merle was a real ranch wife. She cooked for big crews, go out of an evening and milked the cows before the crews came in. They always milked a bunch of cows. She was a real ol' ranch woman.

"There's a picture around somewhere of ol' Hub and Dad." Buzz's wife Shirley, 1958 Cherry County Fair and Rodeo Queen, quietly perched nearby on a kitchen stool, fetches a photograph album.

Buzz squints at the fading photos. He suffers from progressive macular degeneration, but can still distinguish faces. "We had a doctor friend who took all these pictures. There's Hub and Merle, might have been Hub's 80th birthday. My dad on a horse about 1971. Dad died in '72. That's his old black horse. Last time my dad was on a horse. Duane (Buzz's nephew) was riding the horse. Dad got on to take the picture. He was barely able to get on the horse. This is Hub's nephew, Johnny McMurtrey, worked for Hub all his life. Hub was blind in one eye from when he was a kid. He never did say how it happened. This is an old cattle trader bought a lot of our cattle. That's ol' Hub. He always had a walking stick and a dog."

How did you get the nickname Buzz?

"I've had that so long. Guy was working for my folks, young guy, on the south place before we moved up here, named me that when I was in my crib because I made funny noises. He started calling me that and it stuck with me all my life. I don't even know my real name when somebody greets me with it. When I run for school board the first time I used the name Kenneth. This one guy who was married to one of the McMurtrey granddaughters who died of cancer, Charlie Ward. Good friend. I was walking down the street and he grabbed me by the back of the neck and shook me and said, 'Goddamn you, put an ad in the paper that says Buzz Kime. Everybody around town's wondering who this Kenneth Kime is that's running for school board. I didn't know either 'till I checked it out.' So I changed the ad.

"Hub was a grand man. We were talking about building that school? He could never remember if he finished the third or fourth grade. I don't know what Alf's education was. Hub was always on the school board. Even though he'd grumble and growl about paying his taxes, when they set the budget he'd always ask if that'd be enough. He'd say let's add another thousand or two on the budget. He said, 'Goddamn it, these little kids got to have an education. I never had one, but these kids need one.' That's the kind of person he was. Merle was everybody's friend. Great people."

By now Buzz is on a roll, but I worry he's starving and is too polite to stop the interview for supper. It's also clear he's bone tired after three days of hard use. As much as I'd like to hear Buzz's stories, common decency demands I wrap things up and take my leave. Buzz walks me to the door, tells me to call if I think he can be of further help. On the way to my car I dodge a bullet by giving the giant, spiny cactus wide berth.

I'm thinking when Eric Rapp said, "Buzz Kime is solid" he wasn't just blowing smoke.

I debate taking another stab at interviewing Edson and Barbara Gale, but decide dusk is not the time to start that journey. The hired man's 4 X 4 extended cab Ford pickup sits marooned outside Hub and Merle's old house, a warm light shines from the kitchen window. Easy to imagine the smell of Muriel's cinnamon rolls. And not a stretch to see a hurrying man in worn overalls coming at a trot from the barn.

Easing out of the driveway in the crummy SUV that only gets 26 crummy goddamned miles to the gallon, I look for the red and white wooden McMurtrey ranch sign, finally spot it peeking out from behind an April snow drift beside the road, one red trim board gone plumb missing. Maybe one of the heirs will gather up the sign before Turner's men begin converting the ranch to a bison operation.

Chapter 8
CELIA'S KITCHEN

Heidi's got some hillbilly blood in her. She wants to ranch.

— Celia Sandoz Ostrander Barth

After tracing the rise and fall of the McMurtrey ranch I was curious if the descendants of Old Jules Sandoz, founder of perhaps the most famous Nebraska ranching dynasty, were still running cattle in Sheridan County. The Sandoz family would have been subject to the same forces as the McMurtreys: illness, death, divorce, greed. The strenuous physical and considerable financial demands of cattle ranching are perhaps the most common reasons heirs lose interest. Not everyone, even those raised from birth on a Sand Hills ranch, can tolerate the isolation. And sometimes, as was the case with the McMurtrey ranch, multiple heirs find it impossible to get along and selling out becomes the only option. Had Old Jules' descendants overcome the odds and persevered?

The Sandoz family has been ranching since Old Jules, the Swiss patriarch, came to the northwestern corner of the Sand Hills in the 1880s. Jules hunted with the Indians and invited them to camp on his homestead. He located immigrants on new homesteads, battled the open range cattle outfits, like the Spade Ranch, experimented with fruits adapted to the Sand Hills, corresponding with Luther Burbank and other prominent horticulturists. Eventually the Sandoz orchards provided rich harvests for the family and the surrounding area.

After she left home, oldest daughter Marie wrote *Old Jules*, the biography of her remarkable father. It was rejected by publishers and revised 13 times, eventually winning the $5000 Atlantic Prize for nonfiction and becoming a Book of the Month Club selection, netting her an additional $5000. With the publication of *Old Jules* she dropped the e from her name and became Mari Sandoz. Her ground-breaking biography of *Crazy Horse*, along with *The Cattlemen: From the Rio Grande Across the Far Marias*, *The Beaver Men*, *The Buffalo Hunters* and *Cheyenne Autumn* cemented her reputation as one of the most significant historians of the American West. She published 13 additional books of nonfiction, novels and short stories and a stream of book reviews, magazine fiction and historical articles. In spite of her grueling work schedule and chronic migraines, she always found time to encourage young writers.

Although Mari spent most of her writing career far from Sheridan County, Nebraska, her brothers, Young Jules, James and Fritz, and sisters Flora and Caroline, established substantial ranches in the area. Of the surviving Sandoz descendants only Celia Sandoz Ostrander Barth, daughter of Young Jules, and her descendants actively manage working ranches.

The western edge of the Sand Hills. Mid-winter, Sunday afternoon. After arriving at the Pine Creek Ranch, Kathy and I are sitting in Celia's warm kitchen at a long kitchen table, the center of the universe for the Sandoz clan. Just returned from church, Celia, in a stylish peach floral dress, hustles up a pot of coffee while we visit with her husband Lyle, a big ruddy-faced guy. Big hands, broad shoulders, has the look of a man who's done his share of physical labor.

He apologizes for his slow speech, the result of a recent stroke.

Services at the Pleasant Point Community Church, a few miles to the southeast, often lasted all day — morning church worship, followed by a carry-in dinner and a full afternoon of Bible study and hymn singing. Celia and Lyle don't often miss Sunday services and the chance to visit with long-time neighbors like Irene Westover or newer neighbors, like the wife of Ted Turner's hired man, a woman who sometimes plays the church piano "pretty good."

The sprawling two-story ranch house, nestled in the Pine Creek bottoms south of Rushville, faces an impressive two-story barn and extensive corrals. Just to the west lie Celia's garden plot and orchard, which includes the Rag sour cherry trees her grandfather Old Jules Sandoz introduced to the Sand Hills.

The house has been expanded far beyond its original size to accommodate large family gatherings, those gatherings not quite as well-attended since Celia's marriage to Lyle Barth, four years after Orville "Dutch" Ostrander, her first husband, passed away. A large framed color photograph on the living room wall captures Dutch on horseback cutting cattle in the ranch corrals, a photo Celia snapped while perched in the haymow of the barn. Evidence of Celia's photography skills cover the walls of the new addition, competing for space with studio group portraits of her extended family and numerous wedding and graduation photos. As Celia points to each photograph and rattles off educational accomplishments and family connections, I try valiantly to memorize the faces and biographical information. By the time she's finished a complete run down for the third large group photo I am completely overwhelmed, wishing like crazy we'd thought to bring a video camera.

To be in the presence of someone as forthright as Celia is to understand how rare unpretentious honesty has become. Celia's telling of family history papers over nothing. If an anecdote casts an ancestor, a sibling or a descendant in a less than flattering light, so be it. Like Charlie Ward, Bob Childers and Cheryl Ravenscroft, people who also know who they are, Celia sees no reason to mince words. Perhaps she adheres even more closely to the truth than most Sand Hills ranchers because she's had to live with the literary legacy of Mari Sandoz. As much as she respects her aunt for her considerable accomplishments, Mari's habit of making her writing more dramatic and therefore more marketable by adding fictional elements to her versions of family stories, has sometimes made life difficult for Celia and other family members.

"I never knew Grandpa (Old Jules). Dad got along with him. I think Mari was afraid of him. Dad said "I was never afraid of Papa, he just talked rough and had a bad temper." The publishers took out all the nice stuff because they wanted it to sell. It's got to have a lot of problems to make it sell.

"They had me come up to the college (Chadron State College) and talk and they were saying things about Granddad and Aunt Mari that weren't so.

"I said, 'Wait a minute. That's not what my dad told me. I don't believe that. I've got grandkids that have to live with this stuff.'"

"They want me to come to classes and tell these stories to kids and I can't because they're all lies."

Upstairs Celia shows us her large quilting room, awash in colorful, unfinished projects stacked in orderly fashion on the tables below the large windows. A pink, partially finished community quilt occupies the quilting frame in the center of the room.

Lyle leads us to the basement workshop where he builds wooden scale model horse drawn farm equipment. I admire the slide stacker he has under construction, accurate to the last detail. A few months later Celia's granddaughter will deliver a faithful copy to our front door.

Back at the kitchen table, fresh coffee all around, Celia talks about her father and his siblings.

All of Old Jules' children endured the mixed legacy of their famous father, who did more than anyone to settle the new country, standing up to the threats of the open range cattlemen and experimenting with his orchard, producing many fruit varieties particularly suited to the Sand Hills. But he had more wives than was strictly legal, and was both generous and cantankerous with his neighbors, with whom he often feuded over trivial issues.

Mari, after an abbreviated school teaching career and a failed barren marriage (she didn't cotton to being cussed out for the way she opened a pasture gate), escaped to Lincoln, Denver and New York and a successful writing life. She left no children, no family ranch behind, although she doted on her nieces and nephews and helped her siblings financially when she was able.

It was left first to Young Jules, then James, Fritz, Flora and Caroline to build the Sandoz family name in Sheridan County into something synonymous with honesty and hard work.

Celia's talking about her mother's staunch Catholic background. "She went to a Catholic high school in Denver, considered becoming a nun before her father discouraged her because he desired grandchildren. She wanted to teach me catechism, but there was no way my dad would stand for that."

Not a simple task to describe Celia's father:

> *I have been disciplined throughout my life for my nonconformity.*
>
> — Young Jules Sandoz

My maternal grandmother Edith Tupper chose to find redeeming qualities in even the most unlovable. But if she were talking about a neighboring farmer who was both eccentric and likable her eyes twinkled and she'd invariably refer to him as "a caution."

By anyone's definition Young Jules was "a caution." A self-educated free-thinker, who enjoyed arguing his unconventional opinions, he regularly hosted lively kitchen table discussions where neighbors threshed out a full range of issues great and small — religious, political, scientific. Evenings often stretched into early morning as the Sandoz kitchen turned blue with pipe and cigarette smoke, smoke so thick it may still be swirling under the kitchen ceiling in the old ranch house.

He affected a heavy old country accent when it suited him, sometimes played up his eccentricities for effect. Allergic to soap and water, like his father, he often wore his clothes until they were beyond recognition. It usually took a month. Then he'd drive his ramshackle Jeep pickup truck to town, where he walked around with his arms crossed over his chest and his pants tucked inside his boots "like a Cossack." After a grand tour of the downtown, he'd walk into J. C. Penny's, pick out a brand new version of everything he had on his back, leave his old clothes in a festering pile on the dressing room floor.

Intelligent and curious, he read widely, could converse knowledgeably on a host of subjects. He subscribed to the *Congressional Record* and poured over the flimsy pages until they fell apart. He became an expert in geology and could discuss in great detail the Chadron-Cambridge Arch and its impact on water levels in Sheridan County. Although he was fluent in English and German, spoke situational French and exhibited courtly manners around strangers, he could be rough on wives and livestock.

Jules led balky young horses through gates by grabbing their noses with a pair of fencing pliers. If the horse backed up he ripped their nostrils. Many of his horses had shredded noses and short ears. He liked to "ear them down" with his teeth when he broke them. To be fair, Jules often broke wild mustangs, some of them hardened outlaws 7 or 8 years old, and he was often in a hurry, in desperate need of a work horse to plant or harvest a crop and in no position to patiently gentle a horse over a month's time.

Jules gradually built a quality Angus cattle herd, as nervous and flighty as his horses. The man who often charmed guests with his old world manners and wide ranging intellect was capable of hobbling a cow with cruel barbed wire if she refused to mother her calf.

Neighborhood youngsters who helped Jules move cattle remember him cheerfully weaving in and out of the herd in his Jeep pickup, handing the riders cans of warm Mile High beer and chunks of bologna and rat cheese, only to vanish, reappearing an hour later trailing the herd or bouncing along the ridges a quarter mile away. Jules' cattle drives, given his cattle's spooky tendencies, tended to be a little chaotic, although always entertaining. In later years Celia's husband Dutch, who knew a thing or two about organization, took an active role and cattle drives became more orderly.

Jules' path to financial security was long and difficult. He had trouble borrowing money for much of his life. Bankers, who generally have the attention span of gnats, remembered all too well his father's habit of ignoring unpaid bank notes. Young Jules, who consciously aped his father in speech and dress and usually smelled of coyote hounds or worse, found bankers' handshakes to be even colder than usual.

Always careful with his money, he accumulated earnings from day labor, sporadic hog raising, trapping, coyote hunting and ambitious farming projects on rented land. After studying land records he spotted an overlooked parcel of government land and took a small 40 acre homestead smack in the middle of the Spade ranch. After he cashed out his homestead he was able to buy and stock a small ranch closer to his mother's place. Finally, as a man of property, he gained access to credit. He eventually acquired a marshy place (now owned by Celia's son Cash Ostrander) in Willow Creek Valley, which he improved by dredging a channel through the center, creating a valuable ranch with a sizable acreage of highly productive sub-irrigated hay ground. Along the way he, like his siblings, received a $15,000 bequest from Aunt Suzette, his mother's childless sister, and a few strategic contributions from sister Mari, who lived the feast or famine existence of a professional writer, but invariably shared some of her feasts with her family.

Like all of the Sandoz siblings, Young Jules was generous in providing for his heirs. After additional strategic land acquisitions Young Jules was able to give Celia and Dutch a healthy boost, which through hard work and skillful management, they leveraged to good advantage. Celia's brother Ernest suffered from schizophrenia and was never well enough to run a ranch. Celia's younger sister Marguerite lived in a perpetual state of domestic drama. After a couple of failed attempts, Young Jules finally gave up on supplying her with a stake, although he provided generously for both Marguerite and Ernest in his will.

By putting the majority of his resources behind Celia and Dutch, Young Jules engineered a ranch enterprise built to last, the only child of Old Jules to do so.

I'm curious about Celia's aunts and uncles. What sort of lives did they lead after they went out on their own?

Celia rustles around in the dining room, returns with a family genealogy printed on green paper. "Do you know we're related to the Sandoz family in Switzerland? The ones who own the big drug company? Smart people, well-educated. Very successful," which we assume means rich beyond handy comparison.

Son Cash accompanied Celia to Switzerland not long ago to meet her relatives. Someone took a group photo. Cash has an uncanny resemblance to every male Sandoz in the photo. I'm thinking those sturdy Sandoz genes must be dominant.

Celia says the only request she made before the trip was to find a "good Swiss accordion."

Do you play?

"A little. I used to play for dances all the time. My Uncle Boris (Aunt Flora's husband) was a fiddler and we played all over this country."

Would you play us something?

Celia says she's awful rusty. Hard to know how bad it will be.

We beg. Beg some more.

She fetches her accordion, an instrument which turns out to be so incredibly beautiful you wouldn't believe if I told you. Iridescent reds, mother-of-pearl and ivory, all of it genuine. None of your throw away industrial plastics in this baby. Who knew a lowly accordion could be a work of art?

Lyle has a big loopy grin on his face, like something special is about to happen.

Celia straps herself into the harness like she's done it before, then runs through a couple of extended, hesitating, ear wincing, thoroughly discordant riffs.

Uh-oh.

How the hell are we going to get out of this alive, Kathy?

Then Celia hits it full bore, no hesitation, not a note out of place, filling the house to the rafters, not quite a polka, but perky, up tempo, probably some Swiss number. And she's dancing in place and Lyle's dancing in place and soon we're dancing in place, and we're not having the least trouble remembering her grandfather Old Jules' love of music and Mari's story of the Christmas when he spent money he didn't have to buy a mail order Edison phonograph and multiple crates of cylinder records for the enjoyment of the entire neighborhood. Nor is it difficult to picture Celia and her Uncle Boris, back when the country was younger, playing in barns and schools and living rooms, sometimes until dawn, providing more rich fun for this portion of the western Sand Hills than anyone before or since.

I can't recall being surrounded by so much joyful noise and could cheerfully spend the next one thousand years in Celia's magic living room listening to the prized Swiss accordion and dancing in place — one of those unique moments you should never waste because of mundane concerns over jobs and children, because those moments don't come around every damned day.

But we are seven hours from home and waiting chilluns, Kathy has work tomorrow, and although I'm still curious about what happened to the rest of Old Jules' children, we need to get on the road. In retrospect maybe we should have said the hell with it and begged Celia to play until dawn if she were game, let the rest take care of itself. Shoulda, woulda, coulda.

We drive the narrow lane past Celia's orchard, wind along Pine Creek, turn south on the narrow black top headed for Lakeside, Ashby, Ellsworth (headquarters of the old Spade ranch), Hyannis, Arthur, Tryon, North Platte and home. A full moon lights the dunes, revealing the dark shapes of hungry cows meandering over frozen winter range. A slender coyote on important business flickers across the highway at warp speed. We track his straight-line progress over the moonlit landscape until he disappears at the crown of the largest dune on the western horizon.

Inside the warm car with spirits high and hearts preternaturally warm, music from the old country sings in our ears.

Back In Celia's Kitchen

Mid-April. Today I'm flying solo, returning to Sheridan County to interview Celia about her father, Young Jules, and his siblings and to visit with Heidi Ostrander, the granddaughter currently in charge of the day-to-day operation of Celia's ranch.

On the sidewalk leading to the kitchen door I wade through the large herd of hopeful barn cats skulking around empty food pans. The cat herd scatters when a Blue Heeler with his jaws clamped on a long gory strip of fresh afterbirth bolts through the yard pursued by a much larger Australian Shepherd. Calving time on the Pine Creek Ranch.

Celia is distracted by lunch preparations, fetching and thawing food from the freezer, opening jars of home canned vegetables, stirring multiple pots on her large kitchen range. Sometimes she stops between critical operations to answer a question. Usually she doesn't hear the question. Eventually, Lyle, who appears to be fully recovered from his stroke, shows up in the kitchen and rescues Celia from pot stirring duty.

We head back at the kitchen table and are soon hard at work digesting Celia's meticulous genealogical charts.

Celia says James, the son born after Young Jules, was "real quiet," which is how most people who knew him describe him. Always the favorite, James, like Young Jules and younger brother Fritz, learned to trap and hunt from Old Jules, whose skills were legendary. James built his capital with trapping, coyote hunting and hogs, several times partnering with Young Jules farming rented land, until he had enough to buy land and stock it with fine Angus cattle. He married Mary Kearns, a girl with a cleft lip, who was as shy around strangers as her husband. Although all three brothers raised hogs at some point, James had a real affinity for hogs and raised hogs long after his brothers focused exclusively on cattle ranching. James and Mary left their considerable holdings to their two daughters (a son died in infancy), who eventually sold to strangers, not only the family ranch, but also the land they inherited from their Aunt Flora, which would have disappointed Flora had she lived to see it.

Which raises the question of what will happen to Celia's ranch. Although she's only 80-some years old and in excellent health, she's given succession some thought.

"The ranch has all my children's names on it. My son Cash (Ostrander) has his own ranch, my dad's old place. He's got three big strong boys.

My son Jules (Ostrander) is in business with me. He's also a minister. He goes to New York, comes back for a month, gets things organized, then returns to New York. I said I can't tell you what to do. But if he's willing to help me I don't care. Don't know anything about his ministry in New York, but he likes to get up and talk.

"My granddaughter Heidi is in charge of the day-to-day ranch operations. She fixes the fence. If we need some major fence building Jules comes home. All of Jules' family helps put up hay. The old slide stacker, the old tractors. Jules likes the old machinery because he can fix it.

"Heidi wants to find a boyfriend willing to live on the ranch. It's easy to find boyfriends, but not everyone wants to live on a ranch. She's got some hillbilly blood in her. She wants to ranch."

This is not the first time Celia uses the term hillbilly in reference to her family. Her mother's family, the Kicken clan, came from the hill country of North Carolina. Once in Nebraska they made up for a lack of wealth and formal education with a strong set of survival skills. When Celia says her granddaughter has some hillbilly in her she's giving her the highest of compliments, implying Heidi will be able to make a living where others might starve.

All of the children of Jules and Mary Fehr Sandoz grew up to be ambitious hard workers. Mari set her sights on a literary career and, by any reasonable standard, became both famous and successful, while James and Young Jules built ranching operations on a far larger scale than their parents would have thought possible.

Fritz, Old Jules' next oldest son, became the most land acquisitive of all the siblings. His mother initially set him up on a tiny acreage on the family fruit farm, where, according to the neighbors, he "had every color cow and animal you ever heard of," including goats, bees, Banty chickens and ducks. He rented a "4000 acre sand hole clear to hell and gone" 14 miles south of Seneca on the Dismal River before returning a few years later to Sheridan County with a much expanded cattle herd and Blanche, a hard-working wife. He regularly bought new pieces of land, which he enrolled in government land retirement programs, using the payments to gradually retire the debt on the land.

Although Fritz and Blanche had no children, they took in several, raising them as their own, starting some foster children on ranches with leased cows. He also provided a few carefully selected neighborhood couples a start in ranching by renting them ranches and leasing them cows. He usually took his 40 percent share of the calf crop in heifer calves, thinking heifers were more valuable than steers. At the time of his death, the man who kept his business records in his head had so many cattle out on shares with so many different parties in so many states no one was able to conduct anything like an accurate accounting. Although he and his wife made provisions for numerous nieces and nephews, the bulk of his holdings ended up with his favorite hired man, Harold Glasgow, who still operates the home ranch.

When Celia speaks of her Aunt Flora it is with respect and considerable affection. This is, after all, the beneficent aunt who persuaded Young Jules to allow Celia to go to high school and paid for her room and board. Flora was perhaps mindful of the support she received from close neighbors, allowing her to attend high school in town over the strenuous opposition of her father. In assisting with Celia's education, Flora probably remembered the critical financial aid older sister, Mari, and brother, Jules, supplied during her pursuit of a degree in botany from the University of Minnesota. Although she picked up piece work as a seamstress and baked pies in a Pillsbury plant, there were times she came close to dropping out of school. The academic demands of her upper level botany courses and her multiple jobs often conflicted. The occasional money Mari and Young Jules sent kept her in school and allowed her to graduate in three years.

After graduating from college early in the Depression, Flora found jobs in Minneapolis scarce. She returned home to teach country school. After flirtations with a series of handsome beaus, she married Boris Kicken, a dashing musician, who would much rather play for an all-night community dance than wake up before dawn to fix fence. She and Boris rejuvenated the Sandoz fruit farm, which they eventually purchased from her mother's estate with help from her sister, Mari. Flora, whose life was centered on work, gradually became less tolerant of Boris and his nocturnal activities. Boris was a good hand with the orchard, gifted at growing alfalfa, built sturdy fences, but it wasn't enough, and they eventually parted company. Boris reluctantly took his $80,000 share of the enterprise, bought an interest in a dude ranch near Casper, Wyoming, where he later died under suspicious circumstances. He left his share of the dude ranch to Celia.

Flora dug in on her ranch, going through a long line of hired men, who couldn't or wouldn't work hard enough to please her. Her reputation as a "driver" was legendary. Neighbors said Flora always had three hired men, "One coming, one going and one working."

She built up an impressive herd of Hereford cattle, used her knowledge of horticulture to improve the orchards. Over the years she tried pears (which proved unsuitable for the region), hand-grafted plums, cherries, and over 60 varieties of apples. Like her parents, she sold fruit in season to pickers from as far away as Alliance. The vivacious, stylish University of Minnesota graduate who returned to the Sand Hills came to care less about appearances, wore men's shirts and gradually thickened into work-hardened old age. Despite her hermit-like existence and fanatical devotion to the ranch, she remained a social animal, maintaining enduring friendships with neighborhood women, keeping up an active correspondence with far away friends and family and fellow horticulturists and serving as the doting matriarch of the Sandoz clan. The aunt who helped Celia attend high school was also generous to other family members.

I paid a visit to Flora's ranch about 15 years before she died. Mari's grave lies west of the ranch house, halfway up the side of a large dune, overlooking a sub-irrigated meadow and the orchards planted by Old Jules. Just outside the sturdy four-wire fence protecting the grave stood a Hereford bull calf. Shiny coated and fat as butter, he hadn't missed many meals in his young life. After giving his chin a desultory scratching on the top of a post and a curious glance in my direction he strolled off in search of the rest of the herd.

From behind the granite tombstone I studied the valley below, lined by two long columns of dusty fruit trees, heavy with fruit. A wide, level alfalfa field bisected the twin orchards, the southeast orchard littered with unconnected sections of irrigation pipe. Fruit harvest, when it came, would produce not pounds, but tons, an orchard of a scale unknown west of Nebraska City, Old Jules' vision come to full flower.

On a whim I drove down to the humble one-story ranch house, knocked on the screen door. When it opened I found myself staring directly into the hostile eyes of Old Jules as he appeared late in life. Those Sandoz genes are something. Flora was clearly irritated. I must have interrupted important work. After some awkward palaver she invited me inside, gave me iced tea with no ice, talked at length about Mari helping her purchase the ranch by giving her the Book-of-the-Month Club money she received for *Old Jules*. Without her sister's generosity Flora doubted she could have swung the deal.

Flora said after the final cuts had been made in the *Old Jules* manuscript a long section was left out of the published version, a section covering an additional 10 years of Old Jules' life and events in the old neighborhood. Mari left the discarded section of the manuscript in Flora's care with the notion of someday taking it up again and expanding it into a book length manuscript.

"The week she died I took it out and burned it. Nobody needed to read those stories about our neighbors. Mari imagined most of it anyway."

Flora complained about the Hollywood producers who kept pestering her about authorizing a movie version of *Old Jules*. Flora said none of the family was much interested. The family had been mortified by some of the stories in Mari's books, and particularly embarrassed by how their long-time neighbors had been portrayed. A movie version of *Old Jules*, especially after the Hollywood types had messed up the story, was bound to be more trouble than it was worth.

Mari sold the movie rights to *Cheyenne Autumn* for $8000. She needed the money and thought the publicity would be helpful. She had no illusions the studio would be faithful to the book, but the resulting movie was so dreadful (Bronx-born Sal Mineo played Cheyenne warrior Red Shirt) Mari became immune to Hollywood siren calls.

"We've all done well enough we don't need the money."

Still, the idea of a movie version of her father's life was tempting. Which actor did I think would do the best job in the title role?

What about Robert DeNiro, fresh off pretending to be a tough guy immigrant godfather? Flora had never heard of him, and, more importantly, had her own firm ideas. She'd always favored Henry Fonda, but worried he was now too old. She was right, he'd be dead in two years. Hank Fonda as Old Jules. Could he could have mastered the heavy old world accent? It might not have mattered. Sheer foolishness to bet against Hank Fonda fitting himself into a role, or, more likely, fitting the role to Hank Fonda. Who would play the sinister gunman hired by the big ranchers to shoot Old Jules' brother Emile in the back? So many possibilities.

Flora suggested Marlon Brando, another Nebraska boy, might also have the chops for the Old Jules role, but she didn't quite trust him to play it straight.

Flora knew her actors.

Flora encouraged me to return, said I was welcome to explore her stash of Mari's books and personal papers. With apple season only a few weeks away, she could guide me to her high-producing sauce apple trees. Maybe I'd take a few bushels back home. Make enough good sauce to last all winter.

Any lame excuse I might invent for not immediately following up on Flora's kind offer would be woefully insufficient.

Sins of omission are the worst.

Flora, who died childless, willed her ranch to nieces and nephews. Celia ran cattle on her portion of Flora's ranch, which includes Mari's grave and what is left of Old Jules' aging orchards, before grandson Sterling acquired the property.

I'll have to be careful what I say about her, she's still alive.

— Celia Sandoz Ostrander Barth about her
Aunt Caroline

When Celia talks about her Aunt Caroline, her tone undergoes a subtle change, becoming a bit more reserved. Caroline's active promotion of Mari's life and work after Mari's death was viewed with some nervousness by her siblings, who were content living the lives of anonymous cattle ranchers. They had little interest in reliving the public scrutiny they experienced every time Mari published something about their early history. Then there was the falling-out between Caroline and Flora, cause unknown. Although the two sisters continued to speak on the phone occasionally, the relationship was not a warm one.

Caroline, the youngest Sandoz sibling, was born at the end of the brutal winter of 1909-1910, a couple of months after her mother celebrated her 43rd birthday. Mary, once she'd recovered, moved Old Jules' bed out to the lean-to where he slept beside the boys and moved Mari into her bed. As a form of birth control, it worked.

Tow-headed and well-freckled, nicknamed Peggy by the family, Caroline grew up with a mellower Old Jules than the fierce, sometimes violent man Mari knew as a child. Always quick-tongued, Caroline spoke her mind without fear of a hard slap, sometimes leaving her father in a state of grumbling impotence. As Jules aged, Caroline spent more time with him, came to value her father's stories of the old country, his knowledge of history and the mysteries of the natural world.

Caroline first attended school at age 4 in the mammoth barn on the home ranch, with Mari as her teacher. Mari, worried about accusations of favoritism, was particularly exacting with Caroline and siblings James, Fritz and Flora.

A bright student, Caroline attended high school, became a country school teacher, like Mari and Flora before her, teaching for a year, saving her money, attending college the next. In 1935, in the middle of the Depression, she married Robert Pifer, a blue-eyed cowboy who worked on the Margrave ranch. The newlyweds started with a stake of $500, seven head of cattle, a saddle horse and 33 acres farmland rented from her mother.

The young couple scraped by during the hard times, Robert working for larger ranches when he could. Caroline carried a .22 rifle on her daily walks to her mother's place, hoping to fill out the skimpy family larder with a rabbit or two. The Pifers emerged from the Depression with two young daughters and a modest cattle herd. They were able to purchase their own place and in time, assemble a sizable ranching operation.

Caroline did not emulate her father by planting a large orchard, but she did create an extensive arboretum of native and non-native trees which became home to an astonishing variety of song birds.

After Mari's death in 1966, Caroline became her literary executor and the public face of the Sandoz family. Caroline opened her home to visitors, gave talks on Mari's life and conducted tours of Old Jules Country and the noteworthy sites mentioned in Mari's works. She deposited the bulk of Mari's research materials and letters in the Love Library at the University of Nebraska and stored many additional boxes of Mari's letters, unpublished manuscripts and personal memorabilia in the basement of her home south of Gordon, which she turned into a museum.

From 1970-1972 she contributed "Memoranda from Mari Sandoz Letters" to the *Gordon Journal* and later published four volumes of *The Making of a Writer*, annotated collections of Mari's correspondence. She also published *The Great Council*, a draft of material which eventually found its way into Mari's *Crazy Horse* biography, *Ossie and the Sea Monster and Other Stories*, *Cottonwood Chest* and *Victorie*, collections of Mari's previously unpublished short fiction and poetry.

Caroline completed *Recollections*, a short biography of Mari, for the Sheridan County Historical Society, but after considerable soul-searching concluded a full biography of her famous sister was beyond her capabilities. She offered her collection to Helen Winter Stauffer, an English professor from Kearney State College, who was already an established Sandoz scholar. Stauffer later published *Mari Sandoz, Story Catcher of the Plains* (1982) and *Letters of Mari Sandoz* (1992), which decades later remain the two definitive works of Sandoz scholarship.

After Robert died in 1974, Caroline returned to college, in part to better equip herself to deal with Mari's legacy. She graduated from Chadron State College in 1981 at age 71. Young Jules, who was by then a widower and in declining health, came to live with her. They collaborated on his autobiography, *The Son of Old Jules* (1989). She later published Mari's previously unpublished novel *Foal of Heaven* (1992).

In 1997, Caroline developed MS and checked herself into the nursing home in Gordon. She was later afflicted with Parkinson's and dementia. According to Celia, "sometimes she knows you and sometimes she doesn't."

Caroline's daughters, Eleanor and Mary Ann, have lived out of state for many years and are not directly involved in the daily operation of the home ranch, but maintain their ties to the ranch. Celia would be surprised if at least one of the daughters didn't retain ownership of the ranch after Caroline dies, although she doesn't expect either of them to return to the Sand Hills.

Celia hurries back to lunch preparations, sends Lyle to the cellar for one more quart of canned green beans.

Outside Celia's spacious kitchen windows snowflakes the size of duck feathers float to the soggy ground.

The sound of muddy boots scuffling up the sidewalk. Celia's eldest son, Jules Ostrander, just returned from hauling a trailer load of dry cows to the sale barn. Good-sized fellow, full of restless energy.

I am introduced to Jules, briefly explain my presence, settle into a far corner to work on my notes. Jules grabs a newspaper, props his stockinged feet on the window sill, reads and talks. Each news article prompts a soliloquy. Jules, clearly up to date on current events, is also a man with strong opinions, most of which seem perfectly sensible.

More boot scraping outside. Heidi, 27, and her 14-year-old sister Rachel enter laughing. They've spent the morning cutting new cow calf pairs from the herd and driving them to pasture. Heidi's blonde hair is chopped short under a well-worn cowboy hat. Her jeans are missing one rear pocket. The other rear pocket is covered in fresh cow manure, the result of a misadventure with a newborn calf and the reason the sisters are laughing. Rachel, slight-built and shy, wears chaps and a newer cowboy hat. The girls' faces are rosy from the cold.

Heidi asks Jules if he removed the ear tags from the cows before he sold them. Her tone suggests she is not expecting an affirmative answer. Jules says he "got some of them," but the cows moved too fast to get them all. He resumes reading the paper.

Heidi harrumphs her disapproval.

Jules asks me again to explain what I'm doing there.

I supply the short version: a part of what I'm doing is studying ranch families which have survived for several generations. Those kinds of families are becoming scarce as each succeeding generation shows less tolerance for hard labor.

This sets off a round of general merriment.

Heidi says, "Not working has never been an option in this family. What do you think would have happened if one of us said we didn't want to do something?"

The idea is so ridiculous everyone bursts out laughing again.

More boot scraping outside. James Huffman, another of Celia's grandchildren arrives with his wife in tow. James has just moved up from Florida, where he worked for UPS. He says he couldn't stand living around so many people. He has his heart set on joining Celia's operation and she has installed him in a hired man's house on the property. James is clearly more enthused about his return to the Sand Hills than his wife, a Florida native, who will return to Florida permanently a few weeks later.

Celia calls the meal to order. Jules delivers the blessing. I mosey out the door into a driving rain storm and head down the road for an appointment with Jules' wife Lynette.

Heidi and Lynette

Sometimes I wish I could close my eyes and see the same pristine country Jules Sandoz walked when he first arrived in the western Nebraska Sand Hills. His legendary eyesight could spot game animals where I only see blurry distance. Where I find indeterminate weeds and grasses Old Jules, horticulturist extraordinaire, could determine which healthy native plants predicted future agricultural success.

What would he say about Celia's Pine Creek Ranch or the Beguin place, which Celia purchased from a long-time neighbor to house Jules and Lynette Ostrander and their large family? The holdings Old Jules accumulated during his life time would represent a fraction of Celia's expansive range. Old Jules would no doubt appreciate the sub-irrigated meadows on each place, providing dependable crops of hay and fruit and sustainable habitat to fur-bearing animals, a ready source of income.

Pulling into the Beguin buildings I pass a small hired man's house to park in front of an unadorned two-story home. What sort of reception to expect? Before I left Celia's kitchen she phoned Lynette to warn her of my impending arrival and give my research project a limited stamp of approval. "He's probably all right."

Lynette, who grew up in Morris, a small city southwest of Chicago, puts aside her daily routine to sit for an interview with a complete stranger. Her younger girls, their home school lessons completed hours ago, engage in merry, rambunctious play in and out of the house.

I have long been curious about the nuts and bolts of home schooling. The students passing through my public school classroom after spending time in a home school environment were generally well-prepared and diligent, which is why I do not share the education establishment's hysterical alarm at the growing number of home-schooled students. But how does home schooling work on a daily basis? If, as in the case of Jules Ostrander's family, the mother is the teacher, do family members eventually tire of each other's company? Aren't the roles of teacher and parent sometimes at odds? Does the lack of social contact with students from a variety of backgrounds result in socially stunted home schooler? Wouldn't home-schooled students, with no exposure to a variety of teachers, both good and bad, lack some coping experience? Anyone who spends a year or even a semester with an awful teacher has the opportunity to acquire invaluable "dealing with crazy people" skills.

Lynette, who trained as a nurse, began teaching her children at home after moving to Alliance, Nebraska, from Virginia. Her older children had been in private school in Lynchburg, Virginia, where Jules attended seminary, and were considerably more advanced than their classmates in public school. The bullying their son suffered in the Alliance schools gave added impetus to the decision to home school.

Lynette had never taught anyone how to read. She found a phonics-based textbook and went through the book with Carrie in her lap.

"Carrie wanted to read and was inclined to read, which helped. It wasn't long before she was reading fluently."

Eight years later the Ostranders began a second family with the birth of Rachel, followed by Natalie and Sarah. By the time the younger children were ready for school Lynette was an experienced teacher, selecting materials best suited to her students, helping organize a home school network, which sponsors history, science fairs, math and spelling contests. In addition to providing basic education, Lynette searches out enrichment activities, including trips to museums when the family accompanies Jules on his missionary expeditions to New York.

Lynette uses solution manuals when teaching algebra and geometry, which help her understand how problems are done from start to finish. Lynette leaves trigonometry and calculus, which are beyond her comfort level, to her children's college instructors. The children use the internet for research projects and online instruction. Lynette employs computer programs for biology and chemistry and supervises the required experiments in the home kitchen.

"I learn with my children all the time. My daughter Rachel wanted to take a foreign language, but didn't want to take the usual Spanish or French. She decided on Latin. I didn't know anything about Latin. We ordered materials and studied together. You just have to be adventurous sometimes."

Lynette sticks to a nine month school year. "We take summers off. I need a break, the kids need a break. There's gardening and haying. We all need that time."

Lynette's teaching effectiveness might best be evaluated by how her students have fared since leaving home.

Jules, the eldest child, chose a career in the military. Chadron State College required Heidi to earn her GED before being accepted. She graduated with a degree in accounting. Megan considered the GED requirement degrading. Chadron, in part because of Heidi's academic success, agreed to admit Megan based on a superior ACT score. Megan later earned her doctorate in physical therapy. Carrie, who was initially reluctant to leave home, is earning a Master's in equine management from Texas A & M.

Suppressed laughter erupts in the kitchen. One long-legged girl child pursues another up the stairs. Lynette flashes one of those 'everything is right with the world, life is good' smiles. I am thinking any kid would be lucky to have her as a teacher.

How did this gentle, good-natured Illinois native end up home schooling her children on a ranch in the western Nebraska Sand Hills? While Jules attended the University of Nebraska he became involved with the Navigators, an organization devoted to proselytizing a fundamentalist version of Protestant Christianity, mostly on campuses and military bases. The Navigators eventually sent Jules to the Chicago area to experience an urban environment. Lynette, who joined the Navigators while working as a nurse in Bloomington, Illinois, was eventually assigned to Chicago, where she had her car repaired in Jules' car repair shop.

"I was scared to death of him at first. He was opinionated about a woman's place, walked with a bow-legged swagger from being on a horse too much. I had never met a creature like him before. He was very different from my family. But God changed my heart and my mom and dad were happy for me."

Before she married Jules, Lynette traveled to the Sand Hills where she met Young Jules, Celia's father.

"He was staying with Aunt Caroline at the time. As soon as I walked in the door he took my hand and kissed it like a Frenchman would! I never expected anyone from out west to be so gracious.

"He was more European, grew up with music and culture, speaking several languages. My husband's dad was not like that. Dutch didn't come from a cultured home. I would say Jules is more like Dutch than his grandfather Sandoz."

When Young Jules died, leaving a large ranch behind, Celia and Dutch asked Cash and Jules to come home to operate the ranch, split between them. Jules and Lynette lived on the east half of the ranch for five years, built a house and a cow herd, before Jules again felt called to become a preacher. They sold their half of ranch back to Celia and Dutch (who later sold it to Cash) and moved to Virginia to attend seminary at Jerry Falwell's Liberty University in Lynchburg, Virginia.

After graduation, when Jules and his growing family returned to the home ranch for a visit, he successfully interviewed for a pastorate at a Baptist church in Alliance. After serving the church for seven years, Dutch's health deteriorated and Jules moved his family back to Celia and Dutch's ranch. He pitched in on the ranch, did some pastoring on the side. When his father died, Jules became ranch manager but his heart was still set on revival. In the aftermath of the 9/11 attacks he felt compelled to go to New York and pray. He left with $56 and a tank of gas. People helped him along the way. He stayed on Long Island with an acquaintance from seminary. Jules went to Ground Zero, walked around and prayed. He met people, who gave him a place to stay for two years and provide him with housing every time he returns to New York. He started Bible studies, home meetings. People donated money, which he gave to a young widow of a fireman, who had a little baby. For several years he spent roughly six months a year in New York and six months on the ranch, mostly during haying and calving seasons.

Heidi, last seen sitting at Celia's kitchen table, makes her appearance wearing a clean pair of jeans. Lynette excuses herself to tend to her rambunctious children, who may be awaiting a long-delayed lunch.

The first thing you notice about 27-year-old Heidi is two frank blue eyes, brimming with vitality. The second is her calm, forthright manner, typical of people who know who they are. She is talking about her decision to ranch.

"As long as I can remember I wanted to ranch. We'd come here to visit. I liked cows, liked working outside. My intention was to get my college degree and return to the ranch. Dad always said you needed to get away first, then come back. I told him I'd be back in four years. He didn't believe me."

Although Heidi did not grow up with horses, she and her sister Carrie taught themselves to ride. "Catch a horse, throw a saddle on it, ride."

Because their father was opposed to trailering horses to neighborhood brandings Carrie and Heidi became experts at wrestling calves. Eventually neighbors forbade them from wrestling calves until they'd done some roping. "We practiced a little, but it was mostly working in the branding corral around horses and other ropers. It was interesting at times, but how we learn things is when we're forced to do it. Now I love to rope and take a horse to every branding. We do our own doctoring on this place now. We rope our own stuff, doctor it. I have a lot to learn, but I've been there."

Heidi's academic transition from home school to college went smoothly, although the rigid structure, sitting in classrooms for hours listening to lectures and dealing with the subsequent homework on a daily basis was a new experience. Heidi also had to make some social adjustments. "Even though we were sheltered here, I can go out and make friends. But the language college students used... and I had never been around drinking."

Her classmates, even those with ranching backgrounds, thought her crazy to return to the family ranch, which they saw as a life sentence of poverty and hard labor. "But it didn't take long after being around me before they realized I was intent on what I was going to do."

As a requirement for her degree program, Heidi took a summer internship in the bank at Rushville. She also wanted job experience using her college education so she could argue she'd tried it, before returning to the ranch. She met many local people she hadn't known, but her summer at the bank cemented her desire to ranch full time.

"I did not like working in town from 8 a.m. to 5 p.m. I drove back and forth, which wasted so much time I could have used doing more productive things on the ranch. I didn't look forward to cleaning up, dressing up every day. I worked at the bank during the summer, which meant I was inside under air conditioning. I'd much prefer to be outside sweating in 100 degree heat than inside in 60 degrees, freezing my butt off for the whole summer."

Heidi graduated in May of 2003 and was back on the ranch two days later as Celia's hired man, She acquired two heifers and her brand in 2005, the beginning of her own cattle herd. She thinks she has the 'cow sense' cattlemen prize so highly.

"The calving part, if something's wrong, who's going to calve next? Yeah. Learning to judge weights? Yeah. Part of it is being around the herd you know how each cow treated her calf last year. Some of it is born into you. A lot of it comes from experience. You can get it by spending time with the older generation, keeping your mouth shut and listening and watching. How they rope, how they ranch, how they treat a cow. I'd rather learn by watching than by asking too many questions."

Heidi has begun making changes in Celia's operation, dividing the ranch into smaller pastures, using rotational grazing, delaying calving season to limit hay feeding, selecting bulls to eventually lower cow size. "We've been focusing on running a low-input ranch, trying to get the cows to work for us, not us for them."

Growing up in a prominent family with a history of strong personalities can be a mixed blessing. Nor would it be easy to live with some of Mari's more imaginative storytelling. Heidi characteristically sees the glass half full.

"I've been around it my whole life. Old Jules. Mari Sandoz, famous author. You never forget where you're from. Although much of the land has passed out of family hands, it's 'Well, that was Fred Sandoz's or James Sandoz's place.' You have a sense that your family has been in the area a long time. Even if someone might not know you personally, they know your name and that says something about you. The Ostrander name says something. People know the Ostranders are part of the Sandoz clan. People say, 'Well, you're a Sandoz, that's the way you'll be.'

"When you have that importance of family and everyone sees it as a good thing you take pride in continuing what they started, making your own place in that family or tribe."

During our initial visit a few months ago Celia worried about Heidi's search for a suitable husband, one who knew something about cattle and could tolerate the isolation of living in the western Sand Hills. Since that visit Heidi married Brock Terrell, who farms and ranches with his family 30 miles to the east in the Mirage Flats irrigation district south of Hay Springs. During this calving season Heidi and Brock divide their time between the Hay Springs place and Celia's. Going forward they hope to consolidate their responsibilities and eliminate the 40 minute commute.

"Our end goal is to own a place and own our cattle, but neither one of us is going to walk away from family. As long as they need us we'll give them a hand."

Chapter 9
Mr. Water

If there is magic on this planet it is contained in water.

— Loren Eiseley —*The Flow of the River*

I'm staring at a framed black and white photo of a burning building, billowing flames shooting through blackened, vacant windows high into the night sky. A wartime street scene of London during the Blitz? Not exactly.

Jim Goeke, known throughout the Great Plains as Mr. Water, rummages through his PowerPoint presentation files. One set of photos illustrates a talk designed for a Natural Resources District board. Another might be edited for a Rotary meeting. One photo shows rocky outcroppings of the Ogallala aquifer. Another captures an exploratory drilling rig working in a narrow meadow in the western Sand Hills. Once in a while he'll find a piece of paper on his desk to illustrate a point or gesture at a photo on the wall, like one of a burning Old Main on the Colorado State University campus after Vietnam war protestors finished with it.

Jim noticed the Old Main photo on the wall of Crescent Lake Wildlife Refuge's office during a test drilling expedition. After he explained his connection to the photo the Refuge manager, whose brother took the photo, gave it to Jim, who admits he's unsettled every time he sees Old Main engulfed in flames. "I don't even know why I keep it around, not a particularly pleasant memory. My office was in the south corner of the basement in Old Main. Every book, every note, every scrap of paper relating to my PhD research — gone.

"Crazy, awful times. Kent State four days previously. Jackson State a week later. The fatal bombing at the University of Wisconsin that August. At CSU the destruction of Old Main was an isolated event. The CSU campus wasn't nearly as radical as Wisconsin's, but bad things happened anyway."

Faced with restarting his doctoral research from scratch, Jim decided to use his Master's degree in groundwater geology to look for a job. The Army Corps of Engineers offered a position in Vicksburg, Mississippi. Instead, with some trepidation, he chose working in the Geological Survey Division of the School of Natural Resources at the University of Nebraska.

An all-state football lineman and National Merit scholar coming out of high school, Jim was surprised to find himself recruited by Stanford, Nebraska, University of Washington, University of Miami and the University of Illinois among others. Jim accepted an invitation from Colorado State to visit the campus. Although he eventually chose Wisconsin over other colleges or an appointment to West Point, he bookmarked the pleasant CSU campus and its academic strengths in geology and groundwater studies.

During Jim's football career, several academically ineligible teammates at Wisconsin were recruited and awarded scholarships by coach Bob Devaney at Nebraska. During the Devaney era, the Cornhuskers reliably beat the dickens out of Wisconsin. Jim thought college teams should operate by the same rules. Once at Nebraska, Jim kept his distance from NU football until he observed Tom Osborne, Devaney's hand-picked successor, coach his first fall practice. After that Jim made excuses to wander over to Memorial Stadium to watch Osborne coach. "I admired how he related to his players, how he conducted himself on the field. Without any idea of how successful he might become he had my admiration and support."

Less than sixty days after Old Main burned on May 8, 1970, Jim started work at Nebraska. "Within the week I was out on a drill rig near Brewster in the eastern Sand Hills. Three years later I was running a test rig north of Merriman, right on the Nebraska-South Dakota line. I thought it was the most godforsaken place. Remember, I grew up near Chicago, lived in Madison, lived in Ft. Collins, lived in Lincoln. Here I am out in the boonies surrounded by howling coyotes. Not many trees. Now I've come full circle. A big reason I cherish the Sand Hills is I have an idea where it came from, what's under there."

In more laconic southern and western portions of the High Plains, Jim, even at his most relaxed, would be considered a fast talker. When the subject turns to his work and the Ogallala aquifer his speech slips into overdrive and you'd better prop open your ears and pay close attention.

"Lots of people will tell you drilling test holes is a real pain in the ass. It's really, really hard work. Yet it's my thing. Have you ever been around a drill rig? You grind up samples. All the samples come up and it just looks like muddy crap. You have to catch them in a sieve, rinse them off. One person drills the hole. One person collects the samples. Another person describes them. I've got a drill rig picture somewhere. Maybe in this file? Ashworth, the guy who wrote *Ogallala Blue* *, described me as an unmade bed. You read *Ogallala Blue*, right?"

"Yup, you told me to."

"Most reporters compare me to a bear, which doesn't bother me. Ashworth described me as a large unmade bed. He also said I had plumber's 'low pants,' but edited it out of the final manuscript. You don't get dressed up to impress people when you're working and he was out there when we were working.

"The most fun I have is doing this (a photo pops up of Jim at the controls of a drill rig), running the drill bit, a Zen-like experience. You see the drill, be the drill rig. When you've got your hand on the brake and you're letting the drill rig roll, you can actually feel the vibrations, you can hear the sounds. You can see the penetration and do a pretty good job of seeing the subsurface geology.

"See that? (photo of a handful of muck) It's sandstone. See these little dudes? Those are siliceous rootlets. At one time they were organic and the root has been replaced by silica. You find seeds, complete seeds of hackberry trees and grass seeds. Grass seeds come up like small grains of sand and it's hard to tell what they are. If you grab them they're like small light bulbs and you can pop them between your fingers, evidence of what was here five, maybe 20 million years ago.

"M. K. Elias at Ft. Hays State went through the floral assemblages and actually identified what grasses and shrubs grew back then. Now we know when we hit the top of the Ogallala. We get quantitative agents, but not specific. You don't get the specific dates which come with carbon 14. Geologists and hydrologists employ Vision Track, a method of dating using irradiated volcanic ash. We love volcanic ashes. When you drill them up they're very fine, nothing

---

* *Ogallala Blue: Water and Life on the High Plains* by William Ashworth.

but pulverized glass. Get them on your finger and dry them out you see the glitter and you can use it for optically stimulated dating.

"Are you familiar with the term alluvial fan?" I am noncommittal. Jim, failing to determine the true magnitude of my geologic ignorance, decides to soldier on. "As mountains push up and erode, the material washes down the canyons and out on the broad plains and the streams drop their loads. Gradually these alluvial fans get so large they start to mix. Give it 10, 20 million years and those alluvial fans build up a huge deposit of sediment, which is what we call the Ogallala formation.

"The Ogallala is characterized by rapid changes in its composition. Basically it's a garbage dump. You drill a short distance either vertically or horizontally and the character can change significantly. Think of pulses of streams bringing out sediment from the mountains. A high velocity stream during a short flood can bring coarse materials and maybe change paths. Or maybe off the main channel in a backwater you might have quiet water bringing in silts and clays. You could end up with coarse materials in association with fine materials coming from different source areas. That's what's fun about drilling in the Ogallala. It's so unpredictable.

"Underlying the Ogallala formation is what we call the Brule and the Arikaree. The Arikaree is a silty sandstone, the Brule is characterized by reddish brown siltstones to clay stones. The Ogallala was deposited from roughly 19 million years ago to 2 million years ago. Then during the Pliocene to the end of the Tertiary, from 5 million to 2 million years ago, the mountains to the west went through a rejuvenation and what we call the Broadwater gravels came in."

Jim stops talking, checks to see if I'm tracking. He probably can't imagine why I wouldn't be tracking. Any faintly sentient child of 4 these days learns this kind of geological smack talk in pre-school. During my undergraduate years I could just as easily have taken a geology course instead of General Science for Dumbasses 101, the pud course I chose instead. If I'd taken one lousy undergrad geology course I'd surely be able to understand at least 10 percent of what Jim is saying. I curse my laziness, my lack of foresight, my self-imposed ignorance. You just wait, Jim's going to be pounding the Quaternary and the Cenozoic any goddamned minute, maybe throw in the dreaded Oligocene and a few pre-igneous and post-metamorphic rocks for good measure. I smile and nod. Smile and nod. Pretty soon I'm nodding my ass off. Jim sets aside his suspicions and gets back to business. I smile as knowledgeably as humanly possible and nod.

"In Nebraska the Broadwater formation, a thick gravel sequence, overlays the Ogallala in many places. The source area for the Broadwater gravels is the mountains west of Laramie, Wyoming. If you look in that area one of the specific rock types you can find is an anorthosite, a particular kind of feldspar." Feldspar, feldspar. I'm almost certain I've heard of feldspar. It almost has to be some ordinary, every day common kind of rock if I've heard of it, right? I nod my implicit understanding. "Anorthosite oftentimes will have a cleavage face with an iridescent oily blue reflection, almost gem like. We can identify Broadwater gravels by this anorthosite, which we trace to an outcropping west of Laramie, the only source. We have tracked anorthosite from Wyoming all the way across to Northeast Nebraska.

"You're familiar with the test drilling program? No?" Jim aims a pitying glance in my direction. "The test drilling program started in the Republican Basin in 1930. People realized the basin had a unique geology and limited water. The Survey Division finished drilling in the Republican in 1950 and followed up with a series of published reports. Then the Survey people drilled test holes throughout the state, Morrill County, north of McCook, but nobody wanted to drill in the Sand Hills because it would mean deep holes. After I showed up in 1970, until 1980, we filled in the gaps in the Sand Hills. If you want to know how I got to be Mr. Water look at this (map of Sand Hills covered with marked test holes) which shows what I was doing. So far the Survey division has drilled 5436 test holes in Nebraska and we're far from done. I've probably drilled at least 1000 wells myself. We also have drilling logs from private well drillers on a couple hundred thousand other test holes.

"This (photo) is the site in the very northwest corner of Arthur County where Ashworth observed us working. Did I mention he's the guy who described me as a large unmade bed? (Note to self: Refrain from describing Jim as an unmade bed. Instead maybe describe Jim as a guy with enough size to have been a Big Ten lineman?) Ashworth wanted to look at the Ogallala formation, which Darton* identified in 1898 from rock outcrops three miles east of Ogallala, Nebraska. Ashworth came up here and he could see dry rocks, but the only way to understand what was underneath was to watch us drill down to it and clear through it.

"John Jensen owns the ranch we're drilling on. He drove out and apologized because the irrigation well south of his house wasn't a good well and only pumped 2400 gallons a minute. To put that in perspective, 750 gallons a minute is 1,080,000 gallons a day. He said he's got a better well up the valley that pumps 3000 gallons a minute (4,320,000 gallons a day for those of you scoring at home). You hit water in that valley at probably 20 - 30 feet, the top of the saturation zone. They have so much saturated gravel their wells only run 240 feet deep.

At that point they've probably drilled through 100 feet of gravel. We drilled our test well to 960 feet and we hit as much gravel from 240 to 960 feet as there was from the surface to 240 feet."

The saturated zone of the Ogallala aquifer under the 20,000 acre Nebraska Sand Hills ranges from 400 to 1200 feet. In contrast, no portions of the Ogallala aquifer under Colorado or Texas reach a saturated thickness of 400 feet. Kansas and Oklahoma have only a few isolated areas with saturated thicknesses approaching 400 feet. High recharge rates in the Sand Hills, due to permeable sandy soils and numerous wetlands, mean in spite of significant usage for irrigation and domestic purposes, the Ogallala under the Sand Hills contains roughly two-thirds of the underground water resources of the entire Great Plains.

A common misperception, even among water professionals who should know better, has the greedy, natural resource-wasting denizens of the entire Great Plains sucking bazillions of gallons of irreplaceable water from the same underground lake. In actuality, the portion of the Ogallala under the Nebraska Sand Hills is a distinct and hydraulically separate aquifer. Underground water moves at glacial speed under the Sand Hills through the Ogallala garbage dump of various rock formations, clays, sands, gravels and an occasional bit of anorthosite. Measured in feet per year, water travels to the East-Southeast, effectively stopping at the Republican River. Water from the Ogallala adds significantly to stream flows in the Platte River basin and has limited impact on stream flows in the Republican. Irrigators in the Texas Panhandle or Eastern Colorado have zero effect on water levels under the Sand Hills. Any small threat of human depletion of the Ogallala aquifer

---

* Nelson Horatio Darton (1865-1948)-Pioneer geologist-hydrologist who worked for the United States Geological Survey. Throughout his career Darton had an interest in understanding ground water and how it was influenced by geology. He completed impressive geologic mapping projects in New York, Texas, Arizona, New Mexico, South Dakota, Kansas, Wyoming, Colorado and Nebraska.

under the Sand Hills effectively ended when the mass invasion of center pivot irrigation was stopped by political and economic forces. While other portions of the Great Plains wrestle with the reality of low recharge rates and severely depleted aquifers, the Sand Hills rest above a virtually inexhaustible water supply.

Barring organized water thievery by Lincoln and Omaha or a major climatic event, like the long-term drought which occurred 1000 years ago and dried up thousands of shallow Ogallala fed lakes, trillions of gallons of water in the saturated materials under the Sand Hills will continue to feed lakes and streams with unimaginable gobs left over for livestock and human beings.

Jim, who definitely has enough size and agility to have been a Big Ten lineman, changes PowerPoint files, pops up a slide showing a horizontal view of the Ogallala. "When we drill into the Ogallala it starts at 5 million years and goes down to about 20 million years. While there aren't clear demarcations, most of the water above the Ogallala is younger and often times it's been filtered and slightly mineralized as you might expect from limited exposure to the sediments. The deeper you go the more mineralization you see because the water has had more time to take in minerals in solution. If you get a bunch of calcium magnesium carbonate you are into the calcium magnesium carbonate which binds the Ogallala together. The Ogallala has lots of silica. If you see plenty of silica you're probably in the Ogallala. No firm boundaries or levels. In valleys you might get concentrations of organic materials, hydrogen sulfides, a rotten egg smell to the water because of what once were swamps in the Sand Hills.

"The Sand Hills are a great record of climate change. When they started to run water from Sutherland Reservoir to Lake Maloney in 1935 it broke out and eroded a bottom. Harry Weekly found these trees and did tree ring analysis. This was a forest that had burned. They carbon dated the burn back to about 1520. Weekly developed a climate history from the tree rings which went back to about 1220. Eighteen years of drought, 26 years of drought, 19 years of drought.

"Jim Swinehart (Goeke's long-time colleague, a geologist and dune expert in the Survey Division) has been looking at varied soils in the Sand Hills, studying the last 10,000 years. Anything on the right side of this (slide of a graph) is regionally active dune activity, sand movement, like an active Sahara Desert. Each one of these peaks is a reactivation of the dunes. You can see for the last 10,000 years, long before humans were producing much carbon dioxide, there's been a series of warming periods, lots of activity.

Another completely random photo. An aerial view of the stark white Eclipse Church, and behind, the thin ribbon of the South Fork of the Dismal River running along the northern boundary of the church cemetery, nearly vertical bluffs leading to the sand dunes beyond, twenty cars neatly parked on a newly mowed lot in front of the church.

"We drilled all around this neighborhood. You know about Nellie Snyder Yost?" [*] I name a couple of Snyder's books, *Pinnacle Jake*, *Buffalo Bill Cody*. Jim grunts his approval. Maybe I'm a tiny bit better-informed than the complete ignoramus he's seen so far. "She grew up on a ranch west of Tryon, 11 miles south and a little bit east of this church. We drilled holes, did flow studies on that ranch. The family is still on the ranch and they have a plane. They knew we were getting married, flew over the church, took pictures. They even mowed the parking area for us."

---

* Writer, historian, author of 13 books, including the definitive biography of Buffalo Bill Cody.

Any casual visitor to the Eclipse Church would be charmed. Occupied only for neighborhood Christmas services and on special occasions, like weddings and funerals, it is never locked. The last time Kathy and I stopped at the church an unguarded collection plate filled with crumpled bills sat on one pew, inviting additional donations for church upkeep. The ancient organ and dusty piano patiently awaited the next event. Although the sunlight streaming through the west windows illuminated countless floating dust motes, the entire sanctuary had the feel of expectation rather than abandonment. But there's no getting around the plain fact the Eclipse Church is hard to get to from almost anywhere. No small part of its charm.

Given the remote location how did Jim talk his future wife into getting married at the Eclipse Church?

"Now you put me on a mission. Her name is Karen Amen. Oooh, take a look at those photos. Ever seen a boiling spring? This is the one on Birdwood Creek just north of Paxton and Sutherland. The next one is on the Dismal just east of Highway 97? You've been there? You've been down the Dismal? Seriously?" There could be a look of admiration on Jim's face or perhaps a mixture of pity and alarm. Hard to tell.

"I was on the planning commission here in North Platte for a long time. One of our important projects was extending the Buffalo Bill Ranch across the South Platte River, across the Interstate down to Lake Maloney. Karen's engineering firm assigned her to come out to build a consensus between opponents and proponents. Someone told her to talk to me. We had coffee and hit it off. When I told her about my appointment to West Point she got this shit-eating grin. She was born at West Point. Her dad was Paul Amen, an amazing athlete at the University of Nebraska, football and baseball coach at West Point, Nebraska's golden son, at least until Tom Osborne came along. Paul Amen would be a helluva subject for a book project if you're looking for book projects.

"I took Karen along to Chadron for a presentation on water issues to the Board of Regents. On the way I showed her the Eclipse Church. She walked in and fell in love with this church, sat down and played the organ. Played the piano. Here it is, here's a video of Karen playing the piano. (Karen is indeed playing a slightly out of tune piano). Karen and I know the same people. Karen's family used to regularly visit the Monahan Ranch. Like a lot of Nebraskans her family has a deep and abiding affection for the Sand Hills.

"Two years later we're getting married in the Eclipse Church. Saturday afternoon, June 30th. Hotter than hell. There's no electricity, no water. Certainly no air conditioning. We open the windows. There's a nice breeze. And the choir was meadowlarks."

Another photo. A narrow strip of clear running water, steep sandy bluffs rising abruptly from the stream on one bank, gentle grassy slopes leading off to the hills on the other, a small grove of spindly trees in the foreground. This looks familiar. A section of the upper Dismal? Maybe we passed by here when we were searching for the financially troubled Jack Nicklaus-designed golf course south of Mullen? If I'm right, this place sits on the North Fork of the Dismal about 10 miles upstream from where Kathy and I launched our memorable, some might say heroic Dismal River kayak expedition.

Jim is grinning, impatient to tell me I'm staring at his very own piece of the Sand Hills.

"Look at this map. Here's Mullen. Come down this single lane oil mat road. Right here at the top of the hill the oil mat stops. I own everything right in there. I actually bought it while I was in India. An estate auction. A good friend, now she's a piece of work, M. L. Martin, owns a sizable spread in the area and bid on it for me. If I'd have been present at the sale I would have chickened out. I can't even tell you what I paid for it, I'm too embarrassed. It cost a bloody fortune, but I wanted it. You really want to know what it cost? It cost me $1500 an acre. Why did I buy it? People keep asking me what I'm going to do with it. I'm not going to do anything with it. I have this affection for the Sand Hills and it makes me feel good to own a chunk of that. I know Nate and Sadie Bassett lived on that property and built this soddy (photo of a half-tumbled down soddy nestled in the trees above the Dismal River bottoms). My buddy who likes to fish can go trout fishing in my part of the North Fork of the Dismal. Actually, I think of them as Nate and Sadie Bassett's fish. Ten miles south of this place? The Eclipse Church. I'm pretty sure Nate's buried in the Eclipse cemetery. Maybe Sadie too."

*

Over the next few years Jim and I keep in touch, even after he retired from the university and moved to Lincoln, where he and Karen enjoy an active social life, mostly courtesy of Karen's many long-standing friendships in the community. The last time I visited with Jim by phone he was sitting on the living room floor somewhere in Michigan helping a precocious grandchild assemble a puzzle.

Jim and Karen devote a fair amount of time to an ambitious book project on Nebraska groundwater, focusing on his experiences in the field. Jim also hopes to complete a book on Nebraska rivers. Natural resources districts and other groups concerned with water issues continue to call on Jim, who has always enjoyed explaining just about everything water-related to audiences public and private.

At the height of spirited public debate over the proposed XL Keystone Pipeline, which would pass through the eastern Sand Hills carrying Canadian heavy crude oil to American refineries, Jim penned a newspaper piece using scientific facts to refute some the mythical, highly exaggerated environmental threats opponents were using against the project. Jim, like Galileo before him, discovered dropping facts into a boiling cauldron of irrational argument can sometimes earn you a public flogging. Who knew?

Jim stays current with developments in hydrology and is particularly excited about recent advances in airborne magnetic mapping. To conduct airborne magnetic mapping a single magnetometer sensor is typically mounted on a fixed wing aircraft or helicopter. As the aircraft flies a grid it measures the magnetic field, altitude of the aircraft, GPS position and altimeter data. An onboard computer records the raw data and corrects the magnetic data for aircraft altitude variations. Originally developed as a submarine hunting device during WWII, petroleum and mineral prospectors use airborne magnetic mapping to augment other technology. For a hydrologist the ability to visualize a large expanse of the geological structure of the Earth's upper crust, particularly the spatial geometry of bodies of rock and the presence of faults and folds, offers an entirely new methodology to confirm and augment the results of decades of test hole drilling. You can sense Jim, like a retired race horse, strains at the reins to be back on the drill rig with a state of the art magnetic map in his lap.

Paul Amen (1916-2005), product of Lincoln's close-knit German-Russian community Mari Sandoz depicted in *Capital City,* won nine varsity letters at Nebraska, was a member of the first U.S. Olympic baseball team at the 1936 Summer Olympics in Berlin, coached football under Red Blaik at West Point during the Doc Blanchard-Glenn Davis era. Two of their teams were undefeated national champions. He coached an undefeated Army baseball team, was a founding member of the American Baseball Coaches Association, went on to be ACC Football Coach of the Year at Wake Forest before returning to Lincoln to head his family's banking interests. In 1979, Gov. Charles Thone appointed Amen to head the Nebraska State Banking Department.

In early November 1983, Commonwealth Savings and Loan, an under-insured industrial savings bank patronized by many in the Lincoln German-Russian community, collapsed, wiping out significant portions of customers' life savings. Gov. Bob Kerrey, who succeeded Thone, immediately fired Banking Director Paul Amen. Official inquiries revealed the Copple family which controlled Commonwealth used the bank as the family's personal piggy bank and as a source of loans to influential political friends, including Attorney General Paul Douglas. Gov. Kerrey's family investments were also financed with loans from Lincoln's collapsing savings and loan industry. Several members of the Copple family went to prison. Douglas was impeached and disbarred. Reptilian Gov. Kerrey's political career survived and he went on to serve two terms in the US Senate and launch a disorganized and wildly unsuccessful presidential campaign. Investigators later determined Paul Amen to be blameless.

Chapter 10
The Dune Guy

In the mid-1990s writer John McPhee published a *New Yorker* piece on forensic geology. He described the work of forensic geologists investigating several challenging mysteries, including the kidnapping-murder of beer baron Adolph Coors. Forensic geologists eventually solved the Coors case by tracing the muddy gravel stuck to the undercarriage of a burned out automobile abandoned near a city dump in New Jersey back to the Colorado crime scene. A few years prior to completing the article, McPhee showed up at geologist-stratigrapher Jim Swinehart's office at the University of Nebraska with an assortment of rocks he'd gathered on the banks of the Platte River between Lincoln and Omaha. Swinehart picked up each stone, turned it over, studied a few of them under magnification. He selected two dark stones, held them up, said they originated from calderas in or beyond Rocky Mountain National Park, likely east of Steamboat Springs in the Rabbit Ears Pass area.

Years later, sitting across from me in his office at the Conservation and Survey Division of Nebraska's Department of Natural Resources, Jim Swinehart resembles neither a large unmade bed nor a former Big Ten lineman. Long-legged, angular, brimming with nervous energy, he looks to be a guy who could walk a brisk 30 miles without pausing or even taking a deep breath. His scruffy beard and ponytail might be taken as give-a-shit, but are more emblematic of an ingrained oppositional persistence. All the geology big shots believe proposition A is true, has always been true, will always be true, but, you know what? It smells a little funny to me. Let's dig a little deeper into proposition A and see if I'm right and they're wrong, have always been wrong and will always be wrong unless I can convince them otherwise.

Jim Goeke is widely known as Mr. Water. Jim Swinehart could just as easily be known as The Dune Guy or Mr. Dune, except anyone who knows him simply calls him "Swinehart," which provides all the information anyone could possibly need. Hired by the Survey Division the same year as Goeke, the pair of newbies comprised, at one time, the only "outsiders" in the department.

"Jim (Goeke) grew up in Illinois, had been at Wisconsin and Colorado State. I grew up an Air Force brat, spent three years in Newfoundland, moved all over the country, went to school at Penn State and the University of California. Nebraska hired me as a research geologist to work on ancient river deposits, Cenozoic epoch (the period when continents moved into their present positions, mammals became more diverse species, insects and plants began to interact and savannas spread). I had been in some active sand dune areas in California and Arizona. Dunes are a highly specialized area of sedimentology and at the time I was more interested in river deposits, which Nebraska had in abundance.

"I did my dissertation on much older river deposits adjacent to a sea way and involved coal beds. I never did finish my dissertation, one of my life's failures. I ended up doing enough work, had beaucoup publications, taught enough classes nobody else would teach, the department let it go. Jim (Goeke) doesn't have a PhD either. It's a problem only when we apply for grants from the Feds. Jim and I were promoted to full professor based on research, service and the grant money we brought in. So it's one of those things in the past you say is too bad, but doesn't mean much."

How did a geologist with expertise in ancient river deposits transition to one of the world's most respected dune guys, studying dune formation and stratigraphy in locations as diverse as Hooker County, Nebraska, and Inner Mongolia? "One of the first things Vince Dreezen, then head of the Survey Division, asked me to do after I was hired was to combine information from rock outcrops with information from test holes to produce a better picture of the evolution of Nebraska over the past 35 million years. Outcrops are biased pieces of the puzzle because you get a big outcrop for a reason, maybe it's more resistant to erosion. Plus you're only seeing a small percentage of the rocks that particular age because most of them are buried. In Nebraska we had a really good test hole program, but we hadn't done much looking at the outcrops and tying them in.

"As I'm sure Jim (Goeke) has told you, if you want to understand the hydrology and water resources of an area you have to understand the plumbing system, the architecture of the sediments containing the water. Unless you understand how those aquifers are put together, their irregularities, the different sets of valleys that have been cut and filled though time, how they actually fit together in a three-dimensional way, you're not going to understand groundwater or groundwater flow systems.

"Vince assigned me to work closely with Jim Goeke and the drilling program. Jim's primary function was to look at groundwater and hydrology. I sat on the drilling rig studying the rocks and the nearby outcrops. I was probably the first guy they'd hired who had been trained to look at outcrops. And I had experience with subsurface, working for Shell Oil on shallow drilling projects in Utah and on small drilling projects at Penn State.

"My second summer I went out with Jim and other drillers and our own geologists and hydrologists from the Survey Division. That's when I got my first taste of the Sand Hills. I vividly remember the open space, the beauty of the grasslands. I'd just spent four years in rural Pennsylvania. Pennsylvania has over 12 million people in a state about the size of Nebraska and you can hit a traffic jam on Thursday afternoon even in rural areas. Drive between Hyannis and Fullerton and you might see a pickup.

"I had no inkling there was that much dune sand covered by vegetation sitting in the middle of Nebraska. We're driving in and it's like wow! I'd been in pretty nice dune fields, like the Mojave Desert, but never dunes covered with grass. Of course, we were interested in what was below the dunes. We didn't put a rig on top of the dunes because we'd just be drilling through sand and what did we need to do that for? During the initial drilling I didn't pay close attention to the dunes, but when I got back to Lincoln I started reading about the Sand Hills. There wasn't much to read. The articles in major publications had been done in the 1960s and essentially said 'These vegetated dunes have sat there essentially unchanged since the last glaciation', which meant, and at that time there were still unknowns about the precise dates of the last glaciation, somewhere between 12 and 20 thousand years ago.

"I remember thinking about it, looking at those dunes and thinking, boy! Those dunes look pretty fresh. You don't see much in the way of gullies. You see an occasional sand fan, but if you look at an aerial photo there isn't much erosion. So it came to me, if you were a dune sitting around for 20 million years with 18 to 20 inches of annual rainfall and an occasional gully washer you'd look a lot more cut up. At the time I filed it away because our main emphasis was looking at the rocks under the dunes and the dunes were just in the way.

"A few years later I served as a liaison between our division, the US Geological Survey and an oil drilling project in the Sand Hills. They were looking for the kind of oil-saturated sands they'd found in Colorado, things a hundred, two hundred million years old. That was my first experience seriously looking at dunes and how they were deposited. At the time radiocarbon dating had been around for a while, but just try to find anything within a dune to carbon date, an old piece of bone, anything organic. Dunes are well-oxygenated. Even if a bison or antelope dies and is immediately buried by dune sand it gets eaten up by bacteria. In order to preserve bone you have to bury it deep and keep it from being exposed to oxygen. You need mud. You need a flood that buries it quickly and keeps it wet. But dune sand? Not so much.

"One of our grad students was working on outcrops along the Dismal and Middle Loup Rivers, mostly interested in old lake beds, maybe a couple of million years old. He spent a lot of time walking up and down the Dismal and Middle Loup and the feeder creeks. I became interested in what he was doing. One day he said he had an exposure of peat mix with 60 feet of dune sand on top. I drove out with him, went to his five sites south of Thedford along the Dismal. With peat you usually have actual plant fragments you can carbon date. When we returned to Lincoln, Vince said our peat was older than the carbon dater could date, which then was only about 40 or 45 thousand years. This was before the accelerator came into use. He thought it could be as old as 200,000,000, could be 5,000,000. I didn't think it would be that old. Vince sent off our sample and paid the $250 charge. It came back 6000 years old. Vince thought something was bad wrong, the results were way too young, we must have handled the sample incorrectly. We'd followed all the protocols, but Vince told us to date it again. This particular peat deposit is in a huge cut made by the Dismal, through maybe 70 feet of dune sand. The peat bed was between two and three feet thick and you could follow it for about 300 yards and there were a succession of them, old fluvial deposits, old river deposits. Similar results. A geomorphologist in the geology department said we were wrong, there had to be contamination. We found out the USGS had one of the top radio carbon labs in the world in Denver. We went out to the Dismal early one summer, sampled several sites and took multiple samples at each site. All the samples were younger than 6000 years. In some cases we had 10 feet of dune sand on top. In one case almost 100 feet.

"We wrote it up and submitted it to *Science*, a top journal. We just got trashed, hammered by reviewers. 'This is so far from what everyone else is saying... so sorry.'

Meanwhile Tom Ahlbrandt with the USGS was carbon dating in the Casper and Killpecker dune fields in Wyoming and getting some interesting numbers. He thought the story needed to get out. We presented at the Geologic Society of America. Some people encouraged us, others said we needed to drill holes. Maybe we were only looking at outcrops, maybe we were only seeing skin effects, the river's cut into the dune and deposited some peat, the dune moved a little bit and covered it up.

"Tom said let's write this and we did. 1983. "The Dynamic Holocene Dune Fields in the Rocky Mountain Basin and the Great Plains". He wrote the Rocky Mountain Basin part and I wrote the section on the Great Plains. He was more widely known. Even though we had more dates than he did he was lead author, which was fine. It was peer reviewed, published in *Developments in Sedimentology* and received some comments. The oldest site we cited was actually 9930 years old with no dune sands below. This peat deposit is on the South Fork of the Dismal downstream from the Eclipse Church.

"We put together a summary of everything we'd done. Some activity was really young, maybe 2000 or 3000 years, But the big period of movement was between 5000 and 8000 years. Lots of sand moving.

"People invested in thinking dunes were much older kind of dismissed our work. Kept talking about skin effects. We countered with another article, but it didn't move the needle. We needed to drill down through a dune. Jim Goeke found some money from the USGS for expanded drilling. The University acquired the Gudmundsen Ranch in the mid-1980s and Jim was drilling new stock wells. Someone found some peat, maybe 15 or 20 feet below the level of the bigger flats. Jim said why don't we set up a drill rig on top of one of these dunes on the Gudmundsen?

"We dragged the drill up here, (retrieves a topo map from a neat stack of papers on a side board, points to a high point on the map) right in the middle of this big dune 130 feet high. Sure enough, we drill through about 130 feet of dune sand and now we're at the level of the interdune hay field. We hit some silts and stuff, and then we hit 2 feet of organic rich sediment, I mean black stuff. Pieces of wood. Pieces of plant. One of those yahoo ding-dong deals. Thirteen thousand one hundred sixty years old. Not 3000. That sand dune has to be younger than 13,000 years old. How much younger? It's a huge dune. You're not going to deposit that in 1000 thousand years. So we go back to the numbers. Lots of dune activity around 6000 years ago.

"You can't get a dune to migrate unless it's devoid of vegetation. You have to get down to 20 - 30 percent vegetation and that's one ugly looking dune. No rancher has a pasture with 20 - 30 percent vegetation. Nobody's going to say, "Hey, Slim, you've got a little over-grazing there.' It'd be more like 'what in the shit did you do to your ranch, man? You've ruined it.' Even if it's down to 50 percent vegetation your neighbors are going to give you grief. Most of the landscape out here is 90 percent plus. If the vegetation is there the sand can't move because the sand can't bounce. The idea is we might have had one or two dry periods over the last 15,000 years. We're not talking semi-arid, we're talking desert. There's no way you can get these big dunes, let alone small dunes, to move around without dropping your precipitation low enough to get rid of vegetation. The people who saw the last 10,000 years as fairly stable couldn't understand you could have a couple thousand years so dry you could actually have desert, we're talking major desert."

Doesn't that assume a period of natural warming independent of human activity?

"You betcha. Big time warming has gone on in the past. During the Mesozoic, between 61 and 250 million years ago when dinosaurs were around there were no ice caps. We now know in the late medieval period in Europe they were able to grow grapes where they shouldn't have been grapes. But to stimulate dune activity you need more than warming. You have to reduce precipitation. Wind is a factor, but dryness is crucial.

"You need a thousand years of severe drought to move a big dune like that. (points to photo of a massive dune on his office wall) Smaller dunes can migrate much faster. For the last period of mass movement you've got to look at 700 years ago, 900 A. D. to 1100 A.D.

Tree ring studies back that up. You definitely have a warm period in the Rockies and Great Plains. You can't necessarily tell how dry, but now we have dune records of thousands of square miles of active dunes. Not big dunes, smaller dunes. Maybe the bigger dunes weren't devoid of vegetation. Aside from some blowouts we can't find another period in the last six, seven hundred years where we can see wide spread dune activity. Sure, there have been droughts lasting 10, 15 years. Not of sufficient length to remove enough vegetation to stimulate dune activity.

"I know a dune on top of peat is younger than the peat. When we started this there was no way of knowing how old that sand was. It could have been blown in on top of an existing dune, moved again and reworked, moved again. That's where recent work with luminescence dating (OSL)* comes in. The sand itself is hundreds of millions of years old. The source for most of this sand is the Rocky Mountains in Wyoming and Colorado, been carried in by rivers onto the plains and reworked. I'm pretty sure dunes have been moving around here (the Sand Hills) for a couple of million years."

Swinehart followed his groundbreaking dune dating work with research on a wide range of dune related topics, publishing a steady stream of scholarly articles. He questioned studies which largely credited an absence of long periods of drought, the existence of which Swinehart and many others had previously established, for occasional significant increases in underground water levels. Swinehart postulated intense dry periods resulted in enough sand movement to dam streams, including the Niobrara, the Platte and Blue Creek, sometimes resulting a marked rise in underground water levels, sometimes in the formation of large lakes, sometimes, as in the case of the Platte, promoting significant sand movement across formerly wet stream beds to invade new areas. Swinehart's Sand Hills work led to a four-year research project in Inner Mongolia, where he and several colleagues studied 20,000 years of aridity and dune mobility in Inner Mongolia.

At the top of his game when he retired from UNL, Swinehart remains engaged in his chosen field, appearing at academic conferences and shepherding papers on past research projects through the publication process. Following a move to Missouri Swinehart got married. Jim Goeke served as best man. The former hyperactive dune scientist says he thoroughly enjoys his grandchildren and the relative leisure of retirement, something few of his long-time colleagues would have predicted.

---

* Oxford geologist Stephen Stokes developed optically stimulated luminescence dating. Sand has natural radioactivity. Isotopes give off energy in the form of electrons. When exposed to sunlight the electrons are released. If the sand is left in darkness the sand grains store energy at their core. Sand samples can be dated by exposing long buried sand in black lab light, treating it with hydrochloric acid solution, spreading two or three hundred grains on a little disk, exposing it to LED light, then using a photo multiplier reading with a glow meter.

Chapter 11
Two Poets Talk Sand Hills
Kloefkorn and Welch

Because I could not stop for Death -
He kindly stopped for me -
The Carriage held but just Ourselves -
And Immortality.

— Emily Dickinson
"Because I could not stop for Death"

Until the gathering cirrus
begins to deplete the sun:
the throat of the pulley
when I push back the grave gate
whines. At my ankles
persist lost intentions, lost loves,
while underfoot the grit
or all its eternal shifting never moves.

— William Kloefkorn-stanza from
"Alone in the Sandhills of Sheridan County, Nebraska,
Standing Near the Grave of Marie Sandoz"

We are seated in the Holiday Inn coffee shop south of Grand Island. As a personal favor, Bill Kloefkorn and Don Welch, beloved Nebraska poets and legendary teachers of poetry writing, have agreed to participate in a free-wheeling discussion of the Nebraska Sand Hills, subject of my current book project. I have no idea what they'll say, but I am certain the bill for the coffee when it arrives will be dirt cheap compared to what's about to unfold. No more creative thinkers and wordsmiths anywhere, any time, and as such what they say will be unpredictable. Of course, I would pay good money to sit in the corner listening to Don Welch and Bill Kloefkorn chew the fat on any goddamned subject you could name.

To a casual fellow diner, our table of three elderly men in various states of repair and a much younger, fitter Kathy would be unremarkable. A more observant fellow diner might remember Don's relaxed posture, the genial grin splashed across his face, the distinctive mellifluous voice. A more observant fellow diner would note Bill's mane of white hair, his intensity, his forward posture, the passionate fire in his eyes. The periodic gales of laughter coming from our table could have sparked curiosity even to the farthest reaches of the incurious. Hard to say.

Bill announces the first and most important order of business is to decide which god-damned country we should invade. After a spirited debate we vote for Canada.

They talk about teaching and teachers. Bill's elegant fourth grade reading teacher read twenty minutes a day and hooked him forever on reading. Don has warm memories of his tenure as a poet in residence in a one-room school in Custer County, where he assigned the students to write about a place, secret place, a safe place where no one could find them. While the other students took hold of their assignment a younger boy approached, said he can't think of that kind of place, at least not today, wondered if he could sit on Don's lap.

> *And so the two of us sit under a clock*
> *beside a gaudy picture of a butterfly*
> *and a sweet poem by Christian Rossetti.*
> *And in all that silence, neither one of us*
> *can imagine where he'd rather be.*
>
> — Don Welch-stanza from
> "A Poet in Residence at a Country School"

Don and Bill talk shop, collaborative writing exercises, tricking kids into working with metaphors, even if they don't call them metaphors. Like former Olympic track stars challenged to a sprint, the more they reflect on their teaching lives, the more animated they become, eager to get back in the classroom.

Born two months apart in 1932, children of the Depression, Korean War era veterans, their longtime friendship dates back to the early 1960s and graduate school at the University of Nebraska. Don raises and races pigeons. Bill carves walking sticks. Bill spent extended time on a Cherry County ranch during calving season and, as part of his faculty duties at Nebraska Wesleyan, roamed the Sand Hills in good weather and bad recruiting potential college students. Once hired to teach English at Kearney State College, Don also found himself driving dark Sand Hills roads in search of future college students. During one of Don's high school recruiting visits the last remaining uncommitted student asked Don if he could sing the Kearney State fight song while standing on a teacher's desk. He did and she went to Kearney.

Welch's support was key to Kloefkorn's selection as Nebraska's State Poet, over the strenuous objections of those smug members of the Lincoln arts community who viewed themselves as the final arbiters of the pedigree an acceptable state poet required. Once appointed, Bill, proud winner of the state hog calling contest, traveled tirelessly across the state, connecting with Nebraskans on a visceral level no other poet could have done, precisely why Welch pushed his cause. In later years Bill hosted the popular Friday morning public radio show "Poetry of the Plains," entertaining listeners across the state with vintage Kloefkorn readings and conversations with poets both prominent and obscure.

Welch, genial, soft-spoken, self-effacing, spent 39 years of his professional life teaching at what eventually became the University of Nebraska at Kearney. After his retirement from the Reynolds Endowed Chair in English, Poetry and Creative Writing he signed up to teach classes in the renegade UNK philosophy department for another 15 years. Don wore his abiding loyalty to UNK on his sleeve and returned to the English department long after retirement to clean the stables after one of his politically correct nincompoop successors made a mess of things. Along the way he produced 28 chapbooks and a gem of an instructional book on writing. His statue graces the courtyard near the building where he taught, testimony to his nurturing teaching style.

A child of small town Nebraska, Don had a special relationship with his grandmother, who lived a precarious existence on the eastern edge of the Nebraska Sand Hills. Don's poetry, brilliant nuggets of tightly interwoven perception and intricate language, doesn't always smack you in the face, unless he's angry, when he becomes more direct.

Kloefkorn, whose deep baritone voice Welch once compared to a church organ, grew up in Kansas near the Oklahoma border, deeply rooted in the nuances of small town living, tied inextricably to his stubborn German farmer grandparents. Early exposure to crude Pentecostal revival preaching turned his face from organized religion, although he was generally tolerant of believers and spent over 40 years of his teaching career at Nebraska Wesleyan, a nominal Methodist college. His quixotic public campaign against the distribution of Gideon Bibles in motels evolved into a distinctive running gag.

Bill at Wesleyan, like Don at Kearney, became a campus institution. As the end of Bill's 11 o'clock English class in Room 226 at the far end of Old Main approached, Bill's students came to anticipate the 12 o'clock tolling of the electronic bell in the tower. And they came to anticipate Bill telling them the bell is not a real bell, but an impostor bell installed during a remodeling project. "The real bell," he always said, "was up in that tower for a hundred years covered in pigeon shit and nobody gave a rat's ass. Anybody hungry? How about some goddamned pancakes?" Shortly thereafter Bill, an assortment of hungry students and Bill's teaching buddies trekked down to University Place for some goddamned pancakes. There is, at least for the present, no Kloefkorn statue on the Wesleyan campus, but the Lincoln Public schools had the good sense to name a new elementary school after Bill.

A frustrated novelist, Kloefkorn published 31 poetry books, four memoirs and two short story collections. His memoirs rank with the best prose ever produced on the Great Plains. His poems can be quirky, as when he assumes the character of ludi jr., a wise small town idiot. More often his plain spoken poetry, built with sturdy materials, hits us amidships, exactly where he was aiming.

Bill is bragging about former students, a successful novelist and a pair of young poets he believes will have productive careers. Don does not choose to brag on former students, although he has ample reason. Instead he amiably cedes the floor to Bill, who abruptly switches gears.

"To me the Sand Hills are a kind of special distinctive vastness. You can drive across Montana, for example, on a nice day, and know why they call it Big Sky Country. Nebraska has big skies. At times they seem endless and bottomless. But Montana skies are vaster, more bottomless than our bottomless skies. They're wider. But the Sand Hills have a kind of vastness that's just different from anything. No mountains. Just mounds. I think it's because there's a kind of mysteriousness about it. The sand is always moving, always shifting. Obviously in windstorms, creating occasional blowouts. At the same time, underneath is so solid. You've got 20,000 square miles that are shifting, but not leaving. Always shifting, but not leaving. I suppose you could say the same thing about a mountainous area, always changing, but that's over a long period of time. How long does it take to wear this rock down until it tumbles? Who knows? Maybe a million years? Ten million years? In the Sand Hills how long does it take to shift? Five seconds? Ten seconds? A windstorm comes up and the whole thing changes and yet it sits. It's that combination of shifting and not shifting that's unique. And the little forms of life in that place and underneath it all that water. For God's sake, the biggest goddamned aquifer in the Western Hemisphere."

The four of us meditate for an appropriate time on the biggest goddamned aquifer in the Western Hemisphere.

An Emily Dickinson fan, Don brings up his extended childhood sojourns near Ansley with his beloved grandmother. "Dickinson said there was an overtakelessness with God and for her God was a becoming, not a being. She spent her whole life trying to find out who God was until she wrote that remarkable poem — 'because I could not stop for death, it kindly stopped for me'. She realized the horse's heads were always towards eternity, but it would take them forever to get there. That's what I felt as a kid walking from Berwyn to Ansley. I wanted to get there. I wanted to see Bing Crosby in "Pennies from Heaven." I wanted to suck on penny candy, sit in the weeds and watch that movie splashed on the side of the post office. But the best thing was looking up and seeing all those stars, brighter than any bright in my life. With the Sand Hills there's an overtakelessness, an unendingness. There is a sense of becoming I think is utterly fascinating and mysterious."

Bill raises a sturdy finger. "If you don't like my explanation of the Sand Hills mystery go buy the goddamned *Living Bible*. Whoever did that translation should have his nuts cut off. I'm assuming it's a man, a woman would have more sense. It's an abomination if I might borrow a word from Deuteronomy.

"I think with the Sand Hills you have not one paradox, but a whole bunch of them. I mentioned where it's shifting but not shifting. Another is when people describe the Sand Hills the word vegetated always enters the description. It's the largest collection of vegetated sand dunes in the western hemisphere. Another paradox — all this sand, but all this vegetation. One consequence is some of the richest folks in Nebraska come out of the Sand Hills. The nutrients in the grasses are akin to the nutrients in the grass in the Kansas Flint Hills, so you have these incredible cattle produced in the Sand Hills. I also think the Sand Hills must force people fairly quickly to determine what they think and believe. You can't bail yourself out every day or every other minute. Your neighbor might bail you out, but he might take hours to get there. It forces you to figure out where you stand and who you are."

Don nods in agreement. "I think it does. The wise, wise people of the world always know what to subordinate themselves to. It's the dumb ones who always claim the ordinate, claiming to be up above, so they can look down on others. Wise people are looking up at something more important than they are."

Bill is on a roll. "And it's a place you marvel at because you drive across the Sand Hills and here are hundreds of miles of pristine acreage that humankind, for all of its effort, hasn't screwed up, how incredible that is. What we do, our proclivities, is to screw things up. We will develop an area as much as we can develop it. Pour the concrete, man. But the Sand Hills, we haven't figured out how to screw it up. I know there are people working on it, and probably will succeed, and will probably wipe us out, which is nothing in this scheme of time anyway. We tend to think this life is pretty goddamned important.

"And another thing, the Sand Hills provide a context in which one can better appreciate what lies outside the Sand Hills. I thought of that one time when I was driving up Highway 27 through the western Sand Hills to Gordon to visit Mari Sandoz's grave. Here you are in a goddamned Toyota and the whole thing is crazy. You're in a goddamned Toyota manufactured by the Japanese who killed a lot of us at Iwo Jima and all that gets mixed up in your head. I bought a goddamned Toyota. Why did I buy a goddamned Toyota? I saw *The Sands of Iwo Jima* 27 times, memorized most of John Wayne's lines. I'm driving through the dunes remembering some of John Wayne's lines when the William Tell Overture started up on the car radio. I hadn't listened to it all the way through for a long time and had forgotten how the first half of it is kind of dull to the untrained ear. Slow, slow. I was just arriving at the turn off to the Sandoz ranch when, of course, the whole thing changes and instead of thinking about John Wayne's speeches or goddamned Japanese Toyotas I'm caught up in the music. In what other context could you listen to that and have the same effect. I can't imagine."

Don straightens in his chair, smiles his special "I'm about to talk about my grandmother smile." "That's like having the best of both worlds. I can remember when this began to happen in our lives. My father gave my grandmother a radio. The farm did not have electricity, so she used a car battery. If she were selective and listened only to her favorite programs it would last two weeks before it needed another charge. We had a tough time getting the car battery to town until she came up with the idea of taking a rusty machete and cutting apart an old car tire, making half a car tire with a handle at both ends. We put the battery in the middle and between the two of us, hauled the battery two miles to town, have it charged while we went to the store.

"As much as she loved that place, when the world came into it in the form of Jack Benny, it was an even better world."

*

Nobody can stop time. And even if we could I'm not sure it would be a good idea. But just for today I would like to call a freeze frame, listen to these two old friends chew the fat for maybe the next hundred and fifty years.

As we wind things down, a overweening sense of finality hangs over the parting. When, if ever, will we again be savoring Welch and Kloefkorn, men who know who they are, at their comradely best? Although they have become more fragile, neither seems old. Both are producing the best writing of their lives. But they are not young men. Things happen. As Jack Crabb in the movie *Little Big Man* said just before Custer's 7th Cavalry rubbed out his four Cheyenne wives and newborn son on the banks of the Washita, "sometimes the grass don't grow and the wind don't blow and the sky ain't blue."

Several months later I am sitting across from Bill in El Toro, his favorite Mexican restaurant near his Lincoln home. He seems to be on a first name basis with everyone in the place. He has shrunk since Grand Island, his pants hanging off no hips at all. His breathing, rumored to be a problem, seems mostly okay, except for one time when he can't exhale and struggles for a few moments to get squared away.

I've always had an interest in how creative people create. Exactly how does the process work? Creative people usually have distinctive ways of doing things. For instance, if Bill were to write a poem about lunch at El Toro how would he go about it?

The wheels spin for a fleeting moment. "First of all the poem wouldn't be about lunch at El Toro. So it might start out 'this poem isn't about lunch at El Toro, nor is it about the beef burritos we ate, although we did eat beef burritos,' and go from there."

Bill takes a deep breath, fixes me with a steady gaze, says he doesn't want to pry, but asks about my health. I give him the short version, wonder why he asked the question.

"Things aren't going very well with me. I'm dying, Bryan. This lung thing is some sort of auto immune affliction. Incurable. I can tell I'm losing muscle tone. I hope I can live until January. I have a bucket list and most of the stuff is done. I should be able to see all the new books in print, see my grandson play football this fall. But I have all these papers, unfinished manuscripts. Eloise (Bill married his high school sweetheart) would have thrown it all out years ago. After I'm dead it will be gone. I was wondering if you would take charge of all that stuff, maybe seven boxes? All of my correspondence with my younger brother? He writes a good letter. That correspondence might make a decent book."

I agree to take the job. On the way back to Bill's house, where he will renew his close personal relationship with the oxygen machine, I'm thinking about finding a suitable institutional repository. Love Library at UNL? The Nebraska Historical Society? The Lincoln Public Library? Shouldn't a literary executor be appointed to deal with rights issues? Much to investigate.*

Once he's settled in his favorite chair and hooked up to oxygen, perky, chirpy Eloise flits around the kitchen scrubbing the living crap out of things. I can see why Bill is worried she will pitch his stuff at the first opportunity.

Bill unhooks the oxygen, asks about the Sand Hills project. I am worried about bumbling around and screwing up a treasure trove of priceless material. "You won't mess it up, Bryan. You're a writer." Which just might be the kindest single thing anyone has ever said to me.

---

* Bill exceeded his goal of living until January by five months. After his death in May, Bill's children rescued his papers from the house and consigned them to a designated section of the Cochrane-Woods Library at Nebraska Wesleyan.

*

FUNERAL AT ANSLEY
by Don Welch

I write of a cemetery,
of the perpetual care of buffalo grass,
of kingbirds and catbirds
and cottonwoods;

of wild roses around headstones
with their high thin stems
and their tight tines, and their blooms
pursed in the morning.

I write of old faces,
of cotton hose and flowered dresses
and mouths which have grown up
on the weather.

And I write of one woman
who lies a last time in the long sun
of August, uncramped by the wind
which autumns each of us

under catbirds and kingbirds
and cottonwoods, and the gray-green
leaves of the buffalo grass.

This August morning I am gathering seed from wild iris, last night's rain drops still clinging to the gray-green bulging pods. By collecting wildflower seed I am probably committing a Class IV felony, punishable by a quadrillion dollar fine and several years in the slammer, but on this particular morning I need this menial task too much to care. A thousand feet below, across the broad expanse of Colorado's South Park to the east, a haze of white smoke from the Hayden Pass fire hangs tenaciously along the bordering mountain ridges. I can't remember the last time we had a clear view of Pike's Peak. Six weeks probably. The dogs, instead of wandering off on their own business, as is their habit, hang around observing the seed gathering. They suspect I am scuffling.

Last night we learned Don Welch died at his home in Kearney. The sense of loss is almost unbearable. His classy reluctance to share his health troubles beyond a tight circle of family and close friends somehow adds to the gloom on an otherwise brilliant summer morning. My incurably cheerful teacher and friend is dead and I am struggling to let him go.

A sepia memory of Don Welch doing what he loved. Mid-1980s. I am a newly destitute ex-rancher refurbishing my public school teaching credentials, taking, due to a class registration malfunction, Welch's legendary poetry writing course. Most of the class is made up of senior undergraduates, some of them eager, a few of them not so much. The rest of us, a mixed bag of school teachers gathering graduate school credits, bored housewives and a couple of broke ex-ranchers hoping for a fresh start, soon discover that by landing in Don Welch's class we have hit the jackpot.

Welch loves the English language, loves talking about words. He enjoys nothing more than sending a particularly word-rich phrase mellifluously rolling across the room towards our ears, ears both receptive and tone deaf. He tells stories, mostly teaching stories, sometimes more than once, but nobody is more tickled with a Don Welch story than Don Welch. Any passing absurdity makes his eyes twinkle. And he chuckles. No professor chuckles more often than Don Welch.

After we explore the works of famous poets, paying strict attention to the harmonies of form and meaning, Welch assigns new poetry writing tasks nearly every day. Before each class, Welch hands out copies of our latest scribblings and we follow along as he gives every poem, no matter how humble, the best possible rendition. His critical comments, invariably encouraging, make every student feel like a goddamned poetic genius.

One assignment asks for a poem rendered in iambic pentameter. Not many of us have experience with the form, but, brimming with Welch-inspired confidence, we do our best. Except for one mopey undergrad, who clearly lifts his entire submission from *Twilight of the Sioux* by Nebraska Poet Laureate John Neihardt, the exact selection, if memory serves, Welch chose only two days previously to illustrate the highest and best use of iambic pentameter.

The class responds with a mixture of bewilderment and outrage. What the hell are we hearing? How in blazes does he expect to get away with such obvious plagiarism? What a sleaze! More importantly, how will Welch deal with him?

Welch reads the stolen poem with as much close attention and rich delivery as always. He grins, sets the poem on top of the read poem pile and says, "Well, there you have it. Doesn't get any better than that" and moves on to the next student poem, which turns out to be so awful it immediately dispels any suspicion of plagiarism.

What just happened? Welch is his jovial self, plowing through a stack of ugly examples of iambic pentameter, miraculously discovering in each at least one promising nugget. Anyone of my advanced age with much in the way of college experience has witnessed a professor come unglued for less cause. But clearly Welch assumes the mope plagiarist is no threat to the poetry guild, no threat to Welch's ego, no threat to the human race. If the mope is so lazy he can only muster an obvious copy job it's not worth disrupting the harmony of his classroom to make note of it. No wonder they honored Don Welch with a statue.

On this August morning I am also thinking about the last time I heard from Don, a couple of months ago in June, shortly after I sent him some of Kathy's photos of the broad, riotous swatch of wild iris along Breakneck Pass Road below our cabin. He replied with a smidgen of appropriate haiku and said, "Send more photos."

I add another handful of iris pods to the bag, each one plump with promise. Kathy plans to sow the seeds all around our acreage. But maybe we will pick out a particular spot, just below the grove of young aspen saplings for the majority of the seed. Every June we will see the results, so lovely it will hurt our eyes.

Chapter 12
Celia's Branding

Banking was a job. This isn't a job.

— Heidi Ostrander Terrell

We are on our way north to attend the spring branding on Celia's ranch. We've always been curious about Sand Hills brandings. To people like us who always ran their calves through squeeze chutes to be branded, vaccinated and castrated, the rope and drag process seems like it might be unnecessarily chaotic and rough on both humans and animals. Sand Hills ranchers we have met have a benign view of brandings, a time when the neighborhood gets together and makes short work of a helluva lot of work. Ask them why they don't run cattle through a squeeze chute and they'll give you the kind of a pitying look they might give to a silly alien from Mars who won't eat meat. This will be our first Sand Hills branding.

Lightning criss-crosses the sky. The windshield wipers have trouble keeping up with the downpour. The rain stops just past Maywood. We drive through North Platte, Roscoe, over Kingsley Dam and up the north side of Lake McConaughy, through Arthur, past Hyannis to Ellsworth, then north through the heart of the old Spade Ranch, past Mari Sandoz's grave and the Sandoz orchards to Gordon, nary a single glaring yard light the entire way to mask the massive light show overhead.

We find our Gordon motel room to be more than adequate, none of the minor discrepancies Kathy uncovered in the Gering motel where we stayed on our way to interview Dr. George McMurtrey. However, this room has one major defect: thin walls. We have barely fallen asleep when the guy in the next room begins coughing up a lung. Although he is dedicated to the task and works faithfully all night, frequently calling for Audrie to come help him, he never quite finishes the job.

Drizzly 6 a.m. We head west out of Gordon, then 25 miles south through the hills to Celia's Pine Creek Ranch. Aside from some fresh greening, there is little evidence of last night's 3.57 inches of rain reported by a rancher in the Gordon Gas & Shop. The Sand Hills sponged up the 3.57 inches and sent it straight into the vast belly of the Ogallala aquifer below.

Celia, hard at work on lunch preparations, pauses long enough to direct us vaguely north through a couple of pasture gates to where the early crew has Jules and Heidi's small herd, between 60 and 70 cows, corralled for the first of today's brandings.

Red-cheeked Heidi greets us warmly, points out members of the branding crew, made up of Jules and his daughters, older neighbors, younger men and women friends of Heidi and her husband Brock, Heidi's uncle Cash Ostrander, his wife, Jecca and two sons, Sterling and Steele. Heidi discovers her heavy coat has a faulty zipper, leaving the top and bottom of the heavy coat unzipped and open to the cutting wind. She shrugs and begins assigning jobs.

Anyone who brought a horse is entitled to a roping stint. Heidi, clearly running the show, makes sure the crew doing vaccinations has adequate vaccine supplies. An occasional nod or finger wave switches calf wrestlers to ropers or ropers to branders or wrestlers.

The ropers quietly work their horses in close quarters, weaving their way through the corralled pairs, snaking a rope against the heels of a calf, sliding the rope up and around the leg when the calf obligingly raises his foot, then a slow, drag of the bewildered calf to one of four sets of calf wrestlers. One team of 3 wrestlers between the ages of 8 and 12 has more fun than anyone. Nobody minds the blue hair smoke boiling up from the branding irons in their faces or the blood and gook of the castration process. The wrestlers' constant laughter contrasts with the seriousness of the ropers. Roping in a swirling 30-40 mile an hour wind will concentrate the mind.

Heidi's towheaded sister Carrie, sporting brand new leather chaps and big hoop earrings, is all smiles, whether roping or wrestling. Carrie, once she finishes her MBA at Texas A & M, intends to join Heidi and Brock running Celia's place. Celia does not know this, neither do Carrie's parents. They assume she's headed for a career on a corporate thoroughbred farm in Kentucky.

Jules, Celia's evangelist son, roams around ear-tagging heifer calves. Renegade calves escaping from the ropers get past him. Anxious cows threaten to disrupt the brandings, he doesn't pay much heed.

Cash, Celia's younger son, takes charge of one of two full-time castrator positions. He uses a pocket knife, sharpened occasionally on a communal whetstone. He approaches each calf in the same deliberate manner, no matter how long the calf wrestlers have been waiting, with the familiar slow, straight-backed walk which reminds neighbors of the way his maternal grandfather, Young Jules Sandoz, walked. If the calf is being branded, he cuts, if the calf is being vaccinated, he cuts, if the wrestlers have a loose grip, he waits until they have a tight grip, then he cuts, tossing the testicles over the fence, much to the dismay of the other official castrator, an older neighbor, who hordes every last nut in a plastic five gallon bucket.

Jecca, Cash's wife, is a superb and enthusiastic roper. Clearly, if it were up to her, she would spend the entire day in the saddle dragging calves to the fire.

One hour after the first branding began, operations shift to a new location a few miles away on the north end of one of Celia's larger pastures. Fourteen riders scour the light green hills for strays, sending an intermittent stream of black cows and calves trotting towards the corral — tight quarters for Celia's 450 head cow herd.

Heidi's plans to ease crowding by cutting most of the mother cows back to pasture. Jules, manning the west corral gate, sees a half dozen calves sprint past him. Previously released cows bawl them back towards the hills. A grim-faced Heidi dispatches ropers to retrieve the calves. Three more calves escape through the corral fence to the north. More ropers are dispatched. Heidi takes charge of an especially puny calf with a jerry-rigged rope halter, planning to take him home after the branding for supplemental bottle feeding. Meanwhile, on the east end of the corral, Brock and some helpers have efficiently sorted 300 cows back to pasture while losing and recovering a single calf.

The flatbed pickup truck with propane tank, branding iron cooker and Styrofoam ice chest filled with black leg and shipping fever vaccine lumbers into the corral. The cooker soon has eight branding irons in red hot working condition. Calf wrestlers organize themselves into six branding lines, instead of the four at the first pasture set up.

While Cash Ostrander whets his pocket knife, a pair of older neighbors fill syringes. Heidi nods. Four horses and ropers weave through the herd, roping and dragging sleepy-looking calves to the teams of waiting wrestlers. One wrestler grabs the tail and the rope and jerks upward. The other grabs any available leg. The calf goes down. The wrestler holding the tail sits on the ground pushing the down side back leg forward with a foot while holding the other back leg against the calf's side. Cash strolls straight-backed to the operating theater. Vaccinators descend, inject, mark the calf with a grease stick, yellow for black leg, orange for shipping fever.

Temporarily freed of his ear-tagging duties, Jules skillfully wields a branding iron, working with precision, branding each calf on the side with Celia's kerosene lamp chimney brand, a brand her father Young Jules, drew on a piece of paper using the kerosene lamp on the kitchen table as a model. After each branding, sometimes after two, Jules screws the branding iron into a rusty bucket of tarry oil and gravel, coating the iron before sticking in back on the cooker. The coated iron blazes, burning off the collected hair, making the next branding hotter and easier to read.

During a short break from roping, Jecca, the most stylish woman working the branding, says her oldest son, Stetson, plans to move back to the ranch once he finishes a range management course at Southeast Community College in Beatrice and a summer internship on an Australian thoroughbred horse operation. Although one of Jecca's toes is currently in broken condition from being stepped on by a horse, she has chosen to ride a stallion at this branding "to make sure he remembers his manners." I am thinking if Jecca's stallion knows what is good for him he will remember his manners.

Jecca keeps 20 to 25 quarter horse mares and holds a joint production sale with two other breeders every other year in Ogallala. She hopes to attract another breeder to join the sale as she thinks more horses will attract more buyers.

Kathy roams the corral snapping photos. No one seems to notice.

Jules stops by the branding iron cooker during a hiatus in his branding duties. He says he is eager to return to his New York ministry, a $300 airline ticket burning a hole in his pocket, a flight out of Denver scheduled for next week. "Time on the ranch heals me up. Now I'm ready to round up lost souls in New York."

Cash, responding to a general request, begins roasting four calf testicles on top of the branding iron cooker. Salt and pepper shakers magically appear. As workers eat them and pronounce them tasty, he adds more to the cooker top.

Celia and Lyle show up outside the corral. Mindful of the clouds and cold wind Celia is swaddled in a heavy coat and a black Russian style fur hat. She takes photos for an hour before heading home to finish preparations for lunch.

All but a few straggler calves branded and vaccinated, Heidi finally takes a break. She laughs when asked if she thinks branding is hard work. "I had a banking job once. Now that was a job. I always wanted to work somewhere soft, like here. Banking was a job. This isn't a job."

Celia, Lyle and Lynette have a massive lunch ready for the branding crew. Stewed watercress fresh from Pine Creek, ham, roast beef, chicken, mashed potatoes and gravy, rolls, baked beans, vegetable rice casserole, sauerkraut, a raw vegetable tray, two flavors of Jell-O salad, deviled eggs, lemonade, coffee, iced tea and wash tubs full of iced pop. For dessert — nine pies, the majority contributed by Jecca and Celia's sister Marguerite: apple, peanut butter cream, blueberry, banana cream, peach, chocolate, coconut cream, cherry and strawberry-rhubarb.

Fifty-eight men, women and children pass through the line at least once. Jules takes his heaping plate to the long table in the dining room. While neighbors listen intently Jules shares his thoughts on random subjects. He quickly falls into the easy cadence of call and response preaching:

"If you love your man you'll put clean folded laundry in his drawers, cook his meals." A couple of older, wiser men at the table sneak a glance in the general direction of the kitchen. Not spotting any eavesdropping wives, they nod in agreement.

"People aren't loved. What people are looking for is how to correct the sins of their past, how to say they're sorry. Even Muslims." This draws a chorus of blank looks. Nobody nods.

Someone asks why Jules goes to New York instead of Denver or St. Louis or any other large city.

"Why go to New York? New York has the second largest population of Hebrews on planet earth. The largest is in Israel. Whatever is going to happen to the earth will happen to the Hebrews first, because even though they have a different religion than we do, they are God's chosen people. Where did 9/11 happen? New York. What city is the richest on earth? New York." Everyone at the table agrees New York has a helluva lot of money.

"When I heard about 9/11, I went, took $50. I always take $50. I stay with people, good people, but they don't know how to cook. The refrigerator might have a jar of mayonnaise and a package of nitrate filled meat and some soda pop (makes a face). They find out I like Kellogg's Raisin Bran and they buy me Raisin Bran and some milk." Good idea. Kellogg's Raisin Bran and milk, nature's perfect food.

"People ask me how I can live on $50. Three reasons: we don't buy our kids cars, don't put them through college, don't pay for weddings." I'm thinking this is much easier to pull off if Celia is paying the college tuition bills.

"You know Long Island?" Nobody claims to know anything about Long Island. "It's got millions of people, good people, all packed together. You go on the freeway at rush hour and you're happy to move three or four miles an hour! Three or four miles an hour! We all agree three or four miles an hour would be awful.

"Everyone in New York is pulling out of the stock market and looking for alternative investments. What about gold?"

Jules looks around the table. A couple of neighbors shrug their shoulders.

"If you stack up gold, where are you going to put it? Under your mattress? People hear you cashed out of the stock market they'll come and take your gold and kill you." One listener nods agreement.

"Every day people ask me what to do with their money. I tell them to buy a piece of land. Nobody will come in the night and steal your land." I'm thinking Jules should tell that to the pre-Revolution land owners in Russia or China. Tell that to the Cuban land owners before the murderous Castro boys came along. But today Jules has the floor and his audience, land owners one and all, nods and murmurs general agreement.

Laughter breaks out in the kitchen. I wander out to exchange my empty plate for one loaded with a substantial slab of toothsome strawberry-rhubarb pie. The baker who made this pie knows a thing or two about pie crust. Heidi and her sisters, red-faced and nearly out of breath, are sharing stories and teasing each other.

On the way back to the dining room I pass Cash resting on the living room sofa, seemingly oblivious to his brother's lecture in the next room or the laughter in the kitchen. He amiably agrees to visit with me at his ranch later on this evening.

In the dining room Jules still has the floor. "Everyone in New York is stashing food and water, expecting the apocalypse." I wonder if Jules tells people in New York everyone in the Nebraska Sand Hills is preparing for the apocalypse.

"People in your neighborhood will know you have food and they'll come and kill you for your food. Your only chance is to distribute your food to hungry crowds. Then you won't have any food either." This last nugget is enough to make my head hurt, but the neighbors listen politely. Several chime in with their own apocalypse-beating strategies.

I'm thinking about the sack of stale potato chips rusting away in our pantry. Would a starving apocalpyser kill me for stale potato chips? Most likely. What about Kellogg's Raisin Bran? I'll bet we have an ancient box of wrinkly old Kellogg's Raisin Bran just sitting around not doing a damn thing. Clearly I need to give the approaching apocalypse more thought, develop a strategic master plan.

Even though Jules can make my head hurt he's an interesting fellow, a fellow with healthy curiosity, who continually comes up with novel theories. Not a mean or deceptive bone in his body. He may be grounded in his version of modern fundamental Christianity, but he's not looking for reasons to condemn anyone to the fiery furnaces. Easy to see why a complete stranger might take him home and top him off with milk and Kellogg's Raisin Bran. Clearly he is a doting, if absentee father. He and Lynette are raising as cheerful and clear-eyed a set of children as breathe. I've always been a big believer happy children tend to be raised in happy homes. And while his grandfather Young Jules Sandoz frowned on religion, I'm beginning to wonder just how deep the similarities run.

Jules abruptly changes gears, asks me about my research project. When he learns about my interest in the nearby Rex Ranch, owned by the Mormon Church, he fetches his son-in-law Brock Terrell, a guy with work experience on the Rex Ranch, a guy presently minding his own business in Celia's kitchen.

Next to Ted Turner's bison ranches, the ranch holdings of the Mormon Church are the largest in the state of Nebraska. Neighboring ranchers have a more generous attitude toward the Rex Ranch than they do Turner's operations. This is primarily due to Turner's highly publicized land acquisitions, always accompanied by breathless news accounts of how many zillion acres he owned before this latest addition. The perception of Turner as a rich dilettante, once married to a ditsydoodle, left-wing nut moron is shared by many Sand Hills residents. Turner's Sand Hills bison operations experienced problems during the startup phase, before the installation of adequate fencing. Tales of Turner bison herds showing up in neighbor's front yards only grew in the telling. Eventually, as Turner's operations gained a better understanding of the challenges of bison ranching in the Nebraska Sand Hills and placed more importance on being good neighbors, local ranchers became more accepting, although residual resentment has not entirely disappeared.

The Mormons acquired their 228,000 Sand Hills acres without fanfare and, from the beginning, established a cordial working relationship with neighbors. The Rex Ranch is not a single entity, but a conglomeration of several ranching operations under the ownership and management of the Church of Latter Day Saints. Rex Ranch employees, who may or may not be of the Mormon faith, attend neighborhood brandings, even those two hours away, unlike Turner employees, who have little reason to exchange work with neighbors. Rex Ranch managers travel the Sand Hills, speaking at cattlemen's meetings, where they make new friends and explain their low-input ranching philosophy.

Brock grew up south of Hay Springs on his family's farm/ranch. After taking a course in range management at South Dakota State University he served a short internship on the Rex Ranch before becoming a full-time herdsman. His manner, like his wife Heidi's, is direct. When he talks about the cattle and grass business it soon becomes apparent he knows his subject.

Brock describes the Rex Ranch managers as progressive, continually conducting research on cattle nutrition and reproduction. "Rex Ranch philosophy," he says, "is holistic, including grass, wildlife, cattle and people, with the primary emphasis on low-input production and easy calving.

"When I worked on the ranch assisted calving births only ran 1 percent per year. That meant I provided some level of assistance with the births of 10 calves from the 1000 cows I was assigned. Ten might be a little high. The last calving season I worked on the ranch I had maybe five. Or maybe as low as three." In addition to the 1000 mother cows, Brock and an intern had primary responsibility for 1500 yearlings. Calving lasted three weeks. After 21 days the cows that had yet to calve were sorted off and sent to a different area. "Basically you manage 1000 cows and they're your cows. You decide where on the ranch to calve. How many times a day to check the herd. Bonuses were tied to weaning percentages and cow death loss. Herd health and genetic decisions came from higher in the food chain."

At the time Brock worked on the ranch the herd was a composite of Hereford, red Angus, Simmental and Gelbvieh breeds, most adult cows weighing between 1100 and 1200 pounds. The ranch aimed for low milk production. "It costs less to put feed directly in the calf than to put feed into the cow to maximize milk production. A cow producing 15 pounds of milk per day consumes less feed than one producing 25 pounds of milk per day." The ranch also experiments with later calving dates to coincide more closely with greening spring pastures. Since nutrition requirements escalate after calving, later calving dates limit expensive supplemental feeding.

Brock says greater milk production and heavier weaning weights have been the dominant trends in the beef industry for well over half a century, coinciding with the introduction of larger, heavier milking European breeds. "In the competition for heavier weaning weights many cattlemen ignored their increasing production costs. Heavier, bigger framed cows take more feed. Often they cannot thrive in winter conditions without large quantities of supplemental hay. Our management practices on the Rex Ranch represented a return to cost consciousness and an emphasis not on heavy calves, but on live calves."

I'm thinking I need to make a research trip to the Rex Ranch. A trip north might involve another night in the Gordon Motel. Maybe we can listen to a different guy cough up a different lung. Brock gives me the name and phone number of the Rex Ranch manager he worked under.

Brock and Heidi's plans for the future depend to some extent on what Celia does with her holdings. But whether they maintain a close business relationship with Brock's family, take a more active role on Celia's ranch or strike out on their own, the low-input, holistic model practiced by the Rex Ranch will be the blue print for Brock and Heidi's cattle operation.

I ask Brock if marrying into the Sandoz clan had complicated his life.

"I grew up south of Hay Springs where Grandpa settled on the Flats (Mirage Flats) after World War II. By marrying Heidi I went from being related to nobody in the country to being related to everyone.

"I read *Old Jules* in school. It means something."

We are reluctant to leave Celia's warm kitchen. Most members of the branding crew are hanging around, enjoying the communal bliss. On the counter a lone piece of strawberry-rhubarb pie makes a strong argument for staying. But we need some time to prepare for this evening's interview with Cash Ostrander and while we don't think there are limits to Celia's hospitality, we don't want to find out.

Cash Ostrander

After a quick dinner in Gordon, tape recorder loaded with fresh batteries, we head south through the darkening hills for Cash and Jecca's Willow Creek Ranch, former headquarters of Young Jules, the place where Celia and her siblings grew up. The lane from the highway to the ranch house winds along Willow Creek, past an impressive, recently painted barn and solid corrals holding a set of quality mares and a few young colts and fillies. Cash's house sits just east of Young Jules' former ranch house, which Jecca and Cash operated as a bed and breakfast for a number of years. I am wondering if the kitchen ceiling in the old house still smells faintly of the heavy tobacco smoke from Young Jules and his neighbors chewing the fat into the wee hours.

Cash welcomes us into a remodeled ranch bungalow furnished with carefully chosen antiques. He says Jecca chose most of the antiques. Seated at the kitchen table he talks easily about his sometimes eccentric grandfather.

"This place was a swamp when he bought it from owners who'd rented it to the Spade Ranch for years. He used a shovel to find every spring and eventually ditched the swamp, turned it into productive hay land. He purchased a couple of Caterpillar tractors, used them to push hay stacks across soggy ground. One time a farm equipment dealer from Alliance brought up a new four-wheel drive tractor for Grandpa to try out. After the guy unloaded the tractor Grandpa told him to try to move some hay. He promptly got stuck and Grandpa had to pull him out with a Cat. The guy didn't say a word, loaded up the tractor and drove back to Alliance.

"I wouldn't say Grandpa was the kind of guy a kid would run up and hug. He tended to be brusque, but he never scared me. I never worked around him except for brandings, at a time when he no longer did much physical labor, but he did plenty when he was younger. He always wore rubber boots and coveralls.

"Grandpa was not a mechanic, nor did he get along with livestock. Grandma, on the other hand, got along well with livestock. I might take after Grandpa a little bit. I would rather ride the 4-wheeler than a horse."

Once Cash completed four years in the Marines and a stint in range science school at the University of Wyoming he was ready to return to ranching. By then Celia and Dutch owned Young Jules' ranch on Willow Creek. They helped Cash and his brother Jules by splitting the ranch, each half capable of carrying 350-400 head of cows and enough hay ground to winter them. Cash and Jules assumed the mortgage payments and used Dutch and Celia's equipment in return for helping them put up hay.

When Jules decided to give up his half of the ranch and return to preaching Cash was surprised, but not unhappy. "We were having trouble building a herd on half the ranch. I would assume Jules was having the same problems. Jules was always involved in the church. There are other ministers in the family on Dad's side. Old Jules himself was almost anti-religious. My grandpa, Young Jules, wouldn't allow Grandma to practice her Catholic religion. It wasn't until she was about to die that he allowed a priest to hear her confession."

Over the years Cash dabbled in politics, serving on the local school board, the board of the local education service unit and a term on the Nebraska State Board of Education. He's been a long-time member of the state GOP central committee and was a delegate to the Republican National Convention in 2004 and 2008. Cash made two runs for the Nebraska Legislature. The first time he narrowly lost and vowed never to run again. "We were gone every weekend for parades. Felt like we abandoned the boys."

Cash traveled with Celia and his immediate family to Switzerland to attend the Sandoz family reunion. The Swiss Sandoz family, through the Sandoz Family Foundation, owns a significant chunks of pharmaceutical giant Novartis (annual sales 50.3 USD) and Swiss watch maker Parmigiani Fleurier. The Foundation also owns the famous Geneva luxury hotel Beau-Rivage Palace and underwrites artists and science education in Switzerland. Cash savored the welcome he and his family received from financially powerful distant cousins, cousins he so closely resembled Celia said they looked more like brothers than cousins. Rubbing elbows with his prominent relatives may have helped rekindle Cash's political aspirations.

After incumbent LeRoy Louden's retirement, Cash changed his mind and ran in the newly consolidated 43rd legislative district, currently the largest in the state. The consolidation pitted him against Cherry County rancher John Ravenscroft, husband of Cheryl, long-time neighbors of Hub McMurtrey, and Cherry County rancher Al Davis among others. Cash finished third in a crowded primary field. (Al Davis narrowly defeated John Ravenscroft in the general election).

Cash Ostrander is not a prototypical political animal, antenna constantly alert for the slightest shift in public opinion. He seems to engage in politics because he finds the process interesting and has a whimsical interest in public service. Anyone who has ever served on a rural school board understands the utter thanklessness of that position. No pay and plenty of grief. Anyone requiring public adulation usually seeks other hobbies.

Belonging to the Sand Hills Sandoz clan in contemporary times automatically earns family members the interest and approval of Mari Sandoz scholars and many people in the surrounding region. Long-time neighbors, who ranched near James, Young Jules, Fritz, Flora and Caroline, thought them hard-working ranchers and good neighbors. On the other hand, Old

Jules Sandoz, the family patriarch, made powerful enemies, was not the cleanest guy around, and often clashed with his neighbors over trivial matters. According to *Old Jules*, Mari's biography of her father, he left Switzerland after quarreling with his family over money and the suitability of a lower class girlfriend. Whispered family lore has Jules leaving Switzerland in disgrace after being disowned by his mother for shooting a brother. Cash grew up chronically embarrassed by the notoriety of his famous great-grandfather. "But as an adult I came to see Old Jules, despite his flaws, primarily as a man of vision, a successful community builder."

Cash and Jecca have constructed a ranching operation designed to support at least one family. Stetson, once he finishes his Australian internship, has the academic background and the family genes to be successful. If he takes over as planned and persists he can expect to eventually own Willow Creek Ranch.

Cash's rule: "Whoever works the ranch gets the ranch."

We drive back to Gordon in a driving rain. A white Ford Escort with South Dakota plates is parked in front of the neighboring motel room. We fall into bed. At 11:30 p.m. we are reminded the motel's walls are paper thin when a meth dealer arrives next door. He negotiates in kind payment from the mother of two small children who rented the room. The kids wail while the transaction is completed multiple times. The TV blares. Loud dope-dealing phone conversations continue until 4 a.m. Kathy, who is never at her best when her sleep is cut short, is tired and grumpy from the short night before. She finally reaches her limit, jumps out of bed and pounds on the wall.

Pound, pound, pound.

"Will you just shut up! Shut up! Shut Up! Shut up!"

Pound, pound, pound.

"Will you just shut up! Shut up! Shut Up! Shut up!"

I become fully awake. "Why are you pounding on that wall? The racket is coming from over there." I point to the opposite wall, source of all the drug dealer racket.

"How unfortunate," Kathy says.

Next morning we are loading the car. A heavily tattooed 300 pound motorcycle guy wearing full gang colors comes out of the room next door, the one Kathy mistook for the noisy one. He gives us a long, mean squint before revving his engine excessively, roaring off in a westerly direction.

We spot him standing beside his Harley in the parking lot of the Western Cafe, home to Chinese-American buffets on Friday and Saturday nights and Sunday noon. The biker gives us an additional fish eye when we enter.

We admire the worn lariats hanging from the walls, the tong tattoos on the arms of our Native American waitress. A genial older guy in the next booth visits with a fellow senior citizen.

"I guess people do find love on the internet. Take Linda. She found the love of her life on the internet. She had to list her favorite hobby. She said riding lawn mowers."

"Riding lawn mowers?" asks the companion. "As in riding the lawn mower? Not mowing with the lawn mower?"

"Naw, she just likes riding around on them. Jumps on one and rides it all over the place.

That's perfect with this new honey because he's got 10 or 12 of them just sittin' around."

We dawdle over breakfast, picking up a few more juicy morsels of small town conversation, waiting for the motorcycle guy to leave. The sorehead takes his own sweet time, before finally paying up and exiting the restaurant. We do not give him the satisfaction of making eye contact.

On the long drive south through the greening dunes we are thinking not only of grumpy motorcycle guys, but about the Sand Hills tradition of roping and dragging, how superior it is to the "cram 'em through the chute" model we practiced when we ran cattle. Much less stressful for the calves and a much better excuse to gather the neighbors for fellowship and toothsome strawberry-rhubarb pie and making quick work of a whole bunch of work.

We're also thinking of unlikely lawn mower romances, of our elderly box of Kellogg's Raisin Bran currently under imminent threat from rampaging apocalypters. Hope to goodness daughter Sydney has locked the front door. We're remembering Celia's kitchen, surely one of the warmest, most centered places in the known universe. We're thinking how pleased Old Jules would be to sit in that kitchen in his smelly clothes, smoking his smelly pipe, relishing the conversation, the expansive food, the understated success of his descendants. Just for old times' sake, he'd probably end up arguing with someone. And we're also thinking of Brock and Heidi, talented people who clearly know who they are, launched on a future filled with infinite promise. After months slogging through the debris of what once was the McMurtrey clan we bask in the blessed gift of healing.

Chapter 13
War Comes to the Sand Hills

Leo and Leland

The phone call came just before just dawn that September morning. The agent at the Red Cloud depot, instead of delivering the telegram out to the farm as was his duty, read the contents to Bryan Tupper over the party line, informing the entire neighborhood of son Leo Tupper's death in Sicily. My grandfather mumbled something to the anxious family about Leo being hurt before staggering out to the water pump in the yard to compose himself. The news did not come as a complete surprise to my grandmother Edith, who'd awakened from a nightmare a few nights previously while dreaming her hands were covered with her son's blood. After doing the math a few days later the family determined Edith's nightmare occurred on September 1st, the day Leo was killed.

Little Leo, born prematurely on a Wyoming homestead in the shadow of Devil's Tower, so small and fragile his mother had to build a tent over the stove, set some water to boil and stick Leo's bed under the tent while she worked. Little Leo, who from before he could read, looked at the world through impossibly thick spectacles. Leo, with a quick mind and quicker temper, who never backed away from a fight no matter how much larger his adversary. Clinton, his older, stronger brother, learned early there was no way of ending a fight with Leo short of half-killing him. My grandfather, who reserved his highest praise for the fearless, always said Leo "wasn't scared of too much." Leo, who lent his clear tenor voice to my parents' wedding ceremony beside a blooming lilac bush in the front yard of the Tupper farm on Thompson Creek, north of Riverton.

Leo may have been the most intelligent of the Tupper children, and Bryan and Edith Tupper raised no dummies. He was the first child to graduate from college, where he sparkled academically, joined the livestock judging team and became a member of the Block & Bridle livestock honorary. In Leo, Bryan Tupper, whose brief stint at the University of Nebraska also included courses in livestock judging, had much to brag about — which he did loudly, early and often. Leo was bright all right, but occasionally impulsive. After a couple of years of walking and hitchhiking the 160 miles between the family farm north of Riverton and college in Lincoln, he made a snap decision to purchase a 1939 automobile with a high interest loan. Bryan Tupper promptly paid off the note, but he spread the word loudly, early and often his smart son was a complete bonehead when it came to money, which, with the exception of the decision to buy a car with high interest credit, was completely untrue.

With both hay crops and money in short supply in Franklin County, Leo and a cousin headed west one summer to work in the Sand Hills hay fields. He soon fell head over heels for Sophie King, the beautiful, raven-haired school teacher from Ashby employed as a summer cook at his hay camp. Sophie's mother and father, both former Kinkaiders from western

Cherry County, raised a family of nine children in Ashby on practically nothing. Sophie's sensible, quiet demeanor, reinforced by a hardscrabble childhood and the necessity of hauling herself up by her own bootstraps, did not immediately mesh with Leo's ebullient personality. Sophie's initial impression of Leo was of an opinionated braggart who was "stuck on himself." Leo's stock was not improved by a disastrous date with Sophie when he buried a borrowed automobile in soft sand and had to be pulled out by a neighboring rancher.

Months later, when Leo spoke at the Ashby Town Hall on ranch management, Sophie and her younger sister Shirley attended out of casual curiosity. Leo not only made a favorable impression with his presentation, but talked Sophie into dancing to the music of a local band. To seal the deal, Leo sang a few songs with the band. The courtship began in earnest. Shirley remembers "Leo had a good voice and was, by the way, the nicest man I have ever known."

After Leo graduated from college he served a short stint as assistant extension agent in Dawson County, married Sophie and moved with her to an apartment in Valentine where he assumed his duties as the county extension agent of Cherry County, by far the largest county in the state. Leo spent only a few months on the job when he was drafted just prior to Pearl Harbor.

On December 7, 1941, my mother, working in the kitchen of the Ponca Methodist parsonage, heard the news of Pearl Harbor on the radio. Struck by the overwhelming premonition the coming war meant something awful was going to happen to her kid brother Leo, she sank down on a kitchen chair and sobbed.

Leo trained at Ft. Leonard Wood, Missouri, where he quickly rose to squad leader. He complained the job did not earn him a raise, but did allow him to give more orders than he received. His barracks housed nine American-Japanese GIs and three members of his squad were Japanese, whom he admired for their competency and counted among his best friends. "One of the Japs is a Jiu-Jitsu expert and he showed us a little one night down at the field house." Not hard to imagine Leo enthused about learning a martial art allowing him to overcome a larger, stronger adversary.

Leo volunteered for officer's training and became a 1st lieutenant in the combat engineers, earning a considerable advance in salary and housing benefits for Sophie. He trained for amphibious landings in Virginia and on Cape Cod. Daughter Anita was born shortly before he shipped out for North Africa as a member of the 540th Engineer Regiment, Company B in George Patton's 7th Army. In letters to my mother, who was pinching her own pennies as the wife of an impoverished Methodist minister, he compared the price of a quart of milk in Virginia to what she was paying in Nebraska. Leo scrutinized each pay check to make sure the amount was accurate and constantly worked to earn promotions and increase his pay. He requested a portion of his monthly check be invested in war bonds. In spite of one infamous car transaction Uncle Leo knew the value of a dollar.

After landing in North Africa Leo bragged about stepping ashore from the Army Duck (DUKW) without getting his shoes wet, although he had to threaten the coxswain with his pistol to get him to hit the beach. "I'm feeling fine and didn't get a scratch through all of it. I went for 90 hours on four hours sleep. Our company had the toughest beach in the operation and we were subjected to artillery fire landing all around us in the water and two airplanes strafing the beach. Captain had his pack shot off and Lt. McCracken was wounded, so Captain and I ran the show."

Leo found the French and Moroccan populations friendly. "I wish I knew French and Arabic and some other languages, they would come in handy." Leo spent much of his time in Morocco out of harm's way building and rebuilding railroads. However, he nearly died when he and his buddies swam out to some partially sunken ships, casualties of the invasion, to search for souvenirs. They were caught in a vicious rip tide, which tore the clothes from their bodies and nearly drowned them all.

As a member of Patton's 7th Army, Leo landed at Gela in southern Sicily late on D Day, July 10,1943, before moving with his unit through rugged western Sicily towards the northern coast and Messina. Two weeks after Sicily was officially liberated, near Termini Immerse, up the coast from Palermo, Leo and his driver, Pfc. Louis Gentile, a kid with a huge Italian family back home in Connecticut, were near the beach mapping an area the combat engineers had cleared of mines. When the Jeep passed over a Teller German anti-tank mine which had escaped detection, the world blew up.

Leo's captain:

It happened around supper time. We all heard it and some said, 'I wonder who got that one?' I thought of Tupper, but dismissed the thought. Then in half an hour we knew.

Bryan and Edith commissioned a local photographer to cobble together two separate photos into a colorized portrait of Leo, his wife Sophie and infant daughter Anita. Any visitor to the Tupper home for the next 40 years sat in a gray overstuffed chair beneath that picture. Sophie smiling shyly into the camera, tiny Anita wrapped in blanket, Leo dressed smartly in his 1st lieutenant's uniform, unfocused eyes facing away from the camera into an uncertain distance.

Sophie, a daughter of the Sand Hills, returned with little Anita to the bosom of her family in Ashby, where she bought a small house and taught at the Ashby school. For several months Leo's letters kept arriving, each one setting off a fresh round of flickering hope he might, against all odds, still be alive. Over a rough three year patch she gradually put her life back together. She married veteran naval aviator George Anderson, who spent a portion of his war in the Pacific hunting Japanese submarines. Together they ran a grocery store and gas station in Ashby until moving to California in the early 1950s.

My grandfather, who took exorbitant responsibility for nearly everything, viewed Leo's death as a personal defeat, a tragedy Bryan Tupper, easily the smartest man he knew, ought have been sufficiently prescient to forestall. That he'd tried and failed to convince Leo to request a deferment did not alter his sense of responsibility. Never one to be caught up in periodic waves of emotional patriotism, which he thought too often led to American involvement in overseas conflict, he viewed wars as a piss poor excuse to "kill boys." The "gummit," whether it be the local county commissioners, the state legislature or the current dimwitted authorities in Washington D. C., were too damned incompetent to run a popcorn wagon, let alone oversee a complicated and expensive overseas war. To trust incompetent government with the fate of a valuable son, even one who financed automobiles at exorbitant rates or failed to request a timely draft deferment, but who nonetheless might someday put together a sizable farming operation, was sheer lunacy.

Shortly after his sojourn in Wyoming ended in 1920 Bryan Tupper purchased a quarter section on Thompson Creek in Franklin County with a high interest loan from an insurance company. It took 20 years and the advent of higher farm prices during World War II to pay off the note. My grandfather always said he intended that farm to eventually become Leo's base, strategically located near larger farms likely to come on the market in the future. There was no doubt in my grandfather's mind Leo would have taken that 160 acres and added enough ground to shade any other land owner in Franklin County.

Leo, had he lived, might well have fulfilled his early promise. He demonstrated sound entrepreneurial instincts by raising crops of turkeys to finance his college education. His indisputable willingness to take on risk, which led directly to his challenging rip tides, paired with sharp intelligence and a solid education, all predicted success no matter whether he returned to the Cherry County extension office or launched a farming enterprise as his father hoped.

From before my feet could touch the floor, I sat in the gray overstuffed chair under that eerie cobbled together portrait listening to my grandfather's recounting of the brilliant shooting star that was Leo's life, and felt, rather than heard, the accompanying sense of loss and self-recrimination. No personal triumphs, of which there were many, none of the numerous successes enjoyed by his other offspring, were sufficient to absolve my grandfather of his deep sense of shame for failing to prevent a German land mine from killing Leo. After all, Bryan Tupper was a man who firmly believed people make their own luck.

Only a month old when Leo left for North Africa, Anita's impressions of her father depended on the memories of those who knew him and her father's wartime letters.

"I always wondered what it would have been like if he had survived the war and come back to live his life with my mother and me." She learned his parents and siblings thought him intelligent and a good public speaker. She discovered he sent her flowers the day she was born and more flowers when she was nine days old. Letters from Leo's men after he was killed expressed their deep respect for him. Leo's letters from the front revealed a cheerful optimist with a genuine concern for the men in his command. In his last letter, written to his parents on the day he died, he said he felt well, inquired about his younger twin sisters, voiced confidence in how things were going, but closed with "Pray for me!!!"

Years later, after a revived interest in her father's life led Anita to read the collection of Leo's wartime letters, she stumbled upon Ben Macintyre's *Operation Mincemeat*, which describes a successful scheme by British Intelligence to deceive the Germans by planting forged invasion plans on a corpse and floating the body to shore. On July 10, 2013, Anita, settled in with the book and a cup of coffee, was reading the account of a submarine captain surfacing off Gela to launch a signal buoy critical to the invasion. "Out of the gloom came a flicker of light from the leading destroyer of the mighty invasion fleet. Dark shapes emerged slowly from the shadows."

Anita realized she was reading about the invasion of Sicily precisely 70 years to the day after it had taken place. "I sat for a long time trying to imagine what it was like. I wondered if Leo could have known that 70 years later his baby daughter would be reading about this historic event. I wondered if he thought, as the submarine captain did, 'he had never seen anything so lovely' as the hundreds of ships approaching the beach in an orderly manner. I wondered if he was scared."

Three years later when Anita and husband Bill traveled to Sicily, they were touched by the reaction of the Sicilians upon discovering Anita's father died in Sicily. Mauro, born 40 years after Leo waded ashore at Gela: "Americans brought candy, chocolates, cigarettes, but most of all, Americans ended the war for us. Some in Palermo hoped Sicily would become another member of the United States."

Lorenzo from Agrigento, became teary eyed when he heard of Leo's sacrifice. "He was in hopes Leo was short for Leonardo and was Italian-American."

Barbara, a much younger Sicilian, praised the Americans for ending the war. "It wasn't even their war.'"

Anita and Bill took off their shoes and walked the beach at Gela. Across the highway from the beach Anita spotted German bunkers, bunkers occupied during the landing by Italian soldiers, some who fought bravely, some who surrendered as soon as possible. Operation Mincemeat, which fooled Hitler into expecting the invasion much further east on the islands off the coast of Greece, delayed German reinforcements from aiding the Italian defenders at Gela and the Americans suffered fewer casualties than anticipated while securing the beachhead. Luck.

Just prior to leaving for Sicily, Anita uncovered a letter from Pfc. Louis Gentile, Leo's jeep driver, a letter she had not opened because it was addressed to her grandparents and was from someone she did not recognize. The badly injured jeep driver, writing from his hospital bed, described how Leo died as they drove down to a beach near Termini Immerse on the northern coast of Sicily. Up until reading Gentile's letter, all Anita knew was Leo died somewhere on Sicily. Now she had a place. "All my life I had never known where Leo was killed. Now I wasn't sure I wanted to go to Termini Imerese."

Eventually she felt unseen forces pulling her. By coincidence, Bill and Anita's planned route to Palermo passed by the picturesque city of Termini Immerse. After they arrived in the city, Bill used his phone translator to communicate with the driver. "My wife's father was killed in Termini Immerse during the war. She wants to see where it happened."

The driver's demeanor underwent an immediate transformation. "He was on a mission to help us, took off at a high rate of speed, found some old men sitting on a bench in the town square. After much arm waving and pointing he us drove down towards the beach where we found a memorial to those who lost their lives in Termini Immerse during the war. It came to me I had connected with my father in a special way and he had wanted me to be there all along." Luck.

"When we arrived at the Palermo airport our driver deposited our luggage on the curb, stood before me for a moment, said, 'Thank you for your father and for my freedom.'"

Military veterans often talk about luck. Bad luck might mean being in the wrong place at the wrong time. Like the new guy, who hadn't unpacked his duffle bag before an urgent call of nature sent him scurrying to the latrine where an NVA mortar round brought an abrupt end to his military career.

Good luck, like the random drawing of a cushy wartime assignment, played no small part in Eugene Rider's safe and secure military service. A dashing Wauneta, Nebraska, recruit, Rider spent his entire service time during the Korean War assigned to Ft. Benjamin Harrison near Indianapolis. He not only possessed movie star good looks, old school manners and plenty of spending money, but lived in private quarters and drove a flashy Ford convertible. Memories of his hyperactive war-time social life kept him warm for years afterwards.

Lloyd Frandsen, my Marine veteran father-in-law, might have spent the entire Korean War stuck in a frozen sandbagged trench directly across the valley from hordes of suicidal Chinese Communist soldiers. Instead, in spite of shooting expert during basic training, his truck driving experience got him assigned to driving a Jeep ferrying high-ranking officers, supplies and ammunition to the front lines, duty which limited his exposure to enemy fire. During his time driving a Jeep in Korea, Lloyd encountered not a single mine field. Once, he heard a mortar round descending on his Jeep and sharply accelerated. The explosion on the road behind nearly knocked him out of the Jeep, but did no lasting damage. Driving along a ridge along the front lines he watched helplessly as an enemy artillery shell headed directly for his Jeep. The shell fell just short of the target and Lloyd lived to fight another day. Luck.

Good luck sometimes came as one huge unexpectedness. Uncle Willis Jones happily chose the Army Air Force over sweating out WWII in a claustrophobia-inducing tank. He always said the best day of his life was the day he jumped out of a mortally wounded B-17 over Germany with his prematurely opened parachute gathered up in his arms and, against all odds, his chute miraculously deployed.

Bad luck also came without warning. An engineer's Jeep hits a mine. A silent sniper bullet finds its target. Tom Ohnesorge, my tall, raw boned high school classmate, joined the US Navy during the Vietnam War. Navy duty might have kept him out of harm's way. However, the always soft-hearted Tom volunteered for medical training. What might have seemed like a good idea at the time led to an assignment as a medical corpsman to Company A, 1st Battalion, of the 7th Marines. North Vietnamese and Viet Cong snipers specialized in killing medical corpsmen and 1st Lieutenants, especially those taller than their fellows. Less than two months into his deployment while on patrol near the hamlet of Can Van, an enemy sniper killed 22-year-old Thomas Herman Ohnesorge. Luck.

*

A month after Ted Turner bought the McMurtrey Ranch at auction, I am sitting in Leland and Pat Johnston's living room in a comfortable bungalow on the eastern edge of Thedford 65 miles south of Valentine. Shortly after the McMurtrey sale concluded Johnston promised to share stories of his service in the Pacific during World War II, which is exactly what he's doing.

"Lucky" could have been Leland Johnston's middle name, although he grew up destitute near Elsmere in southeastern Cherry County, the youngest of eight children. "It was the dirty thirties and we nearly starved to death. I started working out when I was 12 years old for 35 cents a day."

Johnston worked on ranches full time after graduating from the 8th grade. In early 1943 he tried, at age eighteen, to enlist in the Army Air Corps, but was deemed too young. His draft notice finally caught up with him on a ranch near Brownlee. One of 200,000 Americans drafted that month, Johnston and another Brownlee kid traveled to Ft. Crook in Omaha for their physical exams. The old Northwestern railroad car, lit by stinking carbide lights, had no heat. "We nearly froze to death."

Airplane engines roaring 24 hours a day at the Martin factory near Ft. Crook kept Leland awake and restless. He and his buddy passed their physicals. "My buddy went directly into the army, ended up getting killed in Germany." Leland temporarily returned to Cherry County to await orders. He ran a pool hall in the railroad town of Seneca, then trucked cattle, lumber and cattle feed until he was shipped to Ft. Leavenworth in the fall of 1943, a month after Uncle Leo died in Sicily.

Following rigorous infantry training at Camp Roberts, north of Los Angeles, Johnston shipped out with 10,000 GIs and 500 WACs on the former U. S. S. America, a ship so fast (top speed-36 knots) it didn't require an escort. Oppressive heat and sea sick soldiers below deck led Johnston to finagle a sweet job on the promenade deck guarding WAC sleeping quarters from marauding officers. He was allowed to eat in the air conditioned officer's mess, instead of sweating in the GI mess line hoping for two meals a day.

"We were on the boat 18 days to Sydney, Australia, unloaded the WACs and took on 500 Aussie soldiers. We did not get off the ship."

The GIs eventually disembarked at a replacement depot at Milne Bay, New Guinea, where annual rainfall exceeding 200 inches and 110 degree temperatures kept all things, human and material, in various stages of rot. In 1942, Aussie troops, along with a handful of American GIs defeated a Japanese expeditionary force at Milne Bay, the first defeat inflicted on the Japanese in the Pacific Theater by Allied ground forces. By the time Johnston landed at Milne Bay, the victorious allied troops had been dying from malaria for over a year.

A couple of weeks later, Johnston found himself up the coast at the Mappan Bay replacement depot, lined up in formation. Officers counted down alphabetically. Soldiers with last names beginning with A found themselves assigned to the infantry. By the time they arrived at J all infantry openings had been filled. Fortune, not for the first or last time, smiled on Johnston, and he found himself assigned to A battery, 80th Field Artillery. "The luckiest day of my life."

A road ran along the beach by Johnston's encampment. "I remember trucks coming along every day with dead American infantrymen, their hobnailed boots sticking out. We had it so much better."

Johnston spent the bulk of his service time on New Guinea hauling ammunition with a D-6 caterpillar. "We all took turns as perimeter guards. The Japs sometimes strapped on what they called picric acid, threw themselves on our artillery pieces, blowing up themselves and anyone else who got in the way. Lucky for us none of them got through the perimeter."

Johnston escaped the stifling heat by swimming from the beach with his mates, fashioning blow up floaties from their mattress covers. He traded his beer ration for poker money, swapped his cigarette rations to the natives for coconuts. Johnston and his buddies often found themselves assigned to unloading ships, which provided opportunities to liberate tins of fruit and other prized foods. Johnston had little need for money and had most of his Army paycheck sent home to his mother. Like Uncle Leo, he devoted a portion of each check to purchasing war bonds.

Johnston's good fortune continued even after he left New Guinea for the difficult Philippine campaign. He sailed with the invasion forces on board the flagship LST carrying the top brass. "I was lucky, ate in the officers' mess the whole way. We had gold-plated silverware, milk, fresh meat, could go up on deck, had free run of the ship."

He drove a truck loaded with kitchen equipment from the LST onto the beach, "never even got my feet wet." Once ashore, the American infantry moved rapidly, almost always at night.

"We bulldozed trees, pushed up dirt five to six feet high ahead of our guns and dozed a place for ammunition. We were on guard all the time wherever we set up." Johnston didn't spend much time on guard duty exposed to enemy fire because he was busy hauling ammunition with a 6 X 6 truck. "I hauled every round our outfit fired in the Philippines. I was on the road three or four nights a week. One time I was sent clear to Manila, had to spend the night in the ammunition dump. That night a Jap plane came over. It didn't bomb the ammunition dump, but I made up my mind to never sleep in an ammunition dump again."

On his ammunition hauling trips, Johnston accessed other kinds of supplies, like 10 in 1 rations, enough food for 10 men for a day. "10 in 1 rations had cans of bacon, fruit, chocolate bars, C rations, really good food. I gathered up what I could and took it back to the guys on the lines." Johnston's lucky streak continued until the end of the war and through a short post-war assignment in Korea. The only physical damage Johnston incurred during his entire military career was a case of malaria.

After he mustered out of the army in 1946, Johnston went back to the same ranch he'd left for the military. He then took ranch job working for his future father-in-law where a return bout with malaria disabled him for most of a year. After he recovered he began a life-long pattern of changing jobs and careers: ranch hand to forest service worker to heavy equipment operator to feedlot operator to motel owner to livestock order buyer to hay contractor to livestock auction owner to ranch operator to real estate broker and a dizzying array of cattle and ranch partnerships in between. Sometimes Johnston made a great deal of money. Sometimes he lost nearly everything he owned.

Three heart attacks have slowed Leland just a smidgen. But neither malaria nor heart attacks nor making and losing several fortunes have dented his entrepreneurial spirit. Bryan Tupper would be a fan. Johnston order buys cattle for long-time clients. "I've been in the order buying business for over 50 years, done business with people I've never seen or never met, people who trusted me, people I became good friends with over the phone."

If he thinks the stars are properly aligned he runs yearlings on rented pasture or feeds out cattle in custom lots. After selling the Thedford sale barn, he saw a generational change in land ownership on the horizon. He earned his GED and obtained a real estate license, formed a partnership which became Agri Affiliates (the guys in the yellow jackets handling the McMurtrey Ranch auction), then sold his ownership share in Agri Affiliates, and formed another real estate firm before eventually returning to work with Agri Affiliates. Ranchers who know him or his reputation still contact him when they're considering a land sale.

Leland wants to show me something "special." While he searches, Pat graciously shows me around their home, pointing out several of her show-winning oil paintings, most of them Sand Hills landscapes. Easy to see why the art show judges approved. Like most former Sand Hills school teachers, Pat has presence.

We return to the living room where Johnston holds a newspaper clipping and talks about his last few months in the Philippines. Japanese resistance increased as Johnston's outfit got farther from Manila. "I remember a narrow concrete road where our infantry had killed a lot of Japs. They never bothered to move the bodies off the road and there'd been enough traffic driving over those dead Japs there was just the outline of their uniforms and the yellow stain of the picric acid they'd carried."

Towards the end of the war, starving Japanese soldiers, often separated from their outfits, sometimes wandered into American positions and were killed for their troubles. "We were on our way up from Manila when our guys shot this young Jap on our perimeter, I don't know if he was even armed. Probably lost and hungry. The next morning they were digging a grave with a dozer. You didn't lay them out. You dug a hole and shoved them in. He'd been wearing this 1000 stitch belt and nobody else wanted it. It was awful dirty. I washed it. It had a lock of his hair and those stitches and Japanese writing all over it. The belts were always worn next to the skin and contained family history written on pieces of paper and sewed into little pouches across the belt.

"A few years ago I got out my army things and the belt. The belt didn't mean much to our kids, but it would mean a great deal to that young man's family. I wrote our senator in Washington and had him get hold of the Jap Embassy. I sent the belt and they found this soldier's daughter and gave it to her. She later wrote a letter to the Japanese government."

Johnston stares at the newspaper clipping, tears up. He hands me the clipping which contains the daughter's letter.

> *I have received Takitoshi Tsubokura's thousand stitch belt. It looks different to when I saw it in the photograph. I cannot express the feeling I had when I actually held it in my own hands. I am sure that his wish was to fulfill his nation's mission and to return home to his family wearing it against his skin.*
>
> *My mother told me that the last time she saw him I had just turned 2. I embraced my father tightly, shouting "Daddy, Daddy!" somehow sensing I might never see him again. It still brings tears to my eyes when I think of this.*
>
> *My mother passed away 13 years ago. I feel she is in heaven and has asked him to entrust the thousand stitch belt to me. Thank you from the bottom of my heart. Let us hope for world peace.*
>
> *Sincerely yours,*
> *Miyuki Ikuta*
>
> *PS*
> *My sincerest gratitude to the person from Nebraska in the United States who took good care of the thousand stitch belt.*

I'm sitting in Leland and Pat's living room, wondering, probably like you are, what the odds might be of the 1000 stitch belt finding its way from a cozy bungalow in the heart of the Nebraska Sand Hills back to a young Japanese soldier's only daughter over 70 years later?

Luck.

Chapter 14
Autumn Tank Trip on the Middle Loup

River otters (Lutra canadensis) enjoy more sustained, riotous sex
than a pod of dolphins and a barrel of monkeys put together.

— Rex Hebner, Nebraska zoologist

Sunday morning. Late September. We leave McCook under cloudless skies, temps in the high 70s. Kathy reluctantly loads Tony Joe White, her least favorite musician, into the CD player and I crank up the volume on "Steamy Windows." Impossible to get too much volume on "Steamy Windows" — or "Lustful Earl and the Married Woman" for that matter. Consequently, Kathy can't hear her cell phone and misses Jerry's call requesting last minute directions to the Sandhills Motel in Mullen. By the time we get service we're driving through the hills south of North Platte and the signal is breaking up. Near as I can make out he's outside Alliance and making good time, thinks he'll beat us to Mullen, which he does by an even hour.

Jerry, a retired Wyoming highway engineer/bridge inspector, spent a fair amount of his working life hanging under highway bridges over rugged canyons. Now he lives near the Black Hills, does consulting work all over the country, teaching newbie engineers the tell-tale signs of fatal bridge deterioration. His unflappable demeanor and quick dry wit would be a welcome addition to any river expedition.

We arrive in the Sandhills Motel parking lot to find last night's crowd of bleary-eyed hunters preparing for departure. Jerry, who didn't waste his time watching hung-over hunters pack up, describes in some detail his hour-long exploration of the town of Mullen (pop. 509). We've taken the Mullen tour ourselves. The only tourist destination Jerry missed? The infamous table in Red's Cafe which once hosted Ted Turner and Jane Fonda.

Behind the front desk, we find Mitch Glidden, always an upbeat kind of guy, in a particularly good mood. The summer's stock tank/canoe/kayak rental season has been his best ever. This last weekend in September is the first one in months he's been able to take a day off. Yesterday Mitch and wife Patty joined the Junk Jaunt, a massive three-day garage sale covering 300 miles and 40 towns in the eastern Sand Hills, which recently drew 20,000 shoppers from 32 states. Mitch is pumped after scoring a couple of antique block and tackle rigs he'll use during deer season. He's hoping to spend at least two days on the jaunt next year. "Maybe get a room in Grand Island Friday night, work our way west. Dannebrog, Loup City, Taylor, up to Brewster over to Thedford. You can't believe all the stuff. Miles and miles of stuff."

Mitch's pickup leads us to the car drop off beside the Middle Loup River, east of Mullen, where we leave our vehicles and join Mitch in his truck for the drive upriver. The Ogallala fed Middle Loup, which begins its journey in the Sand Hills north of Whitman, is a river of gentle bends and few obstructions. Perhaps the balmy fall weather will allow us to shorten the trip from the usual five hours.

I ask Mitch about the lower portion of Dismal River I'm interested in tackling next summer. He says fallen timber completely blocks the river in many spots, necessitating short portages. The trip from the Seneca bridge to Highway 83 would be "a very long, hard day." What more could you hope for in a river other than maybe spotting a calcified school teacher's head popping out of an odd patch of quicksand? Kathy, who has been listening to me describe the lower Dismal as "a piece of cake" for the past several months, rolls her eyes.

A few miles north of Mullen we pull off Highway 97 into the river park Mitch uses as a launch site. Our round, upside-down, galvanized stock tank, 7 feet in diameter, sits beside a pile of welded steel tank benches. Today we're opting for the kind of low profile lawn chairs people haul to a beach. We flip over the tank, load the chairs and coolers. Mitch helps us push off. We promptly run aground on a sand bar. The tank hesitates, then slowly wheels off into the current, floating free and easy down river. Just like you draw it up. I open a beverage and lean back in my chair. Brilliant fall sunshine warms my bones. Like the lower Dismal River, the Middle Loup is going to be a piece of cake.

We are alone on the river, except for an occasional white tail deer bounding up a dune to the north and one ground-hugging coyote streaking up and over the nearest ridge. A few trash talking ravens eye us from a safe distance, but lose interest as soon as we spin out of sight. Mostly we float, float up on sand bars, rotate off and on downriver in splendid silence. No ubiquitous electronic beepings, no blinking blue lights. IPod buds do not stream noise into our ears. The nearest Facebook (Work of the Devil) account is miles away. In the heart of the Middle Loup Valley, nonexistent cell phone service means no tweets, no texts, no calls.

We regale Jerry with Dismal River stories. My accounts are, as always, factual and understated. Kathy's dramatic retellings over-emphasize insignificant dangers and slight hardships, leaving out entirely the overweening sense of accomplishment enjoyed by the successful Dismal River voyage. Jerry, after carefully weighing the evidence, says, "That doesn't sound like something I'd be interested in doing."

As on the Dismal, rapacious, blood sucking bugs are few and far between. Perhaps the impressive bird populations have something to do with this. The Sand Hills retain significant numbers of virtually every species of critter inhabiting this area before white men arrived. Nature, at least as far as blood sucking bugs are concerned, is in balance.

Large strainers, which make the Dismal so interesting to navigate, aren't as populous on the Middle Loup. We manage to get hung up in most of them. Usually we're able to ease our way clear by pushing off with our paddles. A couple of times, after particularly forceful shoves, Kathy loses her balance and, glancing off various tree limbs and fellow passengers, completes a series of spectacularly noisy ass plants in the bottom of the tank, coming up laughing and spluttering and a little more scratched each time. By the middle of the next week her body looked like it had been run over by a grape truck. Before long, a mess of twigs, broken branches and a sizable crop of ginormous, but friendly garden spiders cover the bottom of the tank.

Up ahead, crouched on the north bank, a reddish-brown critter resembling an overgrown ferret watches us float towards him. Not an animal we've ever seen. We guess it's some kind of otter, mostly because he has the general demeanor of a wiseass. He waits, smirking, until we dig for the camera, before slipping underwater. Neener, neener. He's a river otter all right, with no business hanging around the Middle Loup north of Mullen. By the early 20th century trappers had virtually wiped out Nebraska's river otter population. Twenty years ago the Nebraska Game and Parks Commission reintroduced otters on the Niobrara in Sheridan County and on the South Loup in Custer County. This little fella must have hot-footed his way cross country from one of those colonies. We trust he brought some company and is reproducing like a madman.

We keep watch downriver for the sly little bastard to surface, but he's way too clever.

A mile later the river bottom widens, revealing the side of a massive dune a quarter mile to the south, and just below the ridge, a scraggily line of dead and dying aspen trees. I wonder if "Buffalo Bruce" McIntosh, the prominent Nebraska tree-hugger who keeps track of Sand Hills aspen colonies, has his eye on this one.

We speculate on how our dogs would fare on a Middle Loup tank trip. Jerry has two Westies at home. We have Finlay, a copacetic Westie, and Hudson, a high energy Gordon Setter. Would they stay in the tank? Would they chase the first nervous deer who explodes out of the timber? or a wise-assed river otter? or a bunch of foul-mouthed, trash-talking ravens? Nothing gives Hudson more pleasure than putting the run on trash-talking ravens. We agree it's hard to anticipate what a dog might do, especially a Westie, known for their hard heads and stubborn behaviors. We agree dogs can swim, even if they haven't taken proper instruction. We agree the spiders running amok in all the broken branches in the bottom of the tank are some of the friendliest we've ever encountered. All is infinite sky and sunshine and solitude and general agreement on everything that matters.

Which is why the trip, which ends precisely at the five hour mark, just as Mitch predicted, seems much too short. We slide the tank up the grassy bank for Mitch to retrieve in a few hours.

Jerry, finding himself at loose ends, gazes wistfully downriver. The sun hangs high in the mid-afternoon sky. If only we had another few miles of lazy spinning down the Middle Loup. Perhaps we could observe Kathy duke it out with another recalcitrant strainer or two. He's thinking of driving west to Carhenge, the slightly wacky tourist destination near Alliance. With 38 vintage automobiles, spray painted gray and arranged to mimic England's Stonehenge, Carhenge attracts curious travelers and film makers seeking unusual backdrops. "I've wanted to see that place ever since I heard about it." Jerry reluctantly takes his leave, easing his pickup down the bumpy sand trail towards the highway.

Basking in warm sunshine and surrounded by the occasional cries of contented water birds, we take our time loading our stuff for the trip home. A last long look around for teasing river otters. Nothing at first, then a sudden ripple, a flash of red brown fur and beady spying eyes fifty yards upstream under a small strainer. Then a splash, quickly erased by empty flowing water. Neener, neener.

Mitch and Patty occasionally host friends for nighttime tank floats down the Middle Loup. Aided by star light or, better yet, a full moon, the river would be easy to read. Piece of cake. Maybe next year.

Chapter 15
November Visit to the Spike Box

Once I was traveling across the sky
This lovely planet caught my eye
And being curious I flew close by
And now I'm caught here
Till I die
Till we die
Learning to live together
Learning to live together
Learning to live together
Till we die

— "Space Captain" by Joe Cocker

To manage Turner lands in an economically sustainable and ecologically
sensitive manner while promoting the conservation of native species.

— Mission statement of Turner Enterprises

Any business or organization which requires a public mission statement
to know what it's supposed to be doing doesn't have a clue what it's supposed to be doing.

— Overheard at the Berkshire Hathaway annual
shareholders meeting

Permission to visit a Turner bison operation took several months and a little persistence. I was impatient, but understood the delay. Nobody likes bad press and Turner has received his share. I was hopeful my stated goal, gaining an understanding of the nuts and bolts of a Turner bison operation, was not as likely to cause alarm in Turner's Atlanta headquarters as, for instance, an article focused on Ted Turner's land acquisition spree or on his personal life. In any event, I had no particular interest in aspects of the Turner story other than his bison operations in the Nebraska Sand Hills. Do an internet search on Ted Turner and you'll get well over 38,000,000 hits. It's not like there's a crying need for another exploration of Turner's life and career.

Whether Turner's people in Atlanta did due diligence and decided I was harmless or whether repeated requests wore them down is impossible to know. My ag background might have differentiated my credentials from other reporters. Certainly anyone questioning my "harmless" bona fides was free to read my published works and draw their own conclusions.

Phone conversations with Spike Box manager Terry Purdum and John Hansen, ramrod of Turner's North American bison operations, made clear they were, like me, waiting for a decision from headquarters. After spring and summer expired with no word from Atlanta, I became moderately pessimistic. When Halloween came and went, I began pondering how to write a worthwhile piece without a site visit. Maybe someone could be talked into flying me over the Spike Box in a small plane. I could observe the bison herds from above, maybe see firsthand how the bison were treating the fragile sand dunes. Jim Wright, long time neighbor of the McMurtreys, whose former ranch was now part of the Spike Box, is a pilot with intimate knowledge of the area. He seems like a good guy. Maybe he'd be agreeable. I was working up my nerve to contact Jim when Terry Purdum called with the good news. In short order we'd agreed to a pre-Thanksgiving visit on a day when he and his crew were working bison.

"We'll probably be working the south herd. The guys start showing up at 7 Mountain Time and work until dark."

After Kathy rousts me out of bed at 3 a.m., I spend an hour loading up on caffeine, trying and largely failing to recalibrate an elderly operating system habitually functional only after 6 a.m. Once the coffee kicks in, fresh tape recorder batteries installed, notebooks, pens and maps safely tucked in the briefcase, I point the car north, not quite able to suppress my excitement.

This visit has been at the top of my wish list ever since I launched this quixotic Sand Hills research project. Turner's Nebraska land acquisitions had been big news ever since they began with the Spike Box purchase in 1995. Public fear and loathing accelerated with the acquisition of the 48,000 acre Deer Creek Ranch in 1997, the 67,000 acre McGinley Ranch in 1999 and the 64,600 acre Blue Creek Ranch in 2000. Smaller, less public purchases and the much-publicized acquisition at public auction of the 28,000 acre McMurtrey spread did nothing to quiet the rumor machine.

One popular theory had Turner planning to buy up the Sand Hills and turn the whole shootin' match over to the National Park Service, the United Nations or some wingnut environmental group as a game preserve. This strategy would net him a big income tax deduction and remove the land from the local real estate tax rolls, which would eventually kill every affected real estate tax dependent Sand Hills county government and school deader than the proverbial doornail.

Another, even more popular story, which I heard from several more or less respectable sources, had Turner drilling into the sacred Ogallala aquifer under his vast properties and selling billions of gallons of precious Nebraska water to those greedy lawn-waterin', water-wastin', dope-smokin' weasels in Denver. That there were formidable legal barriers in place to prevent such a scenario did nothing to quash the rumors. After all, billionaires can change an inconvenient law anytime they want.

There is little doubt Turner's land purchases exerted upward pressure on the price of land, which, if you were a rancher wanting to sell wasn't necessarily a bad thing. But if you wished to continue ranching, maybe expand your holdings, eventually hand over your operation to your heirs, rising land prices led to upwardly spiraling real estate taxes, often the largest single annual expense for a rancher, which could easily drive a ranch out of business.

The resentment Turner engendered also had something to do with the sheer magnitude of his wealth. Although not many people fully comprehended the brilliance and hard work he contributed to the creation of Turner Broadcasting, it was commonly understood Turner earned his money through a certain amount of attention to business, unlike the milksop, wingnut Rockefeller heirs and other nogoodnik inheritors of family fortunes. However, to many in the Sand Hills the how of his earned billions didn't matter. At the time he was acquiring large ranches the most common view was Turner possessed so much wealth he could buy any amount of land he goddamned pleased. He might buy your neighbor's place tomorrow, the one you've had your eye on the past 30 years. Hell, he might have already done so. Turner was infamous for quietly buying a ranch before anyone in the neighborhood became aware the ranch was for sale. Few questioned the premise that local realtors were feeding Turner hot tips on ranches which might be in play. In short, Turner represented a dire threat to every Sand Hills rancher who hoped to stay in business. Nenzel rancher Duane Kime, nephew of Buzz Kime, who lost out to Turner in bidding for the McMurtrey Ranch, eventually became surrounded on three sides by Turner land. "I get along well with Turner's ranch managers. They're competent people. I can't say I like him buying up all the land, but he's got a right to do it. You just can't compete if he wants the land."

Other tales described a clueless hobby rancher, who could not stay in business for five minutes if he needed to turn a profit. His practice of tearing out internal fences as soon as he bought a place, returning the land to its "natural state," led to rumors of overgrazing in areas where bison congregated during the annual rut or in periods of intense heat, on the military crests* of large sand dunes, creating blowouts and erosion. His controversial efforts to increase prairie dog populations on some of his ranches, the occasional failure in the early going to keep bison from roaming from his properties and, in a few cases, the initial lack of outreach to neighbors, since largely corrected, also contributed to an unflattering portrait of Ted Turner.

Turner has always been prone to candid, sometimes outrageous public pronouncements. Not for nothing is he known as "The Mouth of the South." He once said the increase of suicides among U. S. forces in the Middle East was a good thing. At various times he's characterized nuclear weapons, Christianity, global warming, humanity and Rupert Murdoch as the greatest single threats to the planet. Not all of his more controversial statements lack utility. He has, for instance, advocated a massive increase in sexual activity as the ultimate solution to the world's problems. However, he does not lack in self-awareness. Turner has been quoted numerous times as saying, "If I only had a little humility I would be perfect." However, his much-rumored skirt chasing, past episodes of public drunkenness and his failed marriage to the deeply unpopular Jane Fonda only serve to substantiate the image of a less than serious human being.

How accurate these widely-held views of Turner might be was not of primary concern to me. I remained focused on how his bison ranches functioned on a daily basis. Either Turner's bison enterprise was serious business or it wasn't. Either his bison business was functioning in spite of a corporate mission statement or it was following a mission statement and was clueless.

You can tell a great deal about a person by studying the people they hire. Humorist Leo Rosen said it best, "First-rate people hire first-rate people; second-rate people hire third-rate people." You don't have to spend much time hanging around a business to learn whether the owner is capable or a complete nincompoop. My conversations with John Hansen and Terry

---

* The military crest of a hill is located below the actual crest and used by observers so they won't be silhouetted against the sky. Plains Indians often traveled along the military crests of hills to avoid detection.

Purdum make me think Turner has a knack for finding talented employees. If Hansen and Purdum are representative of his other managers, Turner's bison venture is a dead serious enterprise. There's only one way to be certain. The upcoming visit to the Spike Box likely represents the only chance to observe at ground zero. I don't want to blow it.

I fill my gas tank at a North Platte Gas N Puke, enter the store, use the rest room, leave without ever spotting a cashier, probably napping in a back room or, more likely, being held hostage by a drooling, dope-smoking weasel.

Three hours later in gray predawn, I turn west on the narrow oil mat to the Spike Box, Turner's initial Nebraska ranch purchase. A couple of miles down the road, the Dry Valley Church appears on my right. A wire gate and a quarter mile of grassed trail across the pasture lead to the modest church. A small grove of gray cedars behind the church marks the cemetery.

Nine miles west and several cattle guard crossings later, the oil mat yields to a wider gravel road. Because the pastures and roadside are composed of powdery sand, it's evident the roadbed has been built up with heavier soil trucked in from elsewhere and overlaid with a thin coat of road gravel, leaving it less susceptible to damage from loaded livestock semis.

As the eastern sky behind the dunes lightens, dark shaggy bison shapes appear on my right, loping easily alongside my vehicle at a steady 20 miles an hour. I pull over and open the windows, the snorty grunting of running bison fills the air. Cows and calves disappear over a dune, another couple of dozen come into view, part of an early morning tour of a 7900 acre pasture. This is nothing more than early morning exercise, some stretching, a little bit of bison yoga.

A few miles later, a sprawling set of working corrals and the headquarters buildings of the Spike Box come into view. As promised, a herd of bison grazes in a small pasture just outside the corrals. These must be remnants of the south herd Spike Box manager Terry Purdum promised would be worked today. He and his crew have been pregnancy testing cows, weaning calves and culling open cows and older herd bulls for the last several weeks. Once the south herd has been processed, it will be moved to fresh winter pasture and the younger north herd will go through the chutes. If the weather holds, Terry hopes to be finished by the first of January.

At 7.00 a.m. sharp, I pull up in front of the small frame house which serves as the Spike Box office, Terry Purdum emerges to greet me. A high energy guy in his mid-fifties, Terry explains briefly what his crew will be doing today. I soon understand why every Sand Hills rancher I've spoken with thinks Terry, even if his boss might be a threat to humanity, is an okay guy. We go inside. I meet Leon, the number one ranch hand with the longest tenure on the Spike Box. I shake hands with Cole, an ex-Navy man like Terry, and Dallas, an Iraq vet. Wanda, Terry's wife, office manager, bookkeeper and records manager, hard at work with the monthly checks, waves from her desk. Ranch workers enter the office, listen to Terry's directives for the morning's work, sometimes ask a question or two before leaving. The atmosphere crackles with testosterone-enhanced energy. Except for Leon, the crew is fairly raw, most coming on board since July, but they seem to know their jobs and set about doing them.

Brenda, a young neighbor woman who helps out during peak bison processing season, enters the office. She says I passed her house and working corrals just east of the Spike Box. Terry introduces her as "'our right-hand do all, carry all, if we get in a bind she's the one we call person.' If we have hunters she may take over from the wife in serving the hunters. Right Brenda?"

"Right," Brenda says, "But I don't think that's my area of expertise."

Yesterday, when Wanda was under the weather, Wanda cooked and Brenda catered meals to the trophy hunters staying in the modest house on the west side of the ranch. It's clear she has no wish to repeat the experience. At first I put this down to either an aversion to domestic chores or an aversion to wealthy trophy hunters. Later I decide she has an aversion to talking to strangers, although I also learn she has an aversion to small children, even though she has first-hand experience with the species. Maybe, like me, she has an aversion to people in general, although she seems to get on well with Terry and Wanda. She has the same economy of speech and movement as most of the Spike Box crew.

From October through January, the Spike Box hosts trophy hunters. The ranch provides large, mature bulls, sometimes weighing over a ton, a hunting vehicle with a DeWeeze bale loader to lift and haul the dead bull to headquarters and transportation for the dead bull to the Valentine locker plant. The hunter pays for processing. In addition to receiving a humongous supply of bison meat, the hunter can also choose to keep the hide and have the head mounted. Paying customers can expect lodging, a box lunch and an evening meal.

Hunting success runs as close to 100 percent as you can get without using a billion decimal points, although Terry talks about one bull that almost got away. "He ran five miles after he was shot. When it was field dressed the outfitter discovered the bull's heart had been grazed by the bullet. Bison blood coagulates rapidly."

The Spike Box receives 60 percent of the fee, outfitter 40 percent. The outfitter gets a list of potential trophy bulls and directions to where on the ranch they might be hanging out. He takes the customer to the bulls and gives him a choice of two or three bulls. Once the bison is shot the outfitter field dresses the animal.

Income from trophy hunting contributes healthy margins to the Spike Box's annual bottom line, as it does on the other Turner Ranches offering trophy hunting and fishing. You can hunt black bear and Desert Bighorn sheep on the 362,885 acre Armendaris Ranch in New Mexico or angle for lunker sea trout on Turner's 24,000 acre San Jose Ranch on Tierra Del Fuego or fish trophy streams on Turner's other Argentinian ranches.

Although I've clearly interrupted Terry's morning office routine, he invites me into his office, situates himself behind a small desk overflowing with paperwork, gives me as much attention as he can spare between urgent phone calls.

He explains the details of this morning's herd processing.

"We pick a random number of cows every year and bleed 'em. We'll FedEx the samples overnight to Bozeman to our vet. He'll spin 'em down, analyze the blood, tell us how the animals are doing, their general condition. He'll also tell us if there are any problems, like blue tongue. We've never had blue tongue in the herd, but deer occasionally suffer from it so we're always on the alert.

"Sometimes we'll run DNA checks for cattle genes, cull if we find anything. Those cattle-bison breeding experiments in the late 19th century still show up occasionally, although it's become rare for us.

"We also vaccinate our replacement heifers for Bangs* and select our replacement bulls as they come through. I look for length, just like a beef guy, height, hindquarters. I also do a certain amount of selection on color. The darker they are the better I like 'em. That's a personal thing. I like darker bison. After our bull calves come through and I've sorted out the replacements the rest go to a feedlot. My bulls go to Lewis Feedlot north of Kearney. We do not castrate.

"Weight isn't a factor. Some will remain on feed longer than others. The heavy end goes to slaughter faster than others. We have a guy by the name of Brian Ward out of Colorado, who runs our feedlot division. Once they leave this place they're under his control. Some of the heifers that don't go into the herd go to the feedlot, others go to the Bluestem Ranch† in Oklahoma where they'll be fed and brought up to weight. They're pampered a little more. Then if there's a place that needs some replacement heifers after John Herd's brought them up to what they should be, let's say the McGinley Ranch needs a pot load of replacement heifers, then John will cut off a set and send them up. The Oklahoma ranch is kind of a heifer station where ranches can pull replacements. Here, again, he makes decisions. Some will go to a feedlot, some will be what we call grass harvested, sold for meat straight off the ranch."

Terry switches the conversation to his hired men. The Spike Box provides housing, but the houses are far apart. Leon, for instance, lives on Jim Wright's former place several miles over the sand dunes to the north. Terry likes this arrangement.

"One of the things that makes us different from other ranches and one of the things I admire about it is the hired men all live on separate places, not grouped in one spot. It makes for a more peaceful situation. They work together 10 hours a day, but can go off to another part of the ranch the rest of the time where it's out of sight, out of mind, until the next day."

Finding good help is always difficult in the Sand Hills. Just like cattle ranchers, Terry has to find employees who can handle hard physical work, long hours and geographical isolation. If he hires a married worker, the spouse needs to tolerate living far from town and survive on one income, since driving long distance to a job often isn't practical. The employees who stick are often those who've grown up on area ranches and know the drill.

Working with bison exposes Turner ranch employees to an additional element of physical danger. Once irritated, bison become impossible to drive. And, given enough distance, they can run a horse into the ground.

"Bison will be running long after a horse has keeled over. Their tongues drop down and to the side, leaving a dryer vent-sized opening for oxygen. Some of these old bulls out here I'm not sure I'd want to be on a horse. An ATV will get you out of a tight spot a little quicker than a saddle horse that's already been ridden eight or nine miles. A lot of times when our guys are working animals, they'll put a 120-130 miles a day on a four-wheeler."

As part of their daily routine, workers make sure the mineral boxes in all the pastures are full. Terry is fanatical about giving bison constant access to adequate mineral. They check and service windmills, check electric fences with a handheld device, repair where needed.

* Brucellosis, also known as Bangs disease or contagious abortion, is caused by an infection of bacterium Brucella abortus, which can also cause undulant fever in humans. Bangs disease infects cattle, elk, bison, moose and a few other wild species. Although there has never been a proven case of bison infecting cattle, there have been many documented cases of elk infecting cattle. The elk and bison populations in Yellowstone Park have high levels of infection, prompting the National Park Service and state wildlife departments to experiment with various methods of eradicating the disease. In cattle or bison only a consistent and comprehensive program of vaccinating young heifers has been found to be effective in controlling the disease.
† Ted Turner purchased the 39,000 acre Bluestem Ranch for $15 million in 2001. It had grown to 43,000 acres before he sold it to the Osage Nation in 2016 for $74 million.

Distances often mean a guy taking off for a few hours on an ATV with a post hole digger and a couple of fence posts will travel 60 miles before he returns.

The winter work schedule features ice breaking in the windmill tanks around the ranch, keeping fences hot, shop work, repairs.

"We break a lot of ice. This ranch has 255 water tanks. Water is my big concern. Everybody says it's my hang-up. Water is the one thing bison can't do without. I've continuously added tanks and windmills over the years."

Terry says the ranch doesn't often feed bison in the winter. "Once the grass turns brown their metabolism changes and calorie requirements drop. If we have a long stretch of snow and cold I may request a few truckloads of extra protein for older animals, but that's about it. A bison will dig through 8 feet of snow to get grass. As long as they have water, if there's no snow to eat, and mineral they can survive, usually much better than beef animals"

Spring involves considerable fence building, but calving is not monitored. "I've never found a calf dead on this place that's died from calving difficulty. Never. I would assume over the millions of years hip lock and stuff like that has been bred out because they just didn't survive. When a bison calf hits the ground it's going to get up and going a little quicker than a beef calf. That comes back to being wild. Newborns can travel real well, keep up with the herd."

Most of October through January is taken up with processing the herd, weaning calves, shipping culls to feedlots or packing plants.

Terry grew up on various Sand Hills ranches where his father worked, which means he is on a first name basis with most of the area ranch families. After a stint in the Navy, which included two tours in the Pacific, he took extensive computer training and became the in-house tech guy for First National Bank in North Platte. His tech expertise later came in handy when he and Wanda helped implement computerized record keeping on Turner's other Nebraska ranches.

Terry and Wanda moved back to the Sand Hills so their children could attend rural schools. Terry drove trucks for a while, had a cabinetry business with Wanda, worked on cattle ranches and eventually joined a fence-building team. He began spending most of his time building miles of high tensile electric fence on Turner's ranches.

"Tim Neal, his son and I generally ran four or five guys on a crew. We tore out the barbed wire fence after we got the new fence up. The first year at Deer Creek we built sixty some miles. At the time a six-strand, five-foot-tall electric fence cost $5000 a mile. It was a learning experience. We use a solar powered charger with a battery back-up. It'll handle about 10 miles of six strand high tensile wire. Just a deep cycle battery. If it gets cloudy or stormy it'll last about three days."

I'm curious if bison sense the fence is hot or if they have to try it out.

"Through the years they've learned. You might notice along a barbed wire fence you'll see cow trails right along the fence. On our fences you'll see the trails quite a bit farther from the fence. These fences are pretty hot. They hurt if you touch them. The bison have learned not to touch the wires. That's not to say if they get shoved they won't go through a fence."

The tedious repetition of fence building and the constant difficulties finding and keeping reliable workers led him to ask John Hansen, then head of Turner's Nebraska bison ranches, for a job. He worked on the Spike Box under Hansen before taking over as ranch manager after Hansen was promoted.

I ask Terry if money were no object and he owned a ranch and had the choice of stocking it with cattle or bison, which would it be?

Wanda, writing checks in the other room, overhears. "Cattle. I'm an old cowgirl. I'd go back to cattle. And Herefords if we have a choice."

Terry chuckles. "I'd probably stay with beef cattle because most years your beef cattle are going to show a higher return. The longer I'm here the better I like the bison, but it's tough to make it with bison. I might have a little of both. There's moneymaking ends on the bison and moneymaking ends on the cattle. And there's guys that do both. I like my beef cattle, but I'd probably have some of these old boys too. I love the meat. Basically we eat bison pretty much all the time.

Since the vet scheduled to oversee today's blood draws has yet to arrive, Terry drives me to a nearby stock tank set up fed by a solar powered pump. He says solar powered pumps are expensive (from $4500 to $10,000), but are cheaper to maintain and becoming common across the Sand Hills. The capacious tank holds enough to water the herd for three days should a rare period of cloudy weather keep the pump from doing its job.

Terry drives to the buildings on the west end of the Spike Box, former headquarters of the Coble Ranch, which Turner purchased the year after he bought the Spike Box. Terry says the owners of the Coble Ranch were killed in a car accident and none of the heirs wished to run the ranch. The former main ranch house serves as Turner's personal residence when he visits. Today the siding is being replaced on the modest ranch-style home. What it's like inside is anyone's guess, and although we'd expect it's been fixed up some, it certainly is not the elaborate billionaire's mansion like you might expect. Another unpretentious ranch house a few yards away houses visiting trophy hunters.

The radio squawks with the news the vet has finally arrived. Terry fusses he's a half hour late, finally wonders aloud if the vet had some unforeseen emergency. Terry expects the vet to be available and on time since he does most all of the Spike Box's veterinary work and sells the ranch vet supplies.

We pull up beside the small pasture leading to the working corrals where about a hundred cows and calves are eyeing the approach of four ranch hands on four-wheelers. A hundred cows and calves represent a small fraction of the 3000 head south herd. Terry says the workers must wear OSHA approved helmets when rounding up bison. If they choose not to wear them while fixing fence that's on them. The high tensile fence for this small gathering pasture is extra hot and the bottom ground wire is fixed lower than on a typical fence. Terry says the bison keep a healthy distance from the fence because it will arc several inches and bite them. The ATVs move towards the bison at full bore, the bison turn, run into the corral. The ranch hands slam the gate. The bison do not seem especially riled. Terry says the older cows which have been through the process are easier to handle. Another gate opens. The herders make a run at the herd, which takes off at full speed. A small red calf, probably three weeks old, loses its footing and gets trampled under. A midsummer calf suffers the same fate. Both are uninjured, but get left behind when the gate slams shut. The herd moves down through the corrals as the left-behinds are gathered and reunited with their mothers.

Once the animals arrive on the north side of the corrals, Cole takes over. Working from a walkway high above the chutes, he cuts out small bunches of cows and calves, opens and shuts gates, moves them to the sorting gates, where he sends cows down one chute and calves down another. The steel chutes, modeled on working facilities on other Turner ranches, are topped by bars 10 feet above the ground. Many are bent upwards from escape attempts.

Two handlers push the sorted cows toward the squeeze chute using plastic paddles filled with BBs. Bison moving through steel chutes make quite a racket, willing to kick sideways as well as backwards. Full grown bison hit the squeeze chute at warp speed. The guy who catches the bison's head in the head gate has to be quick. Once the animal is caught one man slips a nose clamp into the cow's nostrils and snubs her head to the side. The vet collects blood from the exposed neck. Wanda passes a plastic wand over the cow's RFID* (Radio Frequency Identification) ear tag, which brings up the cow's vital statistics on the computer. If the cow is missing any identification she's supplied with a replacement. She is poured for lice, her weight recorded. On the other side of the chute an ultrasound hose is funneled into the cow's rectum and the vet reads the results on a lighted monitor. If a cow is pregnant she's released. If she's open, wet or dry, Wanda will shout out her age, what her last calf weighed. Terry may mouth her, check for missing or damaged teeth, before deciding to cull or not.

I have never seen an ultrasound machine at work. It is not as fast as a vet with a strong arm and experienced hands, but after seeing how quickly and accurately the cows can kick backwards, I think hand preg-checking bison would be geometrically more dangerous, not to mention shitty. After years of reading accounts of the Plains Indians and pioneers cooking over buffalo chips I'm surprised, especially in the fall of the year after the grass has turned dry and brown, to see bison squirting loose bison shit all over the place. A beef cow with a similar diet would not typically be that loose.

Wanda records all new information on the computer. Brenda records all new information on paper. Paper records provide backup. A cow enters the squeeze chute, her head crashes into the head gate and the whole chute bangs and shudders as she slams around inside. When Wanda passes the plastic wand over her eartag an ID number shows up on the computer screen, along with her current weight, 925 pounds. She is a 5-year-old cow who originated on the Circle D Ranch in Montana, was sent to the Blue Stem Ranch in Oklahoma, before being moved to the Spike Box. If the legendary pre-white man Montana herd had been combined with the pre-white man Texas herd, this cow's travels since birth would mirror their historic migration patterns. Terry snaps the nose clamp into her nostrils, snubs her head to the side. The vet draws a blood sample. The cow stops struggling. Brenda shoots some lice dope on her back. Leon threads the ultrasound up her ass. She kicks viciously three or four times. As he adjusts the hose, the image of a bison fetus comes up on the screen. It appears to be moving around inside the cow as much as the cow is moving around inside the chute, but this might be an optical illusion.

Terry calls lunch break, although the crew clearly would rather finish working the few head of bison left in the chutes. Perhaps Terry is being an overly conscientious host and figures I'm starving. Maybe he's just hungry. The hands reluctantly abandon their posts. The vet disappears down the road. Terry wonders why, says the doc is always a big eater, even though he's skinny.

---

* (RFID) Radio-frequency identification uses electromagnetic fields to identify and track tags attached to objects or livestock. Information stored on the tags can be read by interrogating radio waves from an RFID reader.

A pickup with a DeWeeze bale loader travels west on the gravel road. Terry says the trophy hunters are going to lunch. He's surprised they haven't shot their bulls. He wonders if the outfitter took them to the correct pasture location where the bulls were supposed to be.

We troop into the spare metal building which serves as the ranch break room. Wanda explains employees take turns bringing lunch. She says the only rule is the lunch has to fit in a crock-pot. Today Jessica, wife of Dallas, brought a large crock-pot of chili. Dustin, their handsome, precocious 2-year-old son, is along for the ride.

Wanda looks in the crock-pot, decides there's not quite enough chili to feed the entire crew and sets to work whipping up some beef salad sandwiches out of some prepared beef, ground pickles and Miracle Whip salad dressing. She packs an inch thick layer of beef salad between two slices of Wonder Bread. She says Beau*, Turner's son who was deer hunting on the Spike Box last week, won't touch anything with mayonnaise. I am eating excellent chili across the table from Brenda, who is still shy, probably worried I'll ask her a question and publish the answer. Dallas says Brenda should babysit Dustin. Brenda says she's not big on kids until they are older. Dallas says Dustin can already do sums and knows the alphabet. Brenda harrumphs a noncommittal. The kid may be a genius, but she's not biting.

I feel guilty for eating someone's rightful food portion, someone who's done demanding physical work today. The chili would have been more than enough. The beef salad sandwich way more than enough. I wade through both. Workers lose their shyness to take an extra sandwich or work on the last of the chili. The last guy in line opens the crock-pot to gaze mournfully at the empty pot. I should have skipped something.

I wonder if I'm expected to interview everyone en masse. In my experience, private interviews are apt to yield the best results. But there's an expectancy in the air, like folks are waiting for me to break the ice. Instead, I ask Wanda a harmless question: does she feed visiting trophy hunters gourmet meals?

"Heavens no," she says, "they get plain ranch food like everybody else. I don't cook anything fancy." Since I won't be grilling them on the record the crew relaxes. A half dozen animated conversations get under way.

With the crew mostly fed, Jessica and Dustin sit down across from me to eat. Jessica, cheerful and outgoing, graduated from Thedford High School, 50 miles southeast of the Spike Box. She and Dallas moved from near Tacoma, Washington, where Dallas mustered out of the Army, to the Spike Box, 30 miles from town. Isolated living is nothing new for Jessica, who lived 30 miles from town during her high school years. About once a week she makes the trip to Valentine.

"It takes about an hour and a half each way. The adjustment from living in Washington was easy for us. I have never had a vision of having to live close to a Walmart or a Taco Bell.

"We have phone and internet. I have friends from high school and friends in Valentine. My family is close and Dallas' family is close. I know Dallas isn't headed back to Iraq, he's going to be coming home every night. Knowing that and being close to family makes it easier to live out here. You don't have to worry about being robbed and it's just a nicer environment, very quiet."

---

* Turner's youngest son and Chairman of the Board of Trustees for the Turner Endangered Species Fund and Director of Natural Resources for Turner Enterprises. In 1999, Beau Turner married Gannon Hunt, socialite descendant of legendary oil billionaire H. L. Hunt. He owns a minority interest in the NBA Atlanta Hawks and hosted "Beau Knows Outdoors" on the Sportsman's Channel.

Dallas is an edgy guy, constantly on the move, changing seats, refilling his drink, making pronouncements. He gathers Dustin on his lap, while Dustin digs into one of Wanda's soft cookies which magically appeared on this plate a few moments ago.

Brenda, carrying her empty plate, disappears, magically reappears next to Wanda on the opposite side of the room.

Growing up near Dunning, 30 miles east of Thedford, Dallas worked on his father's ranch and sometimes on his grandfather's ranch near Brewster. After moving with his mother to Arnold on the southern edge of the Sand Hills, he spent his senior year in high school working part time for an area rancher. After graduation, he spent the next eight years in the US Army as a communications specialist.

During his first tour in Iraq, his unit provided escort services for Iraqi and US officials. The next time Dallas landed in Iraq, his unit patrolled Baghdad, cleared houses, searched for weapons caches.

"We slept in tents. Sometimes we patrolled for 18 hours, slept a couple, got up and did it again."

Did he consider making a career of the Army?

"It crossed my mind what would happen if I stayed in 12 more years and retired. I'd been in Iraq twice. Afghanistan was heating up. No telling what war we might be involved in before I retired. A couple of months before I got out I heard Terry had a job opening and gave him a call, came back here for an interview. He told me I had the job and it was waiting for me when I got out.

"I knew what I was getting into from my ranch background. Of course, bison are different from cattle. They have serious tempers. But after you're here a while you learn how to handle them. Any ranch work is going to be hard. Bison are more physically demanding, take a lot of patience, but no harder than working almost around the clock in Iraq in 120 degree heat.

"I might still be here in 10 or 15 years. Something I learned in the army is to never, never plan ahead, because everything gets ruined. I joined the army for schooling and then the Iraq thing kicked off. Who knows, I might use the GI bill to go back to school a get a computer degree. I'll do whatever is best for my family."

Terry stands up, fires a few questions, gives directives for the afternoon's tasks after the bison are worked. The crew tidies up and heads back to the chutes. Elapsed time for lunch — 38 minutes.

Terry wants me to see a nine mile stretch of the North Fork of the Middle Loup Turner fenced to keep the bison from eroding the banks. We head out in his massive Dodge 4 X 4 pickup. We need every bit of clearance on the sugar sand trail with the high grassed center. In places where the bison have followed the trail they've churned it into deep mush. Sharp little hooves on those critters. We drive past the 800 acre dune Turner ordered fenced for a deer reserve. Terry says the reserve is crawling with deer. The irregular, jagged top of the dune differs from most Sand Hill dunes, which have smooth, gentle crests. University of Nebraska geologist Jim Swinehart says these jagged tops are the result of a later dune formation laid over the top of an older, smoother dune. I wonder how he knows this, but, since it comes from Jim Swinehart, one of the world's most knowledgeable dune experts, I suspect it might be true.

The nearest steep dune is pockmarked by a few partially healed blowouts. Makes me wonder what this dune looked like before the buffalo were fenced out. Was it much, much worse? Were the neighbors who whispered about the early Turner experiments with wide open grazing, allowing bison to congregate near the tops of dunes in hot weather and turning them to mush on target? Was the "deer reserve" mostly an attempt to correct the damage? Or were the trophy mule deer hunts Turner markets to well-heeled hunters the motivation? In any case, if Turner caused a problem with his romantic vision of bison roaming his ranches without interior fencing, it's since been corrected.

Terry loves his job, mostly because he can make decisions and because he lives on a 134,000 acre ranch far from civilization.

"Wanda has to remind me when it's been a month since we've been to town. If it were up to me I'd never go." He cites a new golf course being constructed south of Valentine as an example of the looming invasion of urbanites, who will deplete the Ogallala aquifer for their silly golf courses and become permanent residents, making his worst nightmare of a populated Sand Hills a reality. Terry hates going to town, even nearby Mullen, population 509. The problem with towns? "Too many people."

We drive through several hundred recently worked cows standing passively near a closed gate. Terry says they are impatient to be moved to winter pasture. "They know it's time," he says. The cows at the gate stand on a large culvert Turner had installed so the herd can cross the Middle Loup to winter pasture without trampling stream bank vegetation.

From the small meandering North Fork of the Middle Loup, Terry points to a valley intersecting from the northwest. "That's Mud Creek. Once it joins the Loup, things get a lot bigger." And it does. Within a half mile the combination of Mud Creek and additional spring water changes the North Fork of the Middle Loup into a respectable river, easily navigated by kayak or canoe.

Terry says he has something special to show me. We pop over a rise to see the North Fork of the Middle Loup flowing over a substantial waterfall. "Look at that water," Terry says, "have you ever seen a Sand Hills stream so clear?" And sure enough, the water flowing over Horseshoe Falls is as crystal clear as any mountain stream.

Terry points to a low place in the bank marked by churned sand and a smattering of bison tracks. "That's where the entire herd crossed before we installed the culvert. Bison have probably crossed this stream at this exact place for hundreds of years. Hard to break old habits."

Terry would like to be manager of the Spike Box 10 years down the road. He can't imagine liking any other job as well. But he has one dream he'd like to fulfill before he gets too old. "I'd like to go up to the middle of Alaska, build a cabin out in the middle of nowhere and spend the winter. Wouldn't that be neat?" And what does Wanda think about this? "She says to let her know when I get back, she'll be in Florida for the duration."

Terry talks about Plan B. He travels to Point Barrow, where the local Eskimos, for a fee, will build an igloo out on the ice, cook their guests a traditional meal of blubber stew, after which the pilgrim spends the night in the igloo on a snow block bed wrapped in walrus hides. I speculate Wanda probably isn't interested in the igloo deal either. Terry confirms.

We drive back to headquarters, following the long, slow sand trail Leon drives from Jim Wright's former place every day to work. Terry says Leon is the perfect ranch employee who enjoys plenty of elbow room.

The ranch flatbed pickup with a DeWeeze bale loader carrying a large bison bull is parked in front of the machine shed. Terry says a trophy hunter finally got lucky. Dan, the outfitter, uses the bale loader to drop the bull on the driveway. He gets in a near-new John Deere tractor with a bucket and a grapple fork and lifts the bull onto another flatbed truck so it can be hauled to the locker in Valentine for processing. During the lifting the tractor's hydraulic system springs a leak, spilling hydraulic fluid on the floor of the machine quonset. Terry is not happy with the mess. Wants things cleaned up yesterday.

The trophy hunter, pleased as punch, watches his bull being loaded. He holds a plastic Walmart bag. He shows me the bull's heart inside, asks me if I think it's really big. I think it looks about as large as a beef bull's heart, but tell him it's a big 'un. I ask him if he's going to eat the heart raw like a Plains Indian. He looks at me like I have carp wiggling out of my ears, says he wasn't planning on it. I ask him what he's going to do with that extra big heart. He mumbles something, but clearly doesn't have plans other than ownership. He spots a stray piece of bison heart on the driveway, scoops it up and adds it to the Walmart bag.

Terry, still a little grumpy over the hydraulic fluid spill, clearly has things to do and although he would be hospitable for as long as it might take, it's time to grant his release and time for me to head for home.

I ask Terry if there would be any chance to observe the bison calves after they hit the ground in the spring. Or perhaps being too close to the cows when they're calving would interfere with the process?

"No, no. We still have to put out mineral and check water and stuff like that. Just plan on coming up, it won't be a problem. Check with us around the middle of April."

Chapter 16
Blowout Penstemon

One of the best ways to protect the environment is to buy it.
—Ted Turner

We know he put in some prairie dog habitat, if you can believe that.
I didn't think they needed much help.
— Rancher Scott Jones, Midland, South Dakota

You see this big blowout.
You hike up the dune and there's this little bitty bluish penstemon.
And it's already beginning to firm up the sand, heal that gap.
It'll take him quite a while to heal it, but you can watch it happening,
just a little bitty flower sitting in the middle of 20,000 square miles of Sand Hills.
— William Kloefkorn, Nebraska State Poet

Ted Turner's long-standing interest in the native species found on his bison ranches, particularly those in short supply, has led to mostly noncontroversial, mostly successful preservation efforts aimed at the Bolson tortoise, the Aplomado Falcon and the Desert Bighorn sheep among others. More problematic was the decision to preserve and promulgate the Black-tailed prairie dog, better known as the prairie rat, an obnoxious, polygamous, plague-infested grassland-destroying rodent, currently laying waste to thousands of acres in the American west, whose numbers are in no danger of precipitous decline. Turner's prairie dog projects on the Vermejo Park Ranch in New Mexico, the Bad River Ranches in South Dakota and the Z-Bar Ranch in Kansas, intended to provide nourishment for the critically endangered Black-footed ferret, who kills and eats prairie dogs at a prodigious rate, have not endeared Turner to people in the grass business, most of whom are devoted to responsible range management and cheerfully committed to the eradication of any prairie dog found on their properties. Climate alarmists, who fear prairie dog destruction of western grasslands is degrading the region's capacity to absorb carbon dioxide, have also voiced concern.

The population of the typical prairie dog colony, unless checked by varmint hunters, plague or natural predators, expands until it overflows, forcing intrepid members to migrate far and wide, invading fresh swatches of grassland, which they quickly despoil with countless burrows and unsightly, grass-killing dirt mounds. Neighbors bordering the Spike Box have been understandably wary Turner will dump a few thousand prairie dogs on his Sand Hills properties, which might lead to hordes of prairie dogs invading neighboring ranches, undoing multi-generational progress towards prairie dog eradication.

Scattered prairie dog colonies presently exist in the Sand Hills, usually in narrow interdune valleys where the sand is tightly packed and often intermingled with organic matter and sedimentary soils. According to Gregg Wright, wildlife biologist at the Halsey National Forest, prairie dogs have difficulty migrating from an interdune colony across more loosely composed sand dunes. Prior to human settlement numerous prairie dog colonies tended to extend up and down the ribbons of narrow valleys, without taking root on the tops of the dunes.

Reestablishing the Black-footed ferret in the Sand Hills would require, if U.S. Fish & Wildlife Service guidelines were followed, a prairie dog colony of at least 1500 acres, something Turner could probably establish were he willing to risk the wrath of his neighbors. To date, the Spike Box and other Turner Sand Hills ranches have been spared, perhaps because of Turner's desire to remain on good terms with his neighbors. The fact that the soft, sugary sand underlying much of the Turner range is less than optimal prairie dog habitat might also be a consideration. However, Turner has not entirely neglected the Spike Box when it comes to preserving endangered species.

Not long after Ted Turner purchased the Spike Box and his crews were well on the way to converting it to a bison operation, James Stubbendieck, an earnest range scientist, showed up on the ranch in search of the elusive blowout penstemon (*Penstemon haydenii*). The blowout penstemon, with its fragrant, nectar rich, milky lavender flowers, is among the first pioneer species to occupy fresh sand dune blowouts, typically caused by drought, range fire and/or overgrazing. Once established, the blowout penstemon stabilizes the sand, leading to the invasion of less adaptive plants. The penstemon is a poor competitor and gradually succumbs to more vigorous successor plant species as the blowout gradually revegetates.

Increased moisture and improved range management since the 1930s dramatically decreased the incidence of blowouts and restricted the blowout penstemon's ideal environment. By 1987, when James Stubbendieck, UNL Professor of Rangeland Ecology, began cataloging the blowout penstemon population, the plant's range, which once stretched across the central Sand Hills region (University of Nebraska botanist Raymond Pool's survey, (1911-1912) had shrunk to portions of four counties inside a radius of 50 miles, which included the Spike Box Ranch). Stubbendieck initially catalogued 600 plants in the Sand Hills, although he thinks as many as 800-900 could have gone uncounted. In 1987 Stubbendieck and others successfully lobbied to have the blowout penstemon placed on the Federal endangered species, the only Nebraska plant so designated.

Stubbendieck, his colleagues and graduate students first tried collecting and planting seeds, but few plants survived. Only a small percentage of penstemon seeds are viable and it habitually reproduces by rhizomes, which also help stabilize fragile sand dunes. However, the plant thrived in the UNL greenhouses in Lincoln and Stubbendieck found, once replanted in a blowout, transplants had a much better survival rate, sometimes as high as 50 percent.

The blowout penstemon recovery project engaged the curiosity of then Spike Box ranch manager John Hansen and his crew, who soon developed a keen interest in the plant's survival and propagation. The work also captured Ted Turner's attention and he eventually supported Stubbendieck's project by personally helping with the replantings and supplying needed funding through his Endangered Species Foundation, headed by son Beau.

By the time Stubbendieck retired, the blowout penstemon population in the central Nebraska Sand Hills had grown to 44,000, an astonishing recovery and a source of intense personal and professional satisfaction for Stubbendieck. However, the ongoing disappearance of blowouts from the Sand Hills continues to eliminate blowout penstemon habitat. Absent the occurrence of long-term severe drought, active repopulation efforts will likely be required to ensure the blowout penstemon's survival. The National Forest Service at Halsey currently produces penstemon plants, which are being transplanted at a rate of 3000 per year, some on the Valentine National Wildlife Refuge and a majority on the Crescent Lake National Wildlife Refuge, which offers a good supply of blowout habitat.

Turner does not limit his curiosity about the Spike Box to endangered plants and animals. On the recommendation of Dr. Stubbendieck, he invited "Mr. Water," preeminent Ogallala aquifer guru and UNL hydrogeologist Jim Goeke, to visit the Spike Box and talk about what lies underneath, not only the Spike Box, but all of Turner's Sand Hills properties.

Goeke prepared one of his patented PowerPoint presentations, along with matching handouts, superimposing the outlines of Turner's Sand Hills holdings, including the recently acquired McMurtrey Ranch, on a succession of maps: topographic map, regional soils map, maps showing the bedrock geology and the configuration of the base of the aquifer, native vegetation map, water table contour map with the location of test holes, saturated thickness map, transmissivity map and an up-to-date map showing post-irrigation development changes in groundwater levels. This last map provided perhaps the most salient information for Turner, showing as it did, irrigation development in and near the Sand Hills since the 1970s had negligible impact on groundwater levels under any of Turner's ranches. Whether he'd known what he was getting when he began buying Sand Hills grassland or not, the map made clear he had chosen one of the rare areas on earth with virtually inexhaustible groundwater. Goeke says he had an attentive audience of Turner, son Beau, ranch manager Terry Purdum, other bison ranch managers and ranch personnel. Turner, in particular, asked pertinent questions showing a keen understanding of what he'd been shown.

Turner's academic interest in the hydrology under his Nebraska ranches could be taken as proof by conspiracy buffs he intends to pump and sell water to out of state interests. However, on the remote chance Turner would ever consider such a thing, he would first have to lobby the Nebraska legislature into changing current water law. Good luck with that. The public firestorm would be unimaginable.

At least for the present, Turner appears content with returning significant numbers of bison to the Great Plains, preserving endangered species and employing his billions in creative ways. If Turner can turn a profit in the process, which he seems to be doing, so much the better.

Chapter 17
Bad Day at Wood Lake

*That's not flying
that's just falling with style*
— Woody, from the 1996 movie *Toy Story*
regarding Buzz Lightyear.

Poor Jim Van Winkle. Minding his own business in his ranch house west of Wood Lake, 25 miles southeast of Valentine, catching up on a hundred different projects. The phone rings. He should have let it ring. I wish he had let it ring. But Jim is nothing if not polite. As a long-serving Cherry County commissioner he likes to be available to his constituents. How could he have known one brief phone interview about his work with the Sandhills Task Force would lead to a nearly fatal airplane crash, costing him his beloved Piper Super Cub and disrupting his life for many months?

Jim first crossed my radar screen while I was researching the McMurtrey Ranch. Dianne Yarbrough, one of the McMurtrey heirs, had good things to say about Jim's helpfulness and expertise. "There's not much about the Sand Hills Jim Van Winkle doesn't know."

My kind of guy.

The McMurtrey brothers, like many early settlers, dredged channels in their wetlands in order to add productive hay acreage. Over time, as water levels dropped, the sub-irrigated meadows diminished in size. The loss of wetland habitat meant lower numbers of water birds and other swampy critters dependent on wetlands to make a living.

Jim Van Winkle, in his capacity as projects coordinator for the Sandhills Task Force, drove over the McMurtrey with Buzz Kime, made note of a well-managed ranch with a few areas which could be improved.

At the time, the McMurtrey Ranch was still recovering from Judge Moursund's tendency to leave his cattle on pastures until not much was left. The eventual restoration plan included some cross-fencing and partial dams, fencing off abused areas, recreating bends in the creek and raising the water table.

Jim is a worker bee with three full-time jobs. There's the cow-calf operation near Wood Lake he operates with his wife Myki. He's been a Cherry County commissioner for several terms, which means long hours dealing with roads, constituents and county employees. He's also project coordinator for the Sandhills Task Force, a unique organization composed of environmental groups, working ranchers and government agencies. Initiated by the Nebraska Cattlemen's Association to find common ground with the folks who too often misunderstood working ranchers, the Task Force eventually partnered with the Nature Conservancy, the Nebraska Department of Environmental Quality, the US Fish and Wildlife Service, the

Nebraska Environmental Trust, the Nebraska Game and Parks Commission and the Natural Resources Conservation Services on restoration projects affecting thousands of acres in the Sand Hills. The cooperation between environmental groups and working ranchers has been so successful organizations in other states are looking at duplicating the arrangement.

In my Sand Hills travels, I'd heard several people cite Jim Van Winkle as a superb pilot. In an area lousy with skilled pilots Jim is known for his ability to land and take off from relatively tiny pastures, a handy thing for his planning and oversight work with the Task Force. Maybe I can interest Jim in flying me over the Spike Box and the McMurtrey.

He is talking about various projects and the Spike Box in particular. "I'm familiar with the ranch. I hunted, fished and trapped it as a kid. I fly my Super Cub nearly every day. I don't know if I'd be allowed to snoop from the ground but I snoop all the time from the air."

Any chance I could ride along? Look at that fragile dune area on the Spike Box above Horseshoe Falls, maybe get an overview of the McMurtrey while we're at it?

"Yeah, as serious as you are it sounds like your kind of project. We'll have to find time to make that happen."

Bingo!

February didn't work out. Too many deadlines, too much inclement weather. We finally settle on the first week in March, weather permitting.

When I arrive at Jim's place shortly after noon the skies have cleared. Seventy-two degrees and almost calm, the sky a forgettable blue. Perfect flying weather.

Despite a nagging sense of foreboding, I am anxious to get in the air. Jim is not. Whether he was listening to an inner voice, we'll never know. Jim has no memory of this day.

Jim pours me coffee, talks about his land reclamation work as the Sandhills Project Director, about the visionary rancher who first conceived of a working relationship with environmentalists.

Jim is interested in my research, asks me what it's going to look like, talks of people who've written about the Sand Hills, about his deceased mother-in-law, Marianne Beel,[*] who wrote a newspaper column for over three decades and edited a two-volume history of Cherry County. "She thought it was a preface for work that needed to be done. She did it with no technology, took years of her life to do it. She felt bad about the things that weren't quite right. She had high hopes of doing a Sand Hills book until her health failed her.

"Lots of people thought the Sand Hills too vast a topic and couldn't figure out how to nibble at it. The folks who have done their version of a definitive Sand Hills book have all failed."

Except maybe for C. B. McIntosh?

"Yeah, that was a pretty cool thing he did. His book is certainly a reference for me."

I am thinking about McIntosh's masterpiece, presently resting on the book shelf just

---

* Marianne Beel, inducted into the Nebraska Sandhills Cowboy Hall of Fame in 2009, began taking pictures of high school rodeo events when daughter Myki joined the circuit. She later submitted photos and articles on high school rodeo events to the *North Platte Telegraph*. The resulting publicity helped re-energize the sport. She later covered national high school rodeo finals and the National Little Britches rodeo for the Associated Press. In addition to her regular Sand Hills columns for the *North Platte Telegraph* and the *Norfolk Daily News*, she paired with Joan Burney to write "Bull and Beef," a regular column for the *Nebraska Cattleman Magazine*. Towards the end of her life she began compiling a book of past newspaper and magazine columns, which was published posthumously as *Sand in My Shoes: Four Decades of Sandhills Stories and History*. To date, the book has gone through two printings.

above my writing desk, nestled between the two-volume *A Sandhill Century: A History of Cherry County, Nebraska*, edited by Marianne Beel and *Old Jules* by Mari Sandoz.

Jim finally quits listening to his guardian angel and stands up. I immediately have the worrisome thought he should keep listening to his angel and send me home with apologies. There's a whisper of bad karma floating around. But this is my big chance, the result of my persistent nagging. No face-saving way to back out now.

I ride with him down to the shop where he retrieves an air bubble. He thinks one of the plane's tires might be low. And it was. Once we get to the hanger, he fills both tires, goes through a meticulous pre-flight check. He points out the balloon tires and the heavy-duty landing gear he added to the plane for landings in rough pastures. To my untrained eye, the 57-year-old white and blue Piper Super Cub is in immaculate condition. I can see Jim is particular about his plane, for which I am grateful. But I am also twitchy to get going, worried we are running out of daylight. I wonder if Jim will need me to spin the propeller to start the engine, like people did in the days of bi-planes.

When Jim finally decides the plane is satisfactory, I crawl into the cramped back seat, not so easy for a fat guy. The plane looks like a tin can from the inside, no padded surfaces, sharp edges all over the place. Jim tells me to fasten my seat belt, which I do reluctantly. At that point I will comply with any request, no matter how silly, for the chance to see the Sand Hills from the air.

Jim starts the engine from inside the cockpit, no dramatic manual propeller spinning required. We taxi out of the hanger, pausing to check this and that, then taxi down the runway towards the highway, splashing through a few puddles left by recent rains. Jim is talking to me through the headphones. Sometimes I can hear, sometimes not. We make an easy U-turn, accelerate back through the puddles.

After a smooth lift off, we effortlessly gain altitude, like a piece of tissue paper in an updraft. I am thinking the people who compare a Super Cub to a helicopter are not far off.

I am snapping photos like a madman, thinking I should unfasten my seat belt to get better angles. I don't, out of respect for Jim's wishes. The northern horizon opens up, undulating dunes stretching north to the Niobrara River. I am thinking this is going to be a day to remember.

Far below, the hanger appears. Something goes bad wrong. The plane hesitates, Jim grabs at a lever near the floor, jerks forcefully on the lever a few times. Jim says, "I think we're going down." And sure enough we are, headed straight for the runway below. I have just enough time to decide I am going to be dead soon. I hope Kathy can get past this.

In retrospect I wish I had paid more attention to what Jim was doing with the controls, not that I would have understood a damn thing. By virtue of some miraculous piloting we go from vertical to horizontal an instant before we hit, no doubt saving our collective bacon. The impact, when it comes, makes an impression. Wow, that smarts! Innards instantly jellified, pushing up against the diaphragm, ribs breaking, head smacking into the back of Jim's seat. Not going to be riding a horse anytime soon. The plane lurches to the right, bounces a couple of times, plows off the runway through a fence and over rough grassland. Just before hitting another fence we spin a neat 180 degrees and stop.

Against all odds, I am alive.

Maybe I'll see Kathy again after all.

Damn, my guts hurt.

Fade to black.

"Bryan. Get out! Get out, Bryan!

"Unfasten your seat belt. Get out of the plane."

The persistent voice comes from far away. I can barely see an out-of-focus Jim Van Winkle sitting on the ground 30 yards away, back against a fence post, legs stretched straight out.

Unfastening my seat belt turns into a process. The plane leans to the side of the broken landing gear. All my lard-assed weight is forced down against the buckle. Trying to heave myself upward involves more pain.

"Get out of the plane. It might burn."

Sure enough, aviation fuel is pouring into the cockpit from the ruptured wing tank. My pants are soaked. I decide I can handle a little more pain. The buckle finally pops. I fall out on the ground like a sack of clumsy cement, crawl over to Jim. Blood is flowing down his face from a wide open slice in his scalp.

He asks how this happened, if I've called anyone, asks if I've called his wife, asks if I've found his glasses, asks if I am all right. "Not so bad," I say, "but we need to get to a hospital, be checked out, we're both hurt." He agrees he might be hurt.

He asks if I've called anyone, if I've called his wife, if I am okay, if I've seen his glasses. I do not know, that like me, Jim can't see diddley squat without his glasses, but I understand my answers aren't registering. However, at no time do I question my own clarity. I too have been unconscious and am no doubt dingy in the head, but I naturally assume my circuits are clear as a bell.

I try my cell phone — no service. I search the plane for eyeglasses, hoping to find my own as well as Jim's. The search might have gone better if I had my glasses. Aviation fuel continues pouring out of a severed pipe in the wing into the cockpit. Thick fumes. Any spark will blow things to kingdom come. How long will it take the tank to empty? Will the fuel explode before it soaks harmlessly into the sand?

I stumble around the plane, find my camera half buried in the dirt, ruined, lens cockeyed. I retrace the plane's trip through the torn up grass and sand back to the point of impact. No glasses. Hours later a kind neighbor will find both pairs of eyeglasses buried in the sand near the plane and bring them to the hospital. It's a wonder I didn't tromp them to pieces during my half-blind search.

I discover daughter Sydney's camera in my jacket pocket, a backup camera to the one with a ruined lens. I've never used it and can't make out the control buttons, but manage a couple of unsteady crash photos before the batteries expire. Jim is still resting against the gate post, trying to clear his bloodied head. He asks if I found his glasses, if I've called his wife.

Kathy at Home Minding Her Own Business

I leave work at 4, arrive home and exchange greetings with Finlay who is due for his walk. As I'm retrieving his leash, the phone rings. I check the caller ID. Time freezes.

CHERRY CO HOSP 4:17, phone number listed below, but who needs that? Everything I need to know is right there on the cracked LED screen. The hospital is calling to say Bryan won't be coming back, just as he suspected. The phone rings a second time. CHERRY CO HOSP 4:17 in block letters. I'm not going to answer it. You can't make me. No. This isn't how it's supposed to be. Sonofabitch.

Third ring. I argue with myself. Do I want to be a grownup and deal with this call? The fourth ring will be answered by the machine. I have to take the call, like it or not.

I don't know the woman on the other end. I'm not terribly patient with her. I realize now she didn't know I already knew why she was calling. She introduces herself, says she is calling from — "I know! CHERRY CO HOSP! Get on with it." She asks if I am the wife of Bryan Jones. Affirmative. She says she is calling because he's been in a wreck but is okay.

She said wreck. Big difference. That means he was reading while he was driving, missed a slight curve, wrecked the car and now we need to figure out whether we're going to trade and/or purchase the wrecked Rav4 because the lease is up. Okay. He's going to be okay. It was a wreck. He really shouldn't drive and read at the same time and, by the way, a seat belt may be in order for future trips.

The woman on the phone says she needs some information and repeats that my husband is okay. She says "It's important for you to know that your husband walked into the hospital on his own.". Okay. She tells me to sit down. Instead I open the door and Finlay bolts out after Mowgli the cat, both running full speed through the neighbor's yard. I would do that differently were I given the chance. I tell the woman she has to wait a minute, put the phone down, retrieve Finlay from the neighbor's.

She asks me if I'm sitting down. I am. She asks me if I'm alone. I tell her I am except for the dog. She says "That's good. Dogs are good. "She repeats that Bryan walked into the hospital on his own and he was in a plane crash.

At that point the slate is wiped clean and I am, again, whirling. A plane crash? No.

She said it happened on takeoff.

That's impossible. He was to take off at 1. It's 4:19 now. She must not have her facts straight. Or perhaps the plane landed somewhere near Turner's bison ranch and was taking off again. That's probably what happened. But she said he walked into the hospital on his own. No one could do that, not even Mr. Tough Guy. People don't walk into hospitals after a plane crash. She needs to stop talking so I can ask her to clarify these things. Instead she says "I need some information about your husband." I fetch the insurance card and Bryan's social security number.

She asks if Bryan is taking any regular medicine. He takes high blood pressure medication and I can find out the dosage by checking the bottle in the medicine cabinet. On the mirror I see that stupid note. He never leaves notes. I go numb and all my blood drops to my feet. Now I know why he showed me that stupid check book and said he'd feel better knowing I knew where he keeps it. If he'd never said that, he'd be okay. If he'd not written the stupid mushy note, he'd be okay. Now it's certain he won't be coming back. It's as if he sealed the deal with the stupid note. Odd and irrational, but it is what it is.

It takes a few seconds to regroup from the note and I fumble around reading every little detail from the prescription label. I go back to the couch with a pen in hand to write down the caller's version of what happened.

He was in a plane. On takeoff the plane crashed. He drove the pilot to Valentine to the hospital and both walked in on their own volition. Amazing, but then again it's him, so why wouldn't it be? She says Bryan is being prepped for tests which would indicate any internal injuries, but on the surface, aside from some cuts, he was fine. She says Jim is in worse shape. I ask if I could talk to Bryan. Yes, briefly, as they are ready to whisk him away.

His voice. It is really his voice. He is alive. She wasn't lying. Amazing what a single word, "Hi", generates. A boatload of tears, overwhelming gratefulness to be allowed to hear that voice again. I look at this conversation as a final gift. I've seen enough TV medical dramas to know people could seem just fine with all sorts of internal injuries. All of a sudden, BAM, they've gone into cardiac arrest and people stand around saying, "I was just talking to him and he was fine. I don't know what happened."

I know he's not fine from his side of the conversation. He says he's not sure he'll be able to get the car back home tonight. I tell him I plan on driving to Valentine. He sounds grateful and said "Thank you. That would be great." Everyone knows he wouldn't give up the wheel that easily. He must be in bad shape. He confirms the crash happened on takeoff. I say something about him knowing this was going to happen and he agreed. Then it was time for him to give the phone back.

I ask about coming up and if he'll be staying. Until the test results are back she can't say if he'll be admitted and suggests I stay put until they call me back. Something else I wish I could do over. Waiting. Not my forte. I call his sisters with what I know, locate daughter Sydney and ask her to come home.

After an hour I call the hospital. They don't know if the test results are in and put me on hold. The person who gets back on the phone is the pilot's wife, Myki. I cannot understand why the hospital staff gave the phone to the pilot's wife. Myki says she talked to my husband and that he is doing okay but her husband is not. He hit his head and they are discussing options. She said she feels terrible about this and can't believe that Jim crashed the plane because he is always so careful every time he flies. She said they still don't have Bryan's test results.

I find out two hours later, when the doctor calls with the test results, that Myki, the pilot's wife, is a nurse at Cherry County Hospital, on duty in another part of the hospital when Bryan and Jim walked into the emergency room. No one at the hospital thinks to tell Myki of the crash. Or perhaps each person she encountered thinks someone else told her. It was only when the doctor bumped into her quite a bit later and asked how she is holding up that Myki asked, "Why?"

Dr. Mulligan-Witt gives me the rundown on Bryan. Broken ribs, the costochondral rib displacement (or something to that effect), deep cuts on the lips, injured liver. She says they want to keep Bryan overnight because this was such a traumatic event. She says both patients were very lucky, repeated that a couple of times. She talks about Bryan's lacerated lips and said she made the decision not to do surgery on them, thought he'd be able to live a normal life with them as they were. She says they are flying Jim to Omaha. Bryan's liver enzymes are high and they would keep an eye on those overnight. I ask about lodging and she says no one will kick us out of the hospital if we show up.

Sydney, after considerable tears when she arrives home and hears the news, immediately starts packing bags with essentials: Bryan's favorite coffee cup, his shaving kit, a book he once told her was a personal favorite. She is calm while I am in a cyclone. Friend Traci takes Finlay to her home for the duration.

On the drive up to Valentine, I try calling the hospital a couple of times. No cell service. I hope he will last until we get there. We arrive in Valentine to a dead-quiet hospital. When we walk in Bryan's room I am so relieved he hasn't died while we were on the road.

*

Immediately after the crash, while I'm searching for our eyeglasses, Jim gathers his wits, tries unsuccessfully to stand up. Attributing his weakness to post-crash head fuzz and being completely oblivious to the terrific damage his legs have suffered, I grab an arm I don't know is broken and give him an energetic assist. He staggers off to his shop building to staunch the bleeding and clean himself up prior our trip to the hospital.

I fetch my car from Jim's house, pull close to the shop, again try 911 on my cell phone. Still no service. I should probably try the land line in the house, but I worry an ambulance crew would insist on transporting both of us and I would be without a car after being checked over, given two aspirin and released. My clear, level-headed brain is thinking I will drop Jim off at the hospital and boogie for home.

Jim stands at a sink in the shop, doing the best he can with the blood from his head wound. Once he partially stops the flow, he opens the car door, hesitates, worried his aviation fuel-soaked jeans will damage the upholstery. He grudgingly accepts my assurance not to worry about it.

I am grateful Jim is riding shotgun. Even with a bad concussion Jim gives accurate directions to the hospital, as cheerful as a body can be with a bunch of broken bones, a sliced up head and his favorite possession a twisted wreck back at the ranch. I let him off outside the emergency room, suggest he tell the first person he sees that he'd been in a plane crash. Hoisting himself out of the passenger seat, bad as he was hurt, must have cost him a fortune, but he never even grunted. Jim walks up to the emergency room doors like he's taking a casual stroll down main street on a sunny afternoon. Not a guy you'll likely catch limping in public.

I spend the next five minutes driving around the parking lot searching for an empty parking spot. Busy place. By the time I walk through the entrance to the emergency room Jim is not in evidence. Probably not good form to leave for home without checking on him. A serious young nurse accosts me, wants to know my business. "I just delivered Jim Van Winkle and was wondering where he'd been moved."

"Jim said he'd been in a plane crash?"

"Yup, he sure was."

"Where?"

"Right on the ranch, just west of Wood Lake." You could tell she knew Wood Lake, could drive straight to it or could give clear directions to a fellow pilgrim.

"Were you in the crash?"

"Well, yeah," I admitted, "I probably might have been in the crash."

"Are you hurt?"

That was when I made a huge mistake, which I now blame on some kind of undiagnosed concussion. What I should have said, that I was feeling fine, had absolutely no injury symptoms, somehow didn't get said. And it wasn't like I didn't have adequate warning. She was already looking at me like a high energy bird dog on point, nostrils all aquiver. Instead, I weakened, owned up to some minor discomfort, and my hopes for two aspirin and a quick see ya later promptly went straight out the window.

She barked orders in every direction. Before I could mosey off to a quiet corner, a white-clad SWAT team strapped me on a rigid Hindu nail board, wrapped a neck brace around my neck and hustled me into an emergency room bed. I remember telling the nurse multiple times there was not one damn thing wrong with my back or my neck, but she was so busy making the fur fly she must not have heard. Someone wants to cut off my fuel-soaked pants. No goddamned way. I paid the better part of $12 for those babies at Walmart not more than three years ago. Practically new. The white coats humor me, allow me to remove my own goddamned fuel-soaked $12 pants.

Next door, beyond the curtain, I can hear people working on Jim. Once in a while someone asks him a question. Once in a while he'll answer. I find it reassuring he can talk.

A harried male doctor arrives, asks the hovering nurse questions, pokes on me a few times, leaves. A few minutes later a young doctor,* appears from behind Jim's curtain, introduces herself, asks me questions, asks the nurse questions, conducts a thorough examination, says she is ordering a CAT scan, asks if I need anything. I want to talk to Kathy and I want to know when I can leave. She says the nurse will arrange the phone call and says she'll need more information before she can release me.

On what has been a rough day, Kathy's voice couldn't be better medicine. As soon as she rounds up Sydney, they'll be heading to Valentine. Good deal. To me, this will mean one too many family cars in Valentine, but surely I can manage to drive one of them and we can head for home, perhaps yet tonight.

Jim's wife, Myki, drops by. I am surprised to see her. She says she was working her normal shift at the hospital when someone let it slip Jim was in the emergency room. Myki holds my hand, says the doctors think I'm going to be all right. Jim is in much worst shape. She doesn't understand the whys of the plane crashing, says Jim is always so careful. Any minute Jim will be leaving for Omaha on a plane. She intends to ride along. The doctors are particularly worried about his head injuries.

I am also worried about Jim's head injuries. What a royal mess I have made. Why did I insist on nagging Jim into taking me on that goddamned plane ride? Hubris. Stubbornness. They'll get you in trouble every time.

The rest of the afternoon becomes a whirl of white coats wheeling me down long corridors, multiple pale rooms with large, expensive-looking machines, technicians patiently answering my ignorant questions. The nurses cannot be more attentive. A raging thirst is my only complaint. The nurses periodically bring me tepid water, no ice, one tiny plastic glass at a time. I would have no trouble disappearing an entire gallon jug of ice water, or maybe two or three. After repeated requests I assume there is a medical reason why I'm not receiving larger quantities of water. Maybe when Kathy arrives, hopefully within the next five minutes, she will motivate the water people. She is good at motivating people.

When evening comes and the staff turns over, my personal nurse departs and a new one arrives. Because of a staff shortage, Kathy Ormesher has been summoned from her distant home having finished working a double shift only a few hours earlier. In her shoes, I would be grumpy. But she is made of sterner stuff, immediately buckles down to provide the most professional care on the planet. She even brings me almost adequate amounts of tepid drinking water.

Later. Kathy has had time to drive to Valentine two or three times. I cannot understand the delay. Maybe she was so frazzled she wrecked the car. That's probably the deal. The nurses know all about her wreck and won't tell me for fear my condition, which is just fine, thank you very much, will deteriorate. I ask my new favorite medical professional if she's heard anything from Kathy. Negative. Which doesn't mean a damn thing. She's just obeying orders. Loose lips sink ships. She does tell me Jim and Myki have arrived safely in Omaha. At least there's that.

---

* Dr. Michele N. Mulligan-Witt. Jim told me a few weeks later Dr. Mulligan-Witt is not only a skilled physician, but an avid horse person, who tore up a knee rodeoing.

Much later, sometime after 10 p.m., Kathy and Sydney storm into the room like their pants are on fire. Boy, am I glad to see them. Sydney has brought me a favorite book. Who thinks of something like that? I mention some thirst issues. Kathy has an earnest conversation with my new favorite medical professional. Large quantities of water miraculously appear. Better yet, the water contains chunks of life-saving ice. Life is good.

Even though Kathy claims she made a strong case, the hospital refuses to release a perfectly healthy guy. Hospitals can be like that. Kathy and Sydney settle in for the night. Kathy Ormesher hauls in extra chairs, blankets, makes them as comfortable as possible.

The hospital does not turn me loose until the next afternoon. By turning me loose I mean nobody interferes when I make a break for the exit. By then my father-in-law Lloyd and his partner Kathryn have arrived to ferry our extra vehicle back home. I do not let the hospital door hit me in the ass on the way out.

Once the car is safely on the road I open the manila envelope containing my thick check out file. The first sentence of Dr. Mulligan-Witt's case summary refers to me as "an obese, but pleasant gentleman." Gee thanks, Doc.

One Week Later

Jim calls. He is mighty sore, a broken leg, a broken arm, many cracked ribs, a major concussion, cuts all over his body and severe fuel burns on his legs and feet. Laughter is outlawed at his house because it hurts too much to laugh. He is most concerned about how I am getting along and will be second guessing himself forever on what went wrong.

He keeps track of all Super Cub accidents in the United States. Post-crash fuel explosions are the most common cause of death. He doesn't understand why the ruptured fuel tanks didn't explode.

He has no memory of that day, but is hoping the FAA investigators will sort things out.

He seems to be tracking well for guy with a major head injury. Once everyone is healed up we'll get together and resume the interview I was planning after we got back from our flying tour of the Sand Hills.

Three Weeks Later

Jim answers the phone. He's sitting in his house looking through binoculars at a raging blizzard, while his wife Myki, up to her eyeballs in coveralls, drags new born calves into the barn. She's back to working at the hospital, but fortunately had the day off. Anticipating the storm she came home early last night with extra groceries. A neighbor is staying at the house when Myki is at the hospital. Another neighbor feeds at 6 p.m. Sand Hill ranchers know something about neighboring.

Jim drove the pickup on Sunday and is still paying the price. He checked the plane for the first time since the crash. He can see where his head hit the pipes overhead and where his knee put a five inch dent in the steel dash. He hasn't heard back from the National Transpor-

146

tation Safety Board inspectors, who examined the plane after the crash, but thinks he must have taken corrective action for a stall and tried a hard landing, which collapsed the super reinforced landing gear he installed a few years ago for that very purpose. He speculated the reason we don't suffer from whiplash is the plane smacked down first on its belly, he bounced up and hit the pipes, then my fat ass hit the back of his seat, knocking it loose and driving him into the dash. He said he doubted a person with a sledge hammer could knock a dent that deep in the steel dash.

He complained of a sore knee until the docs finally did an MRI and found, in addition to the broken bone just below the knee, the knee joint looks like a bunch of boiled spaghetti. He's going to talk to a surgeon next week, but hopes to put off surgery until the cows are out on grass. He gets around wearing a big brace, can't use crutches because of his broken arm and dislocated thumb. He says the thumb was dislocated for so long before they put it back (he says the Novocain didn't work so well when they put it back), the nerves are still misfiring and the thumb can barely function.

He doesn't have classic whiplash, but suffers off and on from neck pain. The folks at the hospital in Omaha talked about deep muscle trauma. How that differs from whiplash he doesn't know. He has suffered only a few headaches, but knows he's not back to normal. He can't watch TV for more than five minutes or read anything longer than article-length stuff. Not that he's complaining. He talks about himself the way you might talk about a science project. And not a shred of blame directed toward the pushy, inconsiderate dipwad who insisted on flying over the Sand Hills and caused this whole mess. He mostly expresses concern for my condition, my state of mind. He also has many questions about why what happened happened. I am too ignorant of flying matters to be much help.

The fuel burns on his feet, legs and butt have largely healed. He was most troubled by the burns on his groin. Now that the skin has sloughed off and been replaced by new skin he says his comfort level has improved 100 percent, although he wears flannel lined Cabela's underwear. Not for the first time I am grateful aviation fuel soaked my pants only to mid-thigh. The marks from the elastic in his socks are still visible on his ankles. He is not sure if aviation gas is more corrosive than regular gas, but intends to find out.

He put himself on unpaid leave from the Sandhills Task Force, says he'll try to get back to doing office stuff in April. He missed his first county commissioner's meeting in 10 years, but intends to get there on Tuesday, even though Myki sometimes reminds him to take it easy.

One Month Later

Jim is in good spirits when he calls. Getting back to work, even if he's not yet 100 percent, has improved his morale. Jim wishes the NTSB inspectors would complete their crash investigation. He's tired of looking at the wrecked plane every time he drives by the hanger hauling a hay bale. He's sent the NTSB reams of plane records, every inspection since the plane was built. The NTSB says they've never seen such complete records on a plane this old, but the NTSB is anal retentive and he expects a final report to take at least a few more months. He just wishes they'd give him permission to dispose of the plane, his blood and hair still stuck to the roof of the cockpit. Does he have a replacement plane in mind? As a matter of fact, he's just learned of a serviceable Super Cub sitting in a hanger on a local ranch. The owner says the plane will be for sale when Jim gets around to needing it.

Since he was too dinged up to make the last county commissioners meeting, Jim wasn't about to allow a little ground blizzard keep him from attending the next one. He drives to Valentine in spite of a broken leg, a broken arm, a shattered elbow he won't tell anyone about because the doctors would operate, a knee made of boiled spaghetti, another knee almost as bad he won't tell anyone about for fear the doctors would operate, and a partially healed dislocated thumb, the painful remnants of what seems a helluva lot like whiplash, in spite of the doctor's opinion. He's sporting moccasins, because putting on cowboy boots is too rough on his knees, wearing a light jacket, because all the splints and braces won't fit under his heavy coat. He leaves his neck brace at home, not wanting his friends and neighbors to think him a wussy. Jim crawls in the family Suburban because his injured legs can't operate the four speed manual transmission of his pickup — a truck always stocked with the tools a working rancher keeps handy.

When asked why he drove himself, he said he wouldn't be much of a county commissioner if he was so dependent on others he couldn't drive himself to one lousy meeting.

Jim says poor visibility and a few sizable drifts kept his speed below 40 miles an hour, barely creeping along. A few miles from his ranch, a whirlwind of blinding snow and spinning cardboard hit the windshield. He slowed to a full stop, mindful of the occasional icy patch. As quickly as it descended, the whirlwind lifted, revealing a Walmart semi on its side in the ditch, apple boxes and five pound plastic sacks of apples strewn over the highway. The decoupled semi cab lay upside down in the deep snow of the barrow pit.

Jim tried his cell phone. Dead zone. The semi cab was badly buggered, but Jim figured there were probably live folks inside.

"What was I supposed to do?"

He zipped up his light jacket and forced his damaged knees through the thigh deep snow to the side of the semi cab. He found a woman passenger hanging upside down, unable to unfasten her seat belt. The driver, smooshed against the roof, doing plenty of yelling, convinced his air cushioned seat was still connected to the semi's air system. When Jim couldn't open the passenger door, he made his way back through the snow to his vehicle in a vain search for tools. He slogged back down to the semi cab, came across a claw hammer in the wreckage and went to work, but couldn't budge the jammed door.

By this time the yelling truck driver was getting on Jim's nerves. He hauled himself back to the Suburban, clambered up on the back bumper, stood tall enough to get cell phone service, ordered up an ambulance.

A few minutes, later a neighbor came by on his way to Valentine with a cow needing a C-section. He and Jim gathered more serious tools and freed the passenger and driver in short order. The woman was in decent shape considering, but the big cut in the top of the driver's head was bleeding at a goodly rate. Jim said it was a dead ringer for the cut on his own head he'd suffered in the plane crash. The rancher and pregnant cow headed to Valentine. Jim gave the semi driver a discarded fast food napkin from under the seat of the Suburban to clamp on his bleeding head and off they went, met the ambulance about 10 miles outside of town. Jim handed over the patients and arrived at the commissioners meeting only a little bit late.

Big crowd. Plenty of old and new business. The meeting lasted until 8 o'clock in the evening. Jim thought he might have been less attentive than usual, said his neck was killing him.

By the time he drove home the wind had subsided and the roads were mostly clear. He met a pickup piled high with five pound plastic sacks of Walmart apples. Jim said, "Bet there was lots of applesauce eaten in this county the next few days."

And what did his wife Myki think of him driving his badly injured self through ground blizzards to long-winded county commissioner meetings?

"When I got home," he said, "the folks around here weren't too happy with me."

Probably not the best time to ask about another interview, although Jim says he is game. He claims he is eager to meet me, having no memory of ever having done so. He's hoping I can help him figure out what happened. We set a flexible date for early May. I'm thinking this guy is a glutton for punishment. He may not remember what happened the last time I showed up at his ranch near Wood Lake, but I'm betting Myki might.

Chapter 18
John Hansen

Turner runs that kind of operation.
You'd better know who you work for.

— Buzz Kime

The first thing you notice about John Hansen: he completely fills the doorway and then some. Not fat, just big. Steer wrestler big. He also emits that now familiar high testosterone buzz I've come to associate with ranch mangers, making him seem even larger. Would I take orders from this guy? Where do I sign up?

Hansen is doing me an unexpected favor by coming to our house for an interview. We'd discussed doing an interview in his office in Bozeman, but the airplane crash injuries haven't sufficiently healed for me to travel. He's stopping by on his long drive to Blue Stem Ranch in Oklahoma where he'll check on some innovations the manager is trying out.

Kathy has dinner ready, but John spends so much time in his pickup his wife, Jaynee[*], has encouraged him to cut back on road meals. He's also eager to finish this task and resume his journey. He may stop for the night somewhere in Kansas, or if he's feeling strong, drive straight through to the Bluestem.

Sitting upright for extended periods still kicks my ass. After a few minutes the ribs become cranky. That's when Finlay usually does his thing, jumping up beside me and nudging his warm tail bone against the rib doing the most complaining, much more effective than any drug. Friend Jerry Ellerman's two Westies performed the same service for him after a bad motorcycle accident. A word to the wise: if you're headed out there to break a bunch of ribs you might want a Westie or two on hand for the aftercare.

I'm as comfortable as I'm going to get, Finlay's warm tailbone right where it needs to be. If John Hansen has an opinion about a grown man sitting across from him with a West Highland White Terrier growing out of his side he doesn't share, but begins tackling this evening's assignment: describing the nuts and bolts of the Turner bison operation. My task is to pay attention.

Within a couple of minutes I'm finding it difficult to visualize John Hansen scraping and bowing to Ted Turner or anyone else. He probably knows who he works for all right, but this is not a guy who suffers fools or would be easily deterred from following his own counsel. Hansen possesses exactly the right combination of brains and force of nature personality to turn Turner's romantic vision of bison herds roaming pristine prairies into a financially sound reality.

---

* Jaynee Shell Hansen is the daughter of Gail Shell and Jack Ray Shell. Jack, one of the last of the old time cowboys, grew up on an Idaho ranch west of the Snake River, so isolated it could only be reached by boat or by horseback. He managed several large Montana Ranches before spending the last 19 years of his career managing Ted Turner's Bar None Ranch in Montana.

Hansen earned a bachelor's in animal science from Montana State, worked for three years on a cattle ranch, then returned to Montana State for his Master's in range science. "My training was in cattle and horses, pure and simple. I'd never had anything to do with bison. By the way, bison are similar to range horses, how they handle, the way they flock together, like sheep, the way they like to move around gates, that sort of thing.

"When I went to the Spike Box right after it was purchased I'd never worked in the Sand Hills. Never worked with windmills. Never been around bison. It was a big shift. I'd always worked in hard land country, so when I moved down to the Spike Box I had to depend on my neighbors. I had good neighbors. I'd ask questions and they were always willing to give me advice.

"About three weeks after I got to the Spike Box, the trucks rolled in from Montana. Most of the ranch was fenced with older three-wire fences in various states of repair. We picked a couple of pastures that still had some grass left. For the next full year we tried to keep up that fence. We'd go out in the morning on horseback or on an ATV, find the bison, do a rough count, if we were missing some we'd try to predict where they might be. We got so we'd kind of know where they'd gone. We'd try to haze them back. Once in a while they'd get clear over on a neighbor's place. One time there were 150 head on a neighbor and we had to go get them. They never seemed to go out the same place or end up in the same neighbor's pasture. Most times we'd watch the tracks and it was when they'd get shoved into a corner or pushed through. Or something would spook 'em. I don't think there were any dedicated attempts to get out. It was more by accident. They were just shy of a year old when we got them. They were on the Spike Box for the first time. They had no leadership. Sometimes all it would take was a few coyotes howling right next to them to spook 'em. The got settled in and by the next fall they handled a lot better.

"That was the base. Then we got more calves for several years from the Montana ranches.

"By 1997, we had our first calf crop. Eight hundred head the first year. They had calves and we kept replacements. We were already expanding, adding more property. By 1998, we had a whole separate ranch over at Gordon, so we were constantly bringing animals into those ranches until about 2003. That was when we got our last big shipment. By then we were starting to raise significant numbers of our own.

"Ted started accumulating bison about 1990 or 1991. When I came on in 1995 they had the Flying D (113,613 acres, acquired in 1989) up and running in Montana, they also had the Snowcrest Ranch (13,343 acres acquired in 1993) in Montana, where they were taking the bull calves from the Flying D. They'd stocked the Ladder Ranch (156,439 acres acquired in 1992) and the Armendaris Ranch (358,643 acres acquired in 1994) in New Mexico. By 1995, we had three cow-calf operations and a yearling operation. The Bar None was basically an elk hunting and fishing operation with no bison.

"Nobody had any vast experience with bison. Bud Griffith, the manager of the Flying D, a guy who'd run bison for four or five years, was the closest thing for an expert I could call for advice. He said every time you start to think like a cow man, try to think differently. Now that's not strictly true, but you're probably going to have to take a different approach.

"When I started we didn't use ear tags. The first few times we worked bison at the Spike Box there was no tagging, no weighing, none of that. We gave them dewormer and kicked them out, got a head count so we knew whether we'd lost any during the year. Heifer calves were Bangs vaccinated. We didn't have weights or anything. Just our numbers. Once they improved the RFID buttons it was a little easier to run them on the computer. We did hand records operations for several years and I still like to back up the computer with hand records. My wife was one of the first to get set up with RFIDs and use the computer, but she never quit maintaining hand records. And it was a good thing, because we had quite a few computer glitches and crashes at the beginning.

"I worked on the Spike Box for five years until I moved to Montana. Also worked on the McGinley and Blue Creek, then the Deer Creek and Fawn Lake. Actually it was a little bit risky from a corporate management standpoint to have me managing all four ranches. So I kept on them to hire other managers. I told them they were one car wreck away from having to replace a lot of management. When they decided to move me to Montana we decided to put a manager on each place."

Who came up with the design of the Spike Box working corrals? "The corrals at the Spike Box and the other ranches in Nebraska are not perfect, but pretty much the same as the corrals on the Flying D in Montana.

"Our whole operation is a bottoms up deal. We allow a lot of autonomy to our managers and they put their fingerprints on the operation. Guys come in with their own way of looking at things, implement things they want to do. If someone has an idea they run it by me and I run it by Russ Miller. If they want to try it we tell them to keep track of the results, see if it's something we want to adopt.

"Some managers are low key, like to keep things simple, not do a lot with the bison, just keep the records up to date. Then we have managers that look at nutrition, do a lot of culling, that kind of stuff, run their operations like pure bred beef operations. We make our share of mistakes. We try to keep track of those mistakes and not repeat them. It's not like we hit the ground running.

"The bison genome has not been fully mapped. All we test them for is cattle mitochondrial DNA to see if the animal has traces of a cattle background. The incidence in our herd is 5 percent or less. We cull them as we find them.

"There are several smaller producers that are probably just as tough on the selection as we are. There are also sophisticated operations working on grass finishing, marketing on their own web sites. I'd say right now we operate about like a reasonably advanced range cattle operation. We keep fairly good records. You can get five people together and ask them what a good bison looks like and get five different answers. It's not standardized. We've got some managers like to see 'em with a little lower hump and a little longer, just like cattle. We've got other managers who like to see a good, well-defined hump on 'em, a classic buffalo look. We have 15 ranches with 14 devoted to bison. You get those 14 managers together and ask them what constitutes a good bison and you can sit back and listen to the argument rage for hours.

"We're still finding out what works best. It's a never ending process. I did a lot of the initial work and my wife Jaynee did as much or more than I did. Once we got up to three ranches in the Sand Hills I no longer had time to work bison by hand. She was doing the audit by then. She ended up taking over the bison and livestock end of it and I handled the business end. She worked all the bison in the fall. About the first of September they'd start working bison, they'd ship yearlings from all four ranches, then start processing cows and calves, get done about Christmas or shortly after if the weather cooperated. She was working over 10,000 head of animals a year. So I give her all the credit for getting the bison operation started. She's highly organized. She can handle a crew. She understands bison.

"Unfortunately, Jaynee has not been able to work bison for a couple of years. She was riding an ATV on the Blue Creek north of Lewellen when a bull overturned her. The other workers came to her aid or she'd have probably died. She spent a lot of time in the hospital and had to do physical therapy for several years."

Cattle ranchers in the Sand Hills, because of the fragile nature of the sandy pastures, have traditionally practiced tighter management with cattle and grasslands than ranchers in hard grass country. What about bison ranching?

"Raising bison in the Sand Hills we do some different things nutritionally, particularly from what we do in Montana or South Dakota. We might supplement a little more with protein. The jury is still out on how much they actually need. Then bison have that traveling thing. You know bison walk a lot, it's in their nature. Of course, if you don't watch it they can trail things up. That's not something you have to worry about in Montana or New Mexico. You can make mistakes, but they probably have less serious consequences in some of the other states. In the Sand Hills you have to be on top of your game or you really set yourself back. The Sand Hills in some regards are really forgiving, in other ways they are not. You have to change pastures. There's certain pastures you have to watch. They're just real soft and the bison might set up a trailing pattern.

"We found out water didn't work so well as a way to control grazing. If they'd been staying too long at the south end of pastures 30,000 acres in size, I'd shut off the water. They'd walk north, get a drink and walk back south. sometimes they'd cover 10 or 15 miles like it was nothing. It didn't faze them. Our ranches are small compared to the bison's natural state where they had the run of the prairie from Canada to Texas. You'd need a much larger landscape to have free range grazing work out. Twenty miles is nothing to a bison."

What will happen when all of Turner's ranches are fully stocked and more of the annual production needs to be marketed?

"We've been pretty close to fully stocked a couple of times, and then we'll buy more property. We've developed a very simple production model. Back in 2000-2001, the bottom went out of the bison market. We hung in there, worked with some good people and that market now is very strong. We've seen some shifts in demand, but overall demand is good. People who'd eaten bison in restaurants began buying it in stores and cooking it themselves.

"The early years we pretty much kept all the females, didn't use much selectivity. If it was female it got to live and stay on the ranch or go to another ranch to start a herd. As we got closer to being fully stocked we'd keep maybe 20 to 50 percent of the top heifers, send the rest to other ranches or maybe down to Oklahoma, where they've grow them out to two years of age and a feedlot would put a short time finish on them and they'd go to slaughter. That's the way we still do. Most of the managers hold back whatever they determine they need for replacements for cows that have died or culled for age or lack of production or disposition or whatever, just like a beef operation.

"Of course, half the herd is male and we don't need that many bulls. We started running one bull for 10 cows. We're probably closer to one bull for 15 cows, and experimenting with one bull for 20 cows. We don't fertility test bulls. We run a few more bulls than a beef producer would, mainly because all the bulls may not be fertile. Bull calves used to be sent directly to the feedlot, but that didn't work out so well. We started holding bull calves on the ranch and grow 'em out to about 18 months of age. They might go to the feedlot weighing 650 to 700 pounds and kill at somewhere between 1000 to 1100 pounds. Bison will handle fiber better than cattle, but we feed grain to get a consistent product. Range raised meat doesn't always have consistent qualities. Consumers want a predictable product. The American public, if they have a steak today, they want the next one they buy to be just like it. They don't want it any tougher, they don't want the fat any yellower.

"On one of our ranches we have heifers going to slaughter weight on grass. I followed a load of them through the kill plant to the cutting floor with the ranch manager and they graded out phenomenally well. So we do have one ranch, with the right manager and the right complement of grass putting out a finished product wholly with grass. The big question is can we duplicate that on the other ranches. One ranch in New Mexico is thinking of trying it because they have some strong grass. We have one manager here in the Sand Hills that's going to make a test case with just a few head. We'll see how he does.

"Bison are slower maturing. Might calve at three. Might not breed back the first year after she calves. It costs a lot to get them there. Most feedlot beef is killed at 24 months of age, while we're looking to kill ours at 24-30 months. We have to graze them a year extra before we get the calf. We're probably a year to a year and a half behind a beef operation.

"The vast majority of our animals are sold to Rocky Mountain Natural Meats in Denver. Eventually the meat is sold to retail stores like King Soopers, Whole Foods. Some ends up in restaurants, including Ted's Montana Grill. So we sell the meat through several middlemen who sell the product back to Ted. Ted's Montana Grill uses about half or our production. The rest goes to other restaurants and retail stores.

"Some ranches are starting to show a profit after wages and taxes."

Although I'm fairly certain of the answer, I ask if there are significant differences between Montana ranchers and ranchers from Nebraska Sand Hills.

"Ranchers are ranchers all over the west. The only difference is the shape of their hat or maybe the brand of jeans or boots. Some might have a little more farming in their operations. Canada, the Sand Hills, Montana, Nevada, New Mexico, Texas. Cut out all the superficial stuff and they're the same. Hard workers, independent. Same attitude, same values."

It's approaching 10 p.m. and I am worrying about the long drive John has ahead of him. Clearly he would spend as long as it takes to satisfy my curiosity, but I'm not wanting another accident on my conscience. And, truth be told, my ribs have been complaining for the past couple of hours.

How about a cup of coffee for the road? "No thank you, I'm already wired."

Yes he is.

John Hansen fills the doorway one more time and is gone.

Chapter 19
May Visit to the Spike Box and Wood Lake

I was overcome by a certain half melancholy feeling as I gazed on these bison,
themselves part of the last remnant of a doomed and nearly vanished race.
Few, indeed, are the men who now have, or evermore shall have,
the chance of seeing the mightiest of American beasts.

—Theodore Roosevelt, 1889

May morning. The surrounding hills greening with new grass. Terry is waiting for us in the Spike Box office. For a guy who doesn't care to be around people, Terry is a warm and welcoming host. Wanda walks over from their home to the west, explains they'd planned on a foursome, but the big four-door pickup has gone on the fritz.

Kathy and I join Terry in the front seat of a 3/4 ton pickup and head out.

Terry wanted us to come early because it's a long drive to the south end of the ranch where the 3000-head south herd is grazing. The south herd is composed of older animals than the north herd, including cows, who came in the original shipment of 800 heifers from Montana, and older bulls sourced from several Turner ranches. Every fall and winter trophy hunters cull the oldest and most massive bulls from the south herd.

We pass through a pasture gate just west of headquarters by a windmill and an overflowing stock tank. Terry says to remind him to show us something on the way back. There is no road through the hills to the bison, but occasionally we find ourselves driving the old mail track. Terry explains how mail carriers got around the Sand Hills through deep sand before the days of four-wheel drive vehicles. The trick was to under inflate the tires, maybe carry only 15 pounds of pressure, which usually did the job, although everyone packed shovels for emergencies. To negotiate winter snow, the mail carrier added chains to the nearly flat tires. Terry says he used the low pressure tire trick himself when he was a kid and it worked, although the tires wore out pretty quickly.

Terry, a careful driver, mindful of our comfort, picks his way through the hills by the least bumpy route. Without the pickup's oversized tires and four-wheel drive we'd have been stuck several times.

We pass a few scattered bison, mostly bulls and young cows, interested in the pickup because they are still receiving some protein cake. The grass is shorter than optimum, and until the herd is moved to a fresh pasture in a few days it will be supplemented. Like all of Turner's ranch managers, Terry has decision making authority on most matters. If he thinks his herd requires supplemental protein, and he has the money in his budget, it's his call.

Terry points out a cow, who to me, shows no sign of being pregnant. He says the sagging belly is the best indicator of a cow ready to calve. The lower it sinks the closer to calving. A beef cow ready to calve would spring up behind and fill her bag. This particular bison cow has the sagging belly, but little else in the way of leading indicators. Terry says she might be only two or three days away from calving.

I ask about a particular bull meditating nearby, one showing plenty of black and length. Terry says the bull is close to his ideal. He likes the length, which he values when he's selecting herd bulls, and the darker color appeals to Terry's sense of what makes a perfect bison. He says the ranch produced two all black calves this year. He's hoping for more in the future.

Roughly eight miles southwest of ranch headquarters, about a mile from the southern property line, we pop over a rise and a broad valley opens up, revealing most of the 3000-head south herd scattered over a large wet meadow and the surrounding dunes. Terry worries the cows will take their new red calves and skedaddle. He says he never knows how they'll behave. Sometimes they'll hang around the pickup and sometimes they get it into their heads to leave and in a few minutes there won't be a bison in sight.

Because the bison associate the truck with food, a few bulls and dry cows approach the truck. Cows with baby calves ease our way as well, but not as close. Every time I try to take a photo of a calf his mother magically slips between the camera and the calf. We do this little dance for more than an hour, but the cows lose concentration a few times and we bag some photos of newborn bison calves, some so new their umbilical cords haven't fallen off. Terry says a newborn calf, once they've sucked, can keep up with the herd, even at a full gallop.

I am struck by how thick and well-muscled the bison calves are compared to beef calves of similar age. I am thinking back to Heidi and Brock's branding last May, and how easy it was for the men and women and kids to throw month-old Angus calves. Even Heidi's little sisters, who didn't weigh as much as some of the calves, had little trouble holding them down when the hot iron bit into the hide. Working these sturdy bison calves would present a whole different level of difficulty. Perhaps in the late 1880s, when Charlie Goodnight and Buffalo Jones and a few others gathered up a handful of the surviving bison, saving the species from certain extinction, a skilled cowboy from that rugged era could have roped and slapped a brand on a bison calf. But I'll bet an even nickel he'd want plenty of able-bodied assistance, like maybe 10 stout guys with an overly developed sense of adventure.

There's a good deal of friendly bison talk going on. Bison communicate with a huffing sound, a cross between a snort and grunt. If they're relaxed and enjoying life, the huffs have a soothing quality, like purring. If they're alarmed or pissed off, the huffs come faster, flavored with considerable tension. Today, even with several vulnerable baby calves way too near strange, possibly threatening creatures, even if they're sitting in a familiar pickup truck, we are soon surrounded by contented huffing.

Sometimes, if the pressures of budget projections and the management of ranch workers become too stressful, Terry jumps in the pickup and drives until he locates some bison. He kicks back, allowing the sights and sounds and smells to fill his eyes and ears and nose. After a couple of hours, time has slowed to a trickle, earth and sky and prehistoric animals nudge Terry into proper alignment and he returns to work refreshed in body and spirit. We believe him, because although we have been sitting in the middle of this herd for nearly an hour, time stopped shortly after we drove up, and any urgency to be someplace else on any other kind of business disappeared immediately thereafter.

I decide sitting on the ground in the middle of a peaceful bison herd would be a rewarding experience. Terry, reading my mind, says bison can appear calm, but can never be fully trusted. He talks about the day he rode his ATV through the herd while checking fences. An old bull, who'd showed no alarm at his approach, charged and pursued him for several miles, coming dangerously close on several occasions. "I'd have never made it on a horse," he says. "The pace would have killed a horse."

A brief comment on the smell of this herd of 2000 bison on a warm spring day: Last November, with animals jammed together in the sturdy working chutes, fear and anger, which often result in involuntary pissing and shitting, translated into a mildish ammonia smell, not nearly as stout in a dairy confinement set up, or Lord help us, an Arkansas poultry barn in mid-July. Today, the warm southern breeze across the backs of the nearest bison carries with it the faint aroma of smoke and dry manure, suggestive of a Plains Indian cooking fire of buffalo chips, the finest fuel on the planet.

An older cow trots past on a mission. She has misplaced her calf, which is hunkered down 50 yards away. She huffs loudly, trots down to the windmill a quarter mile away. The calf remains still, not about to make itself known to potential predators. Five minutes later the cow is back, circling aimlessly, huffing away. A beef calf would probably get up and go to its mother, do some bawling to let its mother know where it is. This little guy stays quiet in the grass. The cow's circling and huffing alarm the other cows with calves. They head east at a fast walk, taking the lost calf and anxious mother cow with them. They disappear over the hill before the two are reunited. I understand why Terry and his employees keep their distance from the herd during calving season. Terry says rutting season in July and August can be flat dangerous for human observers. Bulls knocking each other around, sometimes with fatal results. Everything looks like a rival to a rutting bull, even a cowboy a half mile away mounted on an ATV.

Hard to guess how long it would have taken before Terry needed to be someplace else. Impossible to know because he's too polite to cut the experience short. We say we have places to be, should have left an hour ago. We're going to be late getting to Jim Van Winkle's place near Wood Lake.

Terry takes the same careful path back through the hills. He shows us places where new cross fencing is being installed, where the bison traffic has churned the grass into a sandy beach. The new fence will help put a stop to that. He says how much a pasture is grazed has nothing to do with whether the bison create trails along the fences. He says if we ever observed a cattle pasture we'd see trails along the fences, they'd just be closer to the fences. His bison respect the electric fences, which sometimes shock animals even if they're not in direct contact. Terry says the electricity sometimes arcs several inches. Bison roam around the perimeter fences, no matter how plentiful the grass. It's what they do.

We stop at the windmill near the main road. Terry says we should look in the stock tank. We see nothing but a few strands of tank slime. He complains the little buggers are hiding. Finally a huge goldfish swims into view, then 20 more, some of them large enough to fillet. Terry says he brought in the goldfish to help keep the tanks free of algae. The fish have thrived, reproduced. He has been able to transplant fish to several other stock tanks. Goldfish in a stock tank might not seem notable. However, this is Terry's project, taken on his own initiative. No one at Turner Enterprises sent him a memo directing him to get into the goldfish business. The philosophy of allowing managers broad discretion in managing their ranches makes for contented managers with a sense of ownership, managers who aren't afraid to innovate.

Back at headquarters we visit with Wanda and Terry for a few minutes. She didn't think much of *Call Me Ted*, the recent Turner biography, thought it showed too much distance between Ted and his extended family.

She and Terry, along with all the other ranch managers, attended Ted's 70th birthday bash in Atlanta several years back. Terry is a reluctant flier. According to Wanda, he spent most of the flight bawling like a baby with his head in her lap. We look at Terry and he's laughing, not denying anything. Wanda says she was most upset to learn she had to wear a dress. The managers wore their cowboy best, shirts, boots, hats, but Wanda and the other wives had to wear dresses. She's happy she went, just bitter about having to wear a dress. She said it was a fabulous party at the Atlanta Civic Center. All of the people who'd helped build Ted's companies were represented, ranch managers, executives from CNN and TBS. All of Ted's wives, children and grandchildren attended and, according to Wanda, got along famously. Beau's wife, whom he'd only recently divorced, showed up as well. Wanda was amazed at the cordial interaction between members of the fractured Turner family. I, too, am surprised. I remember hearing a vague rumor of a cordial divorce in some far away country, but have no personal experience.

We take our leave. Terry and Wanda invite us to come back anytime, but maybe not until late August, after rutting season is over and the bulls regain their sanity. When he learns we are headed to Wood Lake to visit Jim Van Winkle, pilot of the plane, who has no memory of me or the crash, Terry shows great concern, asks for details. Clearly he would not jump at the chance of a small plane flight over the Sand Hills.

Wood Lake

I am certain we can find our way cross-country from the Spike Box to Wood Lake, convinced I have done so once before. Within 15 miles we're dead-ended in a ranch driveway watching horses being loaded into three stock trailers. Not wanting to interrupt preparations for a neighborhood branding with ignorant geography questions, we go back to the last ranch we passed, which turns out to be home to the first 14 carat jackass we meet during the entire research project. A life-long resident of Cherry County, he claims to have never heard of Wood Lake, so, of course, has no idea how to get there. He knows Jim Van Winkle, his county commissioner, but has never heard of Wood Lake, feigns utter amazement after I show him the town on the highway map. Any ranch resident over 10 years of age knows how to follow the meandering sand trails to just about any spot in Cherry County. If they don't they'll spend their days driving far out of their way via the few paved roads. But not this jackass, who pretends ignorance of how to haul his smug carcass cross country to Wood Lake, a town of some importance, established as a cattle shipment center on the Chicago and Northwestern Railroad in early 1882. Wood Lake, where Alf McMurtrey tracked down Rat Peters and his gang of horse stealin' bastards. Chances are better than even this jackass's father drove cattle to Wood Lake. I know he knows. And he knows I know he knows. I can tell by the way his eyes grin when he lies.

Already two hours late for our appointment with Jim, not a guy who waits worth a damn, we retrace our route to the highway and travel the long way up through Valentine and southeast on Highway 20 towards Wood Lake. This is the same Highway 20 I traveled in early March, headed for the Cherry County Hospital with a bloodied Jim in the passenger seat.

Today, on the first glorious Saturday in May, we pass a corral surrounded by a large congregation of pickups and horse trailers — a neighborhood rancher's branding day. Looks like a God's plenty of ropers for the amount of cattle. I think Jim may have tired of waiting and driven over to the branding.

Jim and Myki's house sits a quarter mile off the highway on a side hill, commanding an unimpeded view of the entire valley. The crumpled blue and white Piper Super Cub, right landing gear collapsed, lists to one side in the open hanger.

Jim waits for us on the porch, blue jeans crisply ironed and wearing his cowboy boots. I congratulate him on the boots, knowing he's spent the last couple of months condemned to slippers and moccasins. He says it feels good to be wearing his boots. I suspect it does. I also suspect taking off the boots will make his two knees yell for mercy and he will pay not the slightest attention.

Finlay, his usual social self, quickly makes friends with Jim's dog, a herding dog, who naturally herds Finlay under my chair.

Although we've talked on the phone for several hours since the accident, Jim has no memory of meeting me in the flesh. He gives me the once over. I can't tell if he approves.

Jim says he was about to give up on us, drive over to the neighborhood branding, even though he's still too bunged up to be of any earthly use. He talks about all the good help the neighbors provided while he was laid up during the two month calving season. One guy feeding in the mornings, another feeding at night, a retired rancher taking charge of the overnight calf checks. He sees no way to ever repay them, although he will do his best. Then there's, Myki, just in from feeding an orphan calf. Jim says Myki took care of everything else when she wasn't nursing at the hospital.

I remember Myki from the hospital, remember her holding my hand, comforting a complete stranger while she waited as Jim was readied for the emergency flight to Omaha. She was calmer that night than she is today and it crosses my mind we may be interrupting her feeding chores. Kathy follows Myki into the house to brew up some hot coffee.

Jim says he's getting around much better, can drive the pickup, open gates, crawl up in the tractor and move hay. He carries braces in the pickup in case he gets himself into a dicey situation. "I can ride a horse. Sometimes they (the knees) complain, sometimes they don't. I may have the worst knee fixed sometime in the future, then the other one. But I'm not making surgical appointments any time soon." I notice he sits with his left leg locked straight.

Jim has no memories of the crash or of the next three days, nothing until he woke up in the Omaha hospital. Not knowing what caused the crash drives him crazy. Some of my ignorant suppositions clash with his experience, with how he thinks he and the plane would have behaved. He doesn't believe he would have said "I think we're going down" just as we were going down. He says he always takes off headed for a small notch in the hills north of the house, which would conflict with my memory of beginning a slow turn to the west just before things went bad. I am no longer sure of anything, although I have a clear memory of him reaching below his seat just before he said, "I think we're going down."

We go over it again, like we have on the phone a half dozen times. The two of us visiting over coffee in the house before takeoff, hauling the air bubble down to the hanger, taxiing down the soggy runway.

Jim wants to know what I remember about the takeoff. After looking at the photographs I shot from inside the plane he's almost certain which runway he chose. He says he looked up the weather for March 4 and there was little wind.

"Are you sure I said we're going down?" Jim asks. "I can't see me saying something like that." I can only tell him what I remember and tell him not to put much stock in it.

"Do you remember where were we headed?" Most likely to fly over several of the wetlands restoration projects and perhaps the long ungrazed patch of grass on the wildlife refuge Jim said had gone to hell from underuse. I would have been pleased if we'd flown over the McMurtrey Ranch, seen the pasture on the north end where Muriel McMurtrey's father, Frank Hoffman, homesteaded, built that 10 x 12 foot Kinkaider shack, where the grass was sweet and the McMurtrey work horses could be found every spring when it came time to harness them for haying. I would have nagged Jim to fly over the Spike Box, the junction of the North Loup River and Mud Creek, Horseshoe Falls, the spectacularly irregular dunes and soap weed that mark Ted Turner's 800 acre deer preserve, see if the bison had done any serious damage. And then over Mud Lake at the north side of the Spike Box where the Sandhills Project donated materials for a bank stabilization effort. Given enough time and fuel we might even have ventured as far as Sheridan County to the west, flown over the Sandoz orchards on Flora's old place, returned down the narrow ribbon of the Niobrara, seen it dip into steep canyon walls, join the Snake, become a real river. Those are the sights I hoped to see, but what Jim would have shown me is anyone's guess.

"I just can't figure out where we might have been going." I again offer up the possibilities, but he moves on. After two months of trying out different scenarios, Jim has decided a mechanical problem caused the crash. And he has reasons for saying so. He asked some aviation experts not part of the FAA investigation to look over the plane and the crash site. A couple of them think the propeller was coming loose, prompting the decision to land immediately. Jim's son found the propeller a good distance south of the initial impact point. Jim says the flaps were set at "full flap," which confirms my memory of him yanking on the lever on the floor. He says he would only go the full flap route prior to making an emergency landing. The FAA, he says, is not interested in loose propellers or flaps set for emergency landing, did not put those tidbits in their final report, They have suspended his license temporarily after blaming the crash on "pilot error." He believes the investigators made up their minds before they came out to investigate.

Did I mention Jim has made a study of the FAA reports on every Super Cub crash in history? Most of them involve fire afterwards. Not for the first time I decide our luck was phenomenal.

I assure Jim I have never been grumpy with him over the crash, just frustrated I might not be able to work for a while. He understands, says not being able to work has been the hardest thing to tolerate these past two months. I tell Jim the main emotion I feel these days is gratitude we lived to talk about it.

Sitting on Jim's porch two months later, I'm wondering if the coffee maker has broken down. Myki works at that hospital. She should know the name of the bossy nurse who had me strapped to a Hindu nail board. If Myki and Kathy ever show up with hot coffee I will make inquiries.

Jim says Dr. Michele Mulligan-Witt, the definitely not obese, but nonetheless pleasant doctor who expertly supervised our care at the hospital, is a Cherry County native, who returned after medical school. She tore up her knee, maybe during a goat tying competition, Jim's not sure. She's the one who first suggested he be checked by an orthopedic ace in Omaha, a guy who makes a business of fixing other surgeon's mistakes.

The ace Omaha doc told Jim his knee was a mess, that it would never be right without surgery, surgery that should have been done immediately after the crash. That window had passed and it would be better for Jim to go back home, strengthen the muscles around the knee with special exercises, come back for surgery when the knee is stronger. Jim says he's doing the exercises, just not the other stuff, which would mean driving to the hospital every day for physical therapy. Jim says he doesn't care much for hospitals or doctors, that the only reason he ever goes to the doctor is to suffer through the required flight physicals.

Hot coffee. Staff of life. Kathy and Myki join us on the porch. I suspect they might possibly have been exchanging war stories about difficult husband-patients.

Jim talks about attending high school in Valentine, about the understanding shop teacher who allowed him to check his trap lines during school hours. "I've always loved the Sand Hills, working in the hay fields, running the creeks as a kid, hunting and fishing and trapping. I also wanted to eat, to make a living as a trapper. The fur buying business was good to me. I employed a lot of people in several states, traveled, cut a pretty big swath in that business up through the glory years of the 70s before prices declined."

I have more questions, but although he is too polite to say so, I suspect if we left for home Jim can still make an appearance at the branding while all his neighbors are still in attendance. Myki needs to check on the bottle calf and probably a hundred other chores. We collect Finlay from his hiding place under my chair, ease off the porch, promise to stay in touch.

We stop by the hanger on the way out the drive where Jim's forlorn Piper Super Cub lists to one side, awaiting a trip to the junkyard. Kathy thinks Jim and I were lucky guys.

Chapter 20
Grave Dowsing

James Schilling, when he was growing up near Sidney, Nebraska, became friendly with the local undertaker, whose professional duties sometimes required him to bury a body in the cemetery of a country church. Burial records for rural cemeteries are often spotty and the location of early graves, which might have been marked by transitory wooden markers, cannot easily be retrieved from the community's memory. To avoid planting someone on top of a pre-existing burial, the undertaker used dowsing rods to determine unpopulated areas of the cemetery. He taught young James how to use the rods.

Ten years ago when we read about the Sidney Historical Society's restoration of the old Ft. Sidney cemetery and the employment of a magnetic imaging machine to locate unmarked graves, we contacted James. James said the magnetic imaging machine located graves in exactly the same places where he and his fellow workers had previously dowsed graves and marked them with flags. He volunteered to show us his techniques. Which is why Kathy and I found ourselves trudging around the old Ft. Sidney cemetery long after dark holding bent welding rods.

In the years since we've come to appreciate James' consummate skill. Do you need to find a grave? Just point him in the general direction. Do you want to know if the person in the grave is male or female? He can tell you. He can also tell you if the grave is that of an infant or an adult. If you have a headstone indicating the sex of the inmate, blindfold James and he'll come up with the correct sex. I have no idea why he can do this. There is no scientific basis. You can research the subject until your eyes bleed and not come up with any persuasive explanation. All I know is for James Schilling, and sometimes others, it works.

Over the past 10 years we have located thousands of graves and have gained some confidence in our abilities. Most of the hundreds of people we've taught to dowse caught on quickly, although an occasional complete dunderhead has proven stubbornly incapable. It's always a good idea, if feasible, to leave the dunderheads at home.

One notable dowsing failure occurred at the site of the Beecher Island fight on the Arikaree River in Northeastern Colorado, which given the large number of casualties, should have been a gold mine. The numerous underground springs under the island so interfered with our readings as to make the job impossible. Dowsing the bottoms along Blue Water Creek in Garden County, Nebraska, proved frustrating for the same reason. Other expeditions, as when we were asked to locate six family graves on an abandoned Colorado homestead in Gunnison County, worked out much better.

Cemeteries near frontier boom towns, be they cow towns or mining camps, usually have sections of marked graves and much larger sections composed of unmarked graves. Additional unmarked graves can typically be found outside the cemetery boundaries. These graves belong to those considered unfit for burial next to more proper folk. We're talking about prostitutes, gamblers, horse thieves, Blacks, Mexicans, Chinese, Indians. Prostitutes, who died like flies on the frontier from tuberculosis, venereal disease, alcohol, drugs and violence, were wrapped in a sheet and buried in a furtively dug hole, most commonly in the dead of night. Ad hoc burial parties seldom observed the custom of facing the corpse towards the east, which is why these outside-of-boundary unmarked graves seldom adhere to the normal cemetery spacings and graves face in completely random directions.

Arriving at a frontier cemetery and locating the boundaries is just the first step. We find the "energy" levels to be higher near graves belonging to those who lived interesting lives or died under painful circumstances. The Ft. Sidney Cemetery includes the graves of two unfortunates who were lynched with barbed wire and hung from lamp posts. Walk near those graves with a loose grip on your dowsing rods and interesting things will likely happen. Hold your rods over the outside-the-fence grave of a young prostitute at the Iron City Cemetery near the ghost mining town of St. Elmo, Colorado, and they'll spin like helicopter blades.

Energy can dissipate over time. A burial chamber in the bowels of an 800-year-old Spanish castle might yield nothing of interest. We've tried a few times and failed to raise a pulse. In the near future we hope to dowse Anasazi ruins in the American Southwest dating to the mid-1200s when internecine violence and cannibalism were rampant. Stay tuned.

Even though locating graves with dowsing rods has no scientific basis, thanks to James Schilling the rods have been useful tools for us and we seldom leave home without them. You're on your own.

Chapter 21
Mormon Cows and the Battle of Blue Water

It will be an expensive cow.
— Senator Sam Houston- speech to the
United States Senate January 31, 1855

Mid-April. Finlay and I are tooling along Highway 26 west of Lake McConaughy looking through the windshield at a steady drizzle. The windshield wipers, as always, annoy Finlay. He growls his most ferocious growl, tries to bite them through the glass. The fact that he's never once successfully bitten a wiper through the windshield does not discourage him. Sere pastures grazed short during last summer's drought show a hint of mint green, which encouraged by the rain, seems to be spreading as we drive.

Today's mission, scouting the site of the Battle of Blue Water, promises to be a damp one. No doubt Finlay will be a filthy mess before we're finished. The highway turns sharply north, taking us down past Windlass Hill and into Ash Hollow, the preferred camping place of various Plains cultures for 9,000 years and for weary California-Oregon Trail travelers.

Windlass Hill still bears the scars of the iron shod wheels of wagons being lowered into the valley. No surviving Oregon Trail diaries mention a permanent windlass, but some list a number of temporary creative thingamajigs constructed on the spot. Pilgrims employed ropes attached to sturdy humans, some used teams of horses or oxen and a block and tackle, some locked up their wheels and slid down the precipitous grade.

Once the wagons made it safely to the valley floor the emigrants usually camped, taking advantage of the abundant pure spring water for man and beast and the numerous ash trees for firewood. The ash trees didn't last long and the hardier cedar soon became the main source of fuel for travelers. Heavy repeat usage of the same camp sites meant the ever present threat of deadly cholera.

Finlay scampers up Windlass Hill along the steep concrete walkway, sniffing the roots of soap weed and cedar trees for burrowing critters. With luck, the prairie rattlers who love to sun themselves on the sandstone* ledges of Windlass Hill are hiding from the chilling rain far underground. Finlay's undercarriage is soon decorated with viscous clay mud balls. He'll be sitting on a tarp going home.

The wagon trail stretches far to the southeast horizon but does not continue to the bottom of Windlass Hill. The road where the iron shod wheels creaked down the steep grade gradually eroded into a V-shaped gully, 20 feet deep in places. How many thousand wagons made this track? Not counting the significant traffic by early fur traders and other adventurers, an estimated 500,000 people, some on horseback, traveled this section of the California-Oregon Trail during its glory years (1846-1869). Three people per wagon would add up to around 166,000 wagons creaking over the rocks down to Ash Hollow.

---

* Mostly made up of grains of volcanic ash originating in Northern Nevada and Southern Utah.

The flat area near the bottom of Windlass Hill houses an unknown number of pioneer graves. In 1853 passing travelers told of a row of 20 crude wooden markers near the foot of Windlass Hill, graves from a single cholera outbreak. It only takes a few minutes with the dowsing sticks to locate more than 50 graves, the majority of them female, surely one of the more deadly spots along the Oregon Trail.

Perched on a hillside, Ash Hollow Cemetery overlooks a stretch of the Ash Hollow Creek and the treed ridge beyond. While Finlay waters my already wet tires, I stroll between widely scattered cedar trees and a grand variety of tombstones. For a cemetery buff this cemetery has everything you could want — burials from the current year, graves going back to late 19th century when the area was being settled, graves of pioneers from the Oregon Trail era. It also has an active cemetery preservation society keeping up the place. Metal plaques erected by the Oregon-California Trail Association tell the stories of a handful the older inmates who lost their lives on the way west.

Pioneer cemeteries usually contain as many unmarked graves as those with tombstones. Often these graves can be found outside the cemetery's boundaries. In the case of Ash Hollow, graves are scattered all the way up the sheltering ridge to the top and beyond. It would take several days with dowsing rods and wire flags to do a full survey. A crew with a magnetic imaging machine could go nuts.

Atop a long ridge across Ash Creek valley from the cemetery sits the headquarters and museum of Ash Hollow Historic Park. At the end of a winding path out of sight behind the museum is the entrance to Ash Hollow Cave. The cave and generous spring hosted not only native peoples, but mountain men and other travelers on their way west. Archeologists painstakingly dissected the cave floor, revealing several layers of debris identifying occupiers from four distinct plains cultures spanning at least 3000 years. A nearby excavated bison kill site contained bones of bison one and a half times larger than modern bison and spear points and hide scrapers dating back 6000 to 9000 years. The earliest identified visitors to the cave were members of the Early Archaic Tradition (1000 B.C. - A.D. 500), followed by the Woodland Tradition (A.D. 0-1100), the Central Plains Tradition (A.D. 900-1450), and the Apache, commonly known as the Dismal River Culture (A.D. 1675-1725). Scholars believe some members of the Dismal River culture, under pressure from the Comanche, eventually migrated south to become part of what became the modern Apache.

Exploring historic cemeteries always serves as a reminder of the honest and forthright names parents of long ago applied to their offspring. No confusing, wispy, androgynous names like Willow, London, Cheyenne, August or Brinkley. Willow? What in blazes are those parents thinking? Will the next generation produce a Willow, Jr.? And the next generation a Willow, III? Take a walk through any pioneer cemetery and you'll find the joint overflowing with solid, family sourced names.

I come across a grave from the Oregon Trail era belonging to Rachel Parrison, an unlucky 18-year-old bride who contracted cholera the morning of June 19, 1849, and died that same night. Rachel Parrison. Good name. Solid name. Unlucky name.

Charlotte Lucy Archer Gilliard. Born 40 miles east of Buffalo, New York, in 1833. Married, had children, two of which died in infancy, expired in 1934 at 101 years of age. Charlotte Lucy Archer Gilliard. Can't get any more straight forward than that.

According to the history lesson on a handsome metal plaque, somewhere near here lies J. C. Keeran, cholera victim, and one Sanford Johnson, a wildly optimistic 26-year-old on his way to the California gold fields when smallpox killed him deader than a hammer. May the 26th, 1850. Sanford Johnson. Good name. Honest name.

Determining burial locations in a pioneer cemetery is at best an inexact science. Records may be skimpy to nonexistent. Wooden markers rot and disappear. Headstones fall down and are not always put back where they belong. In the space reserved for Johnson and Keeran and one other unknown person I found not a single male grave, although there were at least three female graves.

A lichen-covered upright stone marks the grave of Pearl Caroline Brown West, 23-year-old woman, who joined the choir in 1910, leaving a husband and unnumbered 'motherless little ones' behind. Pearl. My grandmother Pearl May Black Jones, born in 1886, a year before Pearl Caroline Brown West, also answered to that honest name. She fed hungry grandsons as many slabs of excellent vinegar pie as they would eat. Pearl. Good name. Honest name. Good pie.

Cheyenne. Brinkley. Willow. Makes my head hurt.

In 1854 W. M. F. Magraw erected a trading post and U.S. Mail station in Ash Hollow, which served as a way station on the mail route to Salt Lake City, and stocked trade items for a flourishing business with both Indians and emigrants.

This is where one of the dimmer bulbs in US military history makes his quick entrance and exit.

Grattan Fight

Speaking of dim bulbs, Lt. John Lawrence Grattan, whose honest name may have been his only redeeming quality, graduated near the bottom of his West Point class, after being held back for a year due to miserable grades. A peacetime army had little enthusiasm for a freshly minted officer of such low distinction and he eventually found his way to Ft. Laramie, where he assumed the tenuous position of supernumerary-in-waiting for a vacancy in the regiment. The presence on the North Platte River, a few miles to the east, of thousands of hungry Indians waiting for their promised treaty annuities, served as a constant reminder to the Indian-hating Grattan of the glory he might earn if given half a chance. Meanwhile, he impatiently twiddled his thumbs and thought dark thoughts.

A skeletal, suicidal cow, the unwitting answer to Grattan's bloodthirsty prayers, wandered away from the safety of a Mormon emigrant train and made a beeline into the nearby Brule (Lakota) encampment of Conquering Bear, anointed in 1851 by US representatives without input from his peers, as supreme chief grand poobah of the Brule. High Forehead, a hard-headed visiting member of Minneconjou (Lakota) band, promptly shot the cow. The perpetually hungry Brule, who had waited months for their treaty annuities, were not about to look a gift cow in the mouth. They ignored protruding rib bones and outward indications of chewy livers and promptly ate the entirety of said cow. That, except for the subsequent case of mass indigestion, should have been that.

A whiny-assed pilgrim showing up at Ft. Laramie demanding justice, would, in the normal course of events, have made his complaint to John Whitfield, a seasoned Indian agent. A bureaucrat's bureaucrat, Whitfield would have likely followed the terms of the Horse Creek Treaty of 1851 and either suggested the complainant buck up and get on down the road or made the appropriate investigative noises and promised equitable reimbursement if and when the pilgrim's hysterical story turned out to hold water. Unfortunately, Agent Whitfield was not in residence, having not yet arrived to assume the position. Commanding officer Major O. F. Winship was also out of town on a fort inspection expedition, leaving the case of the devoured cow to be taken up by Lt. Hugh Fleming. Fleming, whose impetuousness nearly cost him his scalp the previous year, could only be regarded as experienced and level-headed when compared to the slobbering Grattan.

Conquering Bear scurried up to the fort to plead his case. He assumed the treaty would be followed and he would be allowed pay off the cow with a horse from his own herd or a cow subtracted from his long awaited treaty annuity. Failing that, he was within his rights when he asked Fleming to wait until the Indian agent arrived to sort things out. Meanwhile, the aggrieved Mormon kept up his whining, insistent on payment of $25 for a cow that likely would not have brought 50 cents at any livestock market in the country.

After some friendly palaver, and just when negotiations were at their most promising, Fleming suddenly turned hostile. Auguste Lucien, the whisky-soaked interpreter long distrusted by the Lakota, twisted the words of both men, resulting in Fleming's imperious demand High Forehead be turned over for punishment. High Forehead was an honored guest of the Brule and, as a Minneconjou, not under Conquering Bear's jurisdiction. The talks broke down and a dispirited Conquering Bear returned to his village expecting a detachment of pissed off soldiers would be arriving on the morrow looking for High Forehead.

Lt. Grattan immediately proposed himself as just the guy to take charge of High Forehead's arrest. Fleming, who should have known better, but angered by Lucien's lies, said "sic 'em, boy."

A half-hearted debate that evening in the Oglala camp about sending the trouble-making Minneconjou on his way ended when nobody had guts enough to volunteer to run him out. Young Crazy Horse, then known as Curly, who had been hanging out with his Uncle Spotted Tail's people, was about to learn an important lesson about trusting white soldiers.

The next morning the supremely confident Lt. Grattan led 29 men of the 6th Infantry and one drunken interpreter out of the fort and eight miles down the river to Conquering Bear's camp. They stopped along the way to load their weapons and two mule drawn artillery pieces.

All the nearby encampments, Minneconjou, Brule, Oglala, containing nearly 5000 men, women and children, were on high alert. Had he known, Grattan wouldn't have much cared, assuming in his puffed up pea-brain that he, 29 members of the United States army and one drunk interpreter were more than a match for 1500 adult Sioux warriors.

A less obtuse officer might have talked with Conquering Bear outside the camp, but Grattan chose to march straight for Conquering Bear's lodge at the very center, making escape virtually impossible if things went wrong. Once again, Conquering Bear tried negotiation. Once again Grattan demanded High Forehead. When consulted, High Forehead emphatically declined the invitation. A sodden Lucien did his part, hurling gratuitous insults at the surrounding warriors, calling them women and bragging they would all soon be dead. Meanwhile, his provocative mistranslations made a peaceful resolution impossible.

In the resulting communication breakdown, one of Grattan's men shot Conquering Bear's brother. Conquering Bear tried to hold back the warriors, thinking the situation could still be salvaged. Grattan ordered his men to fire. Conquering Bear went down. Grattan's artillery blasted the tops off a few tipis before he was chopped to pieces. Trader Jim Bordeaux, who led the burial party, identified what was left of Grattan's body by his watch. Lucien ran for it but was caught and butchered, along with 11 soldiers. The surviving 18 infantrymen jumped on the caissons and into the lone wagon and drove the mules hell-bent for the fort. Legendary Oglala warrior Red Cloud, Curly's Brule uncle Spotted Tail and a large body of Lakota warriors, rode them down and rubbed them out, all except for one badly wounded soldier, his tongue amputated and suffering a slit belly, who somehow made it back to the fort before he expired.

Thirty-one to two, a thumping so lop-sided even a dimbulb like Grattan might have acknowledged it.

The enraged Lakota headed straight for the trading posts of Bordeaux and the American Fur Company where the promised treaty supplies were being kept in storage against the day Agent Whitfield arrived and took charge of distribution. By the next morning every last blanket, bag of sugar and head of livestock owned by the traders was headed north with the fleeing bands of Oglala, Minneconjou and Brule.

For the next year, small groups of warriors launched attacks from their northern sanctuaries on the California-Oregon Trail. The killing of three men and wounding another during the robbery of a mail stage of mules and $10,500 in gold caused the most consternation. They also burned W. M. F. Magraw's post office/trading post in Ash Hollow in April of 1855, causing $2000 worth of damage to the building, corrals and hay stacks. The postal service, never an outfit known for a sense of humor, was not amused, nor was Jefferson Davis, Secretary of War, who was keeping a meticulous count of Sioux misdeeds.

Ft. Laramie commander Major Winship, once he returned to his post, sent ass-covering letters to Jeff Davis exonerating Fleming, Grattan and, by the way, himself and blaming the whole business on the treacherous ingrate Conquering Bear. Agent Whitfield's messages to Washington alternately criticized Grattan or blamed the Sioux, depending on his mood. Winship's official military version naturally carried the most weight, especially with Jeff Davis and President Franklin Pierce. Eastern newspaper reports echoed Winship's fabrications, referring to the boondoggle as a massacre and glorifying the martyred dimbulb Grattan. Noisy editorials braying for revenge enjoyed wide circulation.

General William S. Harney

Urged on by a rabid public, Jeff Davis and Franklin Pierce decided to punish, not only the Indians who'd done bad things, but the entire Sioux nation. Davis, who desired an expanded military, saw a war on the Sioux as the ticket to increased Congressional funding. Gen. Harney, urgently recalled from a snail-eating expedition in France, was chosen for the task.

The irascible Harney, who learned his trade fighting Indians under Andrew Jackson's command, certainly had his quirks*, but he was everyone's #1 choice to wage total war on the incorrigible Sioux.

---

* A civilian court charged Harney with bludgeoning a female slave to death and he was accused more than once of raping young Indian girls at night and hanging them the next morning. During the Mexican War he oversaw the execution of 30 members of the San Patricio Battalion, immigrant Irish Catholic deserters who'd allied with the Mexican army. Harney ordered deserter Francis O'Connor, who'd had his legs amputated the day before, to the scaffold saying "Bring the damned son of a bitch out! My order was to hang 30 and by God I'll do it."

Once he returned from France and received his orders, Harney wasted no time assembling the 600 men of his command. The men who traveled overland from Ft. Leavenworth to Ft. Kearny on the Platte suffered several deaths due to cholera, which broke out at Ft. Leavenworth just as they were leaving. After the entire expedition assembled at Ft. Kearny, Harney pushed them on a rapid, hot, dry march to the confluence of Ash Hollow Creek and the North Platte River. Harney sited the camp in an ideal spot on the flat flood plain below a high ridge under a generous spring. According to some accounts troops, using information supplied by scouts, hiked up the ridge with telescopes to locate Little Thunder's (Conquering Bear's successor) Brule village some seven miles to the northwest up Blue Water Creek. Warriors from Little Thunder's band had been harassing travelers on the Oregon-California Trail. Scouts reported the presence of parties guilty of rubbing out Grattan's command and other misdeeds. Harney could not have been presented with a more inviting target for his initial foray against the Sioux.

By the time Finlay and I trudged up the steep ridge above Harney's camp site, less than a mile northwest of the Ash Hollow Cemetery, the rain had stopped and a brisk wind was drying things out. Finlay's abundant crop of clay dingleberries promptly went into concrete mode.

Let me stipulate even high power binoculars are not military telescopes. I will also stipulate my eyes are not what they were 60 years ago. But if Harney's men spotted Little Thunder's village from this ridge, nestled as it was in the bottom of Blue Water Creek valley seven miles away, hidden from view behind the bordering hills, their eyesight must have been extraordinary. Perhaps on that particular day, due to the ambitious on-going jerky drying operation, gobs of tell-tale smoke floated high above the tipis. Lt. Gouverneur Kemble Warren* stated military observers counted the tipis. Impossible to know.

In the wee hours of September 3, 1855, after a paint-blistering, profanity-laced pep talk, Harney sent his dragoons and horse artillery splashing across the North Platte on a 12 mile flanking maneuver, guided by veteran fur trapper Joe Teason, who positioned them on the east side of Blue Water Creek high above an 11 lodge Oglala camp and Little Thunder's larger Brule village. Harney planned to use his infantry to attack the Sioux from below, driving them into a deadly trap. This military tactic was by no means an invention of Harney's, but the success of the strategy in the Battle of Blue Water made an impression, particularly on George Armstrong Custer. Custer would employ identical tactics in his "victory" against Black Kettle's peaceful Southern Cheyennes on the Washita and in his less successful efforts at the Little Big Horn.

As Harney's infantry, making no effort at concealment, marched up Blue Water Creek from the south, Little Thunder's people became alarmed and began packing to flee. Why they hadn't left earlier when they received word of the approaching army might be explained by

---

* The cerebral Lt. G. K. Warren, called Little Chief by the Sioux because of his diminutive stature, graduated from West Point second in his class and saw his first combat at Ash Hollow as head of a small detachment of engineers. A gifted cartographer and inspiration for Nebraska geographer and cartographer C. B. McIntosh, he later surveyed sections of the Nebraska Sand Hills and produced the first comprehensive map of the United States west of the Mississippi, which enabled railroad engineers to plot the transcontinental railroad. Warren's statue stands at the base of Little Round Top on the Gettysburg battlefield because of his quick action seizing the strategically vital Little Round Top, preventing Confederate artillery from commanding a clear field of fire above Union positions. Known thereafter as "The Savior of Little Round Top," Warren's decisive maneuver changed the outcome of the battle and perhaps the war. Towards the end of the war he was relieved of duty by Gen. Phil Sheridan, who detested him for being overly concerned with the welfare of his troops. He battled for years to clear his name. He died in Newport, Rhode Island, in 1882. His last words: "The flag! The flag!" Three months later a special court of inquiry, after hearing a hundred witnesses, completely exonerated Warren.

the incomplete jerky drying operation, necessitated by a recent successful buffalo hunt. Plains Indian tipis, made from multiple buffalo hides, usually weighed in excess of 250 pounds. Moving them was no small matter. In addition, because the whites had not inflicted military retribution for the Grattan fight the year before, Little Thunder and many others assumed none was coming, in spite of numerous advance warnings from friendly traders. After all, it was dimbulb Grattan who attacked and shot down Conquering Bear for no good reason.

After scouts delivered an invitation from Harney, Little Thunder, Spotted Tail and other leaders rode across the creek to the east to parley with Harney. Harney dismissed their groveling excuses and promises to behave, announcing his intention to attack immediately. At this point Little Thunder finally grasped his predicament. To give the women more time to pack and disappear up the valley, Little Thunder and Spotted Tail returned to the village, scrounged up a white flag and headed back east over the creek. Harney dismounted and walked out to meet them. Little Thunder stood 6 feet 6 inches tall and was an intimidating-looking guy even when he wasn't mounted on a war pony galloping straight at Harney. Little Thunder slid his horse to a dramatic stop, dismounted and offered Harney his hand. Harney refused the offered hand, said he wasn't there for talk, demanded Little Thunder turn over the people responsible for killing the idiot Grattan and his men, also the mail coach robber/murderers and, by the way, the miscreants who'd burned Magraw's Ash Hollow mail station over there just across the river. At this point Little Thunder could have surrendered his entire band of Brules and thrown in some spare visiting Oglalas for effect and it would not have altered Harney's plan to attack. Little Thunder offered excuses. Spotted Tail, guilty of every charge in the indictment, boogied. Little Thunder followed him. Hostilities began shortly after.

By the time the infantry crossed the creek and reached the village, the Brule lodges were largely dismantled and hauled far up the valley. Harney drove straight up the west side of the meandering creek, detaching two units to pursue the Sioux up narrow ravines to the west. They soon encountered warriors, well protected by overhanging ledges, sending musket balls and arrows down on them. Even so, the infantry, largely made up of raw recruits, sustained no casualties during the battle, lack of experience apparently no impediment to self-preservation.

When Phillip St. George Cooke[*] heard firing from below he launched his cavalry attack, driving the desperate Brule and Oglala back towards Harney's approaching infantry. The Sioux tried escaping up narrow ravines past steep sandstone cliffs to the open country to the west, but Cooke's men cut them off. Huddled under sandstone ledges and in a few shallow caves, the Sioux took terrific fire from Cooke's men above and below. Long range fire from rifled muskets and exploding cannon balls turned their refuges into charnel houses. Lt. Warren, an engineer attached to Cooke's dragoons, later wrote, "The sight was heart-rending. Near one of the holes, five men, seven women and three children were killed and several wounded."

As their position under the ledges became untenable the Sioux abandoned many of their dead and wounded and ran down and across Blue Water Creek, suffering horrific casualties while braving withering fire from Harney's infantry and elements of Cooke's command which took positions parallel to the escape route. The Sioux slipped through a slough and up

---

[*] Phillip St. George Cooke (terrific name), sometimes called the father of the U.S. Cavalry, had a long and distinguished military career, serving in both the Mexican and Civil Wars. Early in the Civil War his revisions of Union army cavalry tactics, once adopted, permanently changed the way cavalry forces were used in battle. He has been overshadowed by his more famous son-in-law, dashing Confederate cavalry commander J. E. B. Stuart.

a deep gully, before scattering like quail into the trackless sand dunes to the east. Mounted cavalry followed, slashing the running women and children and a few older men with their sabers. Most Sioux lucky enough to be mounted on ponies fought delaying actions and escaped to regroup at a favored lake far to the northeast. Among the survivors were Spotted Tail, with two saber wounds and two pistol shots through his body, and a badly wounded Little Thunder. In the fight, Spotted Tail lost one wife, a daughter and almost all of his female relation.

Cooke's cavalry, led by Captain Henry Heth,* soon lost contact with their quarry.

Heth's failure to properly position his command to block the Sioux breakout into the dunes earned him considerable scorn from his fellow officers. Harney, however, had a soft spot for Heth and ignored his bolloxed command decisions in the official report.

Harney's buglers summoned them back to Blue Creek for mop up duty. In the confusion, Heth was briefly presumed dead. His premature obituary appeared in newspapers around the country attributing his death to six Sioux arrows. He was reportedly pleased by all the flattering things said about him.

After the fighting ended, soldiers counted 86 dead Sioux and almost as many wounded. Cooke claimed credit for killing 74 Indians and taking 43 captives. The dead Sioux were left for the wolves. Harney's men collected 70 prisoners, all women and children. The wounded were treated for their injuries and all captives taken east to Ft. Kearny. The cavalry suffered four dead, one MIA and seven wounded, four mortally. Most of the trooper casualties were incurred by Captain William Steele's command during the headlong chase into the Sand Hills. Diversionary skirmishes with mounted Indians were no picnic. Harney had the dead soldiers buried without markers near a temporary encampment along the Platte at the mouth of Blue Water Creek.

Troops scoured the battlefield, littered with dead Sioux, most of them women. Not for nothing was General Harney known afterwards as "Woman Killer" Harney. Dead ponies and mules, already bloated and stinking, lined the creek and the escape route to the east. Some soldiers loaded up tipi poles, buffalo robes, fresh jerky and trade goods and hauled them back to camp.

Harney assigned others to discover evidence of past depredations against the whites. They unearthed letters from Spotted Tail's mail coach ambush and assorted bits of army uniforms and bayonets assumed to be from the Grattan fight. Captain B. S. Todd, a cousin to Mary Todd Lincoln, described the recovery of "three tresses of different colors, the scalps of white women murdered on the plains." This 'evidence' was not, of course, subjected to DNA testing. The scalps could have been male, female or none of the above.

Lt. Warren, always a prescient kind of guy, gathered an assortment of nearly a hundred items, including leggings, buffalo robes, beaded dresses and moccasins and shipped them to the Smithsonian Institution in Washington, D. C.

Harney later assigned Lt. Warren to build a 100' x 100' sod fort with walls three feet thick and six feet high near the mouth of Ash Hollow Creek and named it Ft. Grattan, giving lie to the general impression Harney lacked a sense of humor. After the troops stacked some of the appropriated Sioux goods inside, Harney left a small detail to guard the stash and protect

___

* Speaking of dimbulbs, Heth graduated last in the West Point class in 1847. After an unremarkable career on the western frontier, unless you consider becoming hopelessly lost and declared dead remarkable, he joined the Confederate Army where his career could be described as uneven. He was blamed for prematurely starting the Battle of Gettysburg by taking his men into the village of Gettysburg to shop for shoes, alerting nearby Union troops of their presence.

westward travelers. Meanwhile, along Blue Water Creek, troopers piled and burned the remaining tipis, parfleches of fresh jerky, buffalo robes and bloody clothing. The Sioux would have to find another buffalo herd if they were going to eat during the approaching winter.

In 1908, Robert Harvey, chairman of the Nebraska Historical Society's Committee on Historic Sites, began corresponding with General Richard Drum, a Lieutenant in the 4th Artillery at Blue Water. Harvey hoped to learn more about the location of the battlefield and probe Drum's memories for possible atrocities committed against the Sioux during and after the fight. According to Drum, he never saw no stinking atrocities. Harney's soldiers bent over backwards to avoid harming women and children. During the fight when troopers were pouring rifle fire and cannon balls into the Sioux huddled under the ledges "an officer heard the piecing cry of a child and ordered a ceasefire." Drum, by saying "we captured all the women and children" does not concede a single woman or child was killed, although he described women and children who were severely wounded.

By 1908, public opinion had become critical of military campaigns against the Indians. Helen Hunt Jackson's popular *Century of Dishonor* (1881) increased awareness of atrocities committed during and after the Indian Wars. Rampaging prohibitionists and women suffragettes took up the cause. Drum's amnesia concerning the slaughter of women and children during the fight is understandable.

The next year, Harvey contacted General N. A. M. Dudley, nicknamed "The Great American Dudley" by his peers. After the battle, Dudley, a heavy drinker, found himself assigned to a wide variety of sleepy frontier posts. Captain Albert Tracy, who served with Dudley in Utah, was not a fan.

This man has not the slightest conception that he is an ass, and inasmuch as to brain him with a mortar would have no effect to convince him, he will go through life as composedly cheerful as if he were not an ass.

Dudley's extensive correspondence with Harvey revealed no questionable behavior on the part of the troopers. "I repeat, I saw not a single instance of what could be called brutality during the engagement," although he conceded, unlike Drum, "that many squaws were killed and some children... it could not be avoided. They were all huddled together in groups, made no signs of surrender."

However, Dudley took advantage of his role as battle historian to tell tall tales about assuming command of Company E of the Mounted 10th Infantry and directing a masterful, heroic pursuit of the fleeing Sioux for "10 or 12 miles" into the sand dunes. He also took credit for personally escorting the 70 prisoners to Ft. Laramie. (Harney reported the prisoners were taken to Ft. Kearny.)

Like the man said, an ass.

Soldiers who committed their memories of the fight to paper felt Harney's actions were fully justified. This included the soft-hearted Lt. Warren, who labored far into the night after the battle rescuing wounded Sioux women and children. However, the magnitude of the destruction had a sobering effect, especially on the vast majority of Harney's command new to combat. Not a single male Sioux was taken prisoner. Although overall Sioux losses were hard to estimate, given the Indians retrieval of unknown numbers of dead and wounded, Indian casualties almost certainly ran above 60 percent.

By the time Harney's victorious troops set out for Ft. Laramie a few days later any lingering remorse had been replaced by jubilation. As they marched they sang a little made up ditty:

We did not make a blunder
When we rubbed out Little Thunder
And sent him to the other
side of Jordan
On Blue Water Creek

The Battle of Blue Water, a decisive victory for the implacable Harney, dramatically changed the course of the 19th Century Indian Wars on the plains. Harney's wholesale destruction of food and shelter was not an entirely new tactic, but coupled with the significant casualties his troops inflicted on women and children Harney raised the stakes for any Indians thinking of tangling with the army. The earlier strategy of protracted negotiations, patience and retreat gave way to cooperation and abject surrender by some bands and increased hostility and a new found resolve by Red Cloud and Crazy Horse among others to repel the invader at any cost. Blue Water demonstrated to the losers ancient, smooth bore trader muskets were no match for the rifled army muskets firing Minié balls. During the Civil War, when the army was occupied elsewhere, hostile bands regrouped and re-armed. While a steady stream of tribal sub-groups signed treaties and entered reservation life, newly militant bands of Sioux and Cheyenne took part in Red Cloud's War (1866-1868) and the rubbing out of Custer's men on the Little Big Horn (1876). Those victories were, of course, transient, but Blue Water supplied the Indians with strong motivation to roll the dice.

Finlay and I have moved down from the cemetery to the mouth of Ash Hollow Creek and, expecting at any moment to be shot for trespassing, spend fruitless hours searching for any trace of the unfortunately named Ft. Grattan. Perhaps if the fort had been composed of sterner materials.

We drive to a gas station on the east edge of Lewellen where the barely warm, murky coffee tastes of evil and is filmed over with bitter varnish. The cash register guy, chewing on a soggy Swisher Sweet seegar, studies a semi driver filling his tanks at the gas pump. The cash register guy is transfixed by the large numbers adding up on his gas pump monitor. With diesel prices at an all-time record he's looking at totals he's never seen in his life.

Has he ever visited the Blue Water battlefield?

He's heard of a big monument west of town where "all the Indians were killed," but he's never seen it and probably never will.

The classy silver-on-black Nebraska Historical Society marker for the Battle of Blue Water, posted right smack beside the highway, is hard to miss. We backtrack to a well-graveled county road and head north up the east side of Blue Water Creek, passing ranch buildings and corrals built on the flood plain next to narrow alfalfa fields ribboning up the creek and a few irrigated fields littered with last season's corn stalks.

The road crosses the creek and continues north. Sandstone ledges, which would mark the site of the fiercest fighting, remain out of sight to the east. I am uncertain if we should trespass on private property.

A slender older gentleman wearing faded Wrangler jeans and a battered cowboy hat is digging a post hole in the soft sand beside the road. He has the stiff, slightly stooped gait of a man familiar with a horse and saddle. I introduce myself, tell him I'm interested in seeing where the Indians hid under ledges. Some accounts mention caves as well. He is curious, but distant. He pointedly does not introduce himself.

"They call it the Battle of Blue Water. That was no battle. It was a pure massacre. I moved here in the 1939 when I was 10 years old. The government bought our farm, which now lies under Lake McConaughy. Dad used the money to buy this place. I've ridden the creek since I was a kid. Plenty of ledges, plenty of rattlesnakes, but I've never seen a cave. There are no caves. Whoever told you that was wrong. I own some of that. If you come back on a day when I don't have fence to fix I'll show you around. No caves." And no permission to explore his property on my own.

Is Turner's bison ranch much farther up the creek?

"You're only a couple of miles south. You'll notice the unusual fencing even if you don't see any buffalo. Turner came driving down this road just after I'd killed a rattlesnake. Told me I didn't have any business killing rattlesnakes. Said rattlesnakes were part of the balance of nature. Balance of nature my ass.

"You probably heard why he lost out on the Eldred Ranch? No? Big ranch (133,000 acres) up there near the refuge (Crescent Lake Wildlife Refuge). George Eldred was a legend around here. Herded cattle with a helicopter and used horses long after most ranchers went mostly to ATVs. The sugar sand is too fine on his place. ATVs get stuck tighter than Dick's hat band.

"Eldred's kids weren't interested in the ranch. He thought about giving it to the Catholic Church, but the kids talked him out of it. Turner showed up one day out of the blue. Eldred hadn't even listed the place. They talked price around the kitchen table. Turner thought he could offer cash and get a cheap deal. Eldred said Turner should look at a set of newer corrals a few miles away before making a final offer. Turner said he and his men had already seen those corrals when they were checking out the ranch a few days ago and he wasn't too impressed. Of course, Eldred was surprised Turner had trespassed on his ranch. He ordered Turner off the place. Some people say he stuck a hog leg Colt under Turner's nose.

"A few months later Eldred sold the place to the Mormons. They paid him what it was worth."

Do Mormons make good neighbors?

"Yup. They trade work and generally mind their own business. Unlike Ted Turner, they seem to know what they're doing."

The light drizzle turns into a steady rain. I'm thinking of minding my own business instead of slopping around snake-infested battlefields. The rancher trots over to his pickup, pitches the post hole digger in back, drives south. Finlay and I head north through Turner's

Blue Creek ranch. Telltale high tensile electric fences line the road. A few contented bison graze the lush grass along the creek bottom. They are shedding. Gobs of matted mouse-brown hair hang from their humps and sides. Finlay turns his attention from the annoying windshield wipers to the bison. He growls, but not loud enough to attract attention.

A few miles north and west we pass cowboys wearing yellow rain slickers sorting cattle on the former Eldred Ranch, now called the Rex Ranch. Three are mounted on well-muscled bay quarter horses. A half-drowned youngster rides drag astride an ATV. Must not have received the memo on sugar sand. Cross-bred Mormon cows, unlike the suicidal skeleton who wandered into Conquering Bear's camp, are sleek and well-fleshed. Not a protruding rib in sight. The Mormons, it would seem, now know what they're doing.

We are just outside the Crescent Lake National Wildlife Refuge, 45,818 acres of sand dunes and shallow lakes, the largest, most pristine protected dune environment in the United States. With 200 bird species and plenty of deer, raccoons and other critters, Crescent Lake Refuge attracts hunters and an international assortment of birders. The Refuge's lakes and ponds, fed by the Ogallala aquifer are favorite locations for Nebraska geologist Jim Swinehart's wintertime core drilling projects, useful in documenting dune migration patterns. Hard to give up spending time at one of my favorite places on earth.

Perhaps on a day when the windshield wipers aren't having trouble keeping up with the rain and on a day Finlay has given up trying to eat the wipers. Perhaps on a day when torrents of runoff water aren't cutting deep gullies across the road. Perhaps on a day when the road shoulders aren't rapidly dissolving into rivers of liquid sand. Feeling cheated, I manage a convoluted U-turn on the narrow track and head back through the pounding rain for home. No cowboys, ATVs or cattle in evidence at the former Eldred Ranch. The usually dry creek bisecting the Eldred corral is at flood stage.

Back on Blue Water Creek

Hudson, our rambunctious Gordon Setter, is an inexorable black speck tracing wide circles along the western ridges. He will easily cover 30 miles this morning exploring the broad, half-mile wide bottom and surrounding hills of Blue Water Creek. At the rate Hudson is traveling any rattlesnake, lethargic from last night's cold two-inch downpour, will have to be on its toes to coil and strike. At least that's the wildly optimistic hope. Finlay, on the other hand, contents himself with trodding on our heels, no doubt hopeful he will be acquiring a nice collection of ticks today, perhaps even threaten his personal one-day record of 221 ticks.

Kathy, also known as "She Who Doesn't Like Ticks," is in charge of the dowsing rods and the camera. Cousin Warren and his wife, Cathy, keep an eye on Lt. G. K. Warren's detailed map of the battlefield, matching it with the surrounding terrain. I commandeer the binoculars. The usually crystal clear Blue Water Creek, engorged to bank full by last night's downpour, is murky with sandy silt and floating debris. We ford the meandering creek on an ancient bridge with some of its essential parts missing. Finlay takes his sweet time choosing a safe route across.

Mike Fischer has generously given us permission to walk his pasture, site of the opening stages of the Battle of Blue Water. When we received word Kae Carlson, who owns most of the battlefield site, would not allow visitors, I tracked down Mike, who gave us carte blanche.

"You can see most of the battlefield from my pasture. If you look to the north above Carlson's place you can see where the cavalry hid until the battle began."

Because Sand Hills people have always shown me remarkable hospitality and because I'm sometimes tenacious, I took the chance of phoning Kae Carlson. Perhaps the modest request to simply walk the site and get my bearings would work. Maybe I could interest her in the research project, the work already completed, the work yet to do. Perhaps she'd want to be a part of that. But something told me she had made an intractable resolution and I'd be wasting my time. And, truth be told, I am predisposed towards any ranch woman who dislikes random strangers running amok on her property. Chances are a good percentage would be greedy relic scavengers armed with metal detectors, which I would find annoying if I were in her shoes.

Kae Carlson said there were too many liability issues — oodles of rattlesnakes, not one but two people-hating cows, although she said no cattle were currently pastured on the battlefield site. People were always pestering her and if she allowed one visitor she'd have to admit them all. She suggested I read the historical society sign down on the highway. When I said I'd already seen the sign, she suggested I buy an excellent book by this fellow she'd allowed on the ranch 30 years ago. She emphasized the fact he was "a nice guy." I thanked her for her consideration and the book suggestion, said I completely understood her not wanting to be bothered. By the way, I asked, which battle events took place on her land. She said she had no idea, said nobody did. "It went for miles and miles."

A few days later, while reading Fred Werner's book, *With Harney on the Blue Water: Battle of Ash Hollow, September 3, 1855,* I was surprised to discover Kae Carlson had served as Werner's indispensable battlefield guide, pointing out all manner of pertinent landmarks and describing to the "nice guy" in great detail how and where the fight had taken place. Werner's useful book includes a splendid photo of a Sioux jawbone, part of Kae Carlson's personal collection, which also includes shell casings and a large quantity of bullets, some gathered with the aid of Mr. Nice Guy's metal detector.

On this splendiferous April morning, armed with Lt. G. K. Warren's excellent map and Cousin Warren's terrain reading skills, we're hardly even barely pouting about not having access to the complete battlefield. Cousin Warren, who acquired navigation savvy during his service as a helicopter pilot in Vietnam, studies the map, identifies the distinctive bluffs on either side of the creek bottom. Lt. G. K. Warren's quick sketches of the bluffs prove incredibly accurate.

Cousin Warren, not unlike Hudson, makes wide circles on both sides of Blue Water Creek, periodically checking the map against his surroundings. Once he gets his bearings the battlefield emerges.

West of the creek on that wide flat meadow stood Little Thunder's 41 Brule lodges, women drying buffalo meat and stuffing parfleches before being interrupted by Harney's approach. A short distance to the east across the creek from the village, at the base of that steep ridge, the site of Harney and Little Thunder's last palaver. Up the west side of the creek bottom to the northwest, over there under the empty box car-shaped cumulus clouds floating majestically overhead, where Harney's infantry chased the Brule, are the steep ridges and sandstone outcroppings where Cooke's cavalry trapped and pinned down fleeing Brule and Oglala.

Hard against the sturdy barbed wire fence marking the boundary of Carlson's pasture, we take turns with binoculars and the telescopic camera lens searching the ridges for both ledges and caves. Ledges all over the place. Caves prove more elusive, but before we've finished the survey we identify a dozen or more. Not caves in the sense of requiring extensive spelunking, but shallow alcoves with defined openings and enough depth to hide a few terrified Sioux. We can quibble over the definition of a cave, but the guy with the post hole digger who said there were no caves was kinda, almost wrong. We had hoped to dowse the area around the caves and the caves themselves if practical, but today we'll settle for establishing their existence.

Farther upstream, above the Carlson ranch headquarters, the treed ridge where Cooke's men hunkered down, waiting to attack the Oglala lodges until they heard Harney's infantry begin the festivities. The final escape route up the long ravine to the sand dunes to the east, the ravine where Captain Henry Heth failed to set up a blocking position, where the Sioux suffered heavy casualties, remains hidden behind the Carlson ranch. But we have Lt. G. K. Warren's map and, when we get back home, satellite imagery to assist our imaginations.

The boxcar clouds turn deep blue and begin to merge. A faint needle of lightning probes the far southern horizon. Hudson, who is terrified of thunder, dashes down at breakneck speed from a grove of spindly trees, where he's been playing hide and seek with a flock mildly irritated gray birds. He sits impatiently at the back door of the 4Runner waiting to be rescued from the approaching storm. A smug Finlay, loaded up with hitchhiking ticks, a happy dog who clearly considers his work day a success, sits at our feet awaiting instructions.

We take one last look at the wide valley of Blue Water Creek, where so much blood and innocence were lost, a valley soon to receive one more cleansing rain. Sam Houston was right. That crippled up bag-of-bones Mormon cow turned out to be expensive.

Chapter 22
Mormon Cows Revisited

The old saying in our business is progress happens one funeral at a time.

— Burke Teichert

In the mid-1990s, when Ted Turner began acquiring large ranches in the Nebraska Sand Hills, consternation erupted not only in bordering neighborhoods in Cherry, Sheridan and Garden counties, but Omaha and Lincoln newspapers went into a complete tizzy. What the heck was Turner up to? Did he intend to buy up the entire state? Did he have a nefarious plan to mine and sell water from the Ogallala aquifer, depriving Lincoln and Omaha of precious water supplies needed for future growth? Area ranchers, most of them millionaires, were frequently portrayed as helpless victims of Turner's land grab. Every time Turner made a new purchase the state's media recycled the same breathless themes of insatiable megalomanic land greed and potential water theft.

In contrast, initial land purchases by the Mormon Church, beginning in 1990, largely escaped media outrage. However, the Mormon Church's acquisition of the legendary Eldred Ranch on Blue Water Creek in 2004, coming as it did on the heels of Turner's buying spree and attendant media attention, prompted a fresh sense of alarm in the state's newspapers. The Mormons, operators of the largest cattle operations in the world, now owned over 200,000 acres in Nebraska, second only to Ted Turner's holdings. Would any family-owned ranches escape the clutches of Turner or the Mormons? Many were skeptical of Turner's motives and business practices. And what about the Mormons? Were they planning some cultish takeover of the Sand Hills?

In the ranch community, even after the Eldred Ranch purchase, negative response to the Mormons remained muted. In 1990, church officials immediately declared their intention of paying local property taxes instead of claiming the religious property exemption to which they might have been entitled, eliminating the real worry schools and county governments might lose substantial tax revenue. The county assessor in Grant County (pop. 614) has never heard any Mormon Church employee complain about the real estate tax bill. The vast majority of Rex Ranch employees were non-Mormons and many had been working on the same ranches under previous ownership. Neighbors did not see a sudden influx of earnest white shirt and black tie wearing Mormon missionaries. Rex Ranch employees swapped work with their neighbors, unlike Turner's men, who were engaged in the distinct tasks inherent to bison ranching.

Turner Enterprise's improving competency at raising bison in the Sand Hills had limited application. Cattle ranching, which usually yields more dependable profits, remains central to the area's economy. Turner's employees did not necessarily hide the lessons they were learning from the general public, but the market for the information was limited. Bison ranches similar in scale to Turner's holdings do not exist in the Sand Hills. Only widely scattered bison herds of a few hundred head or less are in operation. When Turner eventually determined his Rousseauean idea of free ranging herds over the entirety of a particular ranch created unwanted erosion and uneven pasture usage, he installed cross fencing and strategically placed water wells. He might choose to share that kind of information outside his close circle of ranch managers, but bison ranchers with pastures much smaller than 60,000 acres have limited curiosity about bison ranches with much larger pastures and different problems.

Rex Ranch general manager Burke Teichert, who had overseen several Mormon cattle operations across the US and abroad, took over management of the Nebraska operation in the early 1990s. He brought to the job a wealth of experience in range science, beef genetics, managing employees and cost containment. Teichert's arrival in the Sand Hills came at a time when University of Nebraska range scientists were researching some of the same concepts Teichert had been implementing. The combined educational efforts by UNL researchers, Teichert and his managers would start a revolution in range management practices.

Teichert, while growing up on a ranch in northwestern Wyoming, harbored no ambition to become a key strategist in the Mormon quest for self-reliance. His goal was to operate a cattle ranch. As a kid he mostly worked. "I started working in the hay fields starting in second grade driving a team of horses on a hay rake. My growing up years almost seem as long as the rest of my life. You know how slow time passes when you're a kid."

Every child should have access to a doting grandparent. There is no substitute.

Burke Teichert was blessed with not one, but two influential grandparents. Herman and Minerva Teichert, forced off their Idaho land on the Snake River bottoms by a dam-building project, relocated to Cokeville, Wyoming, in 1927, many years after it had been established as a Mormon outpost by pilgrims from Salt Lake City.

As a kid growing up in Cokeville, Burke Teichert had easy access to both grandparents. His grandfather Herman, possessed of expansive vision, accepted the financial risks entailed in building a large ranch. Even in hard times, he convinced bankers to loan him money to buy cows. He bought land on tax sales. Herman and the young Burke usually drove cows and new calves to summer pastures in the spring, often though unmelted snow drifts. The two-day cattle drives provided plenty of opportunities for conversation and for young Burke to absorb his grandfather's cattle savvy and keen business sense. "My grandfather lived to be 95 or 96. He was hoisting himself in a saddle well into his 90s.

"My dad was probably not quite as good a business manager as my grandfather, but was an excellent operations manager. Both of them got a lot done without many people. They had some fundamental beliefs on how to run a cow. They didn't think you should feed a cow one day if you didn't have to. If she could feed herself you needed to let her. And they stretched the envelope. We lived in snow country and we made the cows work through the snow on both ends of the winter. In the dead of winter we had so much snow we fed hay. But I'm glad I spent most of my career ranching in places where I could graze cattle all winter long."

Teichert's grandmother, Minerva, an accomplished painter, juggled her art career with five children, meals for hired men, selling milk and cream to her neighbors and a letter writing campaign to elected officials in support of equal rights for women. She was, in short, a pistol. "My grandmother would absolutely rebel at the term feminist being applied to her. She was, however, a believer in equal rights for all people. In her time she saw where women were discriminated against when equal amounts or quality of work was performed. I think it became personal because it took so long for her art work to be accepted."

If young Burke found himself in his grandmother's kitchen, he could expect a ginger-snap cookie or a baking powder biscuit lathered with jam. He could also expect his grandmother, a devout Mormon, to provide extended lessons in church history and theology. She also shared her political philosophy, which strongly favored limited government and local solutions to local problems. Minerva set up her easel in the family kitchen and usually talked while painting. Sometimes she asked young Burke to pose beside the painting to give her a better sense of human proportion. Most of her paintings included a horse, whether it was a western landscape or an interpretation of a passage from the Bible.

During the early 1930s, livestock prices plunged and the future of the family's ranch became tenuous. Minerva, whose formal art training included stints at Chicago's Art Institute under the tutelage of famous draftsman John Vanderpoel and in New York under Nebraska-born artist Robert Henri,* took samples of her work to a Salt Lake City art broker. The broker arranged a showing, which led to enough sales and commissioned work to ensure the ranch's future. In addition, she shrewdly traded art for free tuition at Brigham Young University for her descendants and many Cokeville children.

Burke Teichert somehow talked his hard-driving father into letting him play high school football. "All he said was my work had to be done before I went to practice." Teichert played well enough to earn all-state honorable mention honors his senior year. He then enrolled in Brigham Young, where his forward-looking grandmother had arranged free tuition. He interrupted his college career to spend two and a half years on a mission to Brazil, where he became fluent in Portuguese and learned to function in a foreign country.

After returning to BYU, Teichert obtained a BS in ag business. With job prospects unappealing, he enrolled in graduate school at the University of Wyoming where Professor G. Gordon Kearl served as a mentor. "He was the best applied farm-ranch economist to come down the pike. He knew how to look at problems and evaluate them. He took farming, range management, animal science practices, whatever it was, and looked at the cost benefits."

After earning a Master's in ag economics, Teichert served on the Wyoming faculty for a year, sharing an office with Kearl. "He helped me with some analysis work I did for another professor and showed me how to use a computer. That was back in the day of the old main frames."

Teichert then took a job with Carnation Company's Genetics Division, a leader in providing improved genetics to the beef and dairy industries. The genetics education Teichert obtained courtesy of Carnation added an entirely new skill set. "They put me in touch with the best nutritionists, reproductive physiologists and geneticists in the world. I still consult with some of those people."

His next job, working for Harold Schmidt, a Carnation business partner in California, opened Teichert's eyes to correcting genetic flaws with careful breeding and new ways of managing employees, methods he adopted and continues to advocate. "My dad could get a lot done without too many people, but he was more of an authoritarian manager. That's what most of us grew up with. What I learned from Schmidt was you could hire people, and if they

* Author Mari Sandoz published *Son of the Gamblin' Man: The Youth of an Artist* in 1960. The family of Robert Henri, founder of the Ashcan school of art movement, commissioned Sandoz to write the biography of Henri and the story of his controversial father John Cozad. The resulting book, incorporating invented speeches and thoughts, was drubbed by critics and was not a commercial success.

were the right people, you could turn them loose and you didn't have to look over their shoulder every day, every week or even every month. He outlined our jobs and only once in a while would he call me into the office, ask how things were going, maybe make a suggestion, give me an assignment. It was a wonderful revelation for me to recognize you didn't have to boss people. You might give them the training and tools, but good people were self-supervising."

A couple of jobs later, one in California's Imperial Valley and another on a 10,000 cow operation in Washington State, Teichert returned to BYU to take a half-time teaching position, which allowed him to do consulting on the side. He views taking the BYU job as his biggest career mistake because he was leaving an opportunity in Washington to make some serious money. The change was prompted by the hope the move to Salt Lake City would enable him to work back into the Cokeville cattle operation with his father. However, differences in management philosophies, sky high testosterone levels and the hardness of the two particular heads proved too great to overcome. Teichert had to give up his dream of returning with his growing family to Cokeville. Following part-time consulting work for the Mormon Church, he took a job directing the church's food production operations around the world. Teichert, along with a staff of six talented consultants, managed a wide range of projects, from small fruit orchards and produce farms, to large scale farms and ranches.

After his job description changed, Teichert secured a position managing 5,000 cows on church-owned ranches scattered around Utah. Like the ranch he grew up on in Cokeville, most of the Utah range did not suffer from an overabundance of moisture or hay. "Some cows were on high desert winter range. Some cows had hay in the winter, some cows we had to teach to graze in the winter, because they'd been fed hay all their lives. We did everything we could think of to reduce winter hay feeding. In the mid-70s, I became acquainted with Stan Parsons and Alan Savory,* Rhodesians who pioneered planned, time controlled grazing. Both criticized hay feeding as uneconomical." It wasn't long before Teichert began implementing those concepts in the Mormon Church's Utah cattle operations.

Throughout his career Teichert continued his quest for new management practices which might take better care of the environment and increase profitability. He did this by hands on experimentation, almost always in close consultation with other professionals like Don Adams. He became friendly with Adams when he was employed as a nutritionist at the range station at Miles City, Montana. "I called him frequently with all sorts of questions. How much alfalfa hay do I need to supplement cows on this kind of range? Adams had sound research to back up everything he told me. We started feeding supplemental hay to cows in fairly deep snow three times a week. Every neighbor who saw what we were doing thought we were crazy. 'You feed 'em once they'll be down there bellering at the gate.' We didn't feed 'em the next day. The day after that there were a few at the gate, but most of them were out looking for something to eat. We drove them out to where there was some decent grazing, threw out a little alfalfa. Then we skipped two days. Within three weeks the cows wouldn't even start for the gate until they heard the motors. They didn't want to waste the energy. They were busy digging through the snow, grazing grass.

"We determined how much hay they needed for a week, divided into three feedings, Monday, Wednesday and Friday. They got along fine. When I went to Nebraska I'd been

* Savory and Parsons developed systems which mimicked nature's bunched and moving grazing as a methodology to improve grasslands and carrying capacity, and as a means to heal the environment, stating "only livestock can reverse desertification." Their views have been adopted to varying degrees around the world, but remain controversial in some corners of the range management community. Teichert adapted the Savory/Parsons teachings to the particular environments where he was running livestock.

trying that kind of stuff for a while. We didn't have much alfalfa in Nebraska, but we did the same sorts of things with cake and distillers grain and were able to greatly reduce hay feeding from what had been the common practice on the ranches we bought. Meanwhile I've kept in touch with Don (Adams), who moved from Montana to the North Platte station."

Once he took the Nebraska job, Teichert spoke frequently to cattle industry groups, explaining the research-based, low-input, higher profit margin Rex Ranch practices. Teichert served on the board and as a member of the executive committee of the Nebraska Cattlemen's Association, positions not casually awarded to outsiders. Unlike the brash, often bloviating Ted Turner, the uber-competent Teichert impressed Sand Hills ranchers with his relentless thirst for knowledge and his willingness to share that knowledge. Unlike Turner, who grew up as a wild-assed rich man's son, Teichert was born and raised on a hard scrabble cattle ranch and could not only talk the talk, but walk the walk. University of Nebraska range scientists, already engaged in cutting edge low-input beef production research at the Gudmundsen Sand Hills Laboratory, were soon conducting joint research projects with the Rex Ranch and co-publishing the results in scholarly forums.

Ideas for lowering both costs and labor inputs generated immediate currency with ranchers engaged in a capital and labor intensive, low profit enterprise. Promising underlying research, whether done on the Rex Ranch or on the Gudmundsen or on a participating area ranch, was being conducted in the Nebraska Sand Hills, not at a completely foreign location like east Texas or California, with vastly different forage and weather.

Teichert constantly posed questions, then conducted the experiments. If we move calving season back to April from March, how much hay can we save and what effect will the later calving date have on weaning weights? What if we move calving dates even later, from April to May? Can we profitably cull our way to compressed calving dates which maximize our available labor? If a cow has trouble calving unassisted, would we be ahead to cull the cow or should we rebreed her and see what happens? Or, should we rebreed her and sell her to someone not so worried about assisting an occasional birth? Can we improve our bottom line by marketing bred late-calving cows instead of keeping them? Can we eliminate calving problems and still produce a growthy calf? If we force pregnant cows to graze dry grass in winter without extensive supplemental hay feeding will that adversely affect conception rates next summer? What would conception rates look like if we dropped supplemental hay feeding from 750 pounds to 500 pounds per cow?

Rarely, when severe winter conditions warrant, even for the parsimonious, hay feeding becomes a necessity. "The first two years I was in Nebraska we had 20 below temps, 40 mile an hour winds, a wind chill of 60 below for 10 days to two weeks. We fed those cows some. But if you dropped hay in the middle of a pasture they wouldn't come to it. They'd found some shelter in the lee of a hill and you had to drop hay at their toes to get them interested. Some winters we had deep snow early and we fed, but usually there was enough grass the cows could get after it and make a living.

"We wanted high conception rates, unassisted births, a high percentage of live calves. With mature cows we shoot for 85 pounds or less on the bull calves and 75 pounds or less on the heifer calves. With bred heifers we want even lighter calves. We don't care if the cow gives a lot of milk. I've always figured, and had nutritionists tell me this for many years, the conversion from grass to milk to calf is a darn poor conversion. If you need the calf to gain more weight, feed the calf directly. Depending on market and pasture conditions we may keep a number of calves as yearlings, except for the bigger ones, which enables us to move to later calving dates, avoiding winter storms and cutting our hay requirements. I've known other ranchers in Nebraska through my acquaintance with Savory and Parsons, who were far ahead of me. I visited their operations, took our people along. The ranchers were 100 percent open, helped us avoid mistakes.

"If Alan Savory visited our operation, and he's an outspoken person as you know, he might well say, 'Teichert, you're doing this all wrong.' But we're constantly studying how long it takes for the grass to recover. When you take cattle out of a pasture the most important question is not how long did they stay there, but how long before you can put them back. I've worked with other range scientists and studied grass physiology on my own. I wanted to make sure I wasn't listening to a couple of crackpots, that what we were doing was sound from a plant physiology standpoint and sound from an ecological standpoint. After thirty-some years of implementing the program in different regions and environments I have to say, hey, it works."

A key to successfully adopting the Savory-Parsons model of intensive pasture rotation in arid regions is finding ways to water cattle in smaller pastures. "Most of our wells in Nebraska are relatively shallow. We use very little pipeline compared to some regions. Out in the western states, where the water is usually deep, you might spend $15,000 drilling a dry hole and have nothing. Instead, you might go the pipeline route, which is expensive, in order to have a dependable water supply. Most of our water in the Sand Hills is pumped with solar power. We made the pumps and solar panels portable, moving them from pasture to pasture when we move the cattle. Pumps and panels aren't cheap, but one pump serves I don't know how many pastures. It's not a big deal to pull the pumps. Just tie a rope to 'em and pull 'em out hand over hand as quickly as you can. When you first start to pull you're pulling against the water and it makes you grumble a little bit. Don't try to come up too fast with it and you'll be okay."

What about genetics? Each cattle breed, Angus, Hereford, Gelbvieh has its adherents, proclaiming this or that set of traits superior to any other breed. "Hybrid vigor is as close to getting something for free as you're going to get in our industry. We use a composite program, pretty much a three-way cross, so we don't have to worry about which bulls are breeding which cows, although we do have some designated bulls for first calf heifers based on performance criteria. Simmental and Angus occupy three fourths of the composite, breeds with broad genetic bases and good sire summaries. You can select those breeds, put your criteria in a sire search vehicle online and access all of their sires, obtaining a listing the sires meeting your criteria. Beyond Simmental and Angus it gets a little harder to do the research."

Many cattlemen talk about selecting for disposition. And sometimes they do. But too often they may keep a cranky bull with an outstanding pedigree or an evil-tempered cow whose calves top the scales come weaning time. Teichert uses a simple test for disposition and he's not fond of "goofy" cattle. "With a bull, we'll cut out one that meets our other criteria, have him stand between two of us in 60 feet of alley, leave him alone, check for any physical defects that might make him unsound in the future. If that bull can't settle himself in the alley, either tries to run over one of us trying to escape or if he's mean and looking to hurt one of us, he goes straight in the cull pen. There will be some that act calm and you keep 'em and later on they get goofy, but if you cull the goofy ones, over time you'll end up with good dispositioned cattle.

"We do the same test with the heifers we work in the spring. We're always looking for those with physical defects, for those that haven't wintered too well. If a heifer didn't winter well, she'll probably never winter well. At the same time we're looking for disposition. If we see a goofball heading for the back of the alley and when we get close to her she can't stand it and has to bust by we just open the cull gate, doesn't matter how good-looking she is. If you do that you'll have nice dispositioned cattle. Of course, some people aren't competent to work cattle. But if you know how to work cattle quietly and give them half a chance to be good, they'll be good. I don't quite know how to rank it, but disposition is an economically important trait."

Neighbors, impressed with the efficiencies they observed firsthand, began to emulate. Winter hay feeding across the Sand Hills declined in favor of protein supplemented gazing on winter pastures. Ranchers gradually moved February and March calving dates, which require more supplemental feed, to April, even May. The Rex Ranch's intensive, rotating grazing practices, first pioneered by Savory and Parsons, and championed by university and government range scientists, have seen slower adoption rates.

Dave Pratt is one of Teichert's long-time range scientist colleagues. Pratt purchased the Ranching for Profit school from Stan Parsons before Parsons returned to Zimbabwe. Pratt also operates a successful ranch management consulting business. He estimates 50 to 60 percent of Sand Hills operations practice rotational grazing to some extent. "Most would involve eight to ten pastures or fewer. I'd guess 10 percent would do anything like the type of (range) management we espouse, which is at least 15 pastures per herd. Although the 50 to 60 percent adoption rate would be twice the adoption rate in the rest of the country where low-input beef production is also taking hold."

Pratt is an enthusiastic promoter of cell grazing, especially if it's done properly. "We have doubled the carrying capacity on many ranches by using cell grazing. Twenty-five to thirty cells is optimal. In most cases it takes 15 cells to get substantial benefit. Rest periods are important, but the key is to be flexible. Most university research has used too few cells and rigid rotation schedules. Sometimes a three-day rotation is right, sometimes 45 days. Smart managers make decisions based on prevailing conditions. If there's a bunch of long desiccated forage sometimes you feed a little hay, get the herd to liquefy the stuff, crap on it, trample the whole mess into the ground. We put our mineral blocks out on gopher land. That usually takes care of the gophers.

"Cell grazing is not that complicated. Match the rest periods with how fast the grass is growing and keep in mind short grazing periods raise performance. It's also important, depending on moisture and soil type, to maintain the highest possible density of grazing animals. Generally speaking, the bigger the herd, the lower the labor costs, the more improvement you'll see in the pastures."

Managing pastures in a more traditional manner usually means leaving cattle in larger pastures for longer time periods or, on well-run operations, depending on moisture, weather and other factors, until they've consumed from 50 to 60 percent of the available grass. The traditional grazing model is in some ways is easier, and, well, traditional. Competent ranchers anywhere know healthy grass is key to their survival. Allowing livestock to grub pastures into the ground, particularly in the fragile Nebraska Sand Hills, not only earns the active disrespect of neighbors, but usually leads to an early exit from the business. Just because a rancher isn't all in on cell grazing does not mean he or she is a poor operator. Every situation is different. Climates and grass species differ, available labor and available capital vary. How soon a rancher plans to retire can carry significant weight when considering major operational changes. Burke Teichert: "The old saying in our business is progress happens one funeral at a time."

Any operator looking to convert a traditional operation to cell grazing would need to make a sizable investment. The more extensive fencing, the labor inputs required for frequent movement of cattle to different pastures, unless the costs are spread over a large number of animals, and the expense of providing water sources for each truncated pasture have curbed enthusiasm. Even though Sand Hills ranchers have not fully embraced intense rotational grazing, early adopters have been encouraged by higher carrying capacities, healthier herds and improved pastures.

Burke Teichert has never been one to stand on tradition. "We're always trying something new. We've got this ranch in Utah experimenting with various methods of sagebrush control and attempting, at the same time, to increase our wildlife populations. Recently we've been studying more effective methods of compressing calving dates. A tighter calving schedule not only lessens labor demands, but raises overall weaning weights. Older calves weigh more than calves born two months late. We've always culled open cows and late calvers. Now we're culling heifers who don't settle within the first cycle of breeding season. And then there's the other side of the equation — the bulls. If you are buying or keeping a bull out of a 2-year-old heifer he should be born during the first 21 days of calving season. And before you select him as a breeding bull, his mother should calve within the first 21 days of calving season the next year.

"Bulls from early calving females, especially in a low-input operation, will spread that trait to the herd in addition to ideal adult size, milking ability, overall health and temperature and pest tolerance. We know of several producers who range-calve cows and heifers and maybe check them once a day or less. Some don't keep antibiotics on hand. They seldom have to treat sickness, because good health and survivability is bred in.

"We steal ideas from each other all the time. I don't know if I'm much of an original thinker. I owe most of our success in Nebraska to people who were in Nebraska when I got here. I thought I knew something about management, but most of what we've done in Nebraska came from Nebraskans. Actually, most of my ideas come from somebody else. Maybe I have mingled ideas in a way that might be a unique fit to the landscape where I am. Harold Schmidt, Gordon Kearl, Don Adams, friends in Nebraska, mentors in the animal science field have all been extremely helpful to me. I have an inquisitive mind. I may be talking to a researcher and ask if they've ever thought about researching this? Early in my career I didn't have a lot of credibility. But now, when I ask about something sometimes they'll start a research project. Sometimes they'll ask me if I've tried something, refer me to some research, and I'll try it.

"We always operate under the premise there's a better way to do things. We just have to find it. I hate paradigm lock down. Our neighbors, while we're happy they're there, are our competition. If we can produce calves 10 cents a pound cheaper we might stay in business longer."

The combination of the Rex Ranch's profitable example and the promotion of similar practices by university range scientists and Dave Pratt fundamentally changed the beef industry in the Nebraska Sand Hills and beyond. The enthusiasm of early adopters converted others. And although it is not yet possible to determine the full extent of the revolution, longtime observers believe momentum is on the side of low-input, holistic cattle management. Teichert: "Once a producer takes that initial step to limit feed inputs, forcing the cow to make her own living, the rest usually falls in place. The first step changes the mindset and producers begin looking at other ways to cut costs. The reliance on purchased steel and energy is replaced by reliance on sunlight and grass."

Chapter 23
Bull Riders

Don't be afraid to go after what you want to do and what you want to be,
but be willing to pay the price.

— Lane Frost (October 12, 1963-July 30, 1989)

You'd better be square with the bull.

— Rich Boots

Last Sunday in June. Large sections of the Great Plains, including Texas, Oklahoma, eastern Colorado, Kansas and southern Nebraska suffer under relentless skies and stubborn drought unlike anything seen since the 1930s. Movietone News reels in our local movie theater show fences in Oklahoma and Texas buried under drifts of blowing dirt, bone starved cattle trekking hopelessly across the moonscapes in search of something edible. But there is good news. Ike, a guy I particularly like, has put the Korean War on more or less permanent hiatus.

On this blazing hot Sunday, with area dogs finding shade anywhere they can, the Nebraska branch of the Tupper clan, my mother's family, gathers in Kearney's Harmon Park for the annual picnic. Kearney represents a central meeting place for family members coming from Omaha, the Panhandle, central Nebraska counties along the Kansas line, far northeastern Nebraska and a large contingent from the west central Sand Hills, one of the few areas of the state this summer with almost adequate moisture.

While the women flounce checkered table cloths on scootched together picnic tables and organize a spread heavy on fried chicken and potato salad, the younger male cousins explore Harmon Park's elaborate WPA-constructed labyrinth of twisting waterways, fountains, flower beds and concrete and rock goldfish ponds. And the art deco swimming pool! What an exotic sight for those of us from more rural parts of the state. We stare enviously at brash teenagers diving from the high board. Bet we could do that if we only had a swimming suit and maybe enough money for the entrance fee. Chattering girls in tight bathing suits lay out towels and sun themselves along the pool's edge. An extravagantly buxom young woman unsnaps the straps of her bathing suit before lying down. We stare, riveted, hoping for the miracle of gravity.

Our older sisters, badge heavy with delegated authority, fetch us for dinner. My father, one of two Methodist ministers in the clan, takes his turn at giving the blessing. Dad is as brief as the other minister is long-winded. I am hungry and appreciate the brevity. As is the custom, women shepherd the adult men through the food line first, followed by any boy cousin not in diapers. Already a savvy veteran of countless carry-in church dinners, I beeline for the desserts piled on the ass end of the last picnic table. Who knows how long they'll last? I load up three pieces of pie.

My handsome, suntanned Uncle Milton is talking to a suntanned, broad-shouldered man with Brylcreemed hair wearing a cowboy shirt and boots. Some of the Sand Hills men wear straw cowboy hats. All the Sand Hills men wear cowboy boots, which makes them, in my book, exotic. The farmers I know favor overalls and heavy plow shoes when they're working, typical civilian clothes when they're not. I am wondering how these Sand Hills men can tolerate pointy-toed boots which must surely squeeze until they hurt.

My farmer grandfather, wearing his dress shoes, Sunday suit pants, a white shirt and a snap brimmed fedora, fetches me to help carry watermelons. Every year, Bryan Tupper brings enough watermelon to feed the multitude. He produces a galvanized wash tub from his car trunk, likely the same one we use for Saturday night baths when we stay at the farm. I hump the wash tub from his car back to the picnic while he carts a ball-peen hammer and a heavy wet burlap sack containing two large blocks of ice. He gives the burlap sack to Milton, who pounds the crap out of the ice and whatever else is inside. Grandpa and I return to the car for more watermelon. Grandpa says I must be "purty stout" to carry a heavy wash tub all by myself and that I might make a "purty good hand" someday. I am instantly four inches taller and affect an obnoxious swagger.

Grandpa, who never stops talking once he starts, tells how his brother Lucius made good in the Sand Hills. "Lucius went on up 'ere around Ringgold from Franklin County in the 20s, bought a section on contract from a storekeep fella who run a grocery store. Times was hard after the war. I don't imagine anybody ever took care of a dollar better than Lucius Tupper, but by the time the Depression rolled around he was havin' trouble makin' ends meet. The grocery store fella showed up, said this other fella couldn't make payments on another section he'd sold on tick. He wanted to know if Lucius would be interested in takin' it on. Lucius said money was tight, prices was low and he'd just been thinkin' of givin' his section back. They dickered. Lucius ended up tradin' 200 head of gate-cut cattle, a windbroke team of horses and a saddle horse with a fistula for clear title to two sections of good Sand Hills grass." I have heard this story before and, depending on who is doing the telling, details vary. Two sections might be one. The saddle horse with a fistula morphs into a broken down truck, the windbroke team might have been foundered instead, but the point of the story remains the same. I glance at Uncle Lucius over there in the shade of a giant elm talking cattle and interest rates with his brothers with new respect. He must be one savvy operator.

On the next trip to the car, Grandpa harrumphs after overhearing one of the Sand Hills relatives say favorable things about Angus cattle. "The only money ever made in this country on beef, Bryan Lee, was made with yer good whiteface cattle" I have heard this speech many times. It's a speech my grandfather will make right up to the day he buys his first Angus bull.

Once the tub is full of watermelons, Milton dumps the broken ice on top. Now all we have to do is wait impatiently for the wonders of sweet, icy cold watermelon.

Milton introduces me to the Brylcreemed cowboy, Willis Ruby, Aunt Mabel's boy. Willis is named after my great-grandfather, Willis Jay Tupper. Mabel and her husband Guy migrated to the Sand Hills shortly after Oscar Tupper, Grandpa's favorite older brother. Grandpa always says Oscar would have put together "quite a spread if he 'adn't been kilt in that hay feedin' accident. Busted his head wide open on the froze up ground like a muskmelon."

Willis is as soft-spoken as Milton, which is saying something. Like most kids I am impressed with a quiet manner, which forces me to pay attention. A strong, wide hand envelopes mine. His hands have some oddly-shaped bumps and bent fingers, like someone must have worked over his hands with a ball-peen hammer. He is talking about riding bulls. I visualize him riding one of my grandfather's horned Hereford bulls, which always appear to me both enormous and likely dangerous. Milton asks Willis if he's ever been hurt riding bulls. Willis says, not really, nothing to write home about. Milton eventually extracts a slow, grudging recitation of assorted concussions and broken noses. As if I weren't impressed before. I broke my collar bone when I was 2 years old. Does that count?

*

Forty years later. Tupper family picnic. Holdrege, Nebraska. The move from Kearney's Harmon Park to the Phelps County fair headquarters building represents a concession to air conditioned facilities and handier restrooms. The gathering is a shrunken rendition of past annual rituals. Most of the family matriarchs and patriarchs, including my grandfather and Uncle Lucius, and many of the next generation are long dead. Some have moved out-of-state. Fewer representatives willing to drive from the Sand Hills. Most younger family members stay home, some even play golf. I can only imagine what Bryan or Lucius Tupper would say about the golf-playing relatives. One thing for dead certain, they would not be kind. Only dilettante offspring of storekeeps and gummit employees play golf. Only the laziest, most ignorant people they know inhabit country clubs. When not in church, serious people, in other words respectable farmers and ranchers, work.

The family's cadaverous, long-winded minister takes his rightful turn at the pre-meal benediction. Let's concede right off he's a gentle, self-effacing man, not a mean man, not the sort of puffed up preacher who relishes condemning his fellow humans, busy minding their own business, to the ass-blistering fires of hell. However, he's a member of the thanker school of meal blessers, bringing a fevered imagination to the task. He is deeply thankful for today's sunny weather, the state's excellent highway system, the extraordinary skills of his doctors who recently addressed his explicitly described medical issues, also the nurses, hospital orderlies, pink ladies and hospital kitchen workers, the prayers of his congregation for his quick recovery, the Phelps County commissioners for expending scarce tax dollars on this fine facility, the supreme being who personally arranged for each and every one of us to attend, at which point attention wanders. Who can estimate how many trillion gadzillion salmonella bacteria have multiplied in the potato salad while he drones? Just when I began to panic at the realization we're all about to die unlovely deaths due to food poisoning, he wraps things up. I take my place at the end of a short line of hungry men, grab the first three pieces of pie I come across. Shrewd decision. Not many pie bakers left in the family.

Willis Ruby, making a rare trip back to Nebraska from his home near Lander, Wyoming, is the center of attention. I sit close to eavesdrop on Willis's soft drawl. He is telling how he became interested in rodeo. "I started riding milk cows and bucket calves as soon as I can remember. While I was in high school a few of the neighbors paid me to break horses." His first rodeo, in 1946, was held on the 4th of July at Broken Bow. Fearing his parent's reaction he didn't tell them he was participating. "I had to do a lot of sneakin'." Willis kept his gear and a change of clothes in a gunny sack, walked and hitch hiked to Broken Bow.

"At Broken Bow they had some big native 2 and 3-year-old steers. I rode them and barebacks and saddle broncs, made a little money, like $150 or something, a lot of money in those days."

Uncle Milton asks if Willis ever had a pro rodeo card. "I had to buy a professional card in January, 1947. Then it was the RCA, now it's the PRCA. We were travelin' to rodeos in Colorado, South Dakota and Kansas. Even went to Iowa a time or two. I held that card until I had to go to work for a living, about 1953. Then I did amateur rodeo until the early 1960s"

Getting the book on a bull at a rodeo meant talking to other riders or remembering them from past rodeos. Bulls on the current rodeo circuit are much better. "We had some as good, but now every bull is good. They're breeding the buck in 'em, just like the bucking horse program."

After moving to Wyoming in the 1960s to manage a ranch for Tom Morrison and subsequently buying his own ranch, he helped organize the Lander Old Timer's Rodeo Association and returned to the arena. Willis drove back to Nebraska several times to compete in the Old Timer's rodeo in Hyannis. At the age of 50 (teen-aged professional bull riders are more common than bull riders over 30) he was still riding bulls and broncs. He also took up steer wrestling for the first time. Like most rodeo veterans he pleads guilty to harboring some arthritis.

He watches bull riding on television. Isn't sure if he'd wear the protective headgear popular with many current riders. "Maybe if I had my nose broken or something." He's a big fan of North Carolina bull rider J. B. Mauney, whose life time winnings exceed $7 million.

The rodeo gene runs deep in the Ruby family. "My daughters' boys team rope, calf rope. One of them tried bulldogging and kind of quit that. My son's boy was up there pretty good in the bull riding until he went to work for his dad and quit. He's got a little rodeo stock of his own, bulls and bucking horses. My two girls are both barrel racers."

Mid-afternoon. Partially eaten bowls of salmonella-infected potato salad being stowed in coolers for the long trip home. Short good-byes from people hoping to get home in time to check on livestock before dark. I watch Willis Ruby* walk to his car, the one with Wyoming plates. He walks like a guy with a little arthritis.

*

Mid-March. Damp, chilly breeze blowing out of the northwest under stolid gun metal skies. Kathy and I turn into the parking lot of the Eclipse Church on the south fork of the Dismal River. As usual, the free will offering plate inside the unlocked sanctuary overflows with bills. We walk through the cemetery to overlook the always bank full Dismal, innocent as new mown hay as it gurgles its way towards the treacherous, kayak upsetting, domestic arrangement threatening stretches of river south of Mullen. Spring smells of damp sand and awakening roots. We pass by Jim Goeke's holy piece of the Sand Hills, grass greening faintly underneath the bronze and tawny yellows of last year's ungrazed growth. Finlay, who normally spends long car trips in a self-induced coma, has his nose out the window, ears erect, processing the freshening March aromas, hoping to alert us to the presence of potentially dangerous cattle should any appear.

---

* Willis "Bill" Ruby was elected to the Nebraska Sandhills Cowboy Hall of Fame in 2016.

We turn west on a meandering sandy track, on our way to visit with Rich Boots at his cow camp a few miles northwest of the Eclipse Church, where he baches every spring during calving season. Last fall, while visiting with Rod Boots, Rich's brother, at a six-man football game I learned Rich was a pretty good bull rider in his younger days. I also learned Rich named a daughter Nocona Boots and a son Tony Lama Boots. Rod is equally proud of naming a son Justin Boots. Today we are hoping to learn something about bull riding in the early 1960s, more than a decade after Willis Ruby began his career.

At the end of the sandy trail we arrive at the cow camp, composed of a small house on one side and a modest set of corrals and a camper trailer on the other, the corrals sheltered from the sharp wind by steep dunes to the north. We are greeted by smells of wet sand, grass hay, fresh manure and an occasional whiff of ammonia. Finlay's alert suspicions fall on a dozen cows and new calves with barely dried umbilical cords penned in a smaller corral, waiting to be let out on fresh pasture. No better preventative for calf scours than new grass. Finlay, for once, has sense enough to keep his mouth shut. The faint mutter of an ATV engine. Rich Boots rides a muddy ATV into the corral and up and over a ramp straddling both sides of the fence. That ramp must save him countless gate openings and closings.

He dismounts deliberately, showing the effects of 24/7 calving duties. Mid-60s, built from the ground up like a former welterweight with broad shoulders and a low center of gravity, his face red and roughened from long hours in the elements. Rich Boots clearly hasn't spent all his time lollygagging in the nearby camper trailer. He sizes up the situation and invites us to talk in the ranch owner's empty house. He finds a battered percolator and can of coffee in an otherwise barren painted cupboard. While the coffee perks, warming the corners of a cold kitchen with the distinct aroma of mountain grown Folgers, we take seats around a well-worn wooden kitchen table.

"I was born in a house like this. Doctor got there when I was about six hours old."

Rich Boots does not usually feel comfortable invading the ranch owner's house. The terms of his pasture lease do not include the house, which is why he is content to spend the few hours he sleeps during calving season in his tiny travel trailer. "My wife comes out from town once in a while, brings me much better food than I can manage. She doesn't ride horses, but sometimes helps move cattle on the ATV while I use a horse.

"I grew up on a ranch, been on a ranch all my life. We rode colts, bucket calves, cows, anything that bucked we rode. I rode some in high school, won my first all around at Arthur when I was 15. I won the cow riding, bull dogging and placed in the bareback. Ranchers just brought in some old black dry cows that would buck. Some of the real rodeos back then had cow riding instead of bulls.

"When I rode bulls you went to the whole rodeo, you stayed. Then it got to be a business, hit five or six rodeos a week, private jets and all that. Now you can make more with one ride than we made in a couple of years. We was kinda old time and we enjoyed what we did.

"All the Boots family was from the Ashby area. My dad Gerald Boots[*] was born near there."

* Gerald O. Boots grew up in the Ashby area, cowboyed on the Abbott Ranch, roped at rodeos on his famous horse "Smoke," later worked the chutes at local rough stock rodeos and drove a chuck wagon for area cattle drives, earning the nickname "Wishbone." Boots was inducted into the Nebraska Sandhills Cowboy Hall of Fame in 2009.

I am remembering Sophie King Tupper, Uncle Leo's widow, subject of the ghostly cobbled together portrait of Leo in uniform, Sophie and baby Anita which always hung on my grandparent's living room wall. Didn't she have family near Ashby? Move back to Ashby after the war? Maybe ran a grocery store with her second husband George Anderson, before they moved to California?

Any Kings around Ashby when Rich was growing up?

"Charlie Blaylock was married to Myrtle King, a sister to Sophie. They ran the grocery store for several years. Thelma King, Myrtle and Sophie's sister, taught me in second grade. Everybody knew everybody in Ashby." Small world, like just about any place you could name in the Sand Hills.

"After high school my folks sent me down to the University, but I hated it. They wouldn't come get me, so after two months I rode the train home. They said they sent me down there to go to school. It took a while, but they finally let me back in the door. I helped my dad summers in the hay contracting business, started riding bucking horses and bulls, got pretty good at both. I won the South Dakota and Nebraska bull riding championships. By the time I got married I'd done about everything in rodeo I'd wanted to do." After Rich quit rodeo, he, like his brother Rod, a three-time national finals high school steer wrestler and long-time athletic director at Arthur High School, contented himself with making a living and judging rodeos on the side.

"I worked for dad three years and for Pete and Phoenix Becker north of Ashby. They always had horses to break. Eventually worked for Beckers full-time and made foreman. We come over here (Mullen area) about 1979, ran the Helen Farrar place south of Hyannis (38,000 acres) and eventually ran her place south of Mullen (48,000 acres) as well. After she died the heirs sold the land. I leased this place and we moved to town."

The ancient percolator burps a couple of times and falls silent. Rich unearths three mismatched pottery mugs on a sideboard, just the sort of heavy mug to keep coffee hot in a chilly room. We are content with our warm mugs and winter coats.

Rich watches Professional Bull Riders (PBR) competitions on TV. He paid special attention when two-time National Bull Riding Champ Justin McBride* was riding. "He graduated from Mullen, married a local girl. They live in Oklahoma, but come back to see her family fairly often. Like most successful bull riders he's not that big, puny little thing, maybe 135 pounds. That's about what I weighed when I rode. At that weight you don't have a big upper body to keep centered."

I am curious. If he were riding today would he wear the helmet and flak jacket as many current riders do. "I've had a lot of people ask me that. I'd sure wear the jacket. If Lane Frost† would have had one in Cheyenne he'd be alive today. Cody Lambert started promoting those things when his friend Lane got killed and it's saved a lot of lives. I was only hurt one time.

---

* Justin McBride, two-time PBR World Champion, known for riding bulls shortly after he'd been severely injured, was the first bull rider to earn $5 million during his career. He still ranks in the top 10, along with five Brazilian riders in lifetime earnings. After his retirement he launched a successful singing career and announces nationally televised bull riding contests.

† Lane Frost, 1987 PRCA World Champion Bull Rider, had successfully ridden 'Takin' Care of Business' at the 1989 Cheyenne Frontier Days Rodeo for a score of 85. After he dismounted he suffered a glancing blow from the bull's horns, which did not break the skin, but fractured ribs and forced them into his lungs. He got up and attempted to walk, but collapsed and died soon after. Takin' Care of Business continued to appear in rodeos, including the 1990 National Finals. He eventually was retired and died in 1999, 10 years after Lane Frost was killed.

I had one stomp on me. He was spinning and I got underneath him and he come across a time or two, tore some ligaments off my ribs. Helmet-wise? If you had an injury and it was bothering you, yes. But otherwise I don't know if you'd want to change anything. You get on them things you're going to get hurt, they're going to hurt you. I broke my nose once. I think he didn't have horns, but horns won't hurt you. It's them feet coming down on you that does the damage.

"There's a world of difference between the bulls now and the bulls in my day. Back when I rodeoed it was a drawing contest. The contractor usually had two or three really good bulls you could win anytime you got on. Now there's so many good bulls, thousands of them. It's unbelievable how they're breeding them and raising them. We had a few rank bulls. The top five bull riders in Nebraska used to match up with the top five bull riders in South Dakota. They called it the Two-State Finals. I rode a bull there in 1963 that was probably 7 or 8 years old and had never been ridden. It was quite an honor to ride him. Tar Baby. He was rank. I'll never forget it."

Did he always map out what he was going to do before he crawled on a bull? Rich nods. "Like with Tar Baby, you knew he was going to jump out of the chute and come right back at a hundred miles an hour to the left. He'd do it every time. He was mean. He didn't like humans. He'd eat ya. Knowing he was going to circle left I always leaned just a tad going out. When you come out of the chute you want to be a little ahead of the bull. They leave so fast you can't believe it. If you're starting over them that takes the first jump away. Never get in the middle of his back. That's where he'll hurt you. Stay right behind the shoulders and on your rope as much as you can.

"You'd better be square with the bull. You don't ever want to try beatin' him around the circle. When you do that you'll get down in the hole. The centrifugal force is going away from you and it'll drop you inside. If you get outside too far the same thing. You have to stay square. Once you're out of the chute you straighten a little, but you'll always have an arch in your back. If you're too straight up the first thing that happens is your arm flies back like this (demonstrates) and your hips fly out and when that happens you're gone. You're behind. Every time the bull jumps you want to be going forward with him. Get behind and it's over. Every move he makes you just move with him. When he turns, you turn. You'll never catch back up to a spinning bull. That's why you'll see a guy ride a bull plumb easy and the next time on the same bull he might last two seconds.

"It's not strength. I was pretty stout, but strength has nothing to do with it. You can be the puniest guy in the world and ride bulls. It's balance and legs. You want to keep hold of them.

"Ninety-nine percent of bull riders would rather have a bull go into their strong hand. If you ride left-handed you'd rather have them go left. If they buck away from your hand you've got to work much harder. There's guys can ride away from their hand. It didn't bother me too much. Of course, back then we didn't know anything. We mostly got on and tried to ride the damn things. Now they study videos.

"Judges tend to mark a spinning bull higher than a high jumper that goes this way and that, what we call a trashy bull, without a set pattern. A rank spinning bull, if you get in tight with them, is just like sittin' in a rockin' chair. Get behind and they'll drop you. The kind that jump high and kick, go different directions are actually harder to ride because you've got to work all the time to keep up with their moves. But with a good spinning bull, you get tapped off on them and they're the easiest thing in the world to ride. Sounds funny, but you're not even tired when you get through. Eight seconds in a rockin' chair."

Rich cradles his cup in square hands, stares at his dwindling coffee. After a deep breath he talks again about Lane Frost, his first year as a pro, riding the famous bull Red Rock, previously unridden in 309 trips out of the chute. Frost, Rich says, had the build and the skills to have had a long run as a top bull rider.

"Both my boys rodeoed. Tony rode bulls, moved down to North Platte, works as a radio DJ and program director. He got away from ranch life when he got away from me. Tommy[*] was a steer wrestler, finished 11th in the nation at the National High School Rodeo finals. He stuck with it. Worked for a guy who ran rodeo stock, did some rodeo pickup work, got married, started a herd of cattle. No telling where things would be for him now." Rich hesitates, studies his coffee.

"Tommy got killed a few years back helping a buddy in a bar fight out in Wyoming. Bad deal. He was 30 years old." I wonder if Rich is thinking of a grave in the Mullen cemetery, of a large cross fashioned from welded horseshoes on one side, a coiled lariat mounted on a wrought iron stand on the other side.

Rich straightens his back, shuffles his feet. He's been a kind and patient host, but we all know it's past time he needs to be checking his cows. We walk out to the muddy driveway, find Finlay snoozing in the front seat, blissfully unaware of the presence, only a few yards away, of quite possibly dangerous cattle.

The leaden sky, which has threatened to do something all day, begins pelting us with hard sleet. Rich stands next to his ATV, waiting politely for us to leave, changes his mind, beckons us over. "You should come up to the golf course (the Ben Crenshaw-designed course a few miles to the north). Come up sometime this summer. It's a first class operation. There's small cabins on stilts overlooking the Dismal that will sleep a total of maybe 60 people. Great view. You don't have to book a tee time, just wander up to the course when you want, although you might be asked what time you want to get up or when you want breakfast.

"Ben's Porch sits right beside the golf course. That's where my wife and I work sometimes. I grill hamburgers, hot dogs and brats for noon lunch. My wife serves drinks, pop and stuff. Quite a few members fly into North Platte on jets which cost millions. A hundred dollar tip is nothing to these people, but most are good, solid folks and easy to be around. The management won't put up with customers being snooty. They've taken away memberships from people who were rude to waitresses or employees."

Ignorant storekeeps flying into the Sand Hills on zillion dollar jets to play golf? Hundred dollar tips for a hamburger? What would Uncle Lucius or Grandpa Tupper have to say? No way to know, of course, but I'm betting on speechless.

"You two come on up. We'll give you a tour. You might find it interesting."

We pry open our frozen car doors. Rich throws a leg over the ATV, revs the engine, eases up and over the ramps, threads his way past calves huddled against their mothers for protection against the storm. We watch as Rich[†] rides the bucking ATV up the rough, steep sloping dunes through the blinding sleet towards a pasture somewhere to the north.

---

* Thomas A. "Stub" Boots was inducted into the Nebraska Sandhills Cowboy Hall of Fame in 2006.
† Rich Boots was inducted into the Nebraska Sandhills Cowboy Hall of Fame in 2013.

Chapter 24
Renaissance Man

Charles Barron McIntosh
September 5, 1916-May 3, 2007

*To claim that Barron McIntosh is an expert on the Nebraska Sand Hills
is rather like noting that Michael Jordan is an expert on basketball.*
— John C. Hudson, Northwestern University

*Anytime I asked him a question he didn't know the answer to he would be busy the next day
finding out about it. I used to ask him just about anything, because he knew just about everything.*
— Jean Knight, ex-wife and long-time friend

McIntosh's theory of glaciation was complete bullshit.
—James Swinehart, University of Nebraska
geologist

If you spend much time poking around the Nebraska Sand Hills it won't be long before someone asks if you've read "McIntosh's book." This question implies if you'd read the book and fully understood the genius and monumental effort behind it you'd pick a less ambitious project and quit asking all these fool questions. After hearing the same suggestion a half dozen times, I read the book, *The Nebraska Sand Hills: The Human Landscape* (1996). And the questioners are mostly right. McIntosh didn't miss anything, especially in areas of special interest. A skilled geographer, historian, geologist, meticulous cartographer, archeologist, ethnologist, artist, tenacious researcher, McIntosh spent most of his adult life answering the questions his fertile mind churned out in mass quantities. He had no choice. Once a serious question appeared, from whatever source, McIntosh was bound by obsession to do whatever it took to uncover the answer.

The vast majority of those questions had to do with the Nebraska Sand Hills, their creation, the different human occupiers over time, the intrepid explorers, heroes and scoundrels, settlers of widely divergent cultures and ethnicities. The question occupying an out-sized percentage of McIntosh's research was how various federal land dispersement programs evolved and how these programs were used and abused to create large private land holdings. One focus of his research was the Spade Ranch, which in its heyday covered a half a million acres and ran 60,000 head of cattle. The Spade recruited Civil War veterans and widows and ranch cowboys to file on strategic free land. McIntosh showed how Bartlett Richards, owner of the Spade, used 40 acre land patents along his fence lines to effectively enclose thousands of acres of public land. McIntosh also researched the history of Old Jules Sandoz's land acquisitions and the patent history of his father-in-law Harry Lamb's ranch in McPherson County. Title research led McIntosh to spend many summers in tiny Sand Hills county courthouses digging into land records.

McIntosh illustrated the results of his land title research with detailed hand-drawn maps and tables, the kind of attention to detail almost unknown in current scholarship. Colleagues at the University of Nebraska never fail to mention his laboring over maps, how they overflowed his always cluttered roll top desk and covered his office walls. They also mention his prodigious rock collection, which threatened to crowd him clean out of his office.

McIntosh's book answers so many questions it becomes difficult to give a full accounting. Suffice it to say he suffered from wide-ranging curiosity. What underlies the Sand Hills and how and when were they formed? Who were the early occupiers and where did they live? McIntosh collected projectile points from dry washes and dune tops across the Sand Hills, traced their origins and determined time frames of occupation. Where is the trail Spotted Tail's band used to cross the hills? Where did the shell-shocked Brule and Oglala survivors of the Battle of Blue Water assemble afterwards? What about Mormon travelers? Jewish settlers? Irish settlers? Freed slaves? Where were their tracks and settlements and what happened to them? Curious about the convoluted matrimonial history of Old Jules Sandoz? So was McIntosh. Lieutenant G. K. Warren created the first definitive maps of the Sand Hills. What routes did his expeditions follow and why? McIntosh personally retraced Warren's travels.

We have a saying around here: "going down the rabbit hole," which means chancing upon a particularly interesting line of inquiry, following said line of inquiry as far as humanly possible, which may or may not lead to knowledge relevant to the task at hand. Like McIntosh, I've spent a few hours exploring a promising rabbit hole, sometimes months or more.

Shortly after pulling all the files and refreshing my memory with voluminous interview transcriptions and a reacquaintance with McIntosh's published works, I began writing this chapter. A few paragraphs into it, I remembered a humble cardboard box, which we must have stashed somewhere in the garage during our most recent move. An unpretentious box, a well-scuffed box, a box once holding a rot gut brand of tequila, entrusted to my safe keeping by "Buffalo Bruce" McIntosh, Barron's professional environmentalist son. If memory serves, "Big Red Ranch" is written on the outside of the box in red crayon. Well-launched on the writing task and already in possession of more than enough McIntosh material for at least one full blown biography, I groaned. Kathy, upon hearing the box news, groaned. But what are you going to do? Impossible to leave what could be a wealth of fresh McIntosh nuggets unopened. Finding said box took a scant three hours.

Inside? The first draft chapters of McIntosh's autobiography, dozens of photocopies of old photographs, along with multiple rough drafts explaining, in painstaking detail, every photograph.

Most of the photos were taken by McIntosh's beloved paternal Aunt Mabel "Auntie Mame" Souther, with a camera given her by department store magnate Marshall Field. In 1896, Mabel, 32, and her husband Will, 42, moved from the rough frontier town of Crawford, Nebraska, to the Wyoming Powder River country to manage the famous Pratt & Ferris Big Red Ranch. Shortly before taking the new job, Will and Mabel traveled to Chicago and met Marshall Field, a minority investor in the ranching enterprise. Field wanted photos of his property and ranch activities to better oversee his interests and to decorate his office walls. He gave Mabel an expensive camera, developing chemicals and equipment along with detailed instructions. Mabel, once she arrived in Wyoming, took her task seriously and eventually compiled an impressive collection of ranch photographs: cattle brandings, broad fields covered with shocks of grain, threshings, haying crews, ranch buildings, the arrival of the mail stage coach (armed guard included), group photos of cowboys on horseback, cowboys eating around a chuck wagon, cowboys loading cattle on rail cars.[*]

While growing up in nearby Edgemont, South Dakota, McIntosh traveled to the Souther family headquarters north of Crawford for extended vacations at Auntie Mame's. He remembered taking a short-term job while in college as a wool stomper, packing newly shorn wool into long burlap wool bags and wearing a terrific crop of sheep ticks afterwards. Late in life, with his eyesight almost gone, he decided to research the background for many of Mabel's photos, planning to create in the process an illustrated history of Auntie Mame, the Big Red Ranch and the Souther ranches in Wyoming and northwest Nebraska.

A prime example of McIntosh's obsessive attention to detail was his detective work concerning photos of two wolf hunters, a gray whiskered older man and a punk kid, maybe 12 years old. In the first photo, in front of a mammoth barn, a heavily armed man astride a light-colored horse holds the lead rope on a pack horse loaded with wolf skins. The kid sits on a short-eared horse, armed only with a stout cudgel. Is that an actual goddamned grinning monkey sitting on a pile of wolf pelts? The photo is a little fuzzy, but what I'm peering at looks exactly like a goddamned grinning monkey. The second photo, taken at closer range captures the kid in front of an extensive log corral leading a pack horse, grinning monkey riding a smaller load of wolf skins. Is that goddamned monkey drinking out of a mug? Sure looks like a goddamned monkey drinking out of a mug. How can this be?

I flip through the rough drafts. McIntosh says the Big Red Ranch offered a $5 bounty on wolves, the highest bounty of any ranch in the area. McIntosh, likely through *Buffalo Gazette* (WY) newspaper accounts, identifies the adult wolf hunter as S. A. McIntyre, better known as Rattlesnake Jack, a famous wolf hunter, who habitually carried at least one rattlesnake in a gunny sack and occasionally trapped and sold young bears for pets. The punk kid turns out to be Jack's son, who some months after Mabel took his photo, had to ride 12 miles for help after suffering a rattlesnake bite while setting traps. McIntosh assumes the first photo, lacking shadows, was taken in front of the main barn at Big Red Ranch headquarters under cloudy skies. The short shadows in the second photo indicate a late morning-early afternoon time of day. The presence of a grinning monkey will forever remain a mystery, although McIntosh claims, without attribution, the monkey's drinking mug belonged to Auntie Mame.

After 21 months managing the Big Red Ranch, Will and Mabel Souther returned to Crawford, where Will's exuberant capitalism soon created a variety of profitable commercial and agricultural enterprises, boosted by the booming Crawford economy, which ranked 7th in the state by 1911.

As a young man Will came west as the disgraced son of a wealthy Maine family. While at Bowdoin College, he and a bosom pal, future polar explorer Robert Peary, engaged in overly enthusiastic hazing of lowly freshmen. Bowdoin expelled Will, but allowed Peary to graduate. McIntosh never explains Will Souther's access to a seemingly inexhaustible capital, which funded whatever business opportunities he pursued, often using partnerships to stretch his resources. Chances were his well-to-do family did not continue to shun him, particularly after he experienced notable business and personal success on the American frontier.

---

[*] The Nebraska Historical Society and the American Heritage Center at the University of Wyoming house collections of Mabel Souther's photographs.

The final collection of photos capture the bustling town of Crawford at the turn of the century, made prosperous by proximity to Ft. Robinson and nearby Sioux reservations. Additional photos show sheep feeding and shearing on the Souther's Crawford ranch and on their spread in eastern Wyoming. Once again McIntosh scrutinizes each photo for clues, assigning a place, a rough date, sometimes, if there are shadows to read, even a time of day.

Although we have no way of knowing, had his eyesight not betrayed him, had cancer not killed him, and McIntosh had been able to publish his final manuscript, his valedictory project could well have become a valued addition to our knowledge of turn-of-the-century western history and added luster to his remarkable career. He certainly assembled the raw materials.

Howard, McIntosh's father, learned the druggist trade in Crawford before setting up his own drugstore 60 miles north in Edgemont, South Dakota. Although he married and supported a family, Howard never owned an automobile, preferring the train. He walked to work, opened the store early, took an hour for dinner at 6, returned to the store until 10. His growing family became used to an absentee father.

Charles Barron McIntosh, born in 1916, would have surely upgraded his status from over-achieving Boy Scout to Eagle Scout, if such an elevated rank of scouting had existed. As it was, he excelled in high school academics, music, drama, football, basketball and track. He played the trumpet in the school band and formed a local dance band. He quarterbacked his high football team to an undefeated season. McIntosh's younger brother Roy remembers him as "not so big, maybe 140 pounds, but he was fast and hard to tackle."

All through his school years in Edgemont, McIntosh engaged in a vigorous, but losing scholastic competition with Catherine, whose grade on any assignment invariably shaded McIntosh's. A random 8th grade geography assignment of a hand-drawn map earned McIntosh an A+, edging Catherine by the width of the plus. Although Catherine sniffed she would have had a higher grade if she'd taking the assignment seriously, McIntosh was forever hooked on cartography. He later taught cartography in four different universities.

His music teacher, a Huron College alum, encouraged the McIntosh boys to enroll in Huron after high school. Two of them, Curtis and Barron did so, becoming key members of the Huron "Scalpers" football team. Barron suffered a career-ending knee injury when he was maliciously hit from behind after a play ended. He was bitter about it a half century later when his knee was still giving him grief.

Like many Depression era students, McIntosh had little financial help from his parents and worked his way through college, waiting tables in the college cafeteria and playing in dance bands. Summers, he joined the Burlington Northern section gang out of Edgemont or picked up work on one of the Souther ranches. When he went home, once or twice a year, he hitchhiked or hopped a freight train.

Following graduation from Huron in 1938, McIntosh could have sought employment. He had good contacts with the railroad, which paid better than most employers. Instead he enrolled in the University of Nebraska, where he spent a year earning a B.S. in education. His finances likely were perilous, but he paid his bills with restaurant jobs and dance band gigs.

After receiving his degree in education, he accepted a job teaching math and science at nearby Springfield High School. He enjoyed teaching, and a believer in hands-on learning, kept a menagerie in his classroom for instructional purposes. An occasional bull snake escaped into unknown areas of the school, causing predictable hysterics.

His savings bolstered by a year of teaching wages, McIntosh returned in 1940 to graduate school at the University of Nebraska, where he began working on a Master's degree. On a trip to visit his family in Edgemont, McIntosh drove through North Platte, Nebraska, where he spotted a likely-looking dark-haired young woman walking along Jeffers Street. Something about the determined way she carried herself suggested a firm destination. McIntosh pulled over, discovered Ruby Mabel Lamb was headed to Tryon, 35 miles northwest in the Sand Hills, where her family owned a house where the Lamb children stayed during the school year. By sheer coincidence, Tryon was right on McIntosh's planned route to his home in Edgemont.

By the time McIntosh delivered Ruby to Tryon and later to Harry and Lena Lamb's ranch, he was interested in her and she was interested in him. They took a late afternoon horseback ride into the gently sloping valley west of ranch headquarters and then south into the hills. When they returned after dark, Ruby's sister, Dollie, said the courtship phase had been successfully concluded.

Harry Lamb, Ruby's father, met his future wife Lena while they both were employed by the famous Black Ranch on the Dismal River. Harry's father Restore, better known as R. N., a successful North Platte wholesale grocer and businessman, initially homesteaded west of Stapleton.* Son Harry ran away from home at an early age because he hated herding cattle. He herded plenty of cattle after hiring himself out to neighboring ranchers. He took a job at the lower Horseshoe Bar (Black) Ranch on Wild Horse Flats northeast of Stapleton, where he was assigned all the tasks no one else wanted to do. His future wife Lena, titular head of a family of 11 younger brothers and sisters, cooked for the haying crews at the large scale Black haying operation. Lena and Harry were married in 1909. Lena's parents and siblings were staunch Christian Scientists, a sect suspicious of doctors and medicine. Harry soon converted and became the default family doctor, stitching wounds and setting broken bones.

After marrying Lena, Harry's business ambitions led him to try a variety of enterprises, some of them likely financed by his prosperous father. He ran a grocery store in Stapleton, ranched for a time north of Ringgold, where daughter Ruby Mabel Lamb was born before he sold the place to my Great-Uncle Lucius Tupper on contract. Harry moved his family to North Platte, where he worked as a policeman, sold meat, was the night clerk at the Palace Hotel, all the while dabbling in real estate — residential, commercial and agricultural. Land speculators, cattle buyers and ranchers often stayed at the Palace Hotel and Harry kept his ears open. He picked up tips on cattle buying and selling and increased his knowledge of cattle husbandry. Ranchers and land speculators told of adding to their holdings by purchasing Kinkaid claims from discouraged homesteaders, sometimes for as little as 50 cents an acre. In 1929, Lamb persuaded Arch Tracy, a down-on-his-luck Kinkaider northwest of Tryon, to sell him a section plus a detached 40 acres for $1 and the deed to one of Harry's rental houses in North Platte. He was going back to herding cattle, just as the nation entered the Great Depression.

---

* R.N.'s wife Ada Mary died when Harry was 14 years old. Since there were no cemeteries in Stapleton area she was buried on the family homestead. R. N. later donated three acres, including Ada's grave site, for a community cemetery (present day Loup Valley Cemetery). Harry's mother, Harry, his younger sister Nettie, who committed suicide after an unfortunate romance with a married man, Ruby Mabel Lamb McIntosh, and Charles Barron McIntosh are buried in a straight line on the eastern side of the cemetery, shaded by mature cedar trees. Also buried in the Loup Valley Cemetery are my great uncles Oscar and Lucius Tupper. Perhaps Uncle Lucius and Harry, in their spare time, discuss land swaps, the desirability of gate cut cattle and purchasing cheap Kinkaid claims.

The first order of business was trading Lucius Tupper clear title to the Ringgold section for enough gate cut cattle to stock the new place, an ancient team of work horses and an "experienced" saddle horse. In the trade, Harry also obtained a well-used farm implement or perhaps an old truck or maybe a spool of rusty barbed wire and/or a stupid mongrel dog named Shep who wouldn't herd if you paid him a nickel. The story varies according to the person doing the telling.

Shortly after the land trade, my mother, Mattie Tupper, 18 years old and fresh out of Kearney State Teachers College, arrived to schoolmarm the Ringgold school. She stayed for a time with the Dankers, another family with Franklin County roots, but eventually took her room and board with her Uncle Lucius and Aunt Florence in a house with two bedrooms and four children.

According to Tupper family legend, after acquiring clear title to his section Lucius hunkered down in survival mode in the early 1930s doing what he did best, which was not spending money. He also built a fine cattle herd and gradually added to his holdings, buying out broke homesteaders and smaller ranch holdings, eventually amassing 20 sections of debt-free ranch land.

Harry drove his newly acquired cattle herd and assorted horses from the Tupper ranch to the Archer place northwest of Tryon, no mean feat, since the herd included a few mismatched cows and calves. The newly orphaned calves became unhappy at an overnight camp site and returned home. Once he settled his remaining livestock on the Archer place, Harry moved his family from North Platte into a sod house he built with the help of Lena's brothers.

The first years of the Depression taxed the Lamb family, as it did the Tuppers, but Lena was skilled at subsistence living and cash requirements were low. Harry made strategic additions to the ranch through the Depression years, occasionally repeating the trade of North Platte rental houses for Kinkaid claims, sometimes buying land at tax sales. Prices ranged from 50 cents an acre early in the 30s to almost $2 an acre after cattle prices increased towards the end of the decade. Using the lessons he learned from ranchers and cattle traders in the North Platte hotel, Harry frequently changed his mix of livestock, depending on weather and markets. He might run yearlings one year, manage a cow herd for a spell, then switch back to yearlings.

In 1948, two years before he died, Harry built a showy new house, four bedrooms up, three bedrooms down, complete with a walk-in cooler and walk-in freezer. Eventually Harry amassed 20 sections of debt-free grass in a tight square around his headquarters, which he named the Pioneer Ranch,* where Ruby Lamb and Barron McIntosh sealed their romance and where McIntosh's life-long fascination with the Nebraska Sand Hills began.

In the fall of 1941, Barron entered graduate school in political science and public administration at Louisiana State University. He married Ruby in Baton Rouge in September and supported the new household with a bell hop job at the ritzy Heidelberg Hotel from 11 p.m. to 7 a.m. Following Pearl Harbor, Ruby and Barron made preparations for the inevitable wartime separation. When the draft notice from South Dakota arrived in January, their meager possessions were packed and ready to move.

In spite of his bum knee, the draft induction center in Baton Rouge gave McIntosh their stamp of approval. During the early days of the war, although he'd been drafted, McIntosh had the option of choosing a service branch. He chose the Navy. Ruby left for Nebraska and

---

* A ranch eventually purchased by Linda Rodewald Kemp, granddaughter of my Great-Uncle Lucius Tupper.

Barron soon found himself in San Diego undergoing basic training. Assigned to the Navy's weather service, McIntosh's World War II stateside postings included a blimp base in Massachusetts, and a training base on Roanoke Island, North Carolina. Aboard the USS Core, an escort carrier primarily engaged in anti-submarine warfare, he visited Argentina, Newfoundland, Glasgow, Scotland, Bermuda, Guantanamo Bay in Cuba, passed through the Panama Canal to San Diego and sailed on to the Hawaiian and Philippine Islands.

He mustered out of the service and returned to Tryon without a clear plan or a job. In early November, a local preacher came to the house to ask Barron to substitute for a sick elementary teacher, who taught grades 5-8. In January, the teacher left for North Platte and Barron was hired to finish out the year. He took his students to a local sand pit south of town and taught them to identify soil profiles. At the end of the school year at a county wide meeting of school teachers, Barron was voted the best teacher in the county. At which point the McPherson County Schools at Tryon offered the wildly overqualified McIntosh a permanent teaching position.

After three years, despite lacking geography credentials, he volunteered to teach a geography course. This led to summer school at the University of Nebraska, where his physical geography class dealt with aspects of meteorology and climatology, subjects precisely in McIntosh's wheelhouse. He earned sparkling grades and came to the attention of legendary NU geography professor Leslie "Mr. Great Plains" Hewes, a student of Carl Sauer at Cal Berkeley, who preached "holistic" geography. The holistic approach included cultural, human, physical, political, historical and regional geography as well as cartography. Hewes was the first prominent American geographer to study Plains Indian culture and helped the NU geography department gain a national reputation for advanced scholarship.

Hewes offered McIntosh a graduate assistantship for the fall semester. McIntosh hesitated. Not only was he under contract to teach in Tryon in the fall and had a wife and sons to support, but he had no idea how he would finance his studies. In the end, his new infatuation with geography trumped his trepidation and he moved his family to Lincoln. He acquired another Master's degree, his third, in 1952 and a PhD in 1955.

One of McIntosh's first graduate students at Nebraska hailed from Illinois coal country. He told McIntosh old-timers in the coal mines believed mine explosions were correlated with abrupt weather changes. McIntosh, an expert meteorologist, became intrigued. An intrigued McIntosh was a guy who was about to dig into a question like a badger. The result was his PhD thesis showing coal mine explosions were more likely to occur following passage of a low pressure system during periods of cold dry air. McIntosh published a truncated version of his findings,* which became accepted wisdom in government mine safety circles.

During his doctoral pursuit, he earned a Fulbright fellowship and taught at the University of New Zealand in Christchurch for a year. The family's sojourn in New Zealand included a fateful visit to a local dairy farm, where Ruby contracted tuberculosis. A doctor diagnosed her condition a few years later when she was pregnant with Howard. Had Ruby not been a devoted Christian Scientist her tuberculosis might have been a serious, but treatable condition. By the 1950s the antibiotics streptomycin, developed in 1944, and isoniazid, developed in 1952, had become became commonly used and effective anti-tuberculosis agents. However, because she grew up in a Christian Science home, Ruby resisted treatment, even though she was pregnant with Howard. Although she sometimes relented and met with doctors, she

---

* McIntosh, C. B., "Atmospheric Conditions and Explosions in Coal Mines," The Geographical Review, 1957, Vol. XLVII, No 2, pp. 155-174

would not take medications, except irregularly, and only under constant pressure from her doctors and Barron. Meanwhile, McIntosh moved his family. He took a one-year teaching position at the University of Texas and a two-year posting to Eastern Illinois University before returning to teach at the University of Nebraska.

When Ruby's condition became critical, Barron drove her to the state tuberculosis hospital in Kearney. Again she resisted prescribed medications and quit eating entirely after suspecting the doctors of putting medicine in her food. Ruby died in 1961, after a last ditch lung surgery. Those who knew him well believe McIntosh never fully recovered from Ruby's death.

Howard was a toddler when his mother died. Ruby's sister, Dollie, raised him in North Platte until he was old enough for school. Barron balanced his life as a single father with his duties as a geography professor and researcher. Although he and his own brothers were never particularly close, he tried to foster a tight-knit family unit with his boys. He became adept at cooking one-dish casseroles, and in the interest of frugality, insisted on one helping per person.

Once back at Nebraska with a permanent position in the geography department, McIntosh turned his attention to the Nebraska Sand Hills, publishing papers on Black settlements and the use and abuse of the Forest Lieu Act of 1897 to augment large private ranch holdings. In the late 1960s, with older boys Bruce and Douglas out on their own, McIntosh took sons Howard and Les on his extended summer research trips, often camping at Halsey National Forest, where the boys acquired a long succession of transient, beady-eyed, uber-horny ornate box turtles. Never a big believer in air conditioning, McIntosh advised his boys to eat grapes to combat the heat. Howard remembers many summer hours spent traveling the Sand Hills in the back of a hot station wagon munching on grapes.

McIntosh's interest in land acquisition patterns led him to spend thousands of hours in county courthouses searching land records. He also kept a sharp eye for arrowheads and spear points on the crests of dunes and in the bottoms of dry water courses, tracking down the source of the flint to quarries south of the Knife River in North Dakota and the Alibate flint quarries between Amarillo and Borger, Texas. And he was always alert for geological evidence that might prove his pet theory of glacial activity in the Sand Hills.

McIntosh believed glaciers had sheered off portions of the Chadron-Cambridge Arch, but found the proposition difficult to substantiate. He thought if he could prove the Chadron-Cambridge Arch was continuing to rise it might support his hypothesis. He uncovered evidence of a sudden outbreak of "jumping" water wells along the Arch. Wells would sink into the ground or be forced out of the ground by unseen forces. The wells, even if they initially continued working, eventually became useless. He guessed an upthrusting arch coupled with earthquake activity bore responsibility but proof remained elusive. During the course of his jumping well inquiries he spent time on the Fritz Sandoz ranch visiting with Fritz's widow, Blanche.

McIntosh studied yellowed newspaper collections and sometimes devoted a few days each summer to tracing the routes of early Sand Hills explorers. He was especially interested in Lt. G.K. Warren's early mapping expeditions. He loved talking with old timers, particularly Young Jules Sandoz, brother of Fritz, who shared his wide-ranging curiosity about almost everything. Young Jules knew plenty about the Chadron-Cambridge Arch and had made his own study of Spade Ranch land patents. Not surprising that during his 30 years of Sand Hills land title research, McIntosh became familiar with the histories of most of the prominent ranch families in the Sand Hills.

It didn't take long after McIntosh moved back to Lincoln to feel at home in the collegial atmosphere of the geography department, where his mentor Leslie Hewes still served as department chair. He was, however, tenacious in his beliefs, and would argue into the ground anyone foolish enough to challenge him. In particular, his views on how geography should be taught were immutable. Although willing to have coffee with colleagues and chat about most any subject, no one who taught with him in the department remembers being invited into his cluttered house.

He served briefly as department chairman, but university politics gave him ulcers and he relinquished the job. Over the years, especially after Hewes' retirement, knuckle-headed deans hatched a series of schemes to dismember and de-emphasize the department. McIntosh could always be counted on to vociferously defend his beloved geography department. In later years, if an occasional rotating department chair, like Richard Lonsdale, whose job it was to encourage and monitor faculty research, braved his cluttered office to ask if his Sand Hills research was approaching conclusion he'd smile and say, "I'm just working on things at my own pace."

University teaching agreed with McIntosh and his wide-ranging lectures challenged students' note-taking abilities. As a geography major at the University of Nebraska, future Congressman Doug Beureter* took several upper level classes from McIntosh:

> *I chose him as my senior honors thesis advisor because he was an expert in settlement patterns and because he approved of my work in some of his classes. My thesis dealt with population changes in all of Nebraska's 550 cities, towns and villages and I mapped my findings using different colors. He was a gifted cartographer and I had some difficulty coming up with maps that met with his full approval. I later obtained an advanced degree from Harvard in urban planning. The courses I took under Dr. McIntosh were especially valuable.*

By pure coincidence, McIntosh also served as teacher and mentor to Robert Stoddard, my geography instructor at Nebraska Wesleyan University in the early 1960s. My first impression of Stoddard, a tall, gangly, bespectacled guy, socially awkward, long on earnest and short on humor, did not do the man justice. Well before the first lecture ended, I was captivated. Stoddard brought an enthusiastic, holistic approach to his subject and had I not previously committed to the study of history I would have switched majors on the spot. Fifty some years later, I consider him the rock star professor of my undergraduate years.

After Stoddard earned his doctorate at the University of Iowa, he took, at McIntosh's urging, a position teaching at the University of Nebraska, where he and "Mac" became close colleagues, discussed research projects and went on field trips together. Stoddard's exemplary career at Nebraska included numerous publications and Fulbright lectureships in Nepal and Sri Lanka. Although Stoddard never talked specifically about McIntosh's controversial theories of Sand Hills glaciation, he left the impression he offered his friend sound advice.

---

* Former 13-term congressman from Nebraska, Beureter served on several key House committees, including International Relations, Financial Services and the Permanent Select Committee on Intelligence. Following his retirement from Congress in 2004, Beureter served six years as president and CEO of the Asia Foundation, a San Francisco-based policy group influential in Asian politics.

A few years after Ruby's death, McIntosh married Alice, a librarian he met at Love Library on the Lincoln campus. Despite an optimistic beginning, Alice was never entirely comfortable in McIntosh's small, cluttered house. She was also in pursuit of an advanced degree in library science, which she hoped would lead to career advancement, if not in Lincoln, then someplace else. She had two young boys, one of which got into a fight with Howard. McIntosh paddled both of them with a lath. Alice's son claimed it was a 2 x 4. She left. McIntosh returned to his life as a solitary widower, researcher and maker of one-dish casseroles.

Shortly before he retired from teaching, and while he was still deeply involved in Sand Hills research, McIntosh began attending Elderhostels, where he met Jean Knight, a retired public utility worker from Oklahoma. They eventually married, but Jean's conflicts with Howard and Barron's hopelessly cluttered life-style led to an annulment in 1987. Afterwards they remained close. She kept her residence in Lincoln, stayed with him frequently at his Pine Ridge cabin near Crawford and did most of the driving.

After formal retirement from the university, McIntosh continued to toil in his department office working on his beloved maps and charts. Joyce Hurst, long-time geography department secretary, recalls McIntosh removing his trove of maps and charts from his ancient roll top desk, crawling inside and closing the roll top to take short naps. "He was a little man, nothing to him."

During his sojourns at the Pine Ridge cabin with Jean, McIntosh spent time on his research and completed detailed line drawings of the area's flora and fauna. Wife Ruby, a gifted artist, tutored his drawing and painting efforts while they were married and he continued to hone his skills for the rest of his life. When a dangerous forest fire threatened, forest service workers arrived with an evacuation order. Barron resisted while he and Jean packed up McIntosh's Sand Hills book manuscript, notes and maps and loaded them in the pickup. One of the exasperated forest service men asked McIntosh if a book were more important than his life. McIntosh replied, "This book is my life."

After macular degeneration began to erode McIntosh's sight, Jean took an active role in editing his Sand Hills manuscript. Although she considered him to be a fine writer, small details of punctuation and grammar often needed attention. When the Sand Hills book finally met McIntosh's exacting standards, it was published by the University of Nebraska Press in 1996. He dedicated the book not to his sons or parents or brothers, nor to his professional mentor Leslie Hewes, nor to Jean Knight, who helped shape the final manuscript, but to Ruby and the romantic memory of their first horseback ride across the Lamb family ranch.

To Ruby, who helped saddle the two
horses for our ride across the home
valley and on south into the Hills.

The Nebraska Sand Hills: The Human Landscape received enthusiastic reviews from both geographers and lay people. For some reviewers the book represented a throwback to an era when geographers spent more time in the field and in the library and less time on a computer massaging data. Others cite his obvious affection for his subject and the 30 years he spent researching. Every reviewer, professional geographer or not, makes special mention of McIntosh's 100 illustrative maps and graphs, all done by meticulously by hand, a phenomenon rendered almost extinct years before by computer graphics.

Although the book received awards from his fellow geographers and he was asked to speak at several conferences, McIntosh, as usual, shunned the limelight. Roger Welsch, Nebraska folklorist and host of a popular show on Nebraska public television, tried to get McIntosh to discuss his book on the show. McIntosh always politely declined. Initially he made the excuse he was waiting for the scholarly reviews to come in. Later, he blamed his diminished eyesight. Always the lone wolf, most comfortable making solitary tracks across his beloved Sand Hills, McIntosh had already moved on to other projects.

Between revisits to his Big Red Ranch book project, he self-published a personal journal of his time at the Pine Ridge cabin — *Life on the Pine Ridge* (2001) and his first attempt at proving glaciation in the Sand Hills — *Hypothesis for Sandhillian Glaciation* (2001). His original plans for the Sand Hills book included a discussion of his glaciation theory, but when initial reviewers and geologist friends threw doubt on his theory, arguing it would taint the critical reception of the book, he reluctantly left it out. Jim Swinehart, no stranger to controversial theories and one of McIntosh's favorite geologist sounding boards, did more than anyone to dissuade him from publishing. "McIntosh's theory of glaciation was complete bullshit. I tried to talk him out of it. He relied on old stuff in a gravel pit way before the time he was addressing. If the stuff in the gravel pit came from glaciers, it would have included agate and green stone form Minnesota. The gravel under the Sand Hills came from the west."

By the time the two books were published in 2001, McIntosh's eyesight was mostly gone. He had to piggyback two magnifying glasses to read newspaper headlines and used a computer Howard rigged up to magnify everything on the screen six times. Although he could only see light and shadow out of the corner of one eye, he made another attempt at proving his glaciation theory in the self-published *Intuitive Pattern & Process: Hypotheses for Sandhillian Glaciation* (2004). With son Doug's editorial assistance, he added several new thoroughly researched and mapped "proofs." His mapping of land patents had convinced him some of the higher, dryer sand dunes were produced by glacial activity and in the process been made less desirable and less frequently homesteaded. He also presented evidence of rocks striated by moving glaciers and the presence in the Sand Hills of glacial moraines. He mapped interruptions in the natural courses of streams, like Blue Water Creek. And much, much more. I am not a geologist. He may have proved his theory — or not. However, he did not convince his dubious peers and his pet theory, despite countless hours of investigation and two self-published books, remains an outlier. Not that he probably minded all that much. Proving it to himself would have been the most satisfying part of the entire exercise. For the curious, the books are available. As an added bonus, in his last book McIntosh included a chapter on his coal mine explosion theory and a chapter from his Sand Hills book on land filing activity by the Spade Ranch, more than enough material to keep you out of the bars for a considerable spell. Please let me know if you come to any conclusions about the glaciation theory.

McIntosh underwent successful prostate surgery at the Mayo Clinic in the early 1990s and made a good recovery. Not long after his last glaciation book rolled off the press in 2004, he was diagnosed with colon cancer, a condition complicated by his exclusive diet of cherry nut ice cream. He eventually moved to the Clark Jeary Retirement Center in Southeast Lincoln, which also housed Jean Knight, who was recovering from multiple heart attacks and her own bout with cancer.

As often happens with terminal patients suffering from severe pain, McIntosh spent his last days in a drugged haze, incapable of much communication. His son Howard received a phone call late one night. When the nursing staff tried to remove McIntosh's dentures, a common safety procedure, the patient resisted and the dentures refused to budge. Howard came to the facility and, with some difficulty, convinced the nurses 90-year-old McIntosh was still in possession of every one of his original teeth. Had the nurses known about the remarkable teeth of people born and raised in Edgemont, South Dakota, they might not have been so skeptical.

Dr. Peter Sotherland, who served as a dentist in the Edgemont community for the first years his career: "Edgemont jawbones are profound. I broke several pairs of stainless steel forceps yanking teeth on those old guys."

Sotherland attributes the sturdy jaw socket bones to the presence of significant natural fluoride and optimum amounts of calcium and phosphorous in the Madison aquifer Edgemont taps for municipal water. "If I know a patient is from Edgemont, I know I'm in for it. I've seen old boys with granite heads."

Sotherland says Edgemont's famously healthy teeth have little to do with modern dental hygiene. "Edgemont's standard dental care practices are early 20th century. None of this bullshit about brushing and flossing."

The benefits of Edgemont water, according to Sotherland, are magnified when the water is consumed when the person is 4 years old or younger. "That's when the six year molars and front teeth are being formed. But females are different from males. If a female spends the first 18 years of her life in Edgemont, she is much less likely to develop osteoporosis, although she will likely eventually suffer degradation of bone. If males consume Edgemont water for the first 18 years their bones are good for life."

Charles Barron McIntosh kept his original teeth to the end. Six days after he died his sons buried him in the Loup Valley Cemetery next to Ruby. Cleaning out the house took longer. Maps, charts, his art work, his extensive library, including bound plat maps for many Sand Hills counties, and his elementary school textbooks, papers from high school, maps and charts from his time in New Zealand. And rocks. A basement full of rocks. Rocks moved from his university office to the house. Rocks his father collected and labeled in 1905, after moving to Edgemont. And a notebook with a key to identifying all the rocks. The sons split up the rocks. Nobody knows for certain what happened to the notebook with the key.

Everyone who knew him considers Charles Barron McIntosh a rare person, particularly his unique gifts of wide ranging curiosity, brilliant cartography and obsessive research habits. As far back as his spirited grade school competition with Catherine in Edgemont, McIntosh was always deeply ambitious, not necessarily for public praise or awards, but for learning things no one else knew, and then using the knowledge to educate others.

Would he have been so tunnel-visioned and obsessive had Ruby, the love of his life, survived to distract him? Had she been waiting for him at home would he have spent so many hours at his University office perfecting maps? Would he have spent thousands of hours in Sand Hills courthouses, often past closing time, pouring over land records? Impossible to know. But there is little doubt he was deeply affected by the loss.

In the early 1990s, thirty years after Ruby's death, Mike Farrell, long-time producer and film maker for Nebraska public television, persuaded McIntosh to share his knowledge for "Sandhills Story," a documentary Farrell was filming. Farrell used an old sod house south of Whitman on the border of Arthur and McPherson counties as the back drop for the interview. For two hours they sat on a dune overlooking the sod house and the undulating hills beyond talking about the Nebraska Sand Hills. Farrell's primary motive for the interview was McIntosh's research detailing how large ranches, like the Spade, abused federal land disperse-ment programs. However, Farrell allowed McIntosh to tell the Sand Hills stories he wanted to tell, mostly without interruption, which is what a smart interviewer would do. And McIntosh, although he was 75 years old and well past his prime, talked about an astonishing variety of topics, from how the Indians were forced out of the Sand Hills, to the use and abuse of land patents, to the histories and genealogies of prominent ranch families, why Grant County had to be re-surveyed, the origins and long-term effects of the Kinkaid Act, the ramifications of historic Sand Hills droughts and resulting irrigation projects, the wisdom or lack of same in introducing center pivot irrigation to the Sand Hills.

Towards the end of the interview, Farrell asked McIntosh a particularly intuitive ques-tion, which along with the answer did not make the final cut, "Listening to you today... you love this country, consider it special. What is it about it that you love?"

"I don't know. I don't want to say. Some people are going to say my book is going to be dedicated to my wife. You see, she's been over there in the cemetery since 1961 and that's been one of the... don't make me cry fellows... that's a part of it. And I think (the Sand Hills) are especially beautiful, late in the afternoon when the sun is real low and you can get the hills looking a little on the brown side and the valleys beautifully green."

Chapter 25
Dry Valley Church

No sinner is ever saved after the first twenty minutes of a sermon.

— Mark Twain

Heading north from Whitman (pop. 214) after a rain squall on a crumbling one-lane oiled road you have to keep a sharp eye for horny sand turtles. Rain acts as a potent aphrodisiac on the male sand turtle, also known as the ornate box turtle (*terapene ornata ornata*).Once the skies clear and warm breezes blow, blind lust takes over and the red-eyed male sand turtle launches a frantic, completely random search for satisfaction. The female sand turtle, on the other hand, has learned over the centuries to ignore both rain and rutting males. She and hundreds of her sisters, serenely oblivious to the randy males running amok in the neighborhood, loll on grassy dunes, munching contentedly on a hapless bug or a toothsome shoot of new grass, which, since they have their priorities in proper order, they will continue to do, even during a rare chance encounter with a deranged male.

Swerving between trudging turtles and basking rattlesnakes, you cross three branches of the Middle Loup River, south, middle and north, each rivulet occupying a broad valley lined with massive grassed dune ridges. In crossing the Middle Loup north of Whitman, we bisect the route of Lt. G. K. Warren's 1857 pioneering Sand Hills mapping expedition. In crossing the Middle Loup North of Whitman, we also bisect C. B. McIntosh's path 120 years later when he retraced Warren's route. I am focused on avoiding the unintended murder of turtles, rattlesnakes or any other random critter crossing the narrow black tarmac, mindful that only last week Kathy ran over a squirrel as she was ferrying 14-year-old daughter, Sydney, to her waitressing job. Sydney told Kathy she'd just violated "one of the 'amendments', the one that says you can't kill animals and bugs or whatever."

The air, fresh and sweet with new growth, flows through the open car windows. White puffs of clouds, emptied of water or threat, float regally eastward in a state of impotent suspension, casting fleeting shadows on the dune ridges and depressions below.

As you top the rises and each successive valley opens beneath, revealing impossibly green sand hills and lush wet meadows, alive with ducks and geese and a few fat deer wearing slightly disreputable winter coats, and you're fortunate enough to have Peter Ostroushko's rendition of "Sweet Betsy from Pike" cranked up on the CD player, the blend of sky and earth and wandering critters with the warm cello and piano and the tinny effervescence of Ostroushko's mandolin will overwhelm your synapses, make you beg for mercy. And you're wishing against hope this suspended moment in time will continue uninterrupted for just a little while longer, like infinity plus twenty-four hours.

We have eaten a forgettable lunch in a joint at the north end of Kingsley Dam, the second largest hydraulic fill dam in the world. The dam and Lake McConaughy, 22 miles long, four miles wide, with over 100 miles of sandy beach shoreline, covering 35,700 acres at full storage, are situated near the southern border of the Nebraska Sand Hills. Every summer weekend, like a Biblical plague, thousands of obnoxious, beer-swilling Denverites descend on "Big Mac." On this particular Sunday in late May, we found ourselves in a beer piss-scented saloon, seated next to a long table of squabbling, flabby Denver Visigoths, so ravenous they didn't finish one meal before ordering another, this time with extra fries.

An hour later, as we drift along the oil mat north of Whitman, Memorial Day weekend on the shores of Lake McConaughy and the invasion of 20,000 swaggering, motor boating, jet ski fornicating, RV driving, recklessly sunburned, two-day stubbled, habitually inebriated Denverites becomes a distant annoyance.

We are headed for the Dry Valley Church north of Mullen, which holds a Memorial Day service every year to honor service men and women and members of pioneer families buried in the churchyard cemetery. We hope to arrive before the 7 o'clock services begin, but are traveling on an unfamiliar road and have no idea how long it will take to reach the church.

A few minutes and a half dozen horny sand turtles later, just this side of the Curtis Ranch and the beginnings of North Loup River, we turn east on a well-graveled county road. This is the upgraded county road requested by Texas cattle feeder Paul Engler, soon after he purchased Charlie Kramer's spread and renamed it the Spike Box. You may remember Engler as the fellow who hauled Oprah Winfrey into a Texas courtroom for slandering beef on her television program. Although the lawsuit was unsuccessful, his decision to take the offensive heartened cattlemen who'd suffered innumerable market setbacks at the hands of the food quack lobby.

Engler, owner of Cactus Feeders, an outfit currently feeding 520,000 head of cattle, one of the largest such operations in the civilized world, wanted an improved road for his cattle semis, but was unwilling to give the county an easement, without which any future owner of the Spike Box would be free to close the road. After extended negotiations and exercises in mutual stubbornness, county commissioner Jim Van Winkle and Engler made medicine. A helluva good road resulted, not a straight road in the sense of a perfect grid alignment, but a road efficient at bridging the distance from one ranch to another, fulfilling the main purpose of most Cherry County roads.

After adding the 6,000 acre Roseberry Ranch and going through several managers, Paul Engler sold the Spike Box to Ted Turner, who transformed the ranch into his first Nebraska Sand Hills bison operation. Whether Turner would have closed the road without the easement is an open question. Turner prefers peaceable relations with his neighbors and appreciates good access roads as well as the next person. However, coaxing a couple of thousand wild-ass bison through a two sets of electric fences and across an improved gravel road can be vexing work.

Today we're happy for the easement, happy for Jim Van Winkle's wide stubborn streak, happy for the gravel, without which we would surely be stuck. Dry and firm for long stretches, smooshy and deeply rutted where the severe thunderstorms of the past three days dropped their loads, the improved Cherry County road does the best it can. Nonetheless, our car is soon covered in sandy muck, window washer tank exhausted, leaving our forward vision slightly impaired. Fortunately, we encounter not a single sand turtle in the next 20 miles.

Two elongated white shapes rise up out of a nearby wetlands. Whatever else they might be, they're extremely tall and are giving us the old fish eye. We stop, point the camera. They hunker down, almost out of sight. I take the photo anyway, counting ourselves lucky in spotting two of the 639 trumpeter swans currently occupying the Sand Hills. Since reintroduction 50 years ago, the permanent trumpeter swan population has grown at a leisurely pace. Swans usually winter around Merritt Reservoir or on the Calumus River to the east or near the Birdwood and Blue Creeks to the south. Today a camera shy nesting pair squat behind some wet bunch grass. We have no way of knowing if the swans are shy or up to no good. You can never tell with swans. But we're pretty sure they aren't frightened of us or Finlay, the curious West Highland White Terrier presently sticking his nose out the side window. A male trumpeter can measure six feet from tail to bill, have a wing span of nearly 10 feet and kick the living crap out of just about any predator you'd care send his way.

In the resulting photograph, taken through a powerful telescopic lens and enlarged on the computer screen, the swans appear as two infinitesimal white dots.

A few miles to the east we stop to snap a photo of a windmill against a cloud bank. Ted Turner's standard high tensile, solar powered bison fencing stands between us and the windmill. We have entered the Spike Box, 136,000 acres devoted exclusively to bison ranching. No bison in view, most likely roaming several miles to the north or south on summer range, but they've left plenty of good-sized chips behind. This is the holding area for the older bulls after they've gone through the working chutes in the fall. You can gather some prodigious chips from 2000 pound ungulates. I am stuffing chips in a plastic Walmart sack. A child of three could grasp the profit potential of shrewdly marketed, all-natural, 100 percent organic, full-flavored buffalo chips as the barbecue fuel of choice for the environmentally conscious. Kathy, who prefers her steaks cooked with environmentally incorrect propane or charcoal, does not put her full support behind this potential gold mine.

A mile later we pass a modest set of buildings, Turner's quarters when he and Jane Fonda made periodic visits to the Spike Box. Turner's son, Reed Beauregard "Beau" Turner, enthusiastic hunter and fisherman, who heads up Turner Foundation efforts to revive rare species and promote biodiversity on the 1.5 million acres owned by Turner Enterprises, uses the place every year during deer season. Before his divorce this is where he brought his lovely wife Gannon, great-great niece of legendary oil billionaire H. L. Hunt, and cousin of H. L.'s boys, Nelson and Bunker Hunt.* The other modest house on the site serves as base for occasional hunters who visit the ranch in fall and winter to harvest one ton bulls for trophies or younger cows and bulls for meat.

In quick succession, we pass Spike Box headquarters and the sturdy working corrals a quarter mile to the east. A solitary, massive bull, who looks to be about 12 years old, ignores us from the catch pen. Like other mature bulls of a certain age, who much prefer their own company, he appears to be thinking deepy bison thoughts.

We arrive at the Dry Valley Church 10 minutes early. As cars and pickups turn off the main road and make their way down a sandy track through the rank grass to the distant stone church, a man in a pickup stays behind to guard the open pasture gate against escaping cattle. Sure enough, a curious herd of Angus yearling heifers hangs around the parked vehicles in front of the church. We ease our way through the heifers to a spot along the cemetery fence.

* Oil men and commodity speculators who tried to corner the world silver market right before Fed. Chairman Paul "Cue Ball" Volker unceremoniously stomped on their fingers by raising interest rates to record levels, ruining in the process an entire generation of commodity speculators, farmers and small businessmen.

Finlay betrays unusual nervousness after we leave him behind to be immediately surrounded by 30 inquisitive heifers, sniffing at him through the window and rolling their eyes.

The Dry Valley Church, established in 1909 in a nearby school as a Congregational Church, served the settlers who invaded the area after the Kinkaid Act upped the homestead acreage from 160 to 640 acres. Parishioners immediately got busy on a structure of stone-shaped concrete blocks, manufactured on site from imported cement and plentiful local sand, completing construction in 1911. The adjoining cemetery has been open for business since 1904 and, judging from the dates on the tombstones, did a desultory trade until the church was finished and business picked up. Over the years, as the Kinkaiders left and the home-steads absorbed into larger holdings, the church fell into disuse, the last worship service held in 1958. Shingles departed, the bright tin ceiling rusted and crumbled onto the floor, hail knocked out the windows, the floor swelled and buckled. Benches disappeared, along with the pump organ. The local unwashed sand proved a weak aggregate and the homemade concrete stones began to dissolve. By 1986, the church had nearly reached the point of no return.

Mary Swendener-Kravcisin, who spent much of her life on a ranch just over the rise to the west and has buried two husbands in the soft sand of the Dry Valley Cemetery, published an appeal for action in the local *Hooker County Tribune*. Leonard and Judy Ridenour, from a half dozen miles north, and Vernie and Barb McCully, who live seven miles to the northwest, were among the first to respond. Two years and a new roof later, the church hosted the first of the now traditional Memorial Day services.

In 1995, the year Ted Turner purchased the Spike Box, after windows had been fitted with new frames and new clear glass, the ceiling restored with replica tin, the community hosted the initial Christmas Day evening service. This in a building with no plumbing, no electricity, no forced air furnace.

Vernie McCully says a few visitors have suggested wiring the church to the power line which passes within 50 feet of the front step. In the unlikely event this were to happen, I'm pretty certain it would be over Vernie McCully's dead body. Like most in the Dry Valley community, he much prefers candlelight from the horse shoe candelabras he welded together (occasionally loaned out for wedding ceremonies) and the warm light from the jury-rigged kerosene lantern chandelier hanging just below the shiny new tin ceiling.

This evening the pews are filled to near capacity, a fair number of widows and a few squirmy kids scattered among 70 souls.

On cue, Judy Ridenour, leader of tonight's proceedings, notes the visitors in the congregation and requests them to identify themselves and state their reasons for being in this place. A half dozen strangers, including Kathy and me, comply. Some say they've come out of curiosity, the others because of long distance family connectedness.

Then the congregation takes up pending church business during a remarkably efficient meeting. We learn the church's finances may be sound, but could be somewhat better, that the church books, kept by treasurer Mary Swendener-Kravcisin, have undergone an audit after many years of no audits and, to no one's surprise, have been found accurate to the penny.

Ryan Ridenour, Judy and Leonard's son, carries an American flag down the aisle, seats it in a base to the left of the pulpit.

We place our hands on our hearts and recite the pledge of allegiance to the United States of America.

Through the west windows, backlit by the setting sun, nosy black heifers mill against the cemetery fence, straining to hear what's going on inside. We treat them to a couple of patriotic hymns any Protestant worth his salt would have learned with his mother's milk, "Oh, Beautiful for Spacious Skies" and "Onward Christian Soldiers."

The prodigal pump organ, fully repaired by the itinerant music teacher who carted it off to the wilds of Wisconsin and returned it when he learned the church was back in business, groans enthusiastically from its customary spot.

There are those, accustomed to the intricate stained glass windows of traditional churches, who might pronounce these modest clear glass panes both dull and aesthetically deficient. I would argue stained glass, beautiful and inspiring in most settings, would only interfere with the view. Who would trade glimpses of green dunes and ornery yearling heifers and stolid tombstones for little bits of colored glass?

At this point allow me to state unequivocally: delivering tart commentary on sermons, especially those earnestly delivered by volunteer preachers, serves no purpose. As much as one might wish a Memorial Day sermon, especially one delivered in an historic church, on a perfect spring evening after three inches of welcome rain, might be longer on logic and shorter on nonsense, saying so has no utility.

Even so, although it might sound hypercritical, one might hope tonight's speaker, having spent several years living in cattle country and associating with lifelong ranchers, would refrain from referring to the yearling heifers he passed through on the way to the church as "cows."

Much better to detach, gain perspective, appreciate the difficulties inherent in the pastor's task of melding his standard issue funeral sermon, the one with Hebrews dashing out of the Gaza strip to ford the treacherous six-inch deep Jordan River, with praise of service to country, even if he considers all wars to be tragic and wasteful, unless, of course, you're a desert-crazed Hebrew putting the run on the former residents of the Promised Land, who, up to the very moment the advance guard of the blood-thirsty Hebrew invasion came over the hill, were peacefully minding their own business.

If you stare at the shiny new metal ceiling long enough while the speaker cranks up his long-winded metaphors employing Jordan River stones, a story from the church's early years might creep in, a time when the church, still under construction, had no tin ceiling, only exposed rafters, and the Sunday School superintendent, speaking from the pulpit, in the exact spot where the current preacher holds forth, is smack dab in the middle of an emotional appeal, building toward the inevitable climax, when a huge bull snake, impressive even for those frontier times, grown curious about the racket coming from down below, dropped most of himself from the overhead rafter and looked her squarely in the eye. You might imagine a certain amount of subsequent nervousness, punctuated by random squeals, followed by the pitter-patter of trampling Sunday-go-to-meeting shoes as parishioners fled out the front doors.

Following that successful distraction you might try closing your ears and concentrating attention on the delicate light rays filtered through freshening clouds and the clear glass of the west windows, or, even better, focusing on a particular yearling heifer, the one looking right at you with the white blaze on her chest, and allowing the mind to drift over the possible sources of that stark white mark, perhaps to secret Holstein genes from a long dead, family milk cow bred to an Angus herd bull, the very cow with the bad habit of kicking over the milk bucket every time the ancient tom cat with one chewed ear sauntered past.

Eventually, if you run through enough reveries, you might decide if the folks sitting in the pews with tight smiles on their faces are listening to the sermon without visible complaint then that's the very least you can do. Which is what Kathy whispered to me over an hour ago the first time I grumbled and scuffed the floor.

Murmurings from the back of the church. A long pause in the proceedings. From the Dry Valley cemetery to the north the tentative, trembling first notes of "Taps." The youthful trumpeter, gaining confidence with each note, sends the final haunting tribute into the twilight, far beyond the rolling green valley to the surrounding dry dunes. The warm wool of silence which follows is deafening.

Afterward, we socialize in the dim light of a couple of fat candles and Vernie's horseshoe candelabra. Mary Swendener-Kravcisin, church treasurer extraordinaire, searches us out, thanks us for coming, invites us to return for services the evening of Christmas Day. She knows all the history, points to tops of the trees far the west which mark her ranch, the place she spent her life until she married her second husband and moved to town. Her son lives there with his family. The yearling heifers mowing grass along the cemetery fence belong to him.

We are confronted by a full-scale carry-in dinner, instead of the usual Memorial Day service fare of cookies and finger food. I immediately spot three double deck platters of deviled eggs, more than enough for guilt-free second helpings. Let others chow down on the homemade angel food cake with dewy strawberries, let others risk raging sugar diabetes by indulging in the Peanut Butter Fudge Rice Krispie bars. I plan on sticking to egg protein, created as per universal custom with a few sprinkles of paprika.

Toting heavily-laden plates and cups of fragrant hot coffee fresh out of the stainless steel thermos, we wander around the church visiting with strangers. Spring branding season has not been without casualties. Spooked horses and overturned ATVs result in smashed craniums and splintered femurs. Clearly Sand Hills doctors have had their hands full.

The McCullys and Judy Ridenour share a scrapbook of the restoration process, an engaging story, which rapidly reaches warp speed as words multiply and tumble over one another. I am wishing for the tape recorder.

The light fades. Vernie's candelabra has trouble making up the difference. My poor eyes are having trouble reading the scrapbook notes. We agree to sit down with the scrapbook at a future time in full daylight.

We exit through a church empty of preachers or parishioners, stop by a pickup to chat with Leonard, Judy Ridenour's husband, who's just had knee replacement surgery and is more comfortable in the pickup than sitting in a hard pew. Leonard's cheerful demeanor belies the post-surgery discomfort he must be feeling.

He explains why some Ridenours ended up languishing down in the rich irrigated corn and soybean wasteland of Phelps County, while others stayed and thrived in the grass country of Cherry County. He is far too polite to say so, but he clearly feels sorry for the poor schnooks marooned in Phelps County.

The yearling heifers have moved off a couple of hundred yards, more interested in new shoots of grass than departing cars and pickups. As we stroll towards the car with its patient white dog, the McCullys and Judy Ridenour, not in any particular hurry to leave the Dry Valley Church, linger on the front step discussing the next rehabilitation project.

Bumping south through the pasture, following the long line of taillights towards the graveled county road, I am thinking there are probably less rewarding things to do with your time than to linger on country church steps in the deepening shadows of a late May evening, visiting with people so secure in the knowledge of who the hell they are they can tolerate with equal grace a long-winded preacher or a smart aleck cynic.

Acknowledgments and Apologies

Humbling experiences come in two sizes: Those all too familiar incidents reminding us we're probably not, after all, God's gift to humanity. The other sort of humbling events occur when we encounter human beings secure in their own skins, folks who don't have to conduct a poll to know what they think or who they are and who can be so refreshingly straightforward the sheer novelty can take your breath away. Spend any time in the Nebraska Sand Hills and the second variety of humbling will smoosh any inflated ego you may be harboring down to a whimpering puddle.

During a decade traveling through the Nebraska Sand Hills humbling experiences of the second variety became a constant. Beginning with the McMurtrey Ranch auction, when Jim Wright and other neighbors identified both heirs and bidders to a nosy outsider, to our time at the Dry Valley Church with Mary Swendener-Kravcisin, Vernie McCully and Judy Ridenour, who shared their unique community church and commitment to its preservation, I could not have asked for more helpful or truthful witnesses.

The surviving McMurtrey clan members might not have always gotten along, but they were universally kind to me. Dr. George McMurtrey volunteered his encyclopedic memories of the ranch and his growing up years. Mary Alice McMurtrey Williams proved gracious and helpful as was her daughter Dianne Yarbrough. Dr. George's daughter Rella Hallman, her husband Jerry and Jerry's sister Janice patiently endured hours of questions. Rella also entrusted me with her only copy of the McMurtrey family history, which proved invaluable. Eric Rapp and his mother Vera June Rapp traced the founding of the McMurtrey Ranch and their continuing connection. Dr. George McMurtrey's son-in-law, Charlie Ward, and grandson James Ward provided key insights into the McMurtrey's decline and fall and on the breaking of Hub's trust. A special thanks to the staff of the Cherry County District Court for their able assistance in locating and copying pertinent court documents. Thanks as well to J. Bryant Brooks for translating the legalese into plain English.

Dan McMurtrey shared recollections of his years on the ranch, particularly of the winter of 1948-49, and his experiences as a human guinea pig during nuclear testing in the South Pacific. Dr. Diane Zuckerman of the National Research Center for Women & Families described her sobering work for the Senate Committee investigating exposure of military personnel to life-altering chemicals and nuclear fallout.

Of all the McMurtrey heirs and relatives no one was more knowledgeable or entertaining than Bob Childers, who grew up on the McMurtrey and spent most of his early adult years slaving for and learning from Hub. Bob's later tenure on the Spike Box informed his observations on its transformation to a bison operation. Long before the research ended I owed a tidy sum to Bob and Susan for the rental of the chair I so often occupied in their kitchen. Bob's mother Maribeth McMurtrey Childers, niece to Alf and Hub, helped trace the early history of the ranch and her own family's extended residence on the McMurtrey. Jerry Shelbourn, son-in-law to Maribeth Childers, provided working knowledge of the ranch during the later stages of Hub's life.

Neighbors and McMurtrey Ranch renters Duane and Danita Kime and Buzz and Shirley Kime patiently handled my persistent questions while ignoring more pressing business. Duane Kime, long-time Cherry County school board member, shared his perspective on the future of rural schools. Neighbors Edson and Barbara Kime Gale not only provided memories the McMurtrey and its inhabitants, but shared Gale and Kime family coming-into-the-country stories. Barbara's work with Marianne Beel on the Cherry County history series enriched her knowledge not only of the history of her immediate neighborhood, but of the entire county.

Judge A. W. Moursund's son Will provided key background on Moursund's initial investments in the Nebraska Sand Hills. PECO customer and board member Patrick Cox shared his intimate knowledge of the Pedernales Electric scandal and the long struggle by coop members to uncover the facts. Claudia Grisales' bulldog reporting for the *Austin American-Statesman* provided an invaluable road map to the PECO crimes. Although her investigations earned several prestigious regional awards, if we consider the politically powerful interests who were inconvenienced, she should have received a Pulitzer.

During my visit to the Taylor Lake School Deborah Winter and Cheryl Ravenscroft renewed my faith in the teaching profession by making the incomparable magic intelligent teachers produce when unfettered by intrusive rules and stultifying bureaucracy. Mrs. Ravenscroft, when she wasn't busy with students, graciously shared details of her family's long-term neighborly relationship with the McMurtreys. Jolyne Westover, then principal of all rural Cherry County schools, reflected on the geographic challenges she faced supervising and supporting widely scattered classrooms in a county larger than the state of Connecticut. Jolyne's mother-in-law Irene Westover, who with her husband Cal housed Celia Sandoz and her students during the Blizzard of 1949, opened her home and her excellent memory of those historic events. Nephew Alton Westover, a student of Celia's, recounted his time in Celia's classroom, his life on his aunt and uncle's ranch and his miraculous horseback ride home during the blizzard.

Celia Sandoz Ostrander Barth spent several days and evenings at her kitchen table relating her version of the "Lost School Bus" story and sorting out the history of the descendants of Jules Sandoz. She generously furnished family trees and photos while keeping me far removed from a state of starvation. Sons Jules and Cash Ostrander, daughter-in-law Lynette Ostrander, granddaughter Heidi Ostrander Terrell and her husband Brock Terrell provided a clear picture of why the Sandoz clan, by placing family over material considerations, has not only survived, but thrived. Robert Russell, gifted storyteller and long-time renter of Caroline Sandoz Pifer's ranch, and irascible neighbor Bernice Peterson related their long personal histories with various members of the Sandoz clan. And I would be remiss not to offer abject apologies to the anonymous, long-suffering Hell's Angel who endured without complaint Kathy's noisy, wee hour assault on our shared motel room wall.

Over the decades Mitch and Patty Glidden have not only cheerfully rented us canoes, kayaks and stock tanks, hauled us to various dropping off locations and picked up the survivors, but enthusiastically shared their detailed knowledge of the Dismal and Middle Loup Rivers. Jon Farrar, career editor and writer for *Nebraskaland Magazine,* provided special background on the historic Black Ranch and his relationship with Roe Black. Stewart I. Black Jr., Roe Black's grandson and Black family genealogist, helped trace the origins of Black family members who founded the ranch. Special thanks to Jason Tonsfeldt, Park Superintendent at Buffalo Bill Ranch State Historical Park, for research assistance with Buffalo Bill's Sand Hills ventures and brief film career. Linda Hein at the Nebraska State Historical Society cheerfully volunteered her research on the Blacks and their famous ranch on the Dismal.

Brock Terrell's experience as a herdsman on the Rex Ranch provided understanding of low-input cattle production philosophy and how it is best implemented in practice. UNL's Don Adams shared his research and that of his university colleagues and his long term scientific collaboration with Burke Teichert. Dave Pratt, ranch consultant and disciple of Stan Parsons, was particularly generous with his experience and wisdom. Burke Teichert exhibited remarkable patience educating me on the principles of low-input cattle production. Any failure in translation is certainly not due to a lack of diligence on his part. The story of his artist grandmother Minerva Teichert saving the family ranch during the Depression was perhaps the most inspiring of the heroic family legends I encountered.

Thanks to Ted Turner for unconditional access to the Spike Box and his employees. Spike Box managers Terry and Wanda Purdum were the souls of hospitality. John Hansen made a long trip to Nebraska from Montana for an interview and remained in touch. Dallas and Jessica Wycoff provided honest perspective on working for Ted Turner and the challenges of remote Sand Hills living for a young family. UNL professor James Stubbendieck explained his work researching and repopulating the blowout Penstemon. He also provided some of his excellent blowout Penstemon photos.

I am not and never have been a geologist or a hydrologist, nor have I ever demonstrated the slightest aptitude for either discipline. Jim Swinehart and Jim Goeke, both high-energy, chronically impatient people, took more time than they could spare to hammer the rudiments of their chosen specialties into my impervious skull. Although it is likely their Herculean efforts have not been entirely successful, the inevitable errors and omissions are not in any way their responsibility. However, it is impossible to exaggerate how much valuable knowledge these two innovative scientists have created through tenacious, ground breaking research and not a little hard manual labor.

I am especially indebted to the families, friends and colleagues of "Renaissance Man" Charles Baron McIntosh and his wife Ruby Lamb McIntosh. Sons Douglas, Bruce and Howard shared maps, extensive files and personal reminiscences. "Buffalo Bruce" also provided a guided tour to a threatened aspen grove near Halsey we would never have discovered otherwise. Howard told childhood stories of camping out in the Sand Hills while his father burrowed into land records in neighboring county courthouses. Barron's brother Roy provided a trove of information about their growing up years in South Dakota and Barron's athletic and music careers. Ruby's brother Earl Lamb, who doesn't hear as well as he used to, supplied laboriously hand written responses to a lengthy list of Lamb family questions. Dollie Lamb Schroeder, Ruby's sister, provided details of Barron and Ruby's courtship and Ruby's subsequent tragic health issues. Special thanks to Roy Lamb, Dollie Lamb Schroeder, Milton Tupper and Lavada Tupper Rodewald for their family stories and sometimes conflicting memories of the Lamb-Tupper cattle for land swap. Jean Knight, Barron's one time wife and boon companion during his retirement years, described her supporting role in the production of McIntosh's classic Sand Hills book and provided details of the Pine Ridge fire which nearly consumed his exhaustive notes, hand drawn maps and only copy of the nearly complete manuscript. McIntosh's former geography department colleagues Richard Lonsdale, Robert Stoddard, David Wishart and Douglas Amedeo painted a vivid picture of faculty life in the UNL department of geography and the bruising struggles to save the department from ignoramus budget-cutting weasel administrators during and after McIntosh's tenure. Former congressman Doug Beureter shared his memories of McIntosh as a teacher and mentor.

Special thanks to Hot Springs, South Dakota, dentist Dr. Peter Sotherland for his experiences with the supernaturally strong teeth of Edgemont, South Dakotans. Mike Farrell, nationally recognized producer and documentary film maker for forty years at Nebraska Educational Television, provided a key transcript of McIntosh's appearance in the documentary *Sand Hills Story* and recollections of their collaboration.

Without Mike Fischer's open-handed permission to tromp around his Blue Creek ranch we would have been unable to personally explore the Blue Water battlefield. Warren Jones interpreted Lt. G. K. Warren's detailed maps and battle accounts to identify important landmarks. Thanks as well to historian James Hanson for his insights into Lt. Warren's actions during the conflict and the ultimate ramifications of the engagement.

Leland Johnson endured multiple interviews about his WWII experiences with grace and tolerance. Shirley King Ostrander supplied memories of Uncle Leo Tupper's courtship of Shirley's sister Sophie. I relied on Anita Tupper Snell's account of her reconnection with her father and Milton Tupper's memories of Leo and his death. Special thanks to Ron Jones for tracking down Louise Gentile, daughter of Leo's Jeep driver.

Willis Ruby and Rich Boots helped me understand professional bull riding as it existed prior to million dollar purses and private jets. Rod Palmer, founder and guiding light of the Nebraska Sandhills Cowboy Hall of Fame, shared biographies and photographs. Cotton Rasser supplied entertaining stories of his most famous bulls and his long history with the bucking bull business. Steve and Julie Ravenscroft hosted our visit to their bull breeding operation near Hyannis and showed us, from the relative security of the pickup cab, their next crop of Whitewater Skoal sired bucking bull prospects.

I owe my life to the extraordinary piloting skills of Jim Van Winkle and will always regret my myopic nagging, which finally persuaded him to take me up in his beloved Super Cub. I blame my obsessive curiosity, which is not an excuse, only a lame explanation. Jim's wife Myki Beel Van Winkle comforted a complete stranger in the hospital and later welcomed Kathy and me into their home. Dr. Mulligan-Witt, Nurse Kathy Ormesher and the medical staff at Cherry County Hospital cared for this "obese, but pleasant" pilgrim with extraordinary kindness and competency. I was lucky to have crash landed within easy driving distance.

I will always be indebted to Mark Sanders and Kim Verhines, who rescued the manuscript from an uncertain fate, and to Thomas Sims at Stephen F. Austin State University Press for his diligence.

I have been fortunate in my friends. Don Welch and Bill Kloefkorn encouraged me for most of the journey. The unique combination of inspired teaching and memorable poetry embodied in these two long-time comrades will not pass this way again. I've also been fortunate for the past 30 plus years to have the friendship and steadfast support of prolific and iconic author Linda Hasselstrom, who has nurtured more writers than she can possibly remember. No one on the High Plains has showered more generous patronage on writers, both prominent and unknown, than teacher and poet J. V. Brummels. Ladette Randolph's vigorous support for authors, even those hailing from the parochial, insular regions of both coasts, while at University of Nebraska Press helped an entire generation of writers gain audience and recognition. Her early interest in this project provided the confidence it would not be a wasted effort.

I have also been fortunate in my family: Parents Mattie and Lowell Jones, who preserved our family's oral traditions and encouraged a love of books, my sisters Judith Ann and Miriam Ruth, who labored over multiple rough drafts of the manuscript, and my children Kasey, Erica and Sydney, who maintained a high level of enthusiasm for the enterprise, even when the outcome was in doubt.

When someone says "going down the rabbit hole" around here we mean dropping everything and diving into the bowels of a fresh mystery. How old are the Sand Hills? Are Ted Turner's bison ranches profitable? Where did that goddamned smirking river otter come from? Kathy always has my back, but she's more than once rolled her eyes when I've announced the launch of a new excavation because she knows from experience I will not be fit company until the subject is exhausted. Besides tolerating my eccentricities Kathy is dependably game for the next whimsical Sand Hills journey and can be counted on to lend her far-seeing eyes, love of adventure and innate sensibility to any expedition. If all that weren't enough for an oversized helping of abject gratitude and admiration, she's also adept at fixing pesky computer and formatting issues. Without her considerable techy skills this grumpy Luddite would be scribbling on moldy papyrus with a leaky hollow reed. She's a good 'un.

Sources

CHAPTER 1

DISMAL RIVER:

Black, Roe R. *The Horseshoe Bar Ranch: Remembering a Prairie Childhood.* Lincoln: Media Publishing, 1985.

Bratt, John. *Trails of Yesterday.* Chicago: University Publishing Company, 1921.

Brownlow, Kevin. *The War, the West, and the Wilderness.* New York: Alfred A. Knopf, 1979.

Grinnell, George Bird. *Two Great Scouts and Their Pawnee Battalion: The Experiences of Frank J. North and Luther H. North.* Cleveland: Arthur H. Clark, 1928.

O'Donnell, Jeff. *Luther North: Frontier Scout.* Lincoln: J & L Lee, 1995.

Sandoz, Mari. *Cheyenne Autumn.* New York: Hastings House, 1953.

Snyder, Grace. *No Time on My Hands.* Caldwell, Idaho. Caxton Printers, 1963.

Wilson, Ruby. *Frank J. North: Pawnee Scout Commander and Pioneer.* Athens, Ohio: Swallow Press, 1984.

Yost, Nellie Snyder. *Buffalo Bill: His Family, Friends, Fame, Failures, and Fortunes.* Chicago: Swallow Press, 1979.

——————————. *Pinnacle Jake.* Caldwell, Idaho: Caxton Printers, 1951.

Selected Articles:

"Eclipse Cemetery" outbacknebraska.com, September 15, 2013.

Jacobs, Dean. (August 30, 2014) "They Said I Shouldn't Tackle This Dismal Adventure Alone." *Fremont Tribune.*

Wagner, Greg. (February 25, 2013) "The Rivers Least Floated." *Nebraskaland Magazine.*

CHAPTER 3

MCMURTREY RANCH AUCTION:

Auleta, Ken. *Media Man: Ted Turner's Improbable Empire.* New York: W. W. Norton, 2004.

Shoenfeld, Reese. *Me and Ted Against the World: The Unauthorized Story of the Founding of CNN.* New York: HarperCollins, 2001.

Selected Articles:

Bodo, Pete. (November 24, 2000) "Love for Nature Has Guided Turner's Life." *New York Times.*

Ducey, James E. and North Platte Bulletin Staff. (July 16, 2007) "Turner's Land Holdings Keep Increasing." *North Platte Bulletin.*

Dugan, Joe. (July 22, 1999) "Sandhills Rumble Isn't Just About Bison" *Lincoln Journal-Star.*

Gunther. Marc. (October 4, 2006) "Ted Turner's Montana Adventure: He's Raising Buffalo, Killing Fish, Making Money and Having Fun." *Fortune.*

Hewitt, Bill. (January 17, 2000) "Alone on the Range." *People Magazine.*

Hitt, Jack. (December, 2001) "One Nation, Under Ted." *Outside Magazine.*

Jenkins, Nate. (November 28, 2007) "Ted Turner's Land Grab Generates Suspicion in Nebraska." *Lincoln Journal-Star.*

Miller, Steve. (June 7, 2001) "Turner's Bison Roam Huge Tracts of S. D., Neb." *Rapid City Journal.*

"Montana Land Commission's Trade with Ted Turner Was Arbitrary." *Wildlife News Quarterly*, Winter, 1998.

Roybal, Joe. (February 1, 2002) "Ted Turner Has South Dakota Ranchers Concerned." *Penton.*

CHAPTER 4

A KINKAIDER COMES AND STAYS:

Beel, Marianne ed. *A Sandhill Century Book I—The Land: A History of Cherry County, Nebraska*. Valentine: Cherry County Centennial Committee, 1986.

_____ ed. A Sandhill Century Book II — The People: A History of the People of Cherry County. Valentine, Cherry County Centennial Committee, 1985.

Reece, Charles S. *A History of Cherry County, Nebraska: The Story of Its Organization, Development and People*. Valentine: Plains Trading Company, 1992.

Vackiner, Jean ed. *A Sandhill Century Book III — The Next Twenty-Five: A History of Cherry County, Nebraska*. Valentine: Cherry County Historical Society, 2010.

Selected Articles:

Ducey, James E. (1991) "Ditching of Wetlands in the Nebraska Sandhills: A Case Study of Grant County." *Transactions of the Nebraska Academy of Sciences*, XVIII: p. 1.

_____. (July 15, 2007) "Turner's Land Holdings Keep Increasing." nebraskastatepaper.com.

Samuels, John. (December 15, 2008) "Atomic John: A Truck Driver Uncovers Secrets About the First Nuclear Bombs." *New Yorker*.

"Is Military Research Hazardous to Veterans' Health? Lessons Spanning Half a Century." (December 8, 1994) Staff Report Prepared for the U. S. Senate Committee on Veteran's Affairs.

CHAPTER 5

JUDGE MOURSUND:

Cox, Smith, Matthews Inc. *Pedernales Electric Cooperative Inc. Report of Investigation by Navigant Consulting (PI)*. Austin: Navigant Consulting, 2008.

Caro, Robert A. *The Years of Lyndon Johnson: Master of the Senate*. New York: Alfred A. Knopf, 2002.

_____. *The Years of Lyndon Johnson: The Passage of Power*. New York: Alfred A. Knopf, 2013.

Selected Articles:

Beschloss, Michael. (October 12, 1997) "The Johnson Tapes" *Newsweek*.

Biundo, Jen. (August 20, 2008) "PEC Reveals Old Accounts. Cattleman's Bank Wants Judge to Decide on Texland Money." *The Free Press*.

_____. (August 27, 2008) "Former PEC Leaders Confess Texland Payouts." *The Free Press*.

Cox, Patrick. (September 8, 2001) "Texland Continues to Give Up More Questions Than Answers." valleyspringcomm.net.

Furguson, Earnest B. (Autumn, 2011) "LBJ's Wild Ride." *The American Scholar*.

Germany, Kent. (Summer, 2002) "'I'm Not Lying About That One' Manhood, LBJ, and The Politics of Speaking Southern." *University of South Carolina Scholar Commons*, pp. 32-39

Grisales, Claudia. (July 27. 2008) "New Co-op President Has Many Ties to The Past." *Austin American-States man*.

_____. (October 23, 2008) "Pedernales Electric Cooperative: Ex-Directors Got Nearly $1 Million from Failed Venture." *Austin American-Statesman*.

_____. (June 20, 2009) "Indictments Say Pair Directed Co-op Money to Relatives of PEC Executives." *Austin American-Statesman*.

_____. (August 26, 2015) "Former Co-op Official Begins Serving Jail Term." *Austin American-Statesman*.

Grisales, Claudia and Marty Toohey. (May 2, 2015) "After Reforms, is Electric Co-op Transformed?" *Austin-American Statesman*.

James, Leo. (July, 1973) "The Last Days of the Presidency: LBJ in Retirement." *Atlantic*.

Lehman, Jodi. (May 29, 2008) "PEC Legal Fees Top $2 Million Last Year." *Horseshoe Bay Beacon.*

Rogers, Linda Kaye. (August 19, 2008) "Coming Soon: More Details on PEC's 'Mystery' Bank Account." valleyspringcomm.net.

Swearington, Brian D. (August, 2000) "LBJ's Living Legacy." *Texas Monthly.*

CHAPTER 6

WINTER SCHOOL:

Alleman, Roy V. *Blizzard of 1949.* Grand Island: Nebraska Wealth, 1991.

Sandoz, Mari. *Winter Thunder.* Philadelphia: Westminster Press, 1953.

CHAPTER 8

CELIA'S KITCHEN:

Malmberg-Berndt, Sybil. *Fritz Sandoz: A Paragon of Fate.* Gordon, Nebraska: Sheridan County Publishing, 2002.

Malmberg-Berndt, Sybil, et al. *Flora Rosa Sandoz.* Gordon: Sheridan County Publishing, 2001.

Sandoz, Mari. *Old Jules.* New York, New York: Blue Ribbon Books, 1935.

_____. *The Christmas of the Phonograph Records.* Foreword by Linda Hasselstrom. Lincoln: Bison Books, 1996.

Clark, LaVerne Harrell. *Mari Sandoz's Native Nebraska: The Plains Indian Country.* Chicago: Arcadia Publishing, 2000.

Pifer, Caroline Sandoz. *Mari Sandoz: Making of an Author Vol. 1,* Gordon, Nebraska: Sheridan County Publishing, 1972.

_____. *Mari Sandoz: Making of an Author Vol. 2,* Gordon, Nebraska: Sheridan County Publishing, 1984.

Pifer, Caroline Sandoz and Jules Sandoz, Jr. *Son of Old Jules: Memoirs of Jules Sandoz, Jr.* Lincoln: University of Nebraska Press, 1987.

Stauffer, Helen Winter. *Mari Sandoz: Story Catcher of the Plains.* Lincoln: University of Nebraska Press, 1982.

_____ ed. *Letters of Mari Sandoz.* Lincoln: University of Nebraska Press, 1992.

Richards, Bartlett, Jr, and Ruth Van Ackeren. *Bartlett Richards: Nebraska Sandhills Cattleman.* Lincoln: The Nebraska State Historical Society, 1980.

Van Ackeren, Ruth and Howard Van Ackeren. *Robert M. Lawrence Bixby: Preserver of the Old Spade Ranch.* Caldwell, Idaho: Caxton Printers, 1995.

CHAPTER 9

MR. WATER:

Ashworth, William. *Ogallala Blue: Water and Life on the Great Plains.* Woodstock, Vermont: The Countryman Press, 2006.

Selected Articles:

Chen, X.H. et al. (1999) "Hydraulic Properties and Uncertainty Analysis for an Unconfined Alluvial Aquifer." *Ground Water,* Vol. 37, pp. 845-854.

Fleig, Shelby and Kyle Cummings. (April 15, 2013) "UNL Expert: Ogallala Aquifer Has Little Risk of Keystone Pipeline Oil Spills." *Daily Nebraskan.*

Gosselin, D.C. et al. (1999) "Hydrologic Dynamics of Two Interdunal Valleys in the Central Sand Hills of Nebraska." *Ground Water,* Vol. 37, pp. 924-933.

Wayne, Leslie. (February 15, 1992) "The 1992 Campaign: Personal Finance; Kerrey's Varied Business Ventures Raise Some Questions About Propriety." *New York Times*.

CHAPTER 10

THE DUNE GUY:

Bleed, Ann S. and Charles A. Flowerday. ed. *An Atlas of the Sand Hills*. Lincoln: Conservation and Survey Division, University of Nebraska, Third Edition, 1998.

McPhee, John. *Rising from the Plains*. New York: Farrar, Strauss and Giroux, 1986.

Lageson, David R. et al. *Field Guide: Colorado and Adjacent Areas*. Boulder: Geological Society of America, 1999.

Swinehart, J.B. et al. "Field Guide to Geology and Hydrology of the Nebraska Sand Hills." *Geological Society of America Field Trip Guidebook Professional Contributions*, Colorado School of Mines, 1988.

Selected articles:

Goble. R. J. et al. (2004) "Optically Stimulated Luminescence and Radiocarbon Ages of Stacked Paliosoils and Dune Sands in the Nebraska Sand Hills." *Quaternary Science Reviews*, Vol. 23: pp. 1173-1182.

Loope, David B. and James B. Swinehart (Spring 2000) "Thinking Like a Dune Field: Geologic History in the Nebraska Sand Hills." *Great Plains Research* 10, pp. 5-35.

Mason, J. A. et al. (2004) "Late Holocene Dune Activity Linked to Hydrological Drought, Nebraska Sand Hills USA." *The Holocene*, Vol. 14, pp. 209-217.

McPhee, John. (January 29,1995) "The Gravel Page." *New Yorker*. pp. 44-69.

Nicholson, B. J. and J. B. Swinehart. (2005) "Evidence of Holocene Climate Change in a Nebraska Sandhills Wetland." *Great Plains Research*, Vol. 15, pp. 45-67.

Stokes, S. and James B. Swinehart. (1997) "Middle and Late Holocene Dune Reactivation in the Nebraska Sand Hills." *The Holocene*, Vol. 7, pp. 263-273.

CHAPTER 11

TWO POETS TALK SAND HILLS:

Kloefkorn, William. *Where the Visible Sun Now Is*. Illinois: Spoon River Poetry Press, 1989.

Welch, Don. *Dead Horse Table*. Lincoln: Windflower Press, 1975.

Selected Articles:

Biga, Leo Adam. (July 7, 2010) "A Man of His Words, Nebraska State Poet William Kloefkorn" leoadam biga.com.

ed. (January 9, 2014) "UNK Poet Remembers White Shadows in the Grass." *University of Nebraska Foundation*.

Hasselstrom, Linda M. (May 30, 2011) "Bill Kloefkorn and the Rapture." windbreakhouse.com.

Nelson, Robert. (March 2, 1997) "On a Wing and a Poem." *Omaha World-Herald*.

Rooney, Megan R. (November 18, 2004) "Welch's Writings Made on the Move." *Daily Nebraskan*.

Stillwell, Mary K. (July, 2011) "William Kloefkorn: The Genesis of a Poet" *Prairie Fire*.

CHAPTER 14

AUTUMN TANK TRIP ON THE MIDDLE LOUP:

Selected Articles:

Bottrell, Andrew. (April 28, 2013) "Sandhills River Tradition Gets National Attention; 'Tanking' the Middle Loup Featured in Magazine, Named One of US's Great Rafting Trips." *North Platte Telegraph*.

Bryant, Dawn E. (November 4, 2014) "Winter Tanking of the Middle Loup: Stock Tank Racers Take on the Middle Loup." *McCook Gazette*.

Davis, Mark. (July 8, 2006) "Tanks for the Memories." *Omaha World-Herald*.

Grell, Clark. (December 7, 2104) "Otters in Nebraska a Success Story." *Lincoln Journal-Star*.

Hansen, Matthew. (June 8, 2015) "Hansen: He'll Spend His Summer Searching for River Otter – a Nebraska Wildlife Success Story." *Omaha World-Herald*.

Jenkins, Nate. (November 16, 2008) "River Otters Could Get 2nd Chance in Nebraska; State Biologists Consider Their Reintroduction." *San Francisco Chronicle*.

CHAPTER 15

NOVEMBER VISIT TO THE SPIKE BOX:

Fitzgerald, David and Linda Hasselstrom. *Bison: Monarch of the Plains*. Portland: Graphic Arts Center, 1998.

Franti, T. G. ed. *Bison Poems: Of Bison and the Great Plains*. Lincoln: Center for Great Plains Studies, 2002.

Turner, Ted. *Call Me Ted*. New York: Grand Central, 2008.

Selected Articles:

Aksamit, Nichole. (December 5, 2008) "Sorry for Doubting You, Ted Turner." *Omaha World-Herald*.

"Anthrax Strikes Bison on Turner's Flying D Ranch." cattlenetwork.com, August 6, 2008.

"Beau Turner in Dad Ted's Footsteps." *Atlanta Journal-Constitution*, December 10, 2011.

Brown, Matthew. (January 8, 2010) "Turner Bid for Yellowstone Bison Draws Protest." *Associated Press*.

Hammel, Paul. (February 7, 2008) "Ted Turner 'Almost Done' Buying Ranchland." *Omaha World-Herald*.

O'Neill, Ann. (November 17, 2013) "The Reinvention of Ted Turner." *CNN News*.

Schontzler, Gail. (November 29, 2007) "Hunting Season Ends." *Bozeman Daily Chronicle*.

"Solar Windmills Are Displacing the Old Windmill." *Associated Press*, July 19, 2010.

"The 'Mouth of the South' is No Longer as He Devotes His Time (and $1 Billion) to UN, Jets Between 28 Homes and Four Girlfriends, Misses Jane Fonda and Opens Up to THR About Rupert, Jerry and His Abuse as a Child. Says a Friend: 'He's Definitely Changed.'" *Hollywood Reporter*, February 29, 2012.

"Turner on Meet the Press: KGB 'Honorable Place to Work' US in Iraq 'Naked Aggression' Like Soviets in Afghanistan." nbcnews.com/meet-the-press, November 30, 2008.

"Weddings; Gannon Hunt and Beau Turner." *New York Times*, December 12, 1999.

CHAPTER 16

BLOWOUT PENSTEMON:

Pool, Raymond John. *A Study of the Vegetation of the Sandhills of Nebraska* (1913). Whitefish: Kessinger Publishing, 2010.

Weaver, J. E. *Native Vegetation of Nebraska*. Lincoln: University of Nebraska Press, 1965.

_____. and F. W. Albertson. *Grasslands of the Great Plains: Their Nature and Use*. Lincoln: Johnson Publishing Company, 1956.

Selected Articles:

Caha, Carol. et al. (1998) "Organellar Genetic Diversity in *Penstemon jaydenii* (Scrophulariareae): An Endangered Species." *American Journal of Botany* 85: 1704-1709.

Nebraska Game and Parks. (July 3, 2003) "Blowout Penstemon Makes a Comeback." *Casper Star Tribune*.

Stubbendieck, James. et al. (2007) "Transplanted Seedlings Enhance Populations of Endangered Blowout Penstemon." *Ecological Restoration*, 25:224-225.

_____. et al. (1989) "Blowouts in the Nebraska Sandhills: The habitat of *Penstemon haydenii." Proceedings of the Eleventh North American Prairie Conference*, ed. T. B. Bragg and, 223-225. University of Nebraska.

U.S. Fish and Wildlife Service. (2012) "Blowout Penstemon (*Penstemon haydenii*) 5 Years Review: *Summary and Evaluation."*

CHAPTER 17

BAD DAY AT WOOD LAKE:

Mack, Gene D. (2005) Activity Report of the Sandhills Task Force. Sutherland, *Sandhllls Task Force.*

_____. (May, 2006) Kearney, *Sandhills Task Force Newsletter.*

Selected Articles:

"Plane Crash Near Wood Lake Still Under Investigation." *Ainsworth Star-Herald*, March 22, 2009.

CHAPTER 18

JOHN HANSEN:

Selected Articles:

Doyle, Kevin. (2009) "Rocky Mountain Natural Meats: The Leader in Premium Bison Production." *Food & Drink Digital.*

Jackson, Bill. (June 27, 2009) "Coming to a Plate Near You." *Greeley Tribune.*

CHAPTER 21

MORMON COWS AND THE BATTLE OF BLUE WATER:

Adams, George Rollie. *General William S. Harney: Prince of Dragoons.* Lincoln: University of Nebraska Press, 2001.

Beck, Paul N. *The First Sioux War: The Grattan Fight and Blue Water Creek 1854-1856.* Lanham, Maryland: University Press of America, 2004.

Bray, Kingsley M. *Crazy Horse: A Lakota Life.* Norman, Oklahoma: University of Oklahoma Press, 2006.

Champe, John Leland. *Ash Hollow Cave: A Study of Stratigraphic Sequence in the Central Great Plains.* Lincoln: University of Nebraska Studies, 1946.

Grinnell, George Bird. *The Cheyenne Indians, Vol. 1 & 2.* New Haven: Yale University Press. 1923.

_____. *The Fighting Cheyennes.* New York: Charles Scribner's Sons, 1915.

Hanson, James A. *Little Chief's Gatherings: The Smithsonian Institution's G. K. Warren 1855-1856 Plains Indian Collection and The New York State Library's 1955-1857 Warren Expedition's Journals.* Crawford: The Fur Press, 1996.

Hyde, George. *Red Cloud's Folk: A History of the Oglala Sioux Indians.* Norman: University of Oklahoma Press. 1937.

_____. *Spotted Tail's Folk: A History of the Brule Sioux.* Norman: University of Oklahoma Press, 1961.

Jackson, Helen Hunt. *A Century of Dishonor.* Boston: Roberts Brothers, 1885.

Sandoz, Mari. *Crazy Horse: The Strange Man of the Oglalas.* New York: Hastings House, 1942.

Werner, Fred H. *With Harney On the Blue Water.* Greeley, Colorado: Werner Publications, 1988.

Selected Articles:

McCann, Lloyd E. (March, 1956) "The Grattan Massacre." *Nebraska History*, Vol. XXXVII, Number 1.

CHAPTER 22

MORMON COWS REVISITED:

Selected Articles:

Adams, D.C. et al. (1996) "Matching the Cow with Forage Resources to Improve Profitability." *Rangelands* 18:57-62.

_____. et al. (1994) "Extended Grazing Systems for Improving Economic Returns from Nebraska Sandhills Cow/Calf Operations." *Journal of Range Management.* 47:258-263.

_____. et al. (1999)) "Designing and Conducting Experiments for Range Beef Cows." *Proceedings American Society of Animal Science.*

AgEcon. (2007) "Gordon Kearl, 1927-2007" *Agriculture and Applied Economics Department*, University of Wyoming, Laramie.

Duggan, Joe. (October 2, 2004) "Mormon Land Holdings Rise." *Lincoln Journal-Star.*

Grant, Eric. (February, 2007) "The Forgotten Resource: It's Not Just Land and Livestock. It's People Too." *Angus Journal.*

Gardner, Peter B. (Winter, 2008) "Painting the Mormon Story." *BYU Magazine.*

Gordon, Kindra. (November, 2015) "Teichert's Straight Talk." *Angus Journal.*

Loy, Tim W. et al. (2004) "A System for Wintering Spring-Calving Bred Heifers Without Feeding Hay." *Nebraska Beef Cattle Reports*, Animal Science Department, University of Nebraska-Lincoln.

_____. et al. (2003) "Comparison of Two Heifer Development Systems on a Commercial Nebraska Ranch." *Nebraska Beef Cattle Reports*, Animal Science Department, University of Nebraska-Lincoln.

Patterson, Trey. et al. (2001) "Performance and Economics of Winter Supplementing Pregnant Heifers Based on the Metabolizable Protein System." *Nebraska Beef Cattle Reports*, Animal Science Department, University of Nebraska-Lincoln.

Pinborough, Jay Underwood. (April, 1989) "Minerva Kohlhepp Teichert: With a Bold Brush." *The Church of the Latter Day Saints.*

Sonstegard, Viki. (March 28, 2014) "'I Must Paint...It's a Disease' Minerva Kohlhepp Teichert." *Women Out West: Art on the Edge of America.*

Spro, L. R. et al.(2001) "Review: Factors Affecting Decisions on When to Calve Beef Females." West Central Research and Extension Center, North Platte.

Teichert, Burke. (1993) "Setting Direction and Effective Management Style" *Range Beef Cow Symposium*, Animal Science Department, University of Nebraska-Lincoln.

_____. (December 11-13, 2001) "Considerations When Selecting a Calving Season." *Proceedings, The Range Beef Cow Symposium XVII*, Casper, Wyoming.

_____. (December 9-11,1997) "Empowering People." *Proceedings, The Range Beef Cow Symposium XV*, Rapid City, South Dakota.

_____. (June 1, 2017) "7 'What If' Questions Every Rancher Should Ask." *Beef Magazine.*

_____. (August 3, 2017) "Ten Thoughts on Heifer Development." *Beef Magazine.*

CHAPTER 23

BULL RIDERS:

Flying U Rodeo Company. *Million Dollar Memories: 50 Years with Cotton Rasser and the Flying U. Cotton and Karin Rasser.* Marysville, California, 2007.

Selected Articles:

Crossman, Matt. (March 9, 2017) "The Baddest Bull Rider Has a Secret to Success: Always Pick the Baddest Bull." *Success.*

Myslenski, Skip. (August 6, 1989) "A Rodeo Cowboy's Perfect Ride Ends in Death." *Chicago Tribune.*

Silver, Steve. (October 21, 2008) "Ex-UNLV Star McBride Retires from Pro Bull Riding." *Las Vegas Sun*.

CHAPTER 24

RENAISSANCE MAN:

Hewes, Leslie. *The Suitcase Farming Frontier: A Study in the Historical Geography of the Central Great Plains*. Lincoln: University of Nebraska Press,1973.

McIntosh, Charles Barron. *Life on the Pine Ridge*. Henderson, Nebraska: Service Press, 2001.

_____. *Hypothesis for Sandhillian Glaciation*. Lincoln: Augstums Printing Service, 2001.

_____. *Intuitive Pattern and Formative Process: Hypothesis for Sandhillian Glaciation*. Austums Printing Service, 2004.

_____. *The Nebraska Sand Hills: The Human Landscape*. Lincoln: University of Nebraska Press, 1986.

Schroeder, Betty Carol Neal Rodewald, ed. *McPherson County: Facts, Families, Fiction*. Tryon: McPherson County Extension Clubs Council. 1986.

Selected Articles:

McIntosh, Charles Barron. (1957) "Atmospheric Conditions and Explosions in Coal Mines." *The Geographical Review*, Vol. XLVII, No. 2, pp. 155-174.

_____. (1974) "Forest Lieu Selections in the Sand Hills of Nebraska." *Annals of the Association of American Geographers*, Vol. 64, pp. 87-99.

_____. (1975) "Use and Abuse of the Timber Culture Act." *Annals of the Association of American Geographers*, Vol 65, pp. 347-362.

_____. (1976) "Patterns from Land Alienation Maps." *Annals of the Association of American Geographers*, Vol. 66, p. 572.

_____. (1981) "One Man's Sequential Land Alienation on the Great Plains." *Geographical Review*. Vol. 71, p. 433-434.

_____. (1988) "The Route of a Sand Hills Bone Hunt: The Yale College Expedition of 1870." *Nebraska History*, Vol. 69. pp. 84-94.

Film:

Farrell, Mike, Producer/Director/Writer/Grantwriter. (1993) "A Sand Hills Story." (60 Minutes) and Transcript, Nebraska Educational Television.

CHAPTER 25

DRY VALLEY CHURCH:

Caudill, Troy Jr. *Troy's Journey*. New York: Carlton Press, 1982.

Kloefkorn, William. *Platte Valley Homestead*. Lincoln: Platte Valley Press, 1991.

Welch, Don. *Deadhorse Table*. Orange County: Windflower Press, 1974.

Selected Articles:

"Peak in Winter Population of Trumpeter Swans in the Sandhills." *Wildbirds Broadcasting*, May 26, 2009.

Forsberg, Michael. (June, 2011) "Ornate Box Turtles." *Nebraskaland Magazine*. pp. 22-25.

Osborn, Gerri. (January-February 2008) "Dry Valley Church." *Nebraska Life Magazine*.

Suggestions for Further Reading

County and Local Histories:

Blaine County History Book Committee. *The History of Blaine County, Nebraska*. Dallas: Curtis Media Corporation. 1988.

Cherry County Extension Council. *Potluck Papers: Cherry County Heritage Book*, 1974.

Monahan, Earl H. and Robert M. Howard. *Sandhill Horizons: A Story of the Monahan Ranch and Other History of the Area*. Alliance: Rader's Place. 1987.

Norman, Lisa. Haythorn Land & Cattle: *A Horseman's Heritage*. Keystone: Images West.

Volger, William K. Vanishing Dreams: *The Story of Historical Lisco*, Nebraska. McCook: Morris Media, 2007.

General Sand Hills:

Archer, J. Clark and Richard Edwards. *Atlas of Nebraska*. Lincoln: University of Nebraska Press, 2017.

Atherton, Lewis. *The Cattle Kings*. Lincoln: University of Nebraska Press, 1961.

Beel, Marianne. *Sand in My Shoes: Four Decades of Sandhills Stories and History*. Sioux Falls: Pine Hill Press, 2008.

Carter, John. *Solomon D. Butcher: Photographing the American Dream*. Lincoln: University of Nebraska Press, 1985, 1985.

Farrar, Jon. *Red Deer: Biography of a Sandhills Hunting Club*. Lincoln: Red Deer Hunting Club, 2005.

Flowerday, Charles A., ed. *Flat Water: A History of Nebraska and Its Water*. Lincoln: Conservation and Survey Division, University of Nebraska, 1993.

Hutton, Harold. *Doc Middleton: Life and Legends of the Notorious Plains Outlaw*. Chicago: Swallow Press, 1974.

Johnsgard, Paul A. *This Fragile Land: A Natural History of the Nebraska Sandhills*. Lincoln: University of Nebraska Press, 1995.

_____. *The Niobrara: A River Running through Time*. Bison Books, 2007.

Johnsgard, Paul A. and Bob Gress. *Faces of the Great Plains: Wildlife*. University Press of Kansas, 2003.

Jones, Stephen R. *The Last Prairie: A Sandhills Journal*. Camden, Maine: Ragged Mountain Press/McGraw-Hill, 2000.

Janovy, John Jr. *Keith County Journal*. New York: St. Martin's Press, 1978.

_____. *Back in Keith County*. Lincoln: Bison Books, 1984.

Knue, Joseph. *Nebraskaland Magazine Wildlife Viewing Guide*. Lincoln: Nebraskaland Magazine, 1997.

Kraisinger, Gary and Margaret Kraisinger. *The Western: The Greatest Texas Cattle Trail 1974-1886*. Newton: The Mennonite Press, 2004.

MacKichan, Margaret A. and Bob Ross. *In the Kingdom of Grass*. Lincoln: University of Nebraska Press, 1992.

Owen, David A. *Like No Other Place: The Sandhills of Nebraska*. Chicago: The Center for American Places at Columbia College, 2010.

Sanders, Mark ed. *A Sandhills Reader: Thirty Years of Great Writing from the Great Plains*. Nacogdoches: Stephen F. Austin State University Press, 2015.

Scarlett, Mick. *Those Magnetic Sandhills Vol 1*. Kearney: Morris Publishing, 1997.

Memoirs:

Allan, Tom. *To Bucktail and Back...A Million Miles of Memories*. Omaha: Omaha World Herald, 2002.

Babcock, Robert T. *A Long-Time Cowboy*. Lincoln: Word Services, 1978.

Bliss, D. L. Panhandle Vale—*Sandhill Trail: Reminiscences of a Nebraska Rancher*. New York: Exposition Press, 1960.

Bronson, Edgar Beecher. *Reminiscences of a Ranchman*. Lincoln: University of Nebraska Press, 1962.

Freeman, Willam C. *Wild Bill: The Life of William C. Freeman*. Kearney: Morris Publishing, 2000.

Jackson, Franklin C. *Echoes from the Sandhills*. Lincoln: Word Services, 1977.

_____. *Tangle Tales and Trails from the Sandhills*. Calloway: Loup Valley Queen.

Reyman, Claude L. *Growing Up on a Cherry County Nebraska Cattle Ranch*. Kearney: Morris Publishing, 2006.

Waddill, Olin. *Saddle Strings*. Gordon: Tri State Old Time Cowboys Memorial Museum, 1976.

O'Kieffe, Charley. *Western Story: The Recollections of Charley O'Kieffe 1884-1898*. Lincoln: University of Nebraska Press, 1960.

Index

www.ingramcontent.com/pod-product-compliance
Lightning Source LLC
Chambersburg PA
CBHW080621030426
42336CB00018B/3034